PARKIN/BA

MICROECONOMICS

CANADA IN THE GLOBAL ENVIRONMENT

STUDY GUIDE

Avi J. Cohen *York University*

Harvey B. King *University of Regina*

David E. Spencer *Brigham Young University*

Addison-Wesley Publishers Limited

Don Mills, Ontario • Reading, Massachusetts • Menlo Park, California
New York • Wokingham, England • Amsterdam • Bonn • Sydney •
Singapore • Tokyo • Madrid • San Juan

Dedicated
to Alexis and Madeleine, who teach me as they learn (AJC)
and
to Tracy (HBK)

ISBN 0-201-51367-6

Printed and bound in Canada

B C D E F G -ALG- 95 94 93 92

PROJECT EDITOR: Shirley Tessier
PRODUCTION EDITOR: Valerie Jones
COPYEDITOR: Bonnie Di Malta
TYPESET AND INTERIOR DESIGN: Artplus Design Consultants Ltd
TEXT FORMATTING: Judy Petersiel
COVER DESIGN: Pronk & Associates
COVER ART: Calvin Nichols Paper Sculpture
PRINTER: Alger Press Ltd

CONTENTS

INTRODUCTION

Before You Begin...

Our experience has taught us that what first-year economics students want most from a study guide is help in mastering course material in order to do well on examinations. We have developed this *Study Guide* to respond specifically to that demand. Using this *Study Guide* alone, however, is not enough to guarantee that you will do well in your course. In order to help you overcome the problems and difficulties that most first-year students encounter, we have some general advice on how to study, as well as some specific advice on how to best use this *Study Guide*.

Some Friendly Advice

The study of economics requires a different style of thinking than what you may encounter in other courses. Economists make extensive use of assumptions to break down complex problems into simple, analytically manageable, parts. This analytical style, while not ultimately more demanding than the styles of thinking in other disciplines, feels unfamiliar to most students and requires practice. As a result, it is not as easy to do well in economics simply on the basis of your raw intelligence and high school knowledge as it is in many other first year courses. Many students who come to our office hours are frustrated and puzzled by the fact that they are getting A's and B's in their other courses but only a C or worse in economics. They have not recognized that the study of economics is different and requires practice. In order to avoid a frustrating visit to your instructor after your first test, we suggest you do the following.

Don't rely solely on your high school economics. If you took high school economics, you will have seen the material on supply and demand on which your instructor will lecture in the first few weeks. Don't be lulled into feeling that the course will be easy. Your high school knowledge of economic concepts will be very useful, but it will not be enough to guarantee high marks on exams. Your college or university instructors will demand much more detailed knowledge of concepts and ask you to apply them in new circumstances.

Keep up with the course material on a weekly basis. Read the appropriate chapter in the textbook *before* your instructor lectures on it. In this initial reading, don't worry about details or arguments you can't quite follow — just try and get a general understanding of the basic concepts and issues. You may be amazed at how your instructor's ability to teach improves when you come to class prepared. As soon as your instructor has finished covering a chapter, complete the corresponding *Study Guide* chapter. Avoid cramming the day before or even just the week before an exam. Because economics requires practice, cramming is an almost certain recipe for failure.

Keep a good set of lecture notes. Good lecture notes are vital for focusing your studying. Your instructor will only lecture on a subset of topics from the textbook. The topics your instructor covers in a lecture should usually be given priority when studying. You should also give priority to studying the figures and graphs covered in lecture. Especially if you use the *Graphpad* to insert key figures and graphs in your notes, you will have a clear and concise study aid.

Instructors do differ in their emphasis on lecture notes or the textbook, so ask early on in the course: which is *more* important in reviewing for exams — the lecture notes or the textbook. If your instructor answers that both are important, then ask the following, typically *economic* question: *at the margin*, which will be more beneficial — spending an extra hour re-reading your lecture notes or an extra hour re-reading the textbook? This question assumes that you have read each textbook chapter twice (once before lecture for a general understanding, and then later for a thorough understanding); that you have prepared a good set of lecture notes; and that you have worked through all of the problems in the appropriate *Study Guide* chapters. By applying this style of analysis to the problem of efficiently allocating your study time, you are already beginning to think like an economist!

Use your instructor and/or teaching assistants for help. When you have questions or problems with course material, come to office hours to ask questions. Remember, you are paying for your education, and instructors are there to help you learn. We are often amazed at how few students come to see us during office hours. Don't be shy. The personal contact that comes from one-on-one tutoring is professionally gratifying for us as well as (hopefully) beneficial for you.

Form a study group. A very useful way to motivate your studying and to learn economics is to discuss the course material and problems with other students. Explaining the answer to a question *out loud* is a very effective way of discovering how well you understand the question. When you answer a question in your head only, you often skip steps in the chain of reasoning without realizing it. When you are forced to explain your reasoning aloud, gaps and mistakes quickly appear, and you (and your fellow group members) can quickly correct your reasoning. The Short Answer questions in the *Study Guide* and the Review questions at the end of each textbook chapter are good study group material. You also might get together *after* having worked the problems in the *Study Guide* chapter, but *before* looking at the answers, and help each other solve unsolved problems.

Work old exams. One of the most effective ways of studying is to work through exams your instructor has given in previous years. Old exams give you a feel for the style of question your instructor may ask, and give you the opportunity to get used to time pressure if you force yourself to do the exam in the allotted time. Studying from old exams is not cheating, as long as you have obtained a copy of the exam legally. Some institutions keep old exams in the library, others in the department. Upper year students who have previously taken the course are usually a good source as well. Remember, though, that old exams are a useful study aid only if you use them to *understand* the reasoning behind each question. If you simply memorize answers in the hopes that your instructor will repeat the identical question, you are likely to fail. From year to year, instructors routinely change the questions or change the numerical values for similar questions.

Using the Study Guide

You should only attempt to complete a chapter in the *Study Guide* after you have read the corresponding textbook chapter once and listened to your instructor lecture on the material. Each *Study Guide* chapter contains the following sections.

Chapter in Perspective. The purpose of this first section is to briefly situate the material of a particular textbook chapter in the context of what has come before and what will follow. Since you will see so much detailed information throughout the course, we try to paint the bigger picture for you in broad strokes so that you don't feel lost. This is the "look at the forest instead of the trees" section.

Learning Objectives. This section simply repeats the learning objectives from the first page of each textbook chapter. Think of this as a list of important topics. Perhaps the best use of this list would be when you have finished the *Study Guide* chapter. Go through the list and see if you have, in fact, understood each of the objectives. If not, you have more work to do.

Helpful Hints. Where you encounter difficulty in mastering concepts or techniques, you will not be alone. Many students find certain concepts difficult and often make the same kinds of mistakes. We have seen these common mistakes often enough to have learned how to help students avoid them. These hints point out these mistakes and offer tips for avoiding them. The hints focus on the most important concepts, equations, and techniques for problem solving. We hope that this section will be very useful, since instructors always ask exam questions designed to test these possible mistakes in your understanding.

Key Figures and Tables. In the textbook, key figures and tables are identified with the textbook icon. Here, we group together summaries of the key figure and tables to help you focus your study on the most important diagrams. The summaries in this section are similar to those in the textbook captions, but use slightly different language. If you are having trouble understanding particular figures, these additional summaries should prove helpful. If you have understood the figure or table in the textbook, you may skip or skim the summary here.

Self-Test. Besides the Helpful Hints, this will be the most useful section of the *Study Guide.* The questions are designed to give you practice and to test the skills and techniques you must master to do well on exams. There are plenty of the types of questions you are most likely to encounter on your course exams — True/False and Multiple-Choice questions (at least 20 for each chapter). There are other types of questions, described below, each with a specific pedagogical purpose. Before we describe the five parts of the Self-Test section, here are some general tips that apply to all of the parts.

Use a pencil to write your answers in the *Study Guide.* This will allow you to erase your mistakes and have neat, completed pages from which to study.

Draw graphs wherever they are applicable. Some questions will ask explicitly for graphs; many others will not but will require a chain of reasoning that involves shifts of curves on a graph. *Always draw the graph.* Don't try and work through the reasoning in your head — you are much more likely to make mistakes that way. Whenever you draw a graph, even in the margins of the *Study Guide*, label the axes. You may think that you can keep the labels in your head, but you will be confronting many different graphs with many different variables on the axes. Avoid confusion and label. As an added incentive, remember that on exams where graphs are required, instructors will deduct marks for unlabelled axes.

Do the Self-Test questions as if they were real exam questions, which means do them *without looking at the answers.* This is the single most important tip we can give you about effectively using the *Study Guide* to improve your exam performance. Struggling for the answers to questions that you find difficult is one of the most effective ways to learn. The athletic adage — no pain, no gain — applies equally well to studying. You will learn the most from right answers you had to struggle for and from your wrong answers and mistakes. Only after you have attempted all of the questions should you look at the answers. When you finally do check the answers, be sure to understand where you went wrong and why the right answer is correct.

If you want to impose time pressure on yourself to simulate the conditions of a real exam, allow two minutes for each Multiple-Choice question and one minute for each True/False question. The other types of questions vary considerably in their time requirements, so it is difficult to give generally applicable time estimates for them. However, we believe that such time pressure is probably not a good idea for *Study Guide* questions. A state of mind of relaxed concentration is best for work in the *Study Guide.* Use old exams if you want practice with time pressure.

The five parts of the Self-Test section are:

Concept Review. This part contains simple "recall" questions, designed to check your memory of basic terms and concepts. These questions should build your confidence. If you have understood the terms and concepts in the chapter, you should get very few of these questions wrong. This part is not a test of deep understanding or of mastery of analytical skills.

True or False. These questions test your basic knowledge of chapter concepts as well as your ability to apply the concepts. These are the first questions to challenge your understanding to see if you can identify mistakes in statements using basic concepts.

Multiple-Choice. These more difficult questions test your analytical abilities by asking you to apply concepts to new situations, to manipulate information and to solve numerical and graphical problems.

Read each question and all five choices carefully before you answer. Many of the choices will be plausible and will differ only slightly. You must choose the one *best* answer. A useful strategy in working these questions is first to eliminate any obviously wrong choices and then to focus on the remaining alternatives. Be aware that sometimes the correct answer will be "none of the above choices is correct." Don't get frustrated or think that you are dim if you can't immediately see the correct answer. These questions are designed to make you work to find the correct choice.

Short Answer. Each chapter contains five Short Answer questions. These are straightforward, confidence-building questions about basic concepts. They can generally be answered in a few sentences or, at most, in one paragraph. These questions are useful to answer out loud in a study group.

Problems. The best way to learn to do economics is to do problems. Each Self-Test concludes with 4–6 numerical or graphical problems. In many chapters, this will be the most challenging part of the Self-Test. It is also likely to be the most helpful for deepening your understanding of the chapter material. We have, however, designed the questions to teach as much as to test. We have purposefully arranged the parts of each question to lead you through the problem-solving analysis is a gradual and sequential fashion, from easier to more difficult parts.

Answers. The Self-Test is followed by answers to all of the questions. Be sure not to look at the answers until you have attempted to answer all of the questions. When you do finally look at the answers, use them to understand where you went wrong and why the right answer is correct. The detailed answers to the Problems should be especially usefully in clarifying and illustrating typical chains of reasoning involved in economics analysis. If the answers alone do not clear up your confusion, go back to the appropriate sections of the textbook. If that still does not suffice, go to your instructor's or teaching assistant's office hours, or to your study group members, to get help and clarification.

If you effectively combine the use of the textbook, the *Study Guide*, the *Graphpad*, and all other course resources, you will be well prepared for exams. Equally importantly, you will also have developed analytical skills and powers of reasoning that will benefit you throughout your life and in whatever career you choose.

Do You Have Any Friendly Advice For Us?

We have attempted to make this *Study Guide* as clear and as useful as possible, and to avoid errors. No doubt, we have not succeeded entirely, and you are the only judges who count in evaluating our attempt. If you discover errors, or if you have other suggestions for improving the *Study Guide*, please write to us. In future editions, we will try and acknowledge the names of all students whose suggestions help us improve the *Study Guide*. Send your correspondence to:

Professor Avi J. Cohen
Department of Economics
Vari Hall
York University
Toronto, Ontario M3J 1P3

Chapter 1 What is Economics?

Chapter in Perspective

Text Pages 5–26

This first chapter introduces the *subject* of economics: what kinds of questions and problems economics tries to address and why these questions are interesting and important. The fundamental economic problem is scarcity. Because wants exceed the resources available to satisfy them, we cannot have everything we want and must make choices. This problem leads to economizing behaviour — choosing the best or optimal use of the resources available. Economics, as a subject, is the study of how we use limited resources to try to satisfy unlimited wants.

This chapter also introduces the *method* of economics: how economists use economic theory and models to answer economic questions and to analyze and understand how people and economic systems cope with the fundamental problem of scarcity.

Learning Objectives

After studying this chapter, you will be able to:

- **State the kinds of questions that economics tries to answer.**
- **Explain why all economic questions and economic activity arise from scarcity.**
- **Explain why scarcity forces people to make choices.**
- **Define opportunity cost.**
- **Describe the function and the working parts of an economy.**
- **Distinguish between positive and normative statements.**
- **Explain what is meant by an economic theory and how economic theories are developed by building and testing economic models.**

Helpful Hints

1) The definition of economics (the study of how people use limited resources to try to satisfy unlimited wants) leads us directly to three important economic concepts — choice, opportunity cost, and competition. If wants exceed resources, we cannot have everything we want and therefore must make *choices* among alternatives. In making a choice, we forgo other alternatives, and the *opportunity cost* of any choice is the value of the best forgone alternative. Also, if wants exceed resources, then wants and individuals must *compete* against each other for the scarce resources.

2) In attempting to understand how and why something works (for example, an airplane, a falling object, an economy), we can try and use description or theory. A description is a list of facts about something. But it does not tell us which facts are essential for understanding how an airplane works (the shape of the wings) and which facts are less important (the colour of the paint). Scientists use theory to abstract from the complex descriptive facts of the real world and focus only on those elements essential for understanding. Those essential elements are fashioned into models — highly simplified representations of the real world.

   In physics and some other natural sciences, if we want to understand the essential force (gravity) that causes objects to fall, we use theory to construct a simple model and test it by performing a controlled experiment. We create a vacuum to eliminate less important forces like air resistance.

   Economic models are also attempts to focus on the essential forces (competition, self-interest) operating in the economy while abstracting from less important forces (whims, advertising, altruism). Unlike physicists, economists cannot perform controlled experiments to test their models. As a result, it is difficult to conclusively prove or disprove a theory and its models.

3) Models are like maps, which are useful precisely because they abstract from real world detail. A map which reproduced all of the details of the real world (streetlamps, fireplugs, electric wires) would be useless. A useful map offers a simplified view, which is carefully selected according to the purpose of the map.

   Remember that economic models are not claims that the real world is as simple as the model. Models claim to capture the simplified effect of some real force operating in the economy. Before drawing conclusions about the real economy from a model, we must be careful to consider whether, when we reinsert all of the real world complexities the model abstracted from, the conclusions will be the same as in the model.

4) The most important purpose of studying economics is not to learn what to think about economics but rather *how* to think about economics. The "what" — the facts and descriptions of the economy — can always be found in books. The value of an economics education is the ability to think critically about economic problems and *to understand how* an economy works. This understanding of the essential forces governing how an economy works comes through the mastery of economic theory and model-building.

Key Figure

Figure 1.1 A Picture of the Economy, text page 13

This figure illustrates the flow of goods and services as well as flows of money in the economy. There are three groups of decision-makers (households, firms, and governments) and two groups of markets (goods markets and factor markets). Households supply factors of production to firms through factor markets for which they receive payment of wages, interest, rent, and profits. Firms supply goods and services to households through goods markets for which they receive money payments. Governments collect taxes (money flows) from both households and firms and supply goods and services to both in addition to other benefits (transfer payments) to households and (subsidies) to firms.

This figure is important because it highlights the *interdependence* between households, firms, and governments. What any one group can do depends on what the other groups do. This interdependence is co-ordinated through competition and the market mechanism.

SELF-TEST

CONCEPT REVIEW

1) The fundamental and pervasive fact that gives rise to economic problems is _______________ . This simply means that human wants _______________ the resources available to satisfy them. The inescapable consequence is that people must make _______________ .

2) When we choose an action, the value of the best forgone alternative is the _______________ cost of that action.

3) The process of evaluating the costs and benefits of our choices in order to do the best we can with limited resources is called _______________ or _______________ .

4) An economy is a mechanism that determines _______________ is produced, _______________ it is produced, and _______________ _______________ it is produced.

5) The three groups of decision makers in the economy are _______________ , _______________ , and _______________ .

6) Factors of production are classified under three general headings. The physical and mental resources of human beings are called _______________ . Natural resources are called _______________ . Manufactured goods used in production (for example, machines and factories) are called _______________ .

7) While all economies must have some way of co-ordinating choices, there are two fundamental mechanisms. The _______________ mechanism relies on the authority of some kind of central planning, while the _______________ mechanism relies on the adjustment of _______________ in economic markets. A _______________ economy has elements of both of these fundamental mechanisms.

8) An economy that is economically linked with other economies in the world is called _______________ .

9) Statements about what *is* are called _______________ statements, while those about what *ought* to be are called _______________ statements.

10) The branch of economics that studies the choices of individual households and firms is called _______________ , while the branch which studies the behaviour of the economy as a whole is called _______________ .

TRUE OR FALSE

_____ 1) Scarcity is a problem only for capitalist (market) economies.

_____ 2) Economics is the study of how to use unlimited resources to satisfy limited wants.

_____ 3) Scarcity can be eliminated through co-operation.

_____ 4) The notion of opportunity cost is illustrated by the fact that because Fred studied for his economics examination last night he was unable to see a movie with his friends.

_____ 5) Competition is a contest for command over scarce resources.

_____ 6) The opportunity cost of any action is the cost of all forgone alternatives.

_____ 7) To economists, capital is the money used by businesses to buy assets.

_____ 8) The pair of scissors a barber uses to cut hair is an example of capital as a factor of production.

_____ 9) In an economy in which economic activity is co-ordinated by a command mechanism, the decisions of *what, how,* and *for whom* are the result of price adjustment.

_____ 10) A mixed economy is one in which there is both internal and international trade.

_____ 11) Canada is a pure market economy.

_____ 12) In economics, a closed economy is one in which there is very limited economic freedom.

_____ 13) Canada is an open economy.

_____ 14) Careful and systematic observation and measurement are basic components of any science.

_____ 15) Economics is not a science since it deals with the study of willful human beings and not inanimate objects in nature.

_____ 16) An increase in the income tax rate will cause total tax revenue to fall. This is an example of a positive statement.

_____ 17) Science is silent on positive questions.

_____ 18) A positive statement is about what *is*, while a normative statement is about what *will be*.

_____ 19) Detailed description alone is the key to understanding what makes things work.

_____ 20) Economic models are of very limited value in helping us understand the real world because they abstract from the complexity of the real world.

_____ 21) Models are complete descriptions of reality.

_____ 22) Microeconomics is concerned with the economy as a whole.

_____ 23) Macroeconomics includes the study of the causes of inflation.

_____ 24) Testing an economic model requires comparing its predictions against real world events.

_____ 25) When the predictions of a model conflict with the relevant facts, a theory must be discarded or modified.

MULTIPLE-CHOICE

1) The fact that human wants cannot be fully satisfied with available resources is called the problem of
   a) opportunity cost.
   b) scarcity.
   c) normative economics.
   d) what to produce.
   e) for whom to produce.

2) The problem of scarcity exists
   a) only in economies which rely on the market mechanism.
   b) only in economies which rely on the command mechanism.
   c) in all economies.
   d) only when people have not optimized.
   e) now but will be eliminated with economic growth.

3) When the government chooses to use resources to build a dam, those resources are no longer available to build a highway. This illustrates the concept of
   a) a market mechanism.
   b) macroeconomics.
   c) opportunity cost.
   d) a closed economy.
   e) co-operation.

4) Renata has the chance to either attend an economics lecture or play tennis. If she chooses to attend the lecture, the value of playing tennis is
   a) greater than the value of the lecture.
   b) not comparable to the value of the lecture.
   c) equal to the value of the lecture.
   d) the opportunity cost of attending the lecture.
   e) zero.

5) The opportunity cost to a customer of having a $10 haircut is the
   a) customer's best alternative use of the $10.
   b) customer's best alternative use of the time it takes to get a haircut.
   c) customer's best alternative use of both the $10 and the time it takes to get a haircut.
   d) value to the barber of $10.
   e) value to the barber of the time it takes to give a haircut.

6) *All* decision-makers in an economy
   a) co-ordinate choices between groups.
   b) supply factors of production.
   c) make choices.
   d) produce goods or services.
   e) redistribute income.

7) Which of the following is an example of capital as a factor of production?
   a) money held by General Motors
   b) a General Motors bond
   c) an automobile factory owned by General Motors
   d) all of the above
   e) none of the above

8) All of the following are factors of production *except*
   a) natural resources.
   b) tools.
   c) labour.
   d) government.
   e) land.

9) A closed economy is one that has
   a) more exports than imports.
   b) more imports than exports.
   c) strict government control of production.
   d) no economic links between households and government.
   e) no economic links with other economies.

10) The Canadian economy is best described as a
   a) closed economy.
   b) market economy.
   c) command economy.
   d) mixed economy.
   e) wealthy economy that avoids the problem of scarcity.

11) A normative statement is a statement regarding
   a) what is usually the case.
   b) the assumptions of an economic model.
   c) what ought to be.
   d) the predictions of an economic model.
   e) what is.

12) The rich face higher income tax rates than the poor is an example of
   a) a normative statement.
   b) a positive statement.
   c) a descriptive statement.
   d) a theoretical statement.
   e) both b) and c).

13) Which of the following are included in the basic assumptions of an economic model?
   a) people have preferences
   b) choices are co-ordinated
   c) resource endowments are given
   d) rational choice
   e) all of the above

14) An economic model is tested by
   a) examining the realism of its assumptions.
   b) comparing its predictions with the facts.
   c) comparing its descriptions with the facts.
   d) the Testing Committee of the Canadian Economic Association.
   e) all of the above.

15) Which of the following is *not* a key assumption of an economic model?
   a) People have preferences.
   b) People economize.
   c) People's resource endowments are fixed.
   d) People's technology is given.
   e) People's choices are not co-ordinated.

16) When economists say that people are rational, it means they
   a) do not make errors of judgement.
   b) make the best decision from their perspective.
   c) act on complete information.
   d) will not later regret any decision made now.
   e) do not let emotion influence decisions.

17) The branch of economics that studies the decisions of individual households and firms is called
   a) macroeconomics.
   b) microeconomics.
   c) positive economics.
   d) normative economics.
   e) home economics.

18) All of the following are microeconomic questions *except*
   a) technological change.
   b) wages and earnings.
   c) distribution of wealth.
   d) production.
   e) consumption.

19) Which of the following would *not* be considered a macroeconomic topic?
   a) the reasons for a decline in the price of orange juice
   b) the reasons for a decline in average prices
   c) the cause of recessions
   d) the effect of the government budget deficit on inflation
   e) the determination of aggregate income (GDP)

20) Equilibrium is
   a) a balance of opposing forces.
   b) a situation in which everyone has economized.
   c) a situation where all choices are mutually compatible.
   d) the solution of an economic model.
   e) all of the above.

SHORT ANSWER

1) What is meant by scarcity and why does the existence of scarcity mean that we must make choices?

2) Why will co-operation not eliminate scarcity?

3) If all people would only economize, that would solve the problem of scarcity. Agree or disagree and explain why.

4) Explain the interdependence that exists between households and firms in textbook Figure 1.1 on page 13 (ignore government for this question).

5) Why is the Canadian economy considered to be mixed?

PROBLEMS

1) It takes one hour to travel from Montreal to Toronto by airplane and five hours by train. Further, suppose that air fare is $100 and train fare is $60. Which mode of transportation has the lower opportunity cost for the following people?
   a) a person who can earn $5 an hour
   b) a person who can earn $10 an hour
   c) a person who can earn $12 an hour

2) Suppose the government builds and staffs a hospital in order to provide "free" medical care.
   a) What is the opportunity cost of the free medical care?
   b) Is it free from the perspective of society as a whole?

3) Indicate whether each of the following statements is positive or normative. If it is normative (positive), rewrite it so that it becomes positive (normative).

a) The government ought to reduce the size of the deficit in order to lower interest rates.
b) Government imposition of a tax on tobacco products will reduce their consumption.

4) Suppose we examine a model of plant growth which predicts that, given the amount of water and sunlight, the application of fertilizer stimulates plant growth.
a) How might you test the model?
b) How is the test different from what an economist could do to test an economic model?

ANSWERS

CONCEPT REVIEW

1) scarcity; exceed; choices
2) opportunity
3) optimizing or economizing
4) what; how; for whom
5) households; firms; government
6) labour; land; capital
7) command; market; prices; mixed
8) open
9) positive; normative
10) microeconomics; macroeconomics

TRUE OR FALSE

1) F	6) F	11) F	16) T	21) F
2) F	7) F	12) F	17) F	22) F
3) F	8) T	13) T	18) F	23) T
4) T	9) F	14) T	19) F	24) T
5) T	10) F	15) F	20) F	25) T

MULTIPLE-CHOICE

1) b	5) c	9) e	13) e	17) b
2) c	6) c	10) d	14) b	18) c
3) c	7) c	11) c	15) e	19) a
4) d	8) d	12) e	16) b	20) e

SHORT ANSWER

1) Scarcity is the universal condition that human wants always exceed the resources available to satisfy them. The fact that goods and services are scarce means that individuals cannot have all of everything they want. It is therefore necessary to choose among alternatives.

2) Scarcity is a problem of essentially infinite wants and limited resources. While co-operation is one way to organize our activity, as we confront the problem of scarcity, it cannot eliminate it and therefore cannot eliminate economic problems.

3) Disagree. If everyone economized, then we would be making the best possible use of our resources and would be achieving the greatest benefits or satisfaction possible, given the limited quantity of resources. But this does not mean that we would be satisfying all of our limitless needs. The problem of scarcity can never be "solved" as long as people have infinite needs and finite resources for satisfying those needs.

4) Firms depend on households for the supply of factors of production. In exchange, households depend on firms for income. Households use that income to buy goods and services from firms, while firms depend on the money they receive from household purchases to be able to purchase more factors of production in the next period and start the circular flow all over again.

5) The Canadian economy is a mixed economy because it relies on both the market and command mechanisms. Most co-ordination is carried out through the market mechanism, but there are many economic decisions which are either made or regulated by the government.

PROBLEMS

1) The point here is to recognize that the opportunity cost of travel includes the best alternative value of travel time as well as the train or air fare.
   a) Thus, if the opportunity cost of the time spent travelling is the $5 an hour that could have been earned (but wasn't), the opportunity cost of train travel (in dollars) is the $60 train fare plus the $25 ($5 an hour times 5 hours) in forgone income for a total of $85. In this case, the opportunity cost of air travel is the $100 air fare plus $5 in forgone income, for a total of $105. Therefore, for a person whose best alternative use of time is to earn $5 an hour, the opportunity cost of travelling by train is less than the opportunity cost of travelling by air.
   b) For a person who can earn $10 an hour, the opportunity cost of train travel will be $110 ($60 fare plus $50 in forgone earnings) and the opportunity cost of air travel is $110 ($100 fare plus $10 in forgone earnings). In this case the opportunity costs are the same.
   c) For a person who could have earned $12 an hour the opportunity cost of train travel ($120) exceeds the opportunity cost of air travel ($112).

2) a) Even though medical care may be offered without charge ("free"), there are still opportunity costs. The opportunity cost of providing such health care is the best alternative use of the resources used in the construction of the hospital and the best alternative use of the resources (including human resources) used in the operation of the hospital.
   b) These resources are no longer available for other activities and therefore represent a cost to society.

3) a) The given statement is normative. The following is positive: If the government reduces the size of the deficit, interest rates will fall.
   b) The given statement is positive. The following is normative: The government ought to impose a tax on tobacco products.

4) a) The prediction of the model can be tested by conducting the following controlled experiment and carefully observing the outcome. Select a number of plots of ground of the same size which have similar characteristics and will be subject to the same amount of water and sunlight. Plant equal quantities of seeds in all the plots. In some of the plots apply no fertilizer and in some of the plots apply (perhaps varying amounts of) fertilizer. When the plants have grown, measure the growth of the plants and compare the growth measures of the fertilized plots and the unfertilized plots. If plant growth is greater in fertilized plots, we provisionally accept the model and the theory on which it is based. If plant growth is *not* greater in fertilized plots, we discard the theory (model), or modify its assumptions. Perhaps the effective use of fertilizer requires more water. Then construct a new model which predicts that given more water (and the same amount of sunlight), fertilized plants will grow larger than equivalently watered unfertilized plants. Test that model and continue modifying assumptions until predictions are consistent with the facts.
   b) Economists cannot perform such controlled experiments and must instead change one assumption at a time in alternative models and compare the resulting outcomes. Such differences in outcomes can then only be tested against variations in data that occur naturally in the economy. This is a more difficult and less precise model building and testing procedure than exists for the controlled fertilizer experiment.

Chapter 2 Making and Using Graphs

Chapter in Perspective

Text Pages 27–48

As a science, economics is characterized by systematic observation and measurement as well as by the development of economic theory. In both of these components of economic science, the use of graphs plays an important role.

Economic theory describes relationships among economic variables, and graphs offer a very convenient way to represent such relationships. Indeed, the use of graphs allows us to economize in the sense that we are able to obtain much information with little effort. Graphs give a "picture" of the behaviour of measured economic variables. Representing data graphically can be extremely useful for quickly conveying information about general characteristics of economic behaviour. As we will see in the next few chapters, graphical analysis of economic relationships is especially helpful when we are interested in discovering the theoretical consequences of a change in economic circumstances. Given the pervasive use of graphs in economics, this chapter reviews all the concepts and techniques you will need to construct and use graphs in this course.

Learning Objectives

After studying this chapter, you will be able to:

- **Make and interpret a time-series graph and a scatter diagram.**
- **Distinguish between linear and nonlinear relationships and relationships that have a maximum and a minimum.**
- **Define and calculate the slope of a line.**
- **Graph relationships between more than two variables.**

Helpful Hints

1) The chapters of the text discuss numerous relationships among economic variables. Almost invariably these relationships will be represented and analyzed graphically. Thus an early, complete understanding of graphs will greatly facilitate mastery of the economic analysis of later chapters. Avoid the common mistake of assuming that a superficial understanding of graphs will be sufficient.

2) If your experience with graphical analysis is limited, this chapter is crucial to your ability to readily understand later economic analysis. You will likely find significant rewards in occasionally returning to this chapter for review. If you are experienced in the construction and use of graphs, this chapter may be "old hat." Even in this case, the chapter should be skimmed and the Self-Test in this *Study Guide* completed. The main point is that you should be thoroughly familiar with the basic concepts and techniques of this chapter.

3) Slope is a *linear* concept since it is a property of a straight line. For this reason, the slope is constant along a straight line but is different at different points on a curved (nonlinear) line. When we are interested in the slope of a curved line, we actually calculate the slope of a straight line. The text presents two ways of choosing such a straight line and thus two alternative ways of calculating the slope of a curved line: (1) slope across an arc, and (2) slope at a point. The first of these calculates the slope of the *straight line* formed by the arc between two points on the curved line. The second calculates the slope of the *straight line* that just touches (is tangent to) the curve at a point.

4) A straight line on a graph can also be described by a simple equation. The general form for the equation of a straight line is:

$$y = a + bx$$

If you are given such an equation, you can graph the line by finding the y-intercept (where the line intersects the vertical y-axis), finding the x-intercept (where the line intersects the horizontal x-axis), and then connecting those two points with a straight line:

To find the y-intercept,

set $x = 0$.

$$y = a + b(0)$$
$$y = a$$

To find the x-intercept,

set $y = 0$.

$$0 = a + bx$$
$$x = -a/b$$

Connecting these two points (($x = 0$, $y = a$) and ($x = -a/b$, $y = 0$)) or $(0,a)$ and $(-a/b,0)$ yields the line in Figure 2.1.

Figure 2.1

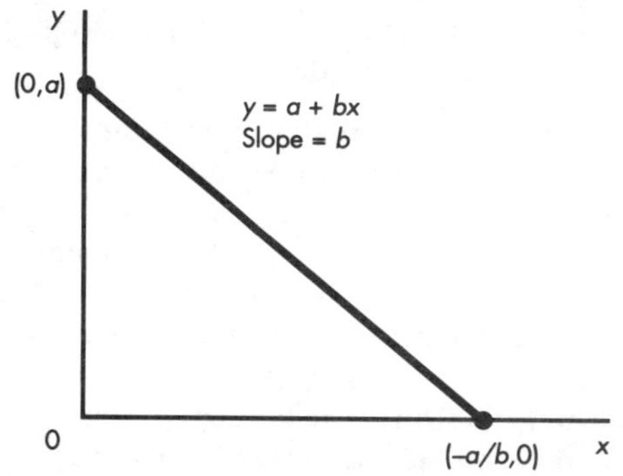

For any straight line with the equation of the form $y = a + bx$, the slope of the line is b.
To see how to apply this general equation, consider this example:

$$y = 4 - 2x$$

To find the y-intercept, set $x = 0$.

$$y = 4 - 2(0)$$
$$y = 4$$

To find the x-intercept, set $y = 0$.

$$0 = 4 - 2x$$
$$x = 2$$

Connecting these two points, (0,4) and (2, 0), yields the line in Figure 2.2.

Figure 2.2

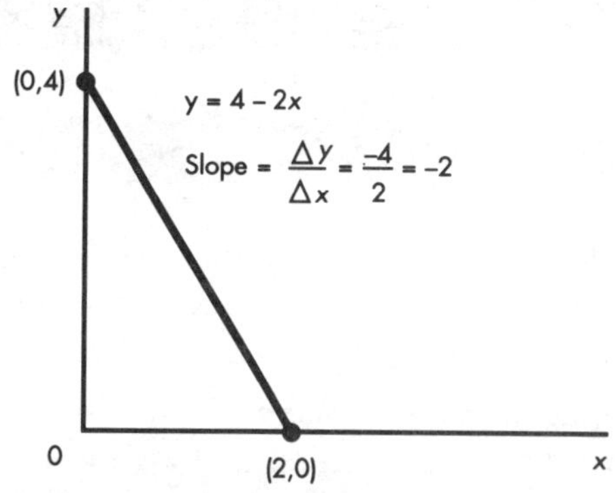

The slope of this line is –2. Since the slope is negative, there is a negative relationship between the variables x and y.

Key Figures

Figure 2.8 Positive Relationships, text page 38
Variables that move up and down together are positively related. Three different positive relationships are illustrated in this figure. In each case, as the variable measured on the horizontal axis increases, the variable measured on the vertical axis also increases. Part (a) illustrates a positive linear relationship, while parts (b) and (c) illustrate positive relationships that are not linear.

Figure 2.9 Negative Relationships, text page 39
This figure is a companion to Figure 2.8 and illustrates negative relationships. Variables that move in opposite directions are negatively related. Three different negative relationships are illustrated in this figure. In each case, as the variable measured on the horizontal axis increases, the variable measured on the vertical axis decreases. Part (a) illustrates a negative linear relationship, while parts (b) and (c) illustrate negative relationships that are not linear.

Figure 2.10 Maximum and Minimum Points, text page 40
The relationship in part (a) reaches a maximum. As the variable measured on the horizontal axis increases, the value of the variable measured on the vertical axis increases, reaches a maximum at point *a* and then decreases. Similarly, the relationship in part (b) reaches a minimum at point *b*.

Figure 2.11 Variables with No Relationship, text page 41
If there is no relationship between two variables, changes in one will have no effect on the other. The two parts of this figure illustrate such a lack of relationship. Part (a) illustrates the fact that changes in the variable measured on the horizontal axis leave the variable measured on the vertical axis unchanged. Part (b) illustrates that changes in the variable measured on the vertical axis leave the variable measured on the horizontal axis unchanged.

Figure 2.12 The Slope of a Straight Line, text page 42
The slope of a straight line tells us how much and in what direction the variable on the vertical axis changes when the variable on the horizontal axis changes. The slope is computed by dividing the change in y (the *rise*) by the change in x (the *run*). When both x and y move in the same direction, as in part (a), the slope is positive and when x and y move in opposite directions, as in part (b), the slope is negative.

Figure 2.13 The Slope of a Curve, text page 43
Slope is a linear concept, so even when we measure the slope of a curve, we do so by calculating the slope of a straight line. This figure illustrates the two ways of choosing a straight line to do this. Part (a) calculates the slope of the straight line that just touches (is tangent to) the curve at a point. Part (b) calculates the slope of the straight line formed by the arc between two points on the curved line.

Figure 2.14 Graphing a Relationship Between Three Variables, text page 44
When graphing a relationship among three variables, we can reduce the problem to graphing the relationship between two variables by holding one of the variables constant and graphing the relationship between the other two. This is illustrated in this figure using as an example the relationship among ice cream consumption, the price of a scoop of ice cream, and air temperature. Part (a) shows the negative relationship between ice cream consumption and the price of a scoop of ice cream if the air temperature is held constant (at 21° C and also at 32° C). Part (b) shows the positive relationship between ice cream consumption and air temperature if the price of a scoop of ice cream is held constant. Finally, part (c) shows the positive relationship between the air temperature and the price of a scoop of ice cream if the consumption of ice cream is held constant.

SELF-TEST

CONCEPT REVIEW

1) A graph that measures an economic variable on the vertical axis and time on the horizontal axis is called a(n) ______________ - ______________ graph.

2) The tendency for a variable to rise or fall over time is called the ______________ of the variable.

3) Suppose the value of one economic variable is measured on the x-axis and the value of a second is measured on the y-axis. A diagram that plots the value of one variable corresponding to the value of the other is called a(n) ______________ diagram.

4) If two variables tend to move up or down together they exhibit a(n) ______________ relationship. Such a relationship is represented graphically by a line that slopes ______________ (to the right).

5) Two variables that move in opposite directions exhibit a(n) ______________ relationship. Such a relationship is represented graphically by a line that slopes ______________ (to the right).

6) Suppose variables *A* and *B* are unrelated. If we measure *A* on the *y*-axis and *B* on the *x*-axis, the graph of *A* as we increase *B* will be a(n) ______________ line.

7) The slope of a line is calculated as the change in the value of the variable measured on the ______________ axis divided by the change in the value of the variable measured on the ______________ axis.

8) A straight line exhibits ______________ slope at all points.

9) To graph a relationship among more than two variables, we simply graph the relationship between ______________ variables, holding all other variables constant.

TRUE OR FALSE

_____ 1) A time-series graph measures time on the horizontal axis.

_____ 2) A time-series graph gives information about the level of the relevant economic variable, as well as information about changes and the speed of those changes.

_____ 3) A graph that omits the origin will always be misleading.

_____ 4) A two-variable time-series graph can help us see if the two variables tend to move together over time.

_____ 5) A one-dimensional graph that represents measured rainfall along a horizontal line is an example of a scatter diagram.

_____ 6) If the graph of the relationship between two variables slopes upward (to the right), the variables move up and down together.

_____ 7) If variable *a* rises when variable *b* falls and falls when *b* rises, then the relationship between *a* and *b* is negative.

_____ 8) If the relationship between *y* (measured along the vertical axis) and *x* (measured along the horizontal axis) is such that *y* reaches a maximum as *x* increases, then the relationship must be negative before and positive after the maximum.

_____ 9) If the value of *y* (measured along the vertical axis) doesn't change as we increase *x* (measured along the horizontal axis), the graph of the relationship between *x* and *y* is horizontal.

_____ 10) The graph of the relationship between two variables that are in fact unrelated will be either horizontal or vertical.

_____ 11) The slope of a straight line is calculated by dividing the change in the value of the variable measured on the horizontal axis by the change in the value of the variable measured on the vertical axis.

_____ 12) The slope of a curved line is not constant.

_____ 13) If we want to graph the relationship among three variables, we must hold two of them constant as we represent the third.

_____ 14) Refer to Figure 2.3. The value of *y* increased between 1970 and 1971.

Figure 2.3

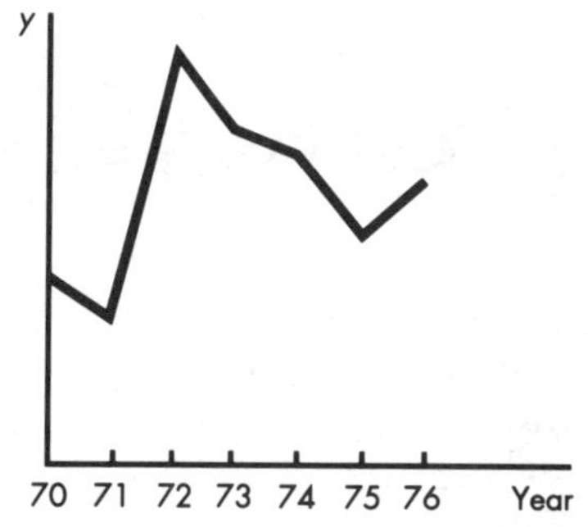

_____ 15) Refer to Figure 2.3. The value of *y* increased much more rapidly between 1971 and 1972 than between 1975 and 1976.

_____ 16) Figure 2.3 is a scatter diagram.

_____ 17) In Figure 2.4, the relationship between *x* and *y* is first negative, reaches a minimum, and then becomes positive as *x* increases.

Figure 2.4

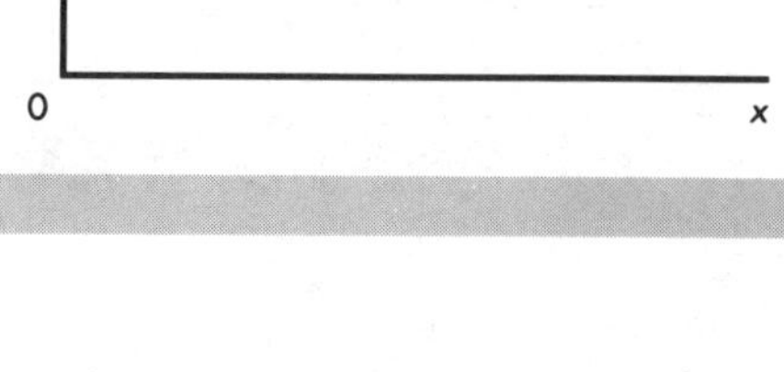

_____ 18) In Figure 2.4, the slope of the curve is increasing as we move from point *b* to point *c*.

_____ 19) In Figure 2.4, the slope of the curve is approaching zero as we move from point *a* to point *b*.

_____ 20) In Figure 2.4, the value of *x* is a minimum at point *b*.

_____ 21) For a point on a two-variable graph, the length of the line running from the point to the vertical axis is the *y*-coordinate.

_____ 22) The slope of a line can be described as "rise over run."

_____ 23) For a straight line, if a small change in *y* is associated with a large change in *x*, the slope is large.

_____ 24) For a straight line, if a large change in *y* is associated with a small change in *x*, the line is steep.

MULTIPLE-CHOICE

1) The behaviour of a single economic variable over time is best illustrated by a
   a) one-variable graph.
   b) two-variable graph.
   c) time-series graph.
   d) linear graph.
   e) scatter diagram.

2) Figure 2.5 is
   a) a one-variable time-series graph.
   b) a two-variable time-series graph.
   c) a scatter diagram.
   d) both b) and c).
   e) none of the above.

Figure 2.5

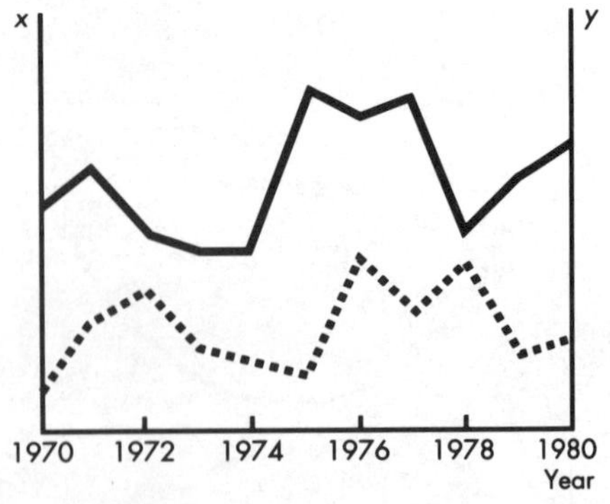

3) The dotted line in Figure 2.5 represents variable *y*. Which of the following statements best describes the relationship between *x* and *y* in Figure 2.5?
   a) *x* and *y* tend to move in opposite directions over time.
   b) *y* tends to move in the opposite direction from *x*, but one year later.
   c) *x* and *y* tend to move together over time.
   d) *x* tends to move in the same direction as *y*, but one year later.
   e) *y* tends to move in the same direction as *x*, but one year later.

4) The data in Table 2.1 could *not* be represented by
   a) two one-variable time-series graphs.
   b) one two-variable time-series graph.
   c) a three-variable time-series graph.
   d) a scatter diagram.
   e) any of the above.

Table 2.1

Year	x	y
1980	6.2	143
1981	5.7	156
1982	5.3	162

5) From the information in Table 2.1, it appears that
   a) *x* and *y* tend to exhibit a negative relationship.
   b) *x* and *y* tend to exhibit a positive relationship.
   c) there is no relationship between *x* and *y*.
   d) there is first a negative and then a positive relationship between *x* and *y*.
   e) there is first a positive and then a negative relationship between *x* and *y*.

6) If variables *x* and *y* move up and down together, they are said to be
   a) positively related.
   b) negatively related.
   c) conversely related.
   d) unrelated.
   e) trendy.

7) The relationship between two variables that move in opposite directions is shown graphically by a line that is
   a) positively sloped.
   b) relatively steep.
   c) relatively flat.
   d) negatively sloped.
   e) curved.

8) What is the slope of the line in Figure 2.6?
a) 2
b) 1/2
c) 3
d) 1/3
e) –3

Figure 2.6

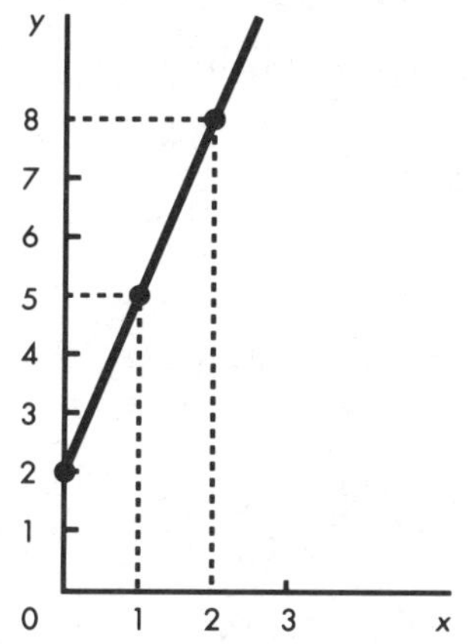

9) If the line in Figure 2.6 were to continue down to the *x*-axis, what would the value of *x* be when *y* is zero?
a) 0
b) 2
c) 2/3
d) –2/3
e) –3/2

10) In Figure 2.7 the relationship between *x* and *y* is
a) positive with slope decreasing as *x* increases.
b) negative with slope decreasing as *x* increases.
c) negative with slope increasing as *x* increases.
d) positive with slope increasing as *x* increases.
e) positive with slope first increasing then decreasing as *x* increases.

Figure 2.7

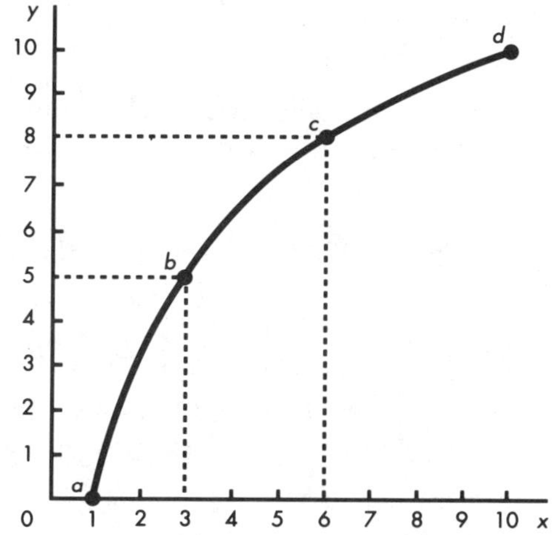

11) What is the slope across the arc between *b* and *c* in Figure 2.7?
a) 1/2
b) 2/3
c) 1
d) 2
e) 3

12) In Figure 2.7, consider the slopes of arc *ab* and arc *bc*. The slope at point *b* is difficult to determine exactly, but it must be
a) greater than 5/2.
b) about 5/2.
c) between 5/2 and 1.
d) about 1.
e) less than 1.

13) If the price of an umbrella is low and the number of rainy days per month is large, more umbrellas will be sold each month. On the other hand, if the price of an umbrella is high and there are few rainy days per month, fewer umbrellas will be sold each month. On the basis of this information, which of the following statements is true?
a) The number of umbrellas sold and the price of an umbrella are positively related, holding the number of rainy days constant.
b) The number of umbrellas sold and the price of an umbrella are negatively related, holding the number of rainy days constant.
c) The number of rainy days and the number of umbrellas sold are negatively related, holding the price of an umbrella constant.
d) The number of rainy days and the price of an umbrella are negatively related, holding the number of umbrellas sold constant.
e) None of the above statements is true.

14) Given the data in Table 2.2, holding income constant, the graph relating the price of strawberries (vertical axis) to the purchases of strawberries (horizontal axis)
a) is a vertical line.
b) is a horizontal line.
c) is a positively-sloped line.
d) is a negatively-sloped line.
e) reaches a minimum.

Table 2.2

Weekly Family Income (dollars)	Price per Box of Strawberries (dollars)	Number of Boxes Purchased per Week
300	1.00	5
300	1.25	3
300	1.50	2
400	1.00	7
400	1.25	5
400	1.50	4

15) Consider the data in Table 2.2. Suppose family income decreases from \$400 to \$300 per week. Then the graph relating the price of strawberries (vertical axis) to the purchases of strawberries (horizontal axis) will
a) become negatively sloped.
b) become positively sloped.
c) shift to the right.
d) shift to the left.
e) no longer exist.

16) Given the data in Table 2.2, holding price constant, the graph relating family income (vertical axis) to the purchases of strawberries (horizontal axis) is
a) a vertical line.
b) a horizontal line.
c) a positively-sloped line.
d) a negatively-sloped line.
e) a positively or negatively-sloped line, depending on the price that is held constant.

17) In Figure 2.8, *x* is
a) positively related to *y* and negatively related to *z*.
b) positively related to both *y* and *z*.
c) negatively related to *y* and positively related to *z*.
d) negatively related to both *y* and *z*.
e) greater than *z*.

Figure 2.8

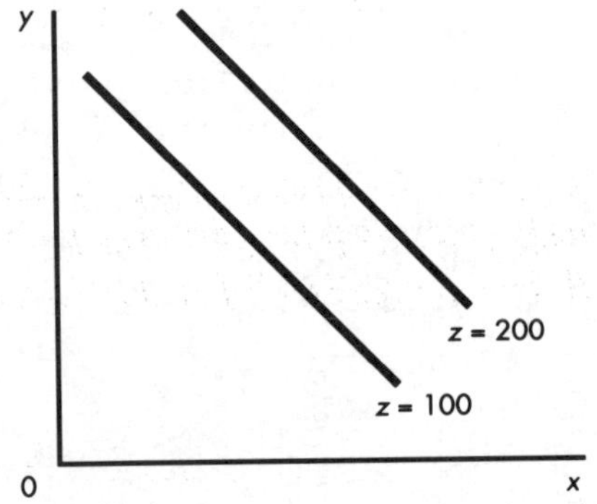

18) In Figure 2.8, a decrease in the value of *z* will cause, *ceteris paribus*,
a) a decrease in the value of *x*.
b) an increase in the value of *x*.
c) an increase in the value of *y*.
d) no change in the value of *y*.
e) both a) and d).

19) If the equation of a straight line is $y = 6 + 3x$, then the slope is
a) –3 and the *y*-intercept is 6.
b) –3 and the *y*-intercept is –2.
c) 3 and the *y*-intercept is 6.
d) 3 and the *y*-intercept is –2.
e) 3 and the *y*-intercept is –6.

20) If the equation of a straight line is $y = 8 - 2x$, then the slope is
a) –2 and the *x*-intercept is –4.
b) –2 and the *x*-intercept is 4.
c) –2 and the *x*-intercept is 8.
d) 2 and the *x*-intercept is –4.
e) 2 and the *x*-intercept is 4.

SHORT ANSWER

1) a) Draw a two-variable time-series graph that illustrates two variables that have a tendency to move up and down together.
b) What would the scatter diagram for these two variables look like?

2) Draw a graph of variables *x* and *y* that illustrates each of the following relationships:
a) *x* and *y* move up and down together
b) *x* and *y* move in opposite directions
c) as *x* increases *y* reaches a maximum
d) as *x* increases *y* reaches a minimum
e) *x* and *y* move in opposite directions, but as *x* increases *y* decreases by larger and larger increments for each unit increase in *x*
f) *y* is independent of the value of *x*
g) *x* is independent of the value of *y*

3) What does it mean to say that the slope of a line is –2/3?

4) Explain how we measure the slope of a curved line
a) at a point.
b) across an arc.

5) How do we graph a relationship among more than two variables using a two-dimensional graph?

PROBLEMS

1) Consider the data in Table 2.3.
a) Draw a time-series graph for the interest rate.
b) Draw a two-variable time-series graph for both the inflation rate and the interest rate.

c) Draw a scatter diagram for the inflation rate (horizontal axis) and the interest rate (vertical axis).
d) Would you describe the general relationship between the inflation rate and the interest rate as positive, negative, or unrelated?

Table 2.3

Year	Inflation Rate (percent)	Interest Rate (percent)
1970	5.4	6.4
1971	3.2	4.3
1972	3.4	4.1
1973	8.3	7.0
1974	11.8	7.9
1975	6.7	5.8
1976	4.9	5.0
1977	6.5	5.3
1978	8.6	7.2
1979	12.3	10.0

2) Compute the slope of the lines in Figure 2.9(a) and (b).

Figure 2.9

(a)

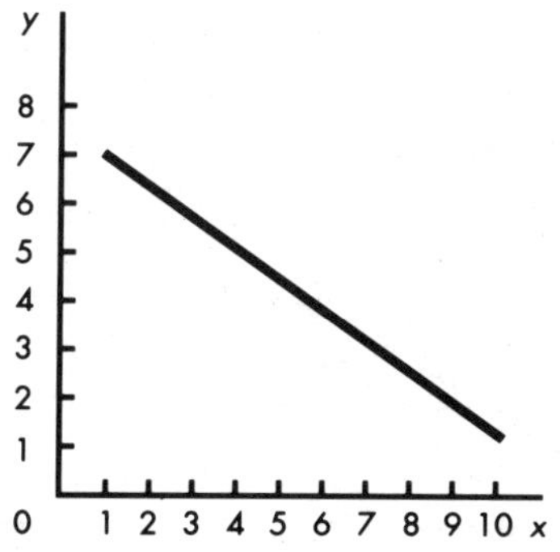

(b)

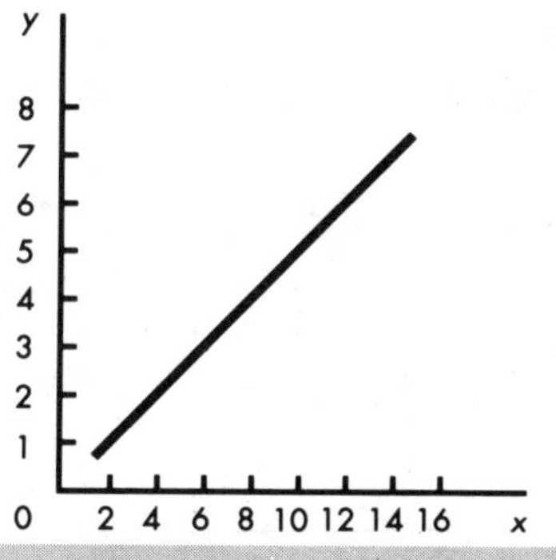

3) Draw each of the following:
a) a straight line with slope –10 and passing through the point (2, 80).
b) a straight line with slope 2 and passing through the point (6, 10).

4) The equation for a straight line is $y = 6 - 2x$.
a) Calculate:
i) the y-intercept.
ii) the x-intercept.
iii) the slope.
b) Draw the graph of the line.

5) Use the graph in Figure 2.10 to compute the slope
a) across the arc between points *a* and *b*.
b) at point *b*.
c) at point *c*, and explain your answer.

Figure 2.10

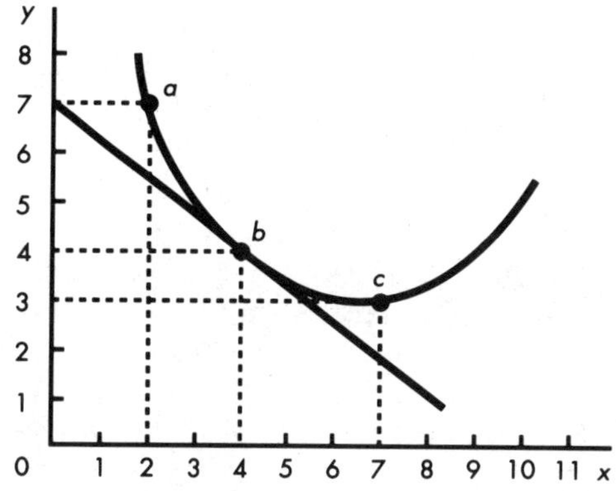

6) In Table 2.4, x represents the number of umbrellas sold per month, y represents the price of an umbrella, and z represents the average number of rainy days per month.

Table 2.4

Umbrellas Sold per Month (x)	Price per Umbrella (y)	Average Number of Rainy Days per Month (z)
120	$10	4
140	$10	5
160	$10	6
100	$12	4
120	$12	5
140	$12	6
80	$14	4
100	$14	5
120	$14	6

6) a) On the same diagram, graph the relationship between x (horizontal axis) and y (vertical axis) when $z = 4$, when $z = 5$, and when $z = 6$. Suppose that, on average, it rains 6 days per month. This implies a certain average relationship between monthly umbrella sales and umbrella price. Suppose that the Greenhouse Effect reduces the average monthly rainfall to 4 days per month. What happens to the graph of the relationship between umbrella sales and umbrella prices?

b) On a diagram, graph the relationship between x (horizontal axis) and z (vertical axis) when $y = \$10$ and when $y = \$12$. Is the relationship between x and z positive or negative?

c) On a diagram, graph the relationship between y (horizontal axis) and z (vertical axis) when $x = 120$ and when $x = 140$. Is the relationship between y and z positive or negative?

ANSWERS

CONCEPT REVIEW

1) time-series
2) trend
3) scatter
4) positive; upward
5) negative; downward
6) horizontal
7) vertical (y); horizontal (x)
8) constant
9) two

TRUE OR FALSE

1) T	7) T	13) F	19) T
2) T	8) F	14) F	20) F
3) F	9) T	15) T	21) F
4) T	10) T	16) F	22) T
5) F	11) F	17) T	23) F
6) T	12) T	18) T	24) T

MULTIPLE-CHOICE

1) c	6) a	11) c	16) c
2) b	7) d	12) c	17) c
3) e	8) c	13) b	18) a
4) c	9) d	14) d	19) c
5) a	10) a	15) d	20) b

SHORT ANSWER

1) a) Figure 2.11(a) illustrates a two-variable time-series graph of two variables with a tendency to move up and down together.
b) Figure 2.11(b) illustrates a scatter diagram for such variables.

Figure 2.11

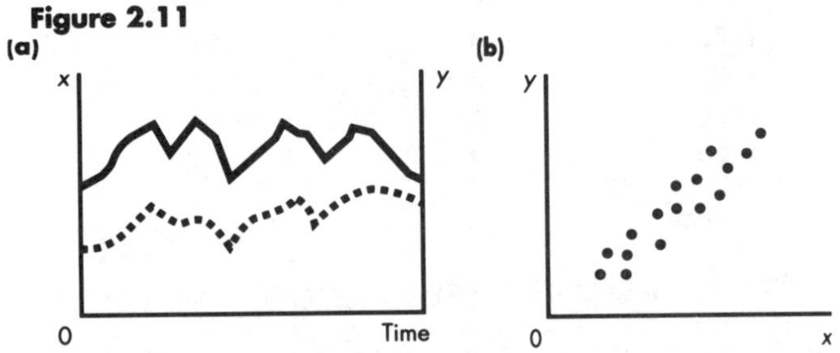

2) Figures 2.12(a) through (g) illustrate the desired graphs.

Figure 2.12

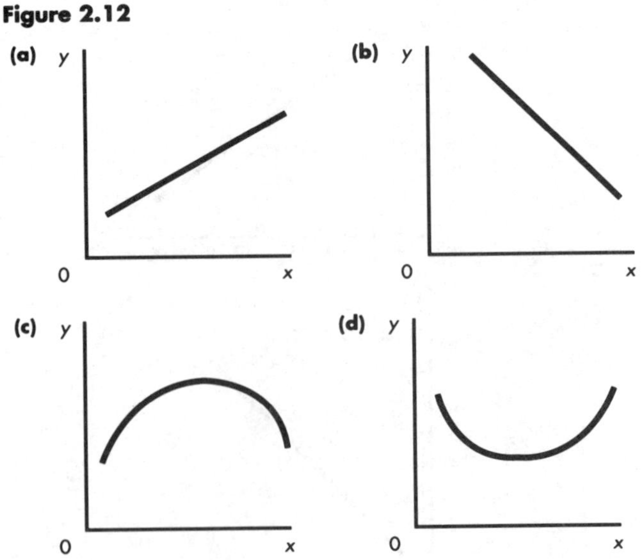

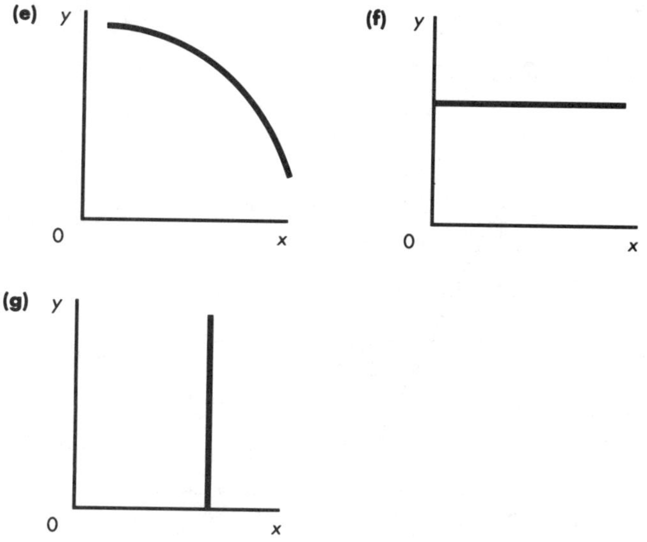

3) The negative sign in the slope of –2/3 means that there is a negative relationship between the two variables. The value of 2/3 means that when the variable measured on the vertical axis decreases by 2 units (the *rise* or Δ *y*), the variable measured on the horizontal axis increases by 3 units (the *run* or Δ *x*).

4) In both cases, we actually measure the slope of a straight line.
   a) The slope at a point is measured by calculating the slope of the straight line that is tangent to (just touches) the curved line at the point.
   b) The slope across an arc is measured by calculating the slope of the straight line that forms the arc.

5) To graph a relationship among more than two variables, we hold all of the variables but two constant, and graph the relationship between the remaining two. Thus, we can graph the relationship between any pair of variables, given the constant values of the other variables.

PROBLEMS

1) a) A time-series graph for the interest rate is given in Figure 2.13(a).
   b) Figure 2.13(b) is a two-variable time-series graph for both the inflation rate and the interest rate.
   c) The scatter diagram for the inflation rate and the interest rate is given in Figure 2.13(c).
   d) From the graphs in Figures 2.13(b) and (c), we see that the relationship between the inflation rate and the interest rate is generally positive.

Figure 2.13

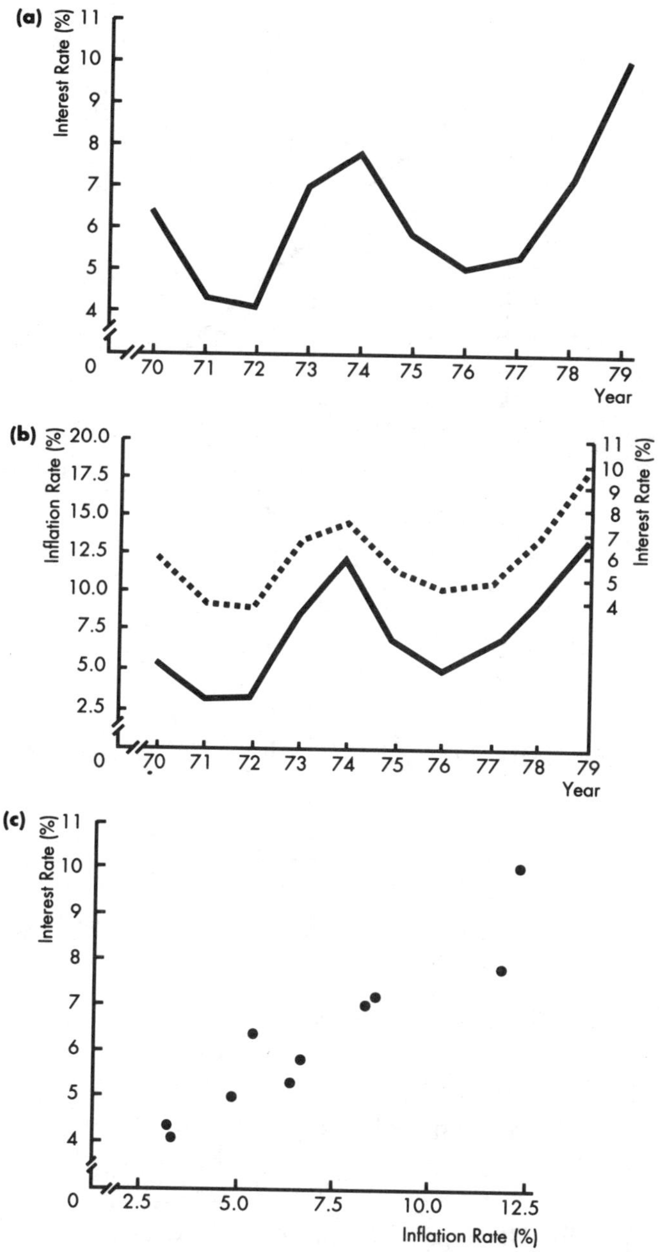

2) The slope of the line in Figure 2.9(a) is –2/3 and the slope of the line in Figure 2.9(b) is 1/2.

3) a) The requested strait line is graphed in Figure 2.14(a) on page 18.
   b) The requested straight line is graphed in Figure 2.14(b) on page 18.

Figure 2.14

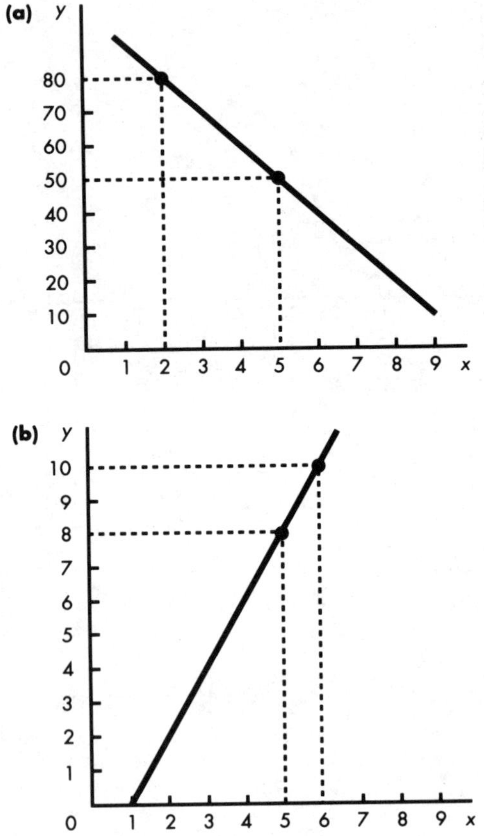

Figure 2.15

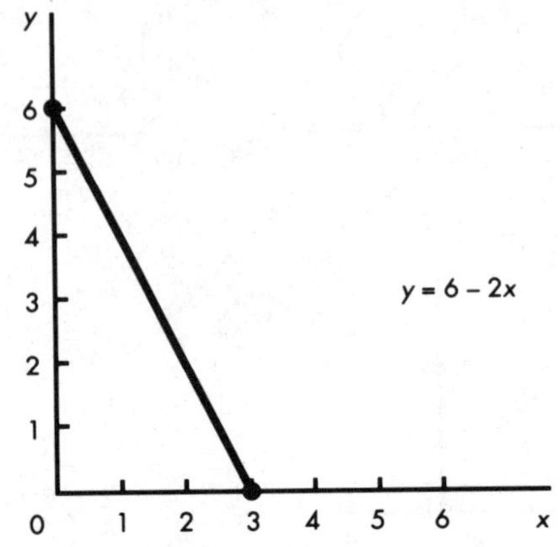

4) a) i) To find the y-intercept, set $x = 0$.

$$y = 6 - 2(0)$$
$$y = 6$$

ii) To find the x-intercept, set $y = 0$.

$$0 = 6 - 2x$$
$$x = 3$$

iii) The slope of the line is –2, the value of the b coefficient on x.

b) The graph of the line is shown in Figure 2.15.

5) a) The slope across the arc between points a and b is –3/2.

b) The slope at point b is –3/4.

c) The slope at point c is zero because it is a minimum point. Nearby a minimum point the slope changes from negative to positive and must pass through zero, to do so.

6) a) The relationships between x and y for $z = 4, 5,$ and 6 are graphed in Figure 2.16(a). If the average monthly rainfall drops from 6 days to 4 days, the curve representing the relationship between umbrella sales and umbrella prices will shift from the curve labelled $z = 6$ to $z = 4$.

b) The relationships between x and z when y is \$10 and when y is \$12 are graphed in Figure 2.16(b). The relationship between x and z is positive.

c) The relationships between y and z when $x = 120$ and when $x = 140$ are graphed in Figure 2.16(c). The relationship between y and z is positive.

Figure 2.16

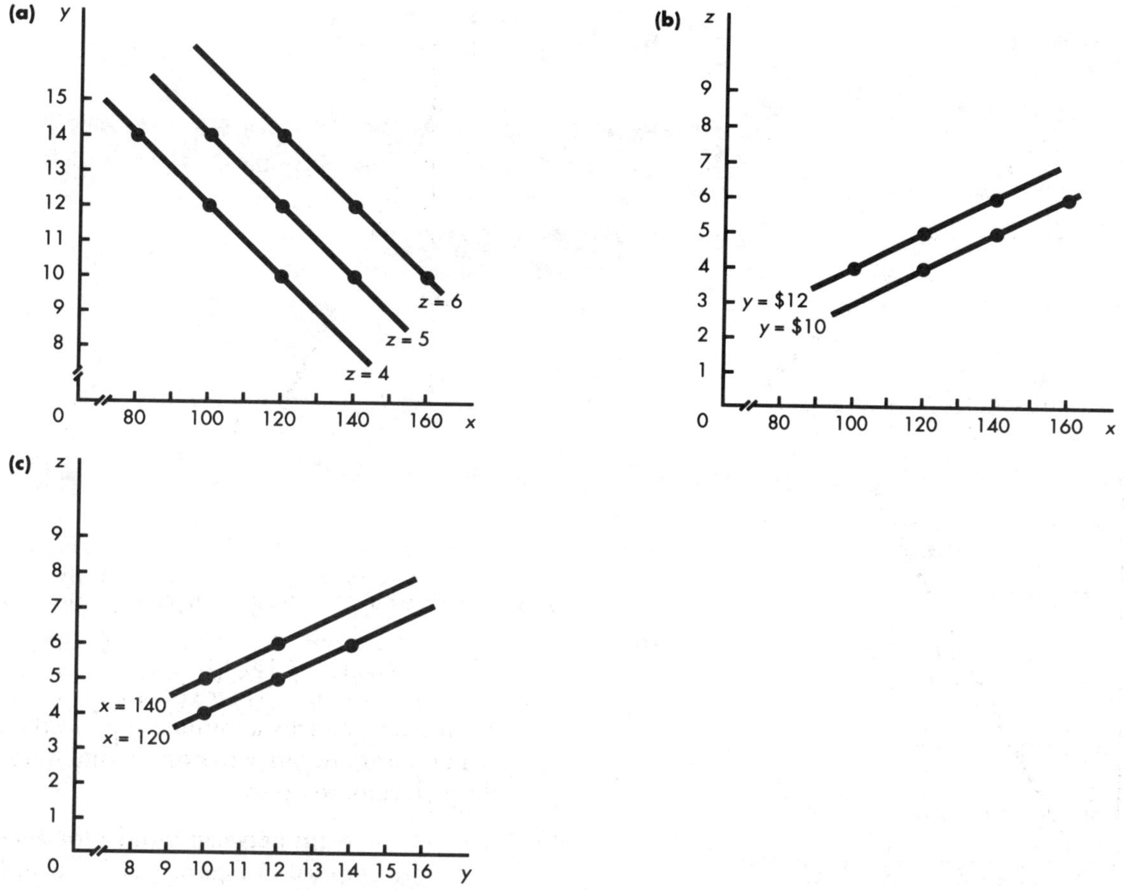
(a)
y
15
14
13
12
11
10
9
8
0
80
100
120
140
160
x
z = 6
z = 5
z = 4
(b)
z
9
8
7
6
5
4
3
2
1
0
80
100
120
140
160
x
y = $12
y = $10
(c)
z
9
8
7
6
5
4
3
2
1
0
8
9
10
11
12
13
14
15
16
y
x = 140
x = 120

Chapter 3 Production, Specialization, and Exchange

Chapter in Perspective

Text Pages 49–68

In the first chapter we learned that the existence of scarcity is the fundamental and pervasive social problem giving rise to economic activity. Because all individuals and all economies are faced with scarce resources, choices must be made, each of which has an opportunity cost. Specialization in production is the key to obtaining maximum output from scarce resources, and leads to lowest opportunity costs. Since workers specialize as producers but consume a variety of goods and services, exchange is a necessary complement to specialization.

This chapter explains why specialization and exchange are the natural consequences of attempts to obtain the most from scarce resources (to optimize). It also discusses the critical role of opportunity cost in explaining why individuals and countries specialize in the production of goods and services and why tremendous gains occur from specialization and exchange.

Learning Objectives

After studying this chapter, you will be able to:

- **Define the production possibility frontier.**
- **Calculate opportunity cost.**
- **Explain why economic growth and technical change do not provide free gifts.**
- **Explain comparative advantage.**
- **Explain why people specialize and how they gain from trade.**
- **Explain why property rights and money have evolved.**

Helpful Hints

1) This chapter reviews the absolutely critical concept of *opportunity cost*— the best alternative forgone— which was introduced in Chapter 1. A very helpful formula for opportunity cost, which works well in solving problems, especially problems that involve moving up or down a production possibility frontier is:

$$\text{Opportunity Cost} = \frac{\text{Give Up}}{\text{Get}}$$

Opportunity cost equals the quantity of goods you must give up divided by the quantity of goods you will get. To illustrate, look again at 3 possibilities on Jane's production possibility frontier in textbook Figure 3.1 on page 53.

Possibility	Corn (kilograms per month)	Cloth (metres per month)
a	20	0
b	18	1
c	15	2

a) First consider an example of moving down the production possibility frontier. In moving from *a* to *b*, what is the opportunity cost of an additional metre of cloth? Jane must *give up* 2 kilograms of corn (20 – 18) to *get* 1 metre of cloth (1 – 0). Substituting into the formula, the opportunity cost is:

$$\frac{\text{2 kilograms corn}}{\text{1 metre cloth}} = \text{2 kilograms corn per metre of cloth}$$

Next, consider an example of moving up the production possibility frontier. In moving from *b* to *a*, what is the opportunity cost of an additional kilogram of corn? Jane must *give up* 1 metre of cloth (1 – 0) to *get* 2 kilograms of corn (20 – 18). Substituting into the formula, the opportunity cost is:

$$\frac{\text{1 metre cloth}}{\text{2 kilograms corn}} = \text{1/2 metre cloth per kilogram of corn}$$

Opportunity cost is always measured in the units of the *forgone good.*

Opportunity cost can also be related to the slope of the production possibility frontier (PPF). As we move down between any two points on the PPF, the opportunity cost of an additional unit of the good on the *horizontal* axis is:

$$\left| \text{slope of PPF} \right|$$

The slope of the PPF is negative, but economists like to describe opportunity cost in terms of a positive quantity of forgone goods. Therefore, we must use the *absolute value* of the slope to calculate the desired positive number.

As we move up between any two points on the PPF, the opportunity cost of an additional unit of the good on the *vertical* axis is:

$$\left| \frac{1}{\text{slope of PPF}} \right|$$

This is the reciprocal relation we saw between possibilities *a* and *b*. The opportunity cost of an additional unit of cloth (on the horizontal axis) between *a* and *b* is 2 kilograms of corn. The opportunity cost of an additional unit of corn (on the vertical axis) between *b* and *a* is 1/2 metre of cloth.

b) Jane's production possibility frontier assumes nonhomogeneous resources, that is, resources that are *not* equally useful in all activities. As a result of this assumption, opportunity cost increases as she increases the production of either good. In moving from possibility *a* to *b*, the opportunity cost per metre of cloth is 2 kilograms of corn. But in increasing cloth production from *b* to *c*, the opportunity cost per metre of cloth increases to 3 kilograms of corn. In producing the first metre of cloth, Jane uses the resources best suited to cloth production. As she increases cloth production, however, she must use resources that are less well suited to cloth production; hence increasing opportunity cost. A parallel argument accounts for the increasing opportunity cost of increasing corn production.

It is also possible to construct an even simpler model of a production possibility frontier, which assumes homogeneous resources, resources that are *equally* useful in all activities. As a result of this assumption, opportunity cost is *constant* as we increase production of either good. Constant opportunity cost means that the production possibility frontier will be a straight line (rather than bowed out). As you will see in some of the following exercises, such a simple model is useful for illustrating the principle of comparative advantage, without having to deal with the complications of increasing opportunity cost.

2) A production possibility frontier represents the boundary between attainable and unattainable levels of production for a fixed quantity of resources and a given state of technology. It indicates the best that can be done with existing resources and technology. Thus, the production possibility frontier will shift out if the quantity of resources increases

(for example, an increase in the stock of capital goods) even if the ability to use those resources does not change. The production possibility curve will also shift out if there is an increase in the ability to produce (a technological improvement) with no change in resources.

3) The text defines absolute advantage as a situation where one person has greater productivity than another in the production of all goods. We can also define ***absolute advantage in the production of one good.*** In comparing the productivity of two persons, this narrower concept of absolute advantage can be defined either in terms of greater output of the good per unit of inputs, or fewer inputs per unit of output.

It is useful to understand these definitions of absolute advantage only to demonstrate that absolute advantage has *no role* in explaining specialization and trade. The gains from trade depend only on differing comparative advantages. People have a comparative advantage in producing a good if they can produce it at lower opportunity cost than others.

4) This chapter gives us our first chance to develop and use an economic model. It is of value to think about the nature of that model in the context of the general discussion about such models in Chapter 1. The model developed in the chapter is a representation of the production possibilities in the two-person and two-good world of Jane and Joe. The model abstracts greatly from the complexity of the real world in which there are billions of people and numerous different kinds of goods and services. The model allows us to explain a number of phenomena that we observe in the world such as specialization and exchange. The model also has some implications or predictions. For example, countries that devote a larger proportion of their resources to capital accumulation will have more rapidly expanding production possibilities. The model can be subjected to "test" by comparing these predictions to the facts we observe in the real world.

Key Figures

Figure 3.1 Jane's Production Possibility Frontier, text page 53

A production possibility frontier is the boundary between attainable and unattainable levels of production for a fixed quantity of resources and a given state of technology. This figure illustrates the production possibility frontier for Jane, who produces corn and cloth. Each point on the frontier shows the *maximum* combinations of corn and cloth she can produce with her resources and technology. Points beyond the frontier are unattainable. Points inside the production possibility frontier are attainable but inferior (they are not maximum combinations of corn and cloth) to points on the frontier. Because the model assumes that capital goods are unchanged (no tool-making), points inside the frontier are inefficient; they represent unemployed or underutilized resources.

Figure 3.2 Jane's Opportunity Cost of Cloth, text page 54

This figure uses information from Figure 3.1 to calculate opportunity costs as we move along the production possibility frontier. Part (a) simply displays the increasing opportunity cost of cloth. Part (b) relates that increasing opportunity cost to movement down the frontier from points *a* to *f* as we increase the production of cloth. In moving from *a* to *b*, we give up 2 kilograms of corn to get 1 metre of cloth; the opportunity cost of the first metre of cloth is 2 kilograms of corn. Similar calculations of opportunity cost as give up/get show increasing opportunity cost as we increase cloth production.

Figure 3.3 Jane's Tool Production Possibilities, text page 57

If resources are used to produce capital goods, for example, tools, productive capacity will increase. This is represented by an outward shift of the production possibility frontier. The greater the proportion of resources used to produce capital goods, the faster the production possibility frontier will shift out. The figure illustrates this concept using the example of Jane's production of corn and cloth. Jane can choose to use all resources to produce corn and cloth (point *e*). In this case, her production possibility frontier remains in its initial position, since Jane's ability to produce will not change. If, however, Jane decides to reduce her current production of corn and cloth in order to produce tools, for example, point *d*, her future productive ability will increase, and so her production possibility frontier will shift out. This figure clearly illustrates the opportunity cost of increasing future production possibilities by producing tools: forgone current production (consumption) of corn and cloth.

SELF-TEST

CONCEPT REVIEW

1) The process of converting resources into goods and services is called ______________.

2) Resources such as iron ore and running rivers are examples of ______________ resources. The skill of a computer programmer and the physical strength of a bricklayer are examples of ______________ resources, and a shoe factory and an olive pitting machine are examples of ______________ resources.

3) The graphical representation of the boundary between attainable and unattainable production levels is called the ______________ ______________ ______________.

4) The ______________ ______________ of a choice is the value of the best forgone alternative choice.

5) Two key activities that can shift the production possibility frontier out are ______________ progress and ______________ accumulation.

6) The opportunity cost of producing capital goods now in order to expand future production is forgone current ______________ goods.

7) If Marta can produce salad forks at a lower opportunity cost than Jill, we say that Marta has a(n) ______________ advantage in the production of salad forks.

8) The economic system that permits private individuals to own the capital resources used in production is called ______________.

9) A system in which goods are traded directly for goods is known as ______________.

10) In order for exchange to take place in such a system there must be a double ______________ of wants.

11) ______________ is defined as a medium of exchange.

TRUE OR FALSE

_____ 1) Increasing opportunity cost results from the equal usefulness of scarce resources in all activities.

Refer to the production possibility frontier in Figure 3.1 for questions 2 – 7.

Figure 3.1

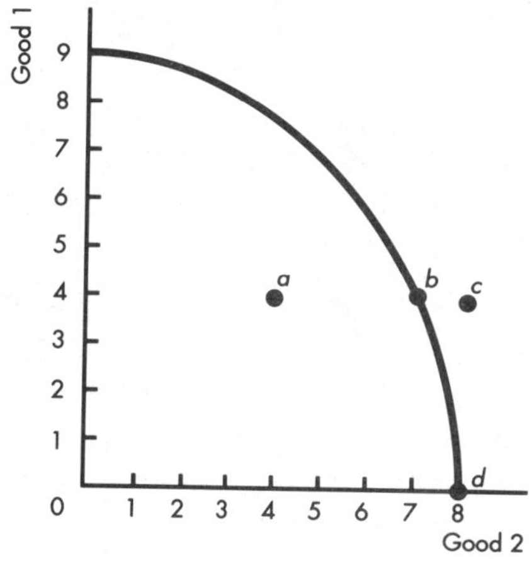

_____ 2) At point *d*, 9 units of good 1 and 8 units of good 2 are produced.

_____ 3) Point *a* is not attainable.

_____ 4) The opportunity cost of increasing the production of good 2 from 7 to 8 units is 4 units of good 1.

_____ 5) Point *c* is not attainable.

_____ 6) In moving from point *b* to point *d*, the opportunity cost of increasing the production of good 2 equals the absolute value of the slope of the production possibility frontier between *b* and *d*.

_____ 7) In moving from point *d* to point *b*, the opportunity cost of increasing the production of good 1 equals the absolute value of the slope of the production possibility frontier between *d* and *b*.

_____ 8) The bowed out (concave) shape of a production possibility frontier reflects decreasing opportunity cost as we increase the production of either good.

_____ 9) Economic growth, by shifting out the production possibility frontier, eliminates the problem of scarcity.

_____ 10) Reducing the current production of consumption goods in order to produce more capital goods will shift the production possibility frontier inward in the future.

_____ 11) In a model where capital resources can grow, points inside the production possibility frontier must represent unemployed resources.

_____ 12) Bill has a comparative advantage in producing good *A* if he can produce more of *A* per unit of inputs than Joe.

_____ 13) Consider an economy with two goods, *X* and *Y*, and two producers, Bill and Joe. If Bill has a comparative advantage in the production of *X*, then Joe must have a comparative advantage in the production of *Y*.

_____ 14) Any time two individuals have different opportunity costs, they can both gain from specialization and trade.

_____ 15) The incentives for specialization and exchange do not depend on property rights but only on differing opportunity costs.

_____ 16) Any system that uses capital in production is a capitalist system.

_____ 17) With specialization and trade, a country can consume at a point outside its production possibility frontier.

_____ 18) With specialization and trade, a country can produce at a point outside its production possibility frontier.

_____ 19) The principle of comparative advantage helps us understand why sooner or later no one in cheap-labour foreign countries will buy Canadian-produced goods.

_____ 20) A monetary exchange system requires a double coincidence of wants.

MULTIPLE-CHOICE

1) If Harold can increase production of good *X* without decreasing the production of any other good, then Harold
   a) is producing on his production possibility frontier.
   b) is producing outside his production possibility frontier.
   c) is producing inside his production possibility frontier.
   d) must have a linear production possibility frontier.
   e) must prefer good *X* to any other good.

2) The bowed out (concave) shape of a production possibility frontier
   a) is due to the equal usefulness of resources in all activities.
   b) is due to capital accumulation.
   c) is due to technological improvement.
   d) reflects the existence of increasing opportunity cost.
   e) reflects the existence of decreasing opportunity cost.

3) The economy is at point *b* on the production possibility frontier in Figure 3.2. The opportunity cost of producing one more unit of *X* is
   a) 1 unit of *Y*.
   b) 20 units of *Y*.
   c) 1 unit of *X*.
   d) 8 units of *X*.
   e) 20 units of *X*.

Figure 3.2

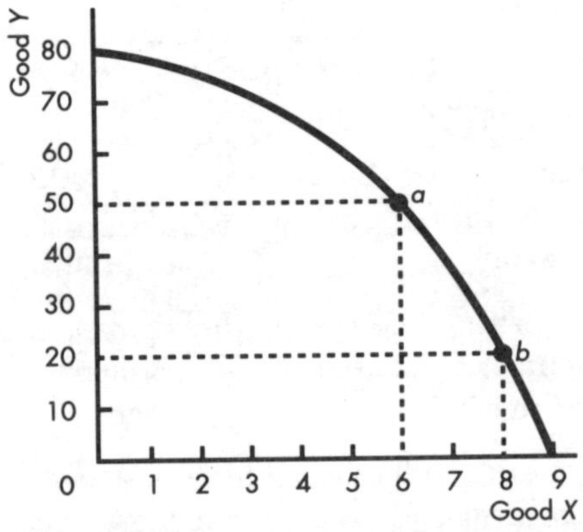

4) The economy is at point *b* on the production possibility frontier in Figure 3.2. The opportunity cost of increasing the production of *Y* to 50 units is
   a) 2 units of *X*.
   b) 6 units of *X*.
   c) 8 units of *X*.
   d) 20 units of *Y*.
   e) 30 units of *Y*.

5) Because productive resources are scarce, we must give up some of one good in order to acquire more of another. This is the essence of the concept of
   a) specialization.
   b) monetary exchange.
   c) comparative advantage.
   d) absolute advantage.
   e) opportunity cost.

6) A movement *along* a given production possibility frontier will result from
   a) technological change.
   b) change in the stock of capital.
   c) change in the labour force.
   d) all of the above.
   e) none of the above.

7) The opportunity cost of pushing the production possibility frontier outward is
   a) capital accumulation.
   b) technological change.
   c) reduced current consumption.
   d) the gain in future consumption.
   e) all of the above.

8) In general, the higher the proportion of resources devoted to technological research in an economy the
   a) greater will be current consumption.
   b) faster the production possibility frontier will shift outward.
   c) faster the production possibility frontier will shift inward.
   d) closer it will come to having a comparative advantage in the production of all goods.
   e) more bowed out will be the shape of the frontier.

9) There are two goods — *X* and *Y*. If the opportunity cost of producing good *X* is lower for Pam than for Gino, then
   a) Pam has an absolute advantage in the production of *X*.
   b) Gino has an absolute advantage in the production of *Y*.
   c) Pam has a comparative advantage in the production of *X*.
   d) Gino has a comparative advantage in the production of *Y*.
   e) both c) and d) are true.

In an eight-hour day, Andy can produce either 24 loaves of bread or 8 pounds of butter. In an eight-hour day, Rolfe can produce either 8 loaves of bread or 8 pounds of butter. Use this information to answer questions 10 and 11.

10) Which of the following statements is true?
   a) Andy has an absolute advantage in butter production.
   b) Rolfe has an absolute advantage in butter production.
   c) Andy has an absolute advantage in bread production.
   d) Andy has a comparative advantage in butter production.
   e) Rolfe has a comparative advantage in bread production.

11) Andy and Rolfe
   a) can gain from exchange if Andy specializes in butter production and Rolfe specializes in bread production.
   b) can gain from exchange if Andy specializes in bread production and Rolfe specializes in butter production.
   c) cannot gain from exchange.
   d) can exchange, but only Rolfe will be able to gain.
   e) can exchange, but only Andy will be able to gain.

12) If individuals *a* and *b* can both produce only goods *X* and *Y* and *a* does *not* have a comparative advantage in the production of either *X* or *Y*, then we know that
   a) *b* has an absolute advantage in the production of *X* and *Y*.
   b) *a* and *b* have the same opportunity cost for *X* and for *Y*.
   c) *b* has a comparative advantage in the production of both *X* and *Y*.
   d) there will be gains from trade.
   e) both b) and d) are true.

13) In a world of *unlimited* private property rights,
   a) slavery would be legal.
   b) the sale of untested drugs would be legal.
   c) taxes would be illegal.
   d) all of the above are true.
   e) none of the above is true.

14) Anything that is generally acceptable in exchange for goods and services is
   a) a commodity.
   b) a medium of exchange.
   c) private property.
   d) a barter good.
   e) called an exchange resource.

15) Which of the following is an advantage of a monetary exchange system over barter?
   a) A monetary exchange system eliminates the basis for comparative advantage.
   b) A monetary exchange system does not require a medium of exchange.
   c) Only in a monetary exchange system can gains from trade be realized.
   d) A monetary system exchange does not require a double coincidence of wants.
   e) All of the above are advantages of a monetary exchange system over barter.

16) Mexico and Canada each produce both oil and apples using labour only. A barrel of oil can be produced with 4 hours of labour in Mexico and 8 hours of labour in Canada. A bushel of apples can be produced with 8 hours of labour in Mexico and 12 hours of labour in Canada. Canada has
a) an absolute advantage in oil production.
b) an absolute advantage in apple production.
c) a comparative advantage in oil production.
d) a comparative advantage in apple production.
e) none of the above.

Suppose a society produces only two goods — guns and butter. Three alternative combinations on its production possibility frontier are given in Table 3.1. Use the information in Table 3.1 to answer questions 17 and 18.

Table 3.1 Production Possibilities

Possibility	Units of Butter	Units of Guns
a	8	0
b	6	1
c	0	3

17) In moving from combination *b* to combination *c*, the opportunity cost of producing *one* additional unit of guns is
a) 2 units of butter.
b) 1/2 unit of butter.
c) 6 units of butter.
d) 1/6 unit of butter.
e) 3 units of butter.

18) According to this production possibility frontier,
a) a combination of 6 butter and 1 gun would not employ all resources.
b) a combination of 0 butter and 4 guns is attainable.
c) resources are homogeneous.
d) the opportunity cost of producing guns increases as more guns are produced.
e) the opportunity cost of producing guns decreases as more guns are produced.

19) In Portugal, the opportunity cost of a bale of wool is 3 bottles of wine. In England, the opportunity cost of 1 bottle of wine is 3 bales of wool. Given this information,
a) England has an absolute advantage in wine production.
b) England has an absolute advantage in wool production.
c) Portugal has a comparative advantage in wine production.
d) Portugal has a comparative advantage in wool production.
e) no trade will occur.

20) Assume that for the production possibility frontier in Figure 3.2, shown in question 4 on page 24, everything that is produced is also consumed. Which of the following statements is *false*?
a) Resources are non-homogeneous.
b) Points inside the frontier represent unemployed resources.
c) Starting at point *a*, an increase in the production of good *Y* will shift the frontier out.
d) The opportunity cost of producing good *Y* increases as production of *Y* increases.
e) Shifts in preferences for good *X* or good *Y* will not shift the frontier.

SHORT ANSWER

1) a) Why is a production possibility frontier negatively sloped?
b) Why is it bowed out?

2) a) In an economy with no tool-making possibilities (constant capital goods), what is the opportunity cost of moving from a point inside the production possibility frontier to a point on the frontier? Explain.
b) In a tool-making economy, what is the opportunity cost of current consumption?

3) Lawyers earn $200/hour while secretaries earn $15/hour. Use the concepts of absolute and comparative advantage to explain why a lawyer who is a better typist than her secretary, will still *specialize* in doing only legal work and will *trade* with the secretary for typing services.

4) Explain how taxes *limit* property rights. If a society must pay for its judicial system and police protection, explain how taxes *enhance* property rights.

5) Explain, using a specific example of exchange, why a monetary exchange system is more efficient than barter.

PROBLEMS

1) Suppose that an economy with unchanged capital goods (no tool-making) has the production possibility frontier shown in Table 3.2.

Table 3.2 Production Possibilities

Possibility	Units of Butter	Units of Guns
a	200	0
b	180	60
c	160	100
d	100	160
e	40	200
f	0	220

a) On graph paper, plot these possibilities, label the points, and draw the production possibility frontier. (Put guns on the *x*-axis.)
b) If the economy moves from possibility *c* to possibility *d*, the opportunity cost *per unit of guns* will be how many units of butter?
c) If the economy moves from possibility *d* to possibility *e*, the opportunity cost *per unit of guns* will be how many units of butter?
d) In general terms, what happens to the opportunity cost of guns as the output of guns increases?
e) In general terms, what happens to the opportunity cost of butter as the output of butter increases? What do the results in part (c) and part (d) imply about resources?
f) If, instead of the possibilities given, the production possibility frontier were a straight line joining points *a* and *f*, what would that imply about opportunity costs and resources?
g) Given the original production possibility frontier you have plotted, is a combination of 140 units of butter and 130 units of guns per week attainable? Would you regard this combination as an efficient one? Explain.
h) Repeat the question asked in part (g) for a combination of 70 units of butter and 170 units of guns.
i) If the following events occurred (each is a separate event, unaccompanied by any other event), what would happen to the production possibility frontier?
   i) A new, easily exploited, energy source is discovered.
   ii) A large number of skilled workers immigrate into the country.
   iii) The output of butter is increased.
   iv) A new invention increases output per person in the butter industry but not in the guns industry.
   v) A new law is passed compelling workers, who could previously work as long as they wanted, to retire at age 60.

2) France and Germany each produce both wine and beer, using a single homogeneous input — labour. Their production possibilities are:

France has 100 units of labour and can produce a maximum of 200 bottles of wine *or* 400 bottles of beer. Germany has 50 units of labour and can produce a maximum of 250 bottles of wine *or* 200 bottles of beer.

a) Complete Table 3.3.

Table 3.3

	Bottles Produced by 1 Unit of Labour		Opportunity Cost of 1 Additional Bottle	
	Wine	Beer	Wine	Beer
France				
Germany				

Use the information in part (a) to answer the following questions.

b) Which country has an absolute advantage in wine production?
c) Which country has an absolute advantage in beer production?
d) Which country has a comparative advantage in wine production?
e) Which country has a comparative advantage in beer production?
f) If trade is allowed, describe what specialization, if any, will occur.

3) Suppose the country of Quark has historically devoted 10 percent of its resources to the production of new capital goods. Use production possibility frontier diagrams like text Figure 3.4 on page 58 to compare the consequences (costs and benefits) of each of the following:
   a) Quark continues to devote 10 percent of its resources to the production of capital goods.
   b) Quark begins now to permanently devote 20 percent of its resources to the production of capital goods.

4) Tove and Ron are the only two remaining inhabitants of the planet Melmac. They spend their 30-hour days producing widgets and woggles, the only two goods needed for happiness on Melmac. It takes Tove 1 hour to produce a widget and 2 hours to produce a woggle while Ron takes 3 hours to produce a widget and 3 hours to produce a woggle.
   a) For a 30-hour day, draw an individual production possibility frontier for Tove; for Ron.
   b) What does the shape of the production possibility frontiers tell us about opportunity costs? about resources?
   c) Assume initially that Tove and Ron are each self-sufficient. Define self-sufficiency. Explain what the individual consumption possibilities are for Tove; for Ron.
   d) Who has an absolute advantage in the production of widgets? of woggles?
   e) Who has a comparative advantage in the production of widgets? of woggles?
   f) Suppose Tove and Ron each specialize in producing only the good in which she/he has a comparative advantage (one spends 30 hours producing widgets, the other spends 30 hours producing woggles). What will be the total production of widgets and woggles?
   g) Now, suppose Tove and Ron exchange 7 widgets for 5 woggles. On your production possibility frontier diagrams, plot the new point of Tove's consumption; of Ron's consumption. Explain how these points illustrate the gains from trade.

ANSWERS

CONCEPT REVIEW

1) production
2) natural; human; capital
3) production possibility frontier
4) opportunity cost
5) technological; capital
6) consumption
7) comparative
8) capitalism
9) barter
10) coincidence
11) money

TRUE OR FALSE

1) F	5) T	9) F	13) T	17) T
2) F	6) T	10) F	14) T	18) F
3) F	7) F	11) F	15) F	19) F
4) T	8) F	12) F	16) F	20) F

MULTIPLE-CHOICE

1) c	5) e	9) e	13) d	17) e
2) d	6) e	10) c	14) b	18) d
3) b	7) c	11) b	15) d	19) c
4) a	8) b	12) b	16) d	20) c

SHORT ANSWER

1) a) The negative slope of the production possibility frontier reflects opportunity cost: in order to have more of one good, some of the other must be forgone.
   b) It is bowed out because the existence of non-homogeneous resources creates increasing opportunity cost as we increase the production of either good.

2) a) In an economy with no tool-making possibilites, a point inside the production possibility frontier represents unemployed or underutilized resources. By moving to a point on the frontier, more output can be produced from the same resources, simply by utilizing the resources more efficiently. Since resources do not have to be withdrawn from the production of any other good, the opportunity cost of moving to a point on the frontier is zero. This is the closest we get to a "free lunch" in the discipline of economics.
   b) In a tool-making economy, we can forgo current consumption to produce capital goods which subsequently increase future production and con-

sumption. By consuming all that is currently produced, we forgo tool-making and, ultimately, increased future consumption.

3) The lawyer has an absolute advantage in producing both legal and typing services relative to the secretary. Nevertheless, she has a comparative advantage in legal services, and the secretary has a comparative advantage in typing. To demonstrate these comparative advantages, we can construct a table of opportunity costs.

Table 3.4 Opportunity Cost of 1 Additional Hour ($)

	Legal Services	Typing
Lawyer	200	200
Secretary	>200	15

Consider first the lawyer's opportunity costs. The lawyer's best forgone alternative to providing 1 hour of legal services is the $200 she could earn by providing another hour of legal services. If she provides 1 hour of typing, she is also forgoing $200 (1 hour) of legal services. What would the secretary have to forgo to provide 1 hour of legal services? He would have to spend 3 years in law school, forgoing 3 years of income in addition to the tuition he must pay. His opportunity cost is a very large number, certainly greater than $200. If he provides 1 hour of typing, his best forgone alternative is the $15 he could have earned at another secretarial job. Thus Table 3.4 shows that the lawyer has a lower opportunity cost (comparative advantage) of providing legal services, and the secretary has a lower opportunity cost (comparative advantage) of providing typing services. It is on the basis of comparative advantage (not absolute advantage) that trade will take place from which both parties gain.

4) Taxes limit property rights directly by eliminating individual control over property, which passes to the government in the form of tax payments. Without income taxes, for example, each individual would have property rights over their entire income. With income taxes, however, the individual retains property rights only over the part that remains after taxes are paid. Taxes enhance property rights by paying for the institutional enforcement necessary for an effective system of property rights. In this sense, taxes are a prerequisite for property rights.

5) The principal reason for the efficiency of a monetary exchange system relative to barter is that the monetary system does not require a double coincidence of wants to complete a successful exchange. For example, suppose you specialize in the production of apples but like to eat bananas. In a barter economy, you would likely not be able to complete an exchange with the first person you found who had bananas to trade. It would be necessary for that person to also want to trade the bananas for apples and not for carrots or some other good. In a monetary economy, you would always be able to make a successful exchange with the first person you found with bananas to trade since that person would be willing to accept money in exchange. Similarly, in a money exchange system, you would be able to sell your apples for money to the first person you found who wanted apples (even if that person did not have bananas to sell).

PROBLEMS

1) a) The graph of the production possibility frontier is given in Figure 3.3.

Figure 3.3

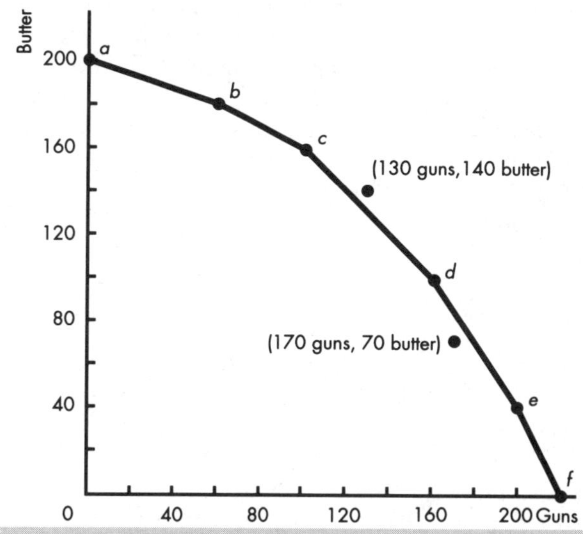

b) In moving from *c* to *d*, in order to gain 60 units of guns, we must give up 160 – 100 = 60 units of butter. The opportunity cost per unit of guns is:

$$\frac{60 \text{ units butter}}{60 \text{ units guns}} = \frac{1 \text{ unit butter per}}{\text{unit of guns}}$$

1) c) In moving from *d* to *e*, in order to gain 40 units of guns, we must give up 100 – 40 = 60 units of butter. The opportunity cost per unit of guns is:

$$\frac{\text{60 units butter}}{\text{40 units guns}} = \text{1.5 units butter per unit of guns}$$

d) The opportunity cost of producing more guns increases as the output of guns increases.

e) Likewise, the opportunity cost of producing more butter increases as the output of butter increases. Increasing opportunity costs imply that resources are non-homogeneous; they are not equally useful in gun and butter production.

f) Opportunity costs would always be constant, regardless of the ouput of guns or butter. The opportunity cost per unit of guns would be:

200/220 = 10/11 units of butter

The opportunity cost per unit of butter would be:

220/200 = 1.1 units of guns

Constant opportunity costs imply that resources are homogeneous, that is, they are equally useful in gun and butter production.

g) This combination is outside the frontier and, therefore, is not attainable. Since the economy cannot produce this combination, the question of efficiency is irrelevant.

h) This combination is inside the frontier and is attainable. It is inefficient because the economy could produce more of either or both goods. Therefore, some resources are not fully utilized.

i) i) Assuming that both goods require energy for their production, the entire frontier shifts out to the northeast as shown in Figure 3.4.

Figure 3.4

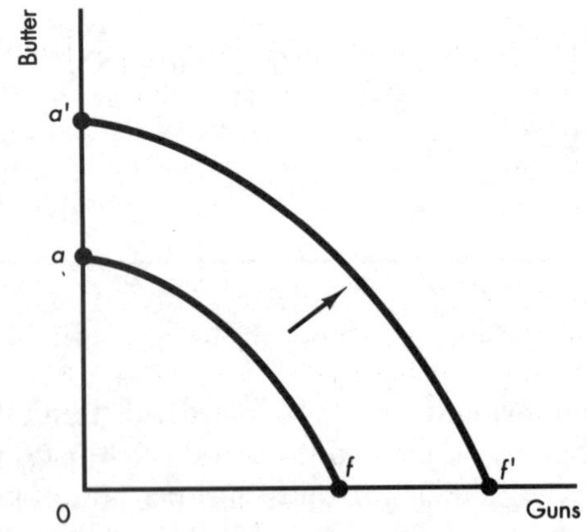

ii) Assuming that both goods use skilled labour in their production, the entire frontier shifts out to the northeast.

iii) The frontier does not shift. An increase in the output of butter implies a movement *along* the frontier to the left, not a shift of the frontier itself.

iv) The new invention implies that for every level of output of guns, the economy can now produce more butter. The frontier swings to the right, but remains anchored at point *f* as shown in figure 3.5.

v) The entire frontier shifts in towards the origin.

Figure 3.5

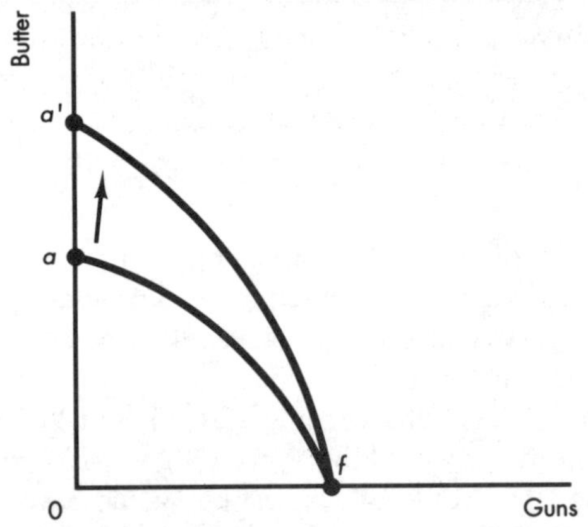

2) a) The completed table is shown here as Table 3.3 Solution.

Table 3.3 Solution

	Bottles Produced by 1 Unit of Labour		Opportunity Cost of 1 Additional Bottle	
	Wine	Beer	Wine	Beer
France	2	4	2 beer	0.5 wine
Germany	5	4	0.8 beer	1.25 wine

b) Germany, which can produce more wine (5 bottles) per unit of input, has an absolute advantage in wine production.

c) Neither country has an absolute advantage in beer production, since beer output (4 bottles) per unit of input is the same for both countries.
d) Germany, with the lower opportunity cost (0.8 beer), has a comparative advantage in wine production.
e) France, with the lower opportunity cost (0.5 wine), has a comparative advantage in beer production.
f) The incentive for trade depends only on differences in comparative advantage. Germany will specialize in wine production and France will specialize in beer production.

3) a) The situation for Quark is depicted by Figure 3.6. Suppose Quark starts on production possibility frontier 1. If it continues to devote only 10 percent of its resources to the production of new capital goods, then it is choosing to produce at a point like *a*. This will shift the frontier out in the next period but only to the curve labelled 2 where, presumably, Quark will choose to produce at point *b*.

Figure 3.6

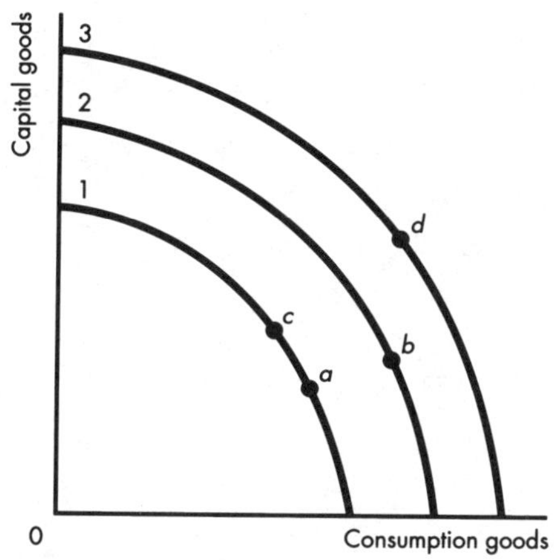

b) Starting from the same initial production possibility frontier, if Quark now decides to increase the resources devoted to the production of new capital to 20 percent, it will be choosing to produce at a point like *c*. In this case, next period's frontier will shift further — to curve 3, and a point like *d*, for example.

Thus, in comparing points *a* and *c*, we find the following costs and benefits: point *a* has the benefit of greater present consumption but at a cost of lower future consumption; point *c* has the cost of lower present consumption, but with the benefit of greater future consumption.

4) a) The individual production possibility frontiers for Tove and Ron are given by Figure 3.7(a) and (b), respectively.

Figure 3.7

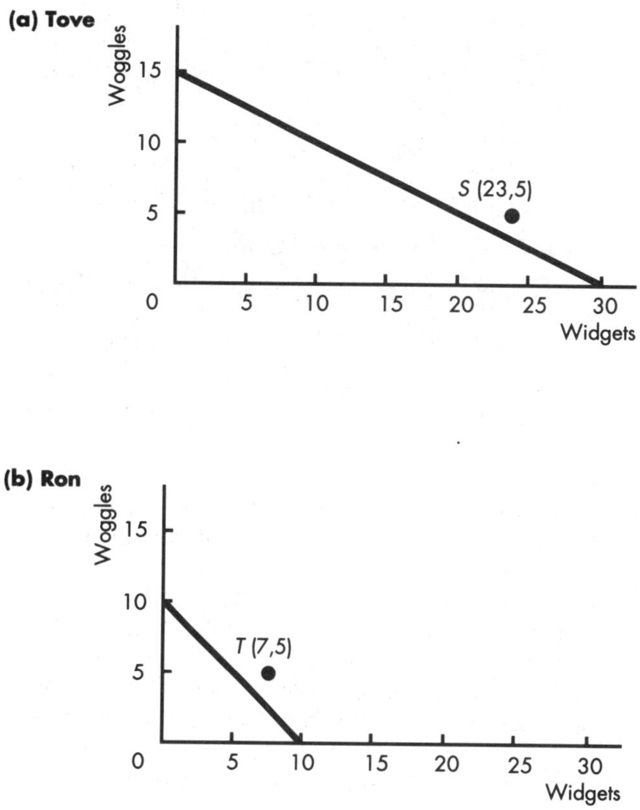

b) The linear shape of the production possibility frontiers tells us that opportunity costs are constant along each frontier, and that resources are homogeneous.

These linear production possibility frontiers with constant opportunity costs abstract from the complexity of the real world. The world generally has increasing opportunity costs, but that fact is not essential for understanding the gains from trade, which is the objective of this problem. Making the model more complex by including increasing opportunity costs would not change our results, but it would make it more difficult to see them.

c) Individuals are self-sufficient if they consume only what they produce. This means there is no trade. Without trade, Tove's (maximum) consumption possibilities are exactly the same as her production possibilities — points along her production possibility frontier. Ron's (maximum) consumption possibilities are likewise the points along his production possibility frontier.

d) Tove has an absolute advantage in the production of both widgets and woggles. Her absolute advantage can be defined either in terms of greater output per unit of inputs or fewer inputs per unit of output. A comparison of the production possibility frontiers in Figure 3.7 shows that, for given inputs of 30 hours, Tove produces a greater output of widgets than Ron (30 versus 10) and a greater output of woggles than Ron (15 versus 10). The statement of the problem tells us equivalently that per unit of output, Tove uses fewer inputs than Ron for both widgets (1 hour versus 3 hours) and woggles (2 hours versus 3 hours). Since Tove has greater productivity than Ron in the production of all goods (widgets and woggles), we say that, overall, she has an absolute advantage.

e) Tove has a comparative advantage in the production of widgets, since she can produce them at lower opportunity cost than Ron (1/2 woggle versus 1 woggle). On the other hand, Ron has a comparative advantage in the production of woggles since he can produce them at a lower opportunity cost than Tove (1 widget versus 2 widgets).

f) Tove will produce widgets and Ron will produce woggles, yielding a total production between them of 30 widgets and 10 woggles.

g) After the exchange, Tove will have 23 widgets and 5 woggles (point S). Ron will have 7 widgets and 5 woggles (point T). These new post-trade consumption possibility points lie outside Tove's and Ron's respective pre-trade consumption (and production) possibilities. Hence, trade has yielded gains that allow the traders to improve their consumption possibilities beyond those available with self-sufficiency.

Chapter 4 Demand and Supply

Chapter in Perspective

Text Pages 69–96

George Bernard Shaw, the renowned British playwright, is reported to have said that one could make a parrot into an economist by teaching it to say "demand and supply." While no parrot has (yet) won the Nobel Prize in economics, Shaw's quip does point out the central role of the concepts of demand and supply in economic thinking. This chapter introduces these basic concepts, which will show up again and again in future chapters.

The previous chapter emphasized the tremendous economic benefits that result from specialization and exchange. Most formal exchange takes place in markets at prices determined by the interaction of buyers (demanders) and sellers (suppliers) in those markets. There are markets for goods (like wheat or textbooks), for services (like haircuts or tattoos), for financial assets (like IBM stock, Canadian dollars, or government bonds). Demand and supply are very powerful tools that economists use to explain how much will be traded and at what price. Careful use of these tools will allow us to explain a wide array of economic phenomena and even predict changes in prices and quantities traded.

Given that demand and supply are so fundamental to economic analysis, extra time and effort spent to truly master the concepts discussed in this chapter will pay large dividends during the rest of the course.

Learning Objectives

After studying this chapter, you will be able to:

- **Explain how prices are determined.**
- **Explain why some prices rise, some fall, and some fluctuate.**
- **Explain how quantities bought and sold are determined.**
- **Construct a demand schedule and a demand curve.**
- **Construct a supply schedule and a supply curve.**
- **Make predictions about price changes using the demand and supply model.**

Helpful Hints

1) When you are first learning about demand and supply, it is useful to think in terms of examples to help build an intuitive understanding. Have some favourite examples in the back of your mind. For example, if the situation calls for the analysis of complementary goods, you may want to think about hamburgers and french fries; if the situation calls for analysis of substitute goods, you may want to think of hamburgers and hot dogs. This will help reduce the "abstractness" of the economic theory.

2) The statement (even if it is uttered by a parrot) that "price is determined by demand and supply" is a shorthand way of saying that price is determined by all of the factors affecting demand (prices of other goods, income, population, preferences) and all of the factors affecting supply (prices of other goods, prices of factors of production, technology). The benefit of using demand and supply *curves* is that they allow us to systematically sort out the influences on price of each of these separate factors. Changes in the factors affecting demand shift the demand curve and move us up or down the given supply curve. Changes in the factors affecting supply shift the supply curve and move us up or down the given demand curve.

   Any demand and supply problem requires you to carefully sort out these influences. In so doing, *always draw a graph*, even if it is just a small graph in the margin of a true-false or multiple-choice problem. Graphical representation is a very efficient way to see what happens. As you become comfortable with graphs, you will find that they are effective and powerful tools for systematically organizing your thinking.

   Do not make the common mistake of thinking that a problem is so easy that you can do it in your head, without drawing a graph. This mistake will cost you dearly on examinations. Also, when you do draw a graph, be sure to *label the axes*. As the course progresses, you will encounter many graphs with different variables on the axes. It is very easy to become confused if you do not develop the habit of labelling the axes.

3) Another very common mistake among students is a failure to correctly *distinguish between a shift in a curve and a movement along a curve*. This distinction applies both to demand and supply curves. Many questions in the self-test are designed to test your understanding of this distinction, and you can be sure that your instructor will test you heavily on this. The distinction between *shifts in* versus *movements along* a curve is crucial for systematic thinking about the factors influencing demand and supply, and for understanding the determination of equilibrium price and quantity traded.

   Consider the example of the demand curve. The quantity of a good demanded depends on its own price, the prices of related goods, income, population, and preferences. The term *demand* refers to the relationship between the price of a good and the quantity demanded, holding constant all of the other factors on which the quantity demanded depends. This demand relationship is represented graphically by the demand curve. Thus, the effect of a change in price on quantity demanded is already reflected in the slope of the demand curve; the effect of a change in the price of the good itself is given by a movement along the demand curve. This is referred to as a *change in quantity demanded*.

   On the other hand, if one of the other factors affecting the quantity demanded changes, the demand curve itself will shift; the quantity demanded at each price will change. This shift of the demand curve is referred to as a *change in demand*. The critical thing to remember is that a change in the price of a good will not shift the demand curve, it will only cause a movement along the demand curve. Similarly, it is just as important to distinguish between shifts in the supply curve and movements along the supply curve.

   To confirm your understanding, consider the effect (draw a graph!) of an increase in household income on the market for compact discs (CDs). First note that an increase in income affects the demand for CDs and not the supply. Next, we want to determine whether the increase in income causes a shift in the demand curve or a movement along the demand curve. Will the increase in income increase the quantity of CDs demanded even if the price of CDs does not change? Since the answer to this question is yes, we know that the demand curve will shift to the right. Note further that the increase in the demand for CDs will cause the equilibrium price to rise. This price increase will be indicated by a movement up along the supply curve (an increase in the quantity supplied) and will not shift the supply curve itself.

   Remember: It is shifts in demand and supply curves that cause the market price to change, not changes in the price that cause demand and supply curves to shift.

4) When analyzing the shifts of demand and supply curves in related markets (for substitute goods like beer and wine), it often seems as though the feed-

back effects from one market to the other can go on endlessly. To avoid confusion, stick to the rule that each curve (demand and supply) for a given market can shift a maximum of *once.* (See Short Answer question 5 and problem 2 on page 41 for further explanation and examples).

5) The relationships between price and quantity demanded and supplied can be represented in three equivalent forms: demand and supply schedules, curves, and equations. The textbook illustrates schedules and curves, but demand and supply equations are also powerful tools of economic analysis. The purpose of this helpful hint is to introduce you to these equations and show you how they can be used to determine the equilibrium values of price and quantity traded.

Figure 4.1 presents a simple demand and supply example in three equivalent forms: (a) schedules, (b) curves, and (c) equations.

Figure 4.1

(a) Demand and Supply Schedules

Price (dollars)	Q_D	Q_S	Shortage (–) or Surplus (+)
1	4	0	–4
2	3	1	–2
3	2	2	0
4	1	3	+2
5	0	4	+4

(b) Demand and Supply Curves

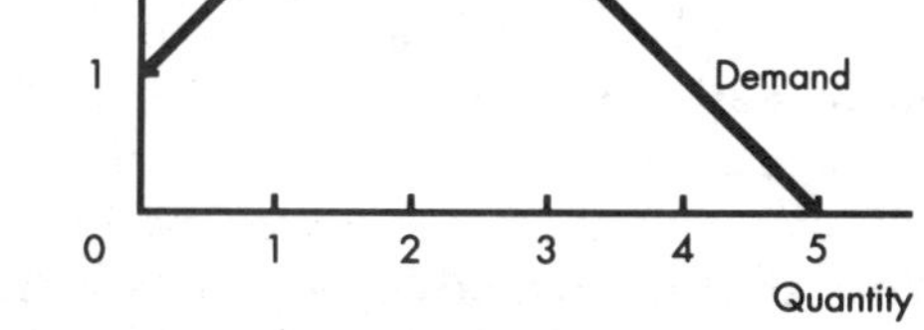

(c) Demand and Supply Equations

Demand: $P = 5 - 1\ Q_D$
Supply: $P = 1 + 1\ Q_S$

The demand and supply schedules in (a) are in the same format as text Figure 4.7 on page 81. The price-quantity combinations from the schedules are plotted on the graph in (b), yielding linear demand and supply curves. What is new about this example is the representation of those curves by the equations in (c).

If you recall (Chapter 2) the formula for the equation of a straight line ($y = a + bx$), you can see that the demand equation is the equation of a straight line. Instead of y, P is the dependent variable on the vertical axis, and, instead of x, Q_D is the independent variable on the horizontal axis. The intercept on the vertical axis, a, is +5, and the slope, b, is –1. The supply equation is also linear and graphed in the same way, but with Q_S as the independent variable. The supply curve intercept on the vertical axis is +1, and the slope is +1. The negative slope of the demand curve reflects the law of demand, and the positive slope of the supply curve reflects the law of supply.

You can demonstrate the equivalence of the demand schedule, curve, and equation by substituting various values of Q_D from the schedule into the demand equation, and calculating the associated prices. These combinations of quantity demanded and price are the coordinates (Q_D, P) of the points on the demand curve. You can similarly demonstrate the equivalence of the supply schedule, curve, and equation.

The demand and supply equations are very useful for calculating the equilibrium values of price and quantity traded. As the schedules and curves both show, two things are true in equilibrium: (1) the price is the same for consumers (the highest price they are willing to pay for the last unit) and producers (the lowest price they are willing to accept for the last unit), and (2) the quantity demanded equals the quantity supplied, so that there are no surpluses or shortages. In terms of the demand and supply equations, this means that *in equilibrium:* (1) the price in both equations is the same. We will denote the equilibrium price as P^* (2) $Q_D = Q_S$ = equilibrium quantity traded. We will denote the equilibrium quantity traded as Q^*. This means that, in equilibrium, the equations become:

$$\text{Demand: } P^* = 5 - 1Q^*$$
$$\text{Supply: } P^* = 1 + 1Q^*$$

These equilibrium equations constitute a simple set of simultaneous equations. Since there are two equations (demand and supply) and two unknowns (P^* and Q^*), we can solve for the unknowns.

Begin the solution by setting demand equal to supply:

$$5 - 1Q^* = 1 + 1Q^*$$

Collecting like terms, we find:

$$4 = 2Q^*$$
$$2 = Q^*$$

Once we have Q^* (equilibrium quantity traded), we can solve for the equilibrium price using *either* the demand *or* supply equations. Look first at demand:

$$P^* = 5 - 1Q^*$$
$$P^* = 5 - 1(2)$$
$$P^* = 5 - 2$$
$$P^* = 3$$

Alternatively, substituting Q^* into the supply equation yields the same result:

$$P^* = 1 + 1Q^*$$
$$P^* = 1 + 1(2)$$
$$P^* = 1 + 2$$
$$P^* = 3$$

Once you have solved for Q^*, the fact that substituting it into either the demand or supply equation yields the correct P^* provides a valuable check on your calculations. If you make a mistake in your calculations, when you substitute Q^* into the demand and supply equations, you will get two *different* prices. If that happens, you know to recheck your calculations. If you get the same price when you substitute Q^* into the demand and supply equations, then you know your calculations are correct.

6) One additional point about the equations for demand and supply. Economists have developed the convention of graphing quantity as the independent variable and price as the dependent variable, and the previous equations reflect this. Despite this convention, economists actually consider real world prices to be the independent variables and quantities as the dependent variables. In that case, the equations would take the form:

$$\text{Demand: } Q_D = 5 - 1P$$
$$\text{Supply: } Q_S = -1 + 1P$$

You can solve these equations for yourself to see that they yield exactly the same values for P^* and Q^*. (*Hint*: First solve for P^* and then for Q^*.) Whichever form of the equations your instructor uses, the technique for solving the equations will be similar and the results identical.

Key Figures and Tables

Figure 4.1 The Demand Schedule and the Demand Curve, text page 72

There are three ways to represent the relationship between the price of a good or service and the quantity demanded: a demand schedule, a demand curve, and a demand equation. This figure illustrates the first two ways. A demand schedule is a table that lists the quantities consumers demand at each price, if everything else remains constant. For example, if the price of a tape is $4, consumers would be willing to buy 3 million tapes per week, assuming that other things (like income and the price of a Walkman) remain unchanged. The law of demand is illustrated by the fact that as the price of a tape increases, *ceteris paribus*, the quantity of tapes that consumers would be willing to buy decreases.

A demand curve is the graphical representation of the relationship between the quantity demanded of a good and its price, holding constant all other influences on consumers' planned purchases. Price appears on the vertical axis and quantity demanded on the horizontal axis. The demand curve tells us how many tapes consumers will be willing to buy in a week at each price, other things held constant. An equivalent interpretation of the demand curve is that it shows the highest price that consumers are willing to pay for the last unit purchased. For example, the highest price that consumers will pay for the 3 millionth tape is $4. The law of demand is reflected in the negative slope of the demand curve.

Figure 4.3 A Change in Demand Versus a Change in the Quantity Demanded, text page 75

This figure distinguishes between a change in demand (represented by a shift in the demand curve) and a change in the quantity demanded (represented by a movement along a given demand curve). Remember that a change in the price of a good or service implies that the quantity demanded changes. Since this is exactly the relationship represented by the demand curve, the change in quantity demanded is represented by a movement along the demand curve. If there is a change in any of the other factors affecting the willingness of consumers to buy at a given price, then we say there is a change in demand, which is represented by a shift in the demand curve itself.

Figure 4.4 The Supply Schedule and the Supply Curve, text page 77

Just as there are three useful ways to represent the demand relationship, there are three ways to represent the relationship between the price of a good or service and the quantity supplied: a supply schedule, a supply curve, and a supply equation. This figure illustrates the first two ways. A supply schedule is a table that lists the quantities that producers will plan to sell at each price, if everything else remains constant. For example, if the price of a tape is $4, producers will plan to sell 5 million tapes per week, assuming that other things (like the technology used to produce tapes) remains unchanged. The law of supply is illustrated by the fact that as the price of a tape increases, *ceteris paribus*, the quantity of tapes that producers plan to supply increases.

A supply curve is the graphical representation of the relationship between the quantity of a good supplied and its price, holding constant all other influences on producers' planned sales. The supply curve tells us how many tapes producers will be willing to sell per week at each price, other things held constant. An equivalent interpretation of the supply curve is that it shows the lowest price that will induce producers to offer the last unit for sale. For example, the lowest price that will induce producers to offer the 5 millionth tape for sale is $4. The law of supply is reflected in the positive slope of the supply curve.

Figure 4.6 A Change in Supply Versus a Change in the Quantity Supplied, text page 79
This figure distinguishes between a change in supply (represented by a shift in the supply curve) and a change in the quantity supplied (represented by a movement along a given supply curve). Remember that a change in the price of a good or service implies that the quantity supplied changes. Since this is the relationship represented by the supply curve, the change in quantity supplied is represented by a movement along the supply curve. If there is a change in any of the other factors affecting the willingness of producers to sell at a given price, then we say there is a change in supply, which is represented by a shift in the supply curve itself.

Figure 4.7 Equilibrium, text page 81
In this figure, the demand and supply curves are combined in the same graph in order to examine the price and quantity traded that leaves both buyers and sellers satisfied. Equilibrium price is defined as that price at which the quantity demanded is equal to the quantity supplied. The equilibrium price ($3 in the example) can be identified using either the table or the diagram. The idea of equilibrium as a point of rest is also illustrated. Note that when the price is below the equilibrium price there is a shortage, which will cause the price to rise toward equilibrium. When the price is above the equilibrium price, there is a surplus, which will cause the price to fall toward equilibrium. Only at the equilibrium price will there be no tendency for the price to change.

Table 4.1 The Demand for Tapes, text page 74
This table specifies the law of demand: the quantity demanded increases as the price of the good or service falls and decreases as the price rises. These changes are represented by movements along the demand curve. The factors that cause changes in demand are also listed. Changes in these factors will cause the demand curve to shift. Note that the table assumes that tapes are a normal good, since a rise in income will cause the demand for tapes to increase. If the good in question is inferior, a rise in income will cause demand to decrease whereas a fall in income will cause demand to increase. As implied by the name, most goods and services are normal.

Table 4.2 The Supply of Tapes, text page 78
In parallel to Table 4.1, this table specifies the law of supply: the quantity supplied increases as the price rises and decreases as the price falls. These changes are represented by movements along the supply curve. The factors that cause changes in supply are also listed. Changes in these factors will cause the supply curve to shift.

SELF-TEST

CONCEPT REVIEW

1) The __________ __________ of a good or service is the amount that consumers are willing and able to purchase at a particular price.

2) The law of demand states that, other things being equal, the higher the __________ of a good, the __________ is the quantity demanded.

3) A demand __________ is a list of the quantities of a good demanded at different __________.

4) A demand curve illustrates the __________ price that consumers are willing to pay for the last unit of a good purchased.

5) The entire relationship between the quantity of a good demanded and its __________ is referred to as demand.

6) The demand curve for most goods will shift to the right if income __________, or if the price of a substitute __________, or if the price of a complement __________, or if the size of the population __________.

7) A good is said to be __________ if the demand for it increases as income increases and __________ if demand decreases as income increases.

8) A decrease in the price of a good will cause an increase in the __________ __________; that is represented by a downward __________ __________ the demand curve.

9) The amount of a good or service that producers plan to sell at a particular price is called the __________ __________.

10) The law of supply states that the __________ the price of a good, the __________ the quantity supplied.

11) A supply curve shows the quantity supplied at each given __________.

12) A decrease in supply is represented by a shift to the __________ in the supply curve.

13) The supply curve will shift to the right if the price of a complement in production __________, or if the price of a substitute in production __________, or if there is a technological __________, or if the price of a productive resource __________.

14) An increase in the price of a good will cause an increase in the __________ __________; that is represented by a (an) __________ movement along the supply curve.

15) The price at which the quantity demanded equals the quantity supplied is called the __________ price.

16) If the price is above equilibrium, a (an) __________ will exist, causing the price to __________.

17) When demand increases, the equilibrium price will __________ and the quantity traded will __________.

18) When supply increases, the equilibrium price will __________ and the quantity traded will __________.

19) If demand increases and supply increases, then we know that the quantity traded must __________; but equilibrium price may increase, decrease, or remain unchanged.

TRUE OR FALSE

_____ 1) If the quantity of a good demanded exceeds the quantity supplied, then the quantity traded will be less than the quantity demanded.

_____ 2) The law of demand tells us that as the price of a good rises, the demand decreases.

_____ 3) The law of demand tells us that as the price of a good rises, the quantity demanded decreases.

_____ 4) The negative slope of a demand curve is a result of the law of demand.

_____ 5) An increase in the price of apples will shift the demand curve for apples to the left.

_____ 6) Hamburgers and french fries are complements. If Burger Bar reduces the price of french fries, the demand for hamburgers will increase.

_____ 7) A supply curve shows the maximum price at which the last unit will be supplied.

_____ 8) A demand curve shows the least that consumers are willing to pay for the last unit.

_____ 9) A demand curve is a graphical representation of the relationship between the price of a good and quantity demanded given the level of income, prices of other goods, population, and preferences.

_____ 10) The law of supply implies that a supply curve will have a negative slope.

_____ 11) A cost-reducing technological improvement will shift a supply curve to the right.

_____ 12) If we observe a doubling of the price of mozzarella cheese (an ingredient in any pizza), we will expect the supply curve for pizza to shift to the left.

_____ 13) When a cow is slaughtered for beef, its hide becomes available to make leather. Thus, beef and leather are substitutes in production.

_____ 14) If the price of beef rises, we would expect to see an increase in the supply of leather and in the quantity of beef supplied.

_____ 15) If the current price is such that the quantity demanded exceeds the quantity supplied, the price will tend to rise.

_____ 16) If demand increases, we would predict an increase in equilibrium price and a decrease in quantity traded.

_____ 17) If potatoes are inferior goods, we would expect an increase in income to result in a fall in the price of potatoes.

_____ 18) A change in demand will cause equilibrium price and quantity traded to move in opposite directions.

_____ 19) A decrease in the supply of a good will result in a decrease in both the equilibrium price and the quantity traded.

_____ 20) Suppose there is a significant decline in the price of iron ore (used in making steel). We would predict that the equilibrium price of steel will fall and the quantity traded will increase.

_____ 21) Suppose the demand for personal computers increases while the cost of producing them decreases. With this information, we can definitely predict that the quantity of personal computers traded will increase and the price will fall.

_____ 22) An increase in the price of avocados and a decrease in the quantity traded is consistent with a decrease in the supply of avocados.

_____ 23) When the actual price is above the equilibrium price, a shortage occurs.

MULTIPLE-CHOICE

1) If an increase in the price of good *A* causes the demand curve for good *B* to shift to the left, then
 a) *A* and *B* are substitutes in consumption.
 b) *A* and *B* are complements in consumption.
 c) *A* and *B* are complements in production.
 d) *B* is an inferior good.
 e) *B* is a normal good.

2) Which of the following could *not* cause an increase in demand for a commodity?
 a) an increase in income
 b) a decrease in income
 c) a decrease in the price of a substitute
 d) a decrease in the price of a complement
 e) an increase in preferences for the commodity

3) If Hamburger Helper is an inferior good, then, *ceteris paribus*, a decrease in income will cause
 a) leftward shift of the demand curve for Hamburger Helper.
 b) rightward shift of the demand curve for Hamburger Helper.
 c) movement up along the demand curve for Hamburger Helper.
 d) movement down along the demand curve for Hamburger Helper.
 e) none of the above.

4) All of the following "other things" are held constant along a demand curve *except*
 a) income.
 b) prices of other goods.
 c) the price of the good itself.
 d) preferences.
 e) all of the above.

5) Good *A* is a normal good if
 a) an increase in the price of a complement causes the demand for *A* to decrease.
 b) an increase in income causes the demand for *A* to increase.
 c) an increase in the price of a substitute causes the demand for *A* to increase.
 d) it satisfies the law of demand.
 e) income and the demand for *A* are negatively correlated.

6) If turnips are an inferior good, then, *ceteris paribus*, an increase in the price of turnips will cause
 a) a decrease in the demand for turnips.
 b) an increase in the demand for turnips.
 c) a decrease in the supply of turnips.
 d) an increase in the supply of turnips.
 e) none of the above.

7) A decrease in quantity demanded is represented by a
 a) rightward shift of the supply curve.
 b) rightward shift of the demand curve.
 c) leftward shift of the demand curve.
 d) movement upward and to the left along the demand curve.
 e) movement downward and to the right along the demand curve.

8) The price of a good will tend to fall if
 a) there is a surplus at the current price.
 b) the current price is above equilibrium.
 c) the quantity supplied exceeds the quantity demanded at the current price.
 d) all of the above are true.
 e) none of the above is true.

9) The fact that a decline in the price of a good causes producers to reduce the quantity of the good supplied illustrates
 a) the law of supply.
 b) the law of demand.
 c) a change in supply.
 d) the nature of an inferior good.
 e) technological improvement.

10) A shift of the supply curve for rutabagas will be caused by
 a) a change in preferences for rutabagas.
 b) a change in the price of a related good that is a substitute in consumption for rutabagas.
 c) a change in income.
 d) a change in the price of rutabagas.
 e) none of the above.

11) A decrease in quantity supplied is represented by a
   a) movement down the supply curve.
   b) movement up the supply curve.
   c) leftward shift of the supply curve.
   d) rightward shift of the supply curve.
   e) rightward shift of the demand curve.

12) If a resource can be used to produce either good *A* or good *B*, then *A* and *B* are
   a) substitutes in production.
   b) complements in production.
   c) substitutes in consumption.
   d) complements in consumption.
   e) normal goods.

13) Which of the following will shift the supply curve for good *X* to the left?
   a) a decrease in the wages of workers employed to produce *X*
   b) an increase in the cost of machinery used to produce *X*
   c) a technological improvement in the production of *X*
   d) a situation where quantity demanded exceeds quantity supplied
   e) all of the above

14) If the market for twinkies is in equilibrium, then
   a) twinkies must be a normal good.
   b) producers would like to sell more at the current price.
   c) consumers would like to buy more at the current price.
   d) there will be a surplus.
   e) quantity traded equals quantity demanded.

15) A shortage is the amount by which quantity
   a) demanded exceeds quantity supplied.
   b) traded exceeds quantity supplied.
   c) traded exceeds quantity demanded.
   d) demanded exceeds the equilibrium quantity.
   e) supplied exceeds the equilibrium quantity.

16) The demand curve for tribbles is $P = 300 - 6Q_D$. The supply curve for tribbles is $P = 20 + 8Q_S$. If the price of a tribble was set at $120, the tribble market would experience
   a) equilibrium.
   b) excess demand causing a rise in price.
   c) excess demand causing a fall in price.
   d) excess supply causing a rise in price.
   e) excess supply causing a fall in price.

17) A surplus can be eliminated by
   a) increasing supply.
   b) government raising the price.
   c) decreasing the quantity demanded.
   d) allowing the price to fall.
   e) allowing the quantity traded to fall.

The market for coffee is initially in equilibrium with supply and demand curves of the usual shape. Pepsi is a substitute for coffee; cream is a complement for coffee. Questions 18-20 concern the market for *coffee.*

Assume that all *ceteris paribus* assumptions continue to hold *except* for the event(s) listed. Answer each question without considering the others.

18) Coffee is a normal good. A decrease in income will
   a) increase the price of coffee and increase the quantity demanded of coffee.
   b) increase the price of coffee and increase the quantity supplied of coffee.
   c) decrease the price of coffee and decrease the quantity demanded of coffee.
   d) decrease the price of coffee and decrease the quantity supplied of coffee.
   e) cause none of the above.

19) An increase in the price of Pepsi will
   a) increase the price of coffee and increase the quantity demanded of coffee.
   b) increase the price of coffee and increase the quantity supplied of coffee.
   c) decrease the price of coffee and decrease the quantity demanded of coffee.
   d) decrease the price of coffee and decrease the quantity supplied of coffee.
   e) cause none of the above.

20) A technological improvement lowers the cost of producing coffee. At the same time, preferences for coffee decrease. The *quantity traded* of coffee will
   a) rise.
   b) fall.
   c) remain the same.
   d) rise or fall depending on whether the price of coffee falls or rises.
   e) rise or fall depending on the relative shifts of demand and supply curves.

21) If *A* and *B* are complementary goods (in consumption) and the cost of a resource used in the production of *A* decreases, then the price of
   a) both *A* and *B* will rise.
   b) both *A* and *B* will fall.
   c) *A* will fall and the price of *B* will rise.
   d) *A* will rise and the price of *B* will fall.
   e) *A* will fall and the price of *B* will remain unchanged.

22) If both demand and supply increase, then
   a) price will rise and quantity traded will increase.
   b) price will fall and quantity traded will increase.
   c) price could either rise or fall and quantity traded will increase.
   d) price will rise and quantity traded could either increase or decrease.
   e) price will fall and quantity traded could either increase or decrease.

23) Which of the following will definitely cause an increase in the equilibrium price?
a) an increase in both demand and supply
b) a decrease in both demand and supply
c) an increase in demand combined with a decrease in supply
d) a decrease in demand combined with an increase in supply
e) none of the above

24) The demand curve for whatnots is $P = 75 - 6Q_D$ and the supply curve for whatnots is $P = 35 + 2Q_S$. What is the equilibrium *price* of a whatnot?
a) $5
b) $10
c) $40
d) $45
e) none of the above

25) Farm land can be used to produce either cattle or corn. If the demand for cattle increases then
a) demand for corn will increase.
b) supply of corn will increase.
c) demand for corn will decrease.
d) supply of corn will decrease.
e) both b) and c) are true.

SHORT ANSWER

1) Explain the difference between wants and demands.

2) Suppose we observe that the consumption of peanut butter increases at the same time as its price rises. What must have happened in the market for peanut butter? Is the observation consistent with the law of demand?

3) The price of personal computers has continued to fall even in the face of increasing demand. Explain.

4) A tax on crude oil would raise the cost of the primary resource used in the production of gasoline. A proponent of such a tax has claimed that it will not raise the price of gasoline using the following argument. While the price of gasoline may rise initially, that price increase will cause the demand for gasoline to decrease, which will push the price back down. What is wrong with this argument?

5) Brussel sprouts and carrots are substitutes in consumption and, since they can both be grown on the same type of land, substitutes in production too. Suppose there is an increase in the demand for brussel sprouts. Trace through the effects on price and quantity traded in both the brussel sprout and carrot markets. (Keep in mind Helpful Hint 4.)

PROBLEMS

1) The information given in Table 4.1 is about the behaviour of buyers and sellers of fish at the market on a particular Saturday.

Table 4.1 Demand and Supply Schedules for Fish

Price (per fish)	Quantity Demanded	Quantity Supplied
$0.75	270	45
$1.00	260	135
$1.25	245	185
$1.50	225	225
$1.75	200	250
$2.00	170	265
$2.25	135	280
$2.50	105	290
$2.75	80	300
$3.00	60	310
$3.25	45	315
$3.50	35	320

a) On graph paper, draw the demand curve and the supply curve. Be sure to label the axes. What is the equilibrium price?
b) We will make the usual *ceteris paribus* assumptions about the demand curve so that it does not shift. List four factors that we are assuming do not change.
c) We will also hold the supply curve constant by assuming that three factors do not change. List them.
d) Explain briefly what would happen if the price were initially set at $2.75.
e) Explain briefly what would happen if the price were initially set at $1.
f) Explain briefly what would happen if the price were initially set at $1.50.

2) The market for wine in Canada is initially in equilibrium with supply and demand curves of the usual shape. Beer is a close substitute for wine; cheese and wine are complements. Use demand and supply diagrams to analyze the effect of each of the following (separate) events on the equilibrium price and quantity traded in the Canadian wine market. Assume that all of the *ceteris paribus* assumptions continue to hold except for the event listed. For both price and quantity traded, you should indicate in each case whether the variable rises, falls, remains the same, or moves ambiguously (may rise or fall).

a) The income of consumers falls (wine is a normal good).
b) Early frost destroys a large part of the world grape crop.
c) A new churning invention reduces the cost of producing cheese.
d) A new fermentation technique is invented that reduces the cost of producing wine.
e) A government study is published that links wine drinking and heart disease.
f) Costs of producing both beer and wine increase dramatically.

3) Table 4.2 lists the demand and supply schedules for cases of grape jelly.

Table 4.2 Demand and Supply Schedules for Grape Jelly per Week

Price (per case)	Quantity Demanded (cases)	Quantity Supplied (cases)
$30	180	60
$40	140	80
$50	100	100
$60	60	120
$70	20	140

a) On the graph in Figure 4.2, draw the demand and supply curves for grape jelly. Be sure to properly label the axes. Label the demand and supply curves D_0 and S_0, respectively.

Figure 4.2

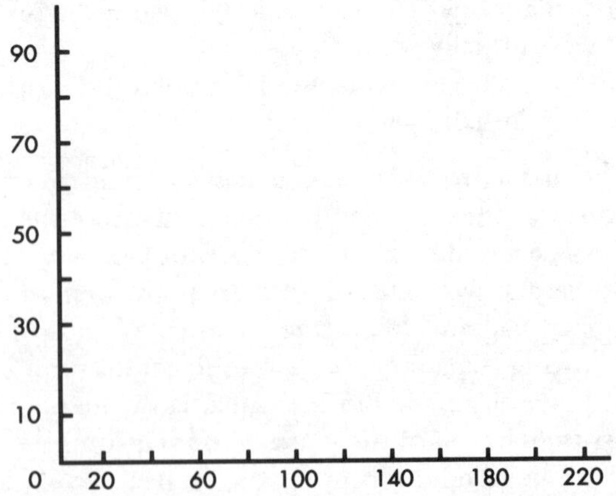

b) What are the equilibrium price and quantity traded in the grape jelly market? On your diagram, label the equilibrium point *a*.
c) Is there a surplus or shortage at a price of $40? How much?
d) The demand and supply schedules can also be represented by the following demand and supply equations:

$$\text{Demand: } P = 75 - 0.25Q_D$$
$$\text{Supply: } P = 0.5Q_S$$

Use these equations to solve the following:
i) equilibrium quantity traded (Q^*)
ii) equilibrium price (P^*)
[Your answers should be the same as those in 3b).]

e) Suppose the population grows sufficiently that the demand for grape jelly increases by 60 cases per week at every price.
i) Construct a table (price, quantity demanded) of the new demand schedule.
ii) Draw the new demand curve on your original graph and label it D_1.
iii) Label the new equilibrium point *b*. What are the new equilibrium price and quantity traded?
iv) What is the new demand equation? [*Hints*: What is the new slope? What is the new price-axis intercept?]

4) The demand equation for dweedles is $P = 8 - 1Q_D$. The supply equation for dweedles is:

$$P = 2 + 1Q_S,$$

where P is the price of a dweedle in dollars, Q_D is the quantity of dweedles demanded, and Q_S is the quantity of dweedles supplied. The dweedle market is initially in equilibrium and income is $300.
a) What is the equilibrium quantity traded (Q^*) of dweedles?
b) What is the equilibrium price (P^*) of a dweedle?
c) As a result of an increase in income to $500, the demand curve for dweedles shifts (the supply curve remains the same). The new demand equation is:

$$P = 4 - 1Q_D$$

Use this information to calculate the following:
i) new equilibrium quantity of dweedles traded
ii) new equilibrium price of a dweedle

d) On the graph in Figure 4.3 on page 43, draw and label: (1) the supply curve, (2) the initial demand curve, (3) the new demand curve.
e) Are dweedles a normal or inferior good? How do you know?

Figure 4.3

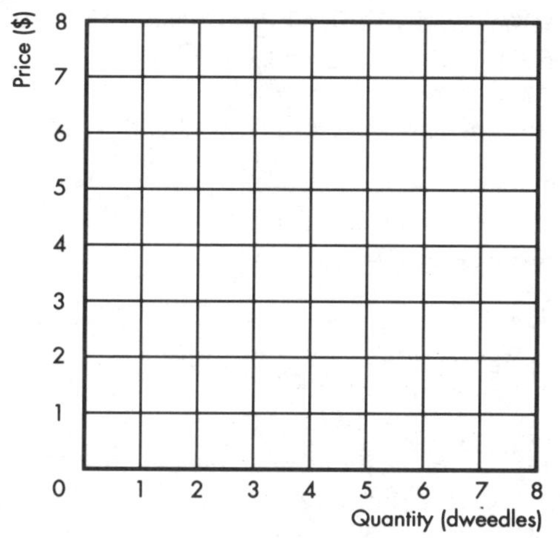

5) The demand equation for flubits is $P = 80 - 2Q_D$. The supply equation for flubits is:

$$P = 50 + 1Q_S,$$

where P is the price of a flubit in dollars, Q_D is the quantity of flubits demanded, and Q_S is the quantity of flubits supplied. Assume that there are *no* changes in *ceteris paribus* assumptions.

a) If the price of flubits was set at $56, calculate the exact surplus or shortage of flubits.
b) Explain the adjustment process that will bring the situation above to equilibrium.
c) What is the equilibrium quantity traded (Q^*) of flubits?
d) What is the equilibrium price (P^*) of a flubit?
e) Now assume that as a result of technological advance, the supply curve for flubits shifts (the demand curve remains the same). The new supply equation is:

$$P = 20 + 1Q_S$$

Use this information to calculate the following:
i) new equilibrium quantity of flubits traded
ii) new equilibrium price of a flubit

ANSWERS

CONCEPT REVIEW

1) quantity demanded
2) price; lower
3) schedule; prices
4) highest
5) price
6) increases; increases; decreases; increases
7) normal; inferior
8) quantity demanded; movement along
9) quantity supplied
10) higher; higher
11) price
12) left
13) increases; decreases; improvement; decreases
14) quantity supplied; upward
15) equilibrium
16) surplus; fall
17) increase; increase
18) decrease; increase
19) increase

TRUE OR FALSE

1) T	6) T	11) T	16) F	21) F
2) F	7) F	12) T	17) T	22) T
3) T	8) F	13) F	18) F	23) F
4) T	9) T	14) T	19) F	
5) F	10) F	15) T	20) T	

MULTIPLE-CHOICE

1) b	6) e	11) a	16) b	21) c
2) c	7) d	12) a	17) d	22) c
3) b	8) d	13) b	18) d	23) c
4) c	9) a	14) e	19) b	24) d
5) b	10) e	15) a	20) e	25) d

SHORT ANSWER

1) Wants reflect our unlimited desires for goods and services without regard to our ability or willingness to make the sacrifices necessary to obtain them. The existence of scarcity means that many of those wants will not be satisfied. On the other hand, demands refer to plans to buy and, therefore, reflect decisions about which wants to satisfy.

2) The observation that the consumption of peanut butter increases at the same time as the price of peanut butter rises is entirely consistent with the law of demand (a negatively-sloped demand curve). It simply reflects the fact that the demand for peanut butter has increased (the demand curve has shifted out to the right).

3) Due to the tremendous pace of technological advance, not only has the demand for personal computers been increasing, but the supply has been increasing as well. Indeed, supply has been increasing much more rapidly than demand, which has resulted in falling prices. Thus, *much* (but not all) of the increase in sales of personal computers reflects a movement down along a demand curve rather than a shift in demand.

4) This argument confuses a movement along an unchanging demand curve with a shift in the demand curve. The proper analysis is as follows. The increase in the price of oil (the primary resource in the production of gasoline) will shift the supply curve of gasoline to the left. This will cause the equilibrium price of gasoline to increase and thus the *quantity demanded* of gasoline will decrease. Demand itself will not decrease; the demand curve will not shift. The decrease in supply causes a movement along an unchanged demand curve.

5) The answer to this question requires us to trace through the effects on the two graphs in Figure 4.4(a) and (b) — one for the brussel sprout market and one for the carrot market. The sequence of effects occurs in order of the numbers on the graphs.

Look first at the market for brussel sprouts. The increase in demand shifts the demand curve to the right from D_0 to D_1 (1), and the price of brussel sprouts rises. This price rise has two effects (2) on the carrot market. Since brussel sprouts and carrots are substitutes in consumption, the demand curve for carrots shifts to the right from D_0 to D_1. And, since brussel sprouts and carrots are substitutes in production, the supply curve of carrots shifts to the left from S_0 to S_1. Both of these shifts in the carrot market raise the price of carrots, causing feedback effects on the brussel sprout market. But remember the rule (Helpful Hint 4) that each curve (demand and supply) for a given market can shift a maximum of *once*. Since the demand curve for brussel sprouts has already shifted, we can only shift the supply curve from S_0 to S_1 (3) because of the substitutes in production relationship. Each curve in each market has now shifted once and the analysis must stop. We can predict that the net effects are increases in the equilibrium prices of both brussel sprouts and carrots, and indeterminate changes in quantities traded in both markets, even though the diagrams as drawn show $Q_2 < Q_0$.

Figure 4.4

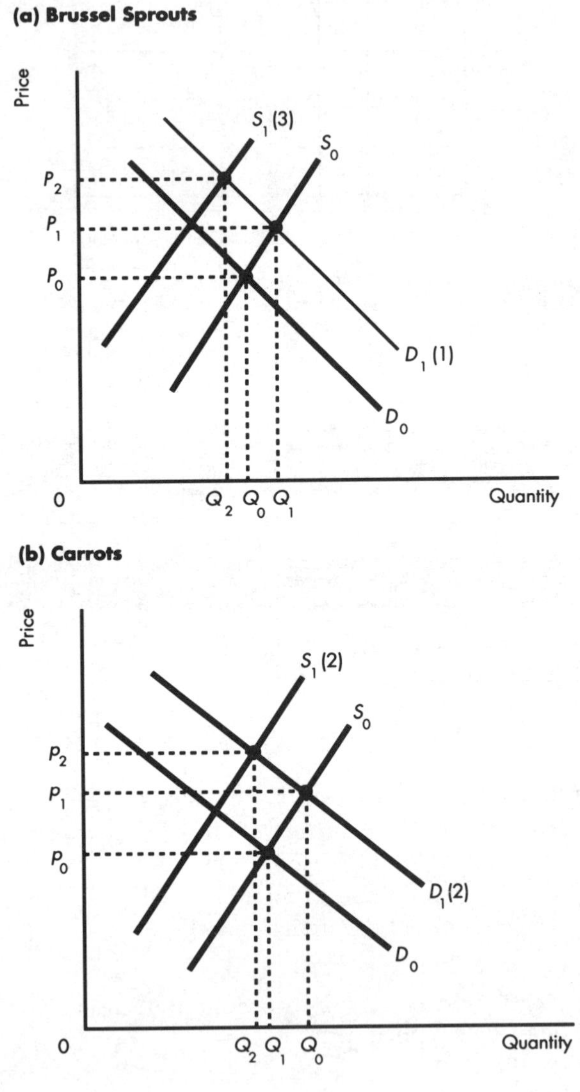

PROBLEMS

1) a) The demand and supply curves are shown in Figure 4.5. The equilibrium price is $1.50 per fish.

Figure 4.5

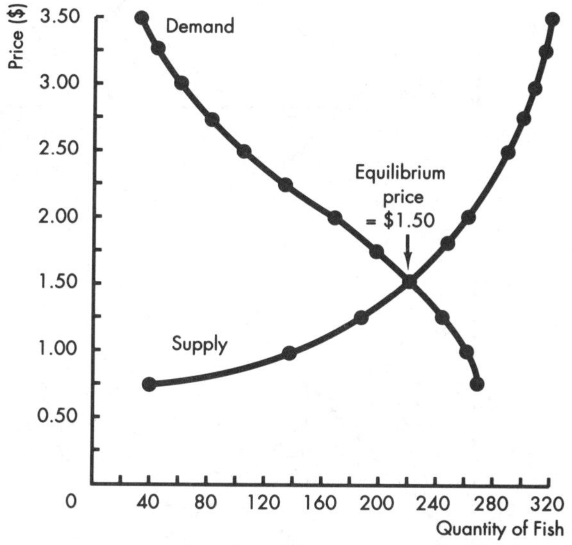

b) Prices of other (related) goods; income; population; preferences.

c) Prices of other (related) goods; prices of factors of production; technology.

d) At a price of $2.75, quantity supplied (300) exceeds quantity demanded (80). Fish sellers find themselves with surplus fish. Rather than be stuck with unsold fish (which yields no revenue), some sellers cut their price in an attempt to increase the quantity of fish demanded. Competition forces other sellers to follow suit, and the price falls until it reaches the equilibrium price of $1.50, while quantity demanded increases until it reaches the equilibrium quantity of 225 units.

e) At a price of $1, the quantity demanded (260) exceeds the quantity supplied (135) — there is a shortage. Unrequited fish buyers bid up the price in an attempt to get the "scarce" fish. As prices continue to be bid up as long as there is excess demand, quantity supplied increases in response to higher prices. Price and quantity supplied both rise until they reach the equilibrium price ($1.50) and quantity (225 units).

f) At a price of $1.50, the quantity supplied exactly equals the quantity demanded (225). There is no excess demand (shortage) or excess supply (surplus), and, therefore, no tendency for the price or quantity to change.

2) The demand and supply diagrams for parts (a) to (e) are shown in Figure 4.6 on page 46.

Questions such as that of problem 2f) require the examination of two separate but related markets — the beer and wine markets. Since this kind of question often causes confusion for students, a more detailed explanation of the answer is given here.

Look first at the beer market in Figure 4.7 (a) on page 47. The increase in the cost of beer production shifts up the supply curve of beer from S_0 to S_1. The resulting rise in the price of beer from P_0 to P_1 affects the wine market since beer and wine are substitutes (in consumption).

Turning to the wine market in Figure 4.7 (b), there are two shifts to examine. The increase in beer prices causes the demand for wine to shift out from D_0 to D_1. The increase in the cost of wine production shifts up the supply curve of wine from S_0 to S_1. This is the end of the analysis, since the question only asks about the wine market. The final result is a rise in the price of wine from P_0 to P_1, and an ambiguous change in the quantity traded of wine. Although the diagram shows $Q_1 = Q_0$, Q_1 may be $\leq$ or $\geq Q_0$.

Many students rightfully ask, "But doesn't the rise in wine prices then shift out the demand curve for beer, causing a rise in beer prices and an additional increase in the demand for wine?" This question, which is correct in principle, is about the dynamics of adjustment, and these graphs are only capable of analyzing once-over shifts of demand or supply. We could shift out the demand for beer, from D_0 to D_1, but the resulting additional rise in beer prices would lead us to shift the demand for wine a *second time.* In practice, stick to the rule that each curve (demand and supply) for a given market can shift a maximum of *once.*

Figure 4.6

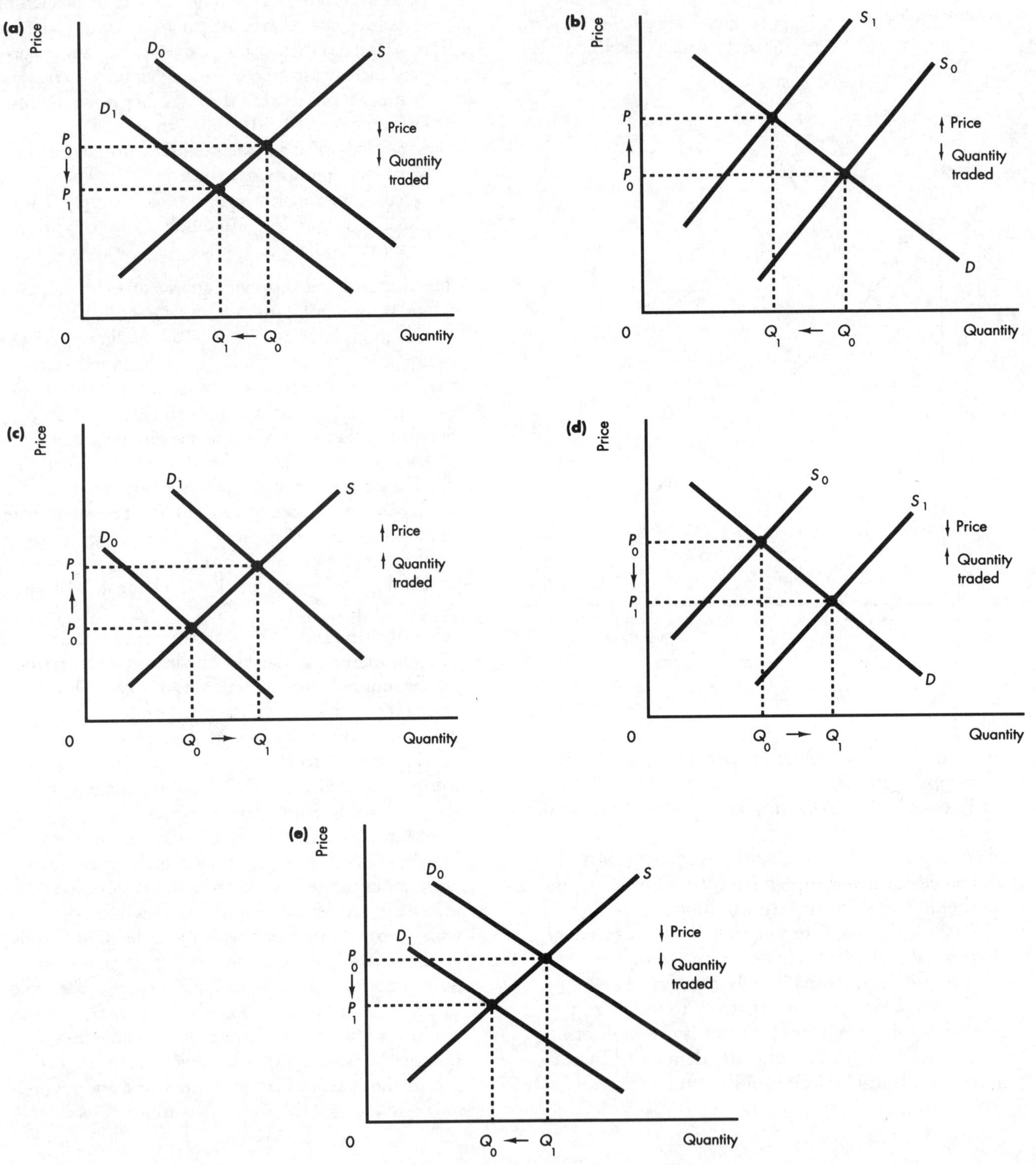
(a)
Price
D_0
S
D_1
P_0
P_1
↓ Price
↓ Quantity traded
0
Q_1 ← Q_0
Quantity
(b)
Price
S_1
S_0
P_1
P_0
↑ Price
↓ Quantity traded
D
0
Q_1 ← Q_0
Quantity
(c)
Price
D_1
S
D_0
P_1
P_0
↑ Price
↑ Quantity traded
0
Q_0 → Q_1
Quantity
(d)
Price
S_0
S_1
P_0
P_1
↓ Price
↑ Quantity traded
D
0
Q_0 → Q_1
Quantity
(e)
Price
D_0
S
D_1
P_0
P_1
↓ Price
↓ Quantity traded
0
Q_0 ← Q_1
Quantity

Figure 4.7

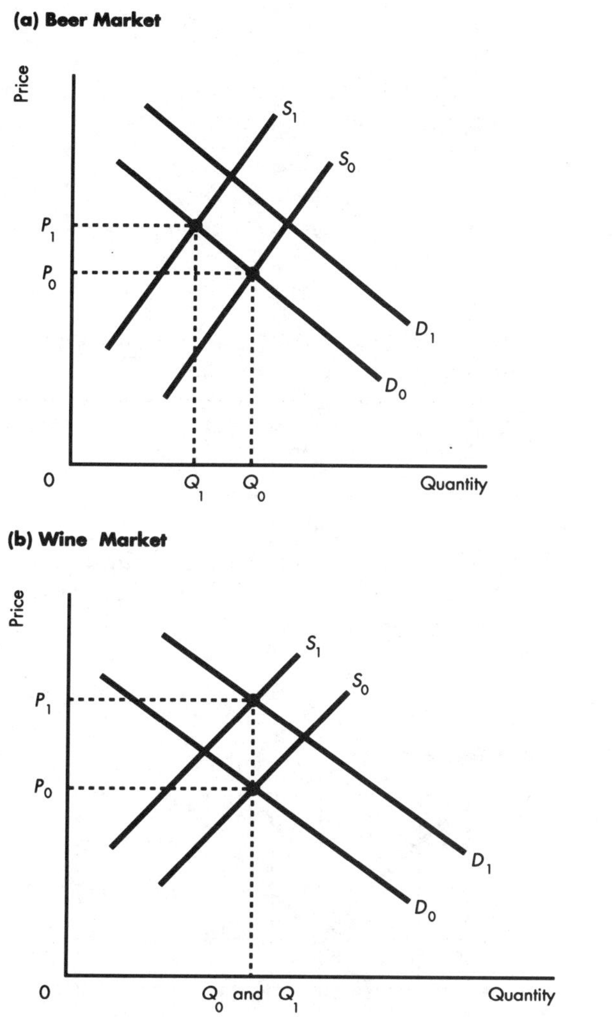

3) a) The demand and supply curves for grape jelly are shown in Figure 4.2 Solution.

b) The equilibrium is given at the intersection of the demand and supply curves (labelled point *a*). The equilibrium price is $50 per case and the equilibrium quantity traded is 100 cases per week.

c) At a price of $40 there is a shortage of 60 cases per week.

d) In equilibrium, the equations become:

$$\text{Demand: } P^* = 75 - 0.25Q^*$$
$$\text{Supply: } P^* = 0.5Q^*$$

i) To solve for Q^*, set demand equal to supply:

$$75 - 0.25Q^* = 0.5Q^*$$
$$75 = 0.75Q^*$$
$$100 = Q^*$$

Figure 4.2 Solution

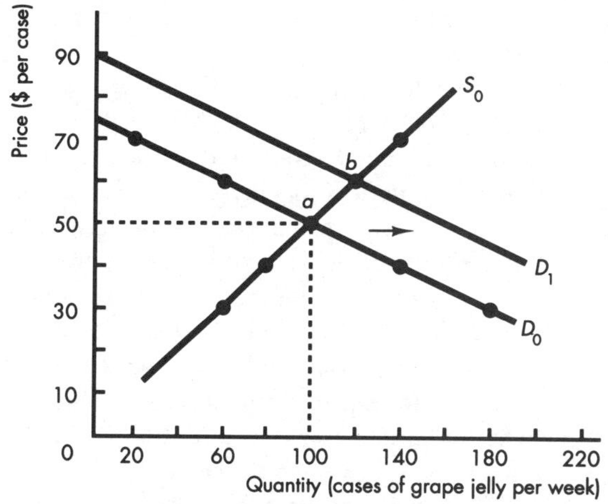

ii) To solve for P^*, we can substitute Q^* into either the demand or supply equations. Look at demand first:

$$P^* = 75 - 0.25Q^*$$
$$P^* = 75 - 0.25(100)$$
$$P^* = 75 - 25$$
$$P^* = 50$$

Alternatively, substituting Q^* into the supply equation yields the same result:

$$P^* = 0.5Q^*$$
$$P^* = 0.5(100)$$
$$P^* = 50$$

e) i) Table 4.3 also contains the (unchanged) quantity supplied, for reference purposes.

Table 4.3 Demand and Supply Schedules for Grape Jelly per Week

Price (per case)	Quantity Demanded (cases)	Quantity Supplied (cases)
$30	240	60
$40	200	80
$50	160	100
$60	120	120
$70	80	140

ii) The graph of the new demand curve, D_1, is shown in Figure 4.2 Solution on page 47.

iii) The new equilibrium price is $60 per case and the quantity traded is 120 cases of grape jelly per week.

iv) The new demand equation is $P = 90 - 0.25Q_D$. Notice that the slope of the new demand equation is the same as the slope of the original demand equation. An increase in demand of 60 cases at every price results in a rightward *parallel* shift of the demand curve. Since the two curves are parallel, they have the same slope. The figure of 90 is the price-axis intercept of the new demand curve, which you can see on your graph. (Remember that the demand equation is the equation of a straight line ($y = a + bx$); in this case, $a = 90$.)

If you want additional practice in the use of demand and supply equations for calculating equilibrium values of price and quantity traded, you can use the new demand curve equation together with the supply curve equation to calculate the answers you found in e)iii).

4) In equilibrium, the equations become:

$$\text{Demand: } P^* = 8 - 1Q^*$$
$$\text{Supply: } P^* = 2 + 1Q^*$$

a) To solve for Q^*, set demand equal to supply:

$$8 - 1Q^* = 2 + 1Q^*$$
$$6 = 2Q^*$$
$$3 = Q^*$$

b) To solve for P^*, we can substitute Q^* into either the demand or supply equations. Look first at demand:

$$P^* = 8 - 1Q^*$$
$$P^* = 8 - 1(3)$$
$$P^* = 8 - 3$$
$$P^* = 5$$

Alternatively, substituting Q^* into the supply equation yields the same result:

$$P^* = 2 + 1Q^*$$
$$P^* = 2 + 1(3)$$
$$P^* = 2 + 3$$
$$P^* = 5$$

c) In equilibrium, the equations are:

$$\text{Demand: } P^* = 4 - 1Q^*$$
$$\text{Supply: } P^* = 2 + 1Q^*$$

i) To solve for Q^*, set demand equal to supply.

$$4 - 1Q^* = 2 + 1Q^*$$
$$2 = 2Q^*$$
$$1 = Q^*$$

ii) To solve for P^*, we can substitute Q^* into either the demand or supply equations. Look first at demand:

$$P^* = 4 - 1Q^*$$
$$P^* = 4 - 1(1)$$
$$P^* = 4 - 1$$
$$P^* = 3$$

Alternatively, substituting Q^* into the supply equation yields the same result:

$$P^* = 2 + 1Q^*$$
$$P^* = 2 + 1(1)$$
$$P^* = 2 + 1$$
$$P^* = 3$$

d) The supply curve, initial demand curve (D_0), and new demand curve (D_1) for dweedles are shown in Figure 4.3 Solution.

Figure 4.3 Solution

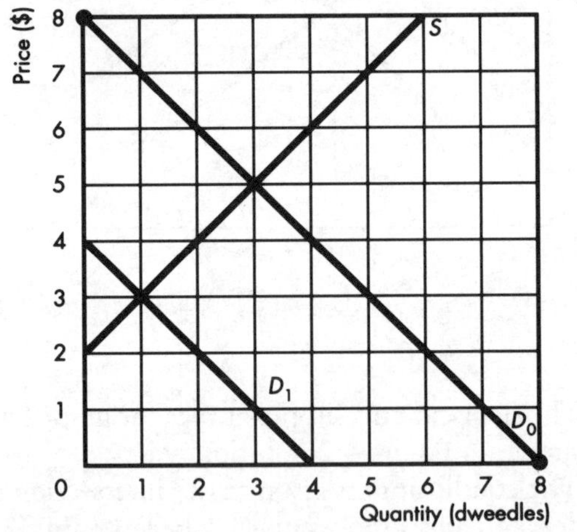

e) Dweedles are an inferior good. An increase in income (from $300 to $500) caused a decrease in demand — the demand curve for dweedles shifted to the left.

5) **a)** Substitute the price of $56 into the demand and supply equations to calculate the quantities demanded and supplied at that price. This is the mathematical equivalent of what you do on a

graph when you identify a price on the vertical axis, move your eye across to the demand (or supply) curve, and then move your eye down to read the quantity on the horizontal axis. Substituting into the demand equation we find:

$$P = 80 - 2Q_D$$
$$56 = 80 - 2Q_D$$
$$2Q_D = 24$$
$$Q_D = 12$$

Substituting into the supply equation:

$$P = 50 + 1Q_S$$
$$56 = 50 + 1Q_S$$
$$6 = Q_S$$

Quantity demanded exceeds quantity supplied by 6 (12 – 6), so there is a shortage of 6 flubits.

b) A shortage means the price was set below the equilibrium price. Competition between consumers for the limited number of flubits will bid up the price and increase the quantity supplied until we reach the equilibrium price and quantity traded.

c) In equilibrium, the equations are:

$$\text{Demand: } P^* = 80 - 2Q^*$$
$$\text{Supply: } P^* = 50 + 1Q^*$$

To solve for Q^*, set demand equal to supply:

$$80 - 2Q^* = 50 + 1Q^*$$
$$30 = 3Q^*$$
$$10 = Q^*$$

d) To solve for P^*, substitute Q^* into the demand equation:

$$P^* = 80 - 2Q^*$$
$$P^* = 80 - 2(10)$$
$$P^* = 80 - 20$$
$$P^* = 60$$

You can check this answer yourself by substituting Q^* into the supply equation

e) The new equilibrium equations are:

$$\text{Demand: } P^* = 80 - 2Q^*$$
$$\text{Supply: } P^* = 20 + 1Q^*$$

i) To solve for Q^*, set demand equal to supply:

$$80 - 2Q^* = 20 + 1Q^*$$
$$60 = 3Q^*$$
$$20 = Q^*$$

ii) To solve for P^*, substitute Q^* into the supply equation.

$$P^* = 20 + 1Q^*$$
$$P^* = 20 + 1(20)$$
$$P^* = 20 + 20$$
$$P^* = 40$$

You can check this answer yourself by substituting Q^* into the demand equation.

Chapter 5 Elasticity

Chapter in Perspective

Text Pages 101–124

The analysis in Chapter 4 showed how changes in demand and supply can explain the *direction* of changes in quantity and price. If, for example, the supply of a good falls, its quantity demanded falls and its price rises. In this chapter, we learn to calculate the *magnitude* of those changes — for example, by *how much* does quantity demanded fall?

The key concept for calculating the magnitude of such changes is *elasticity*. Elasticity is a measure of the quantitative *responsiveness* of quantity demanded or supplied to changes in other key economic variables. Using different applications of elasticity, we will learn to calculate how much quantity demanded will respond to changes in price, income, or changes in the prices of substitutes or complements and, by how much quantity supplied will respond to a change in price. The elasticity concept is one of the most practical concepts in economics. It can help a company decide whether lowering the price of its product will increase or decrease total revenue from sales. It can also help a government policy-maker estimate how much revenue a sales tax will raise.

Learning Objectives

After studying this chapter, you will be able to:

- **Define and calculate the price elasticity of demand.**
- **Explain what determines the elasticity of demand.**
- **Distinguish between short-run demand and long-run demand.**
- **Use elasticity to determine whether a price change will increase or decrease revenue.**
- **Define and calculate other elasticities of demand and supply.**
- **Distinguish between momentary supply, long-run supply, and short-run supply.**

Helpful Hints

1) There are many elasticity formulae in this chapter, but they are all based on the same simple, intuitive principle — *responsiveness.* All of the demand and supply elasticity formulae measure the *responsiveness* (sensitivity) *of quantity* (demanded or supplied) to changes in something else. Thus, percentage change in quantity is always in the numerator of the relevant formula. As you come to understand how quantity responds to changes in price, income, and prices of related goods, you will be able to work out each elasticity formula, even if you have temporarily forgotten it.

2) The complete formula for calculating the price elasticity of demand between two points on the demand curve as shown in Table 5.1 on text page 105 is:

$$\eta = \left| \frac{\%\ \Delta \text{ Quantity Demanded}}{\%\ \Delta \text{ Price}} \right|$$

$$= \left| \left(\frac{\Delta Q}{Q_{AVE}}\right) \Big/ \left(\frac{\Delta P}{P_{AVE}}\right) \right|$$

The law of demand assures us that price and quantity demanded always move in opposite directions along any demand curve. Thus, without the absolute value sign, the formula for the price elasticity of demand would yield a negative number. Because our main interest is in the *magnitude* of the response in quantity demand to a change in price, for simplicity, we take the absolute value to guarantee a positive number. Whenever you see the often-used shorthand term, *elasticity of demand,* remember that it means the absolute value of the *price* elasticity of demand.

3) Elasticity is *not* the same as slope although they are related. Along a straight-line demand curve the slope is constant, but the elasticity varies from infinity to zero as we move down the demand curve. To see that this is the case, look at the formula below, which is just a rearrangement of the elasticity formula in Helpful Hint 2.

$$\eta = \left| \left(\frac{\Delta Q}{\Delta P}\right) \left(\frac{P_{AVE}}{Q_{AVE}}\right) \right|$$

The term in the first parentheses is simply the inverse of the slope. Since the slope is constant everywhere along a straight-line demand curve, so is the inverse of the slope. Consider, however, what happens to the term in the second parentheses as we move down the demand curve. At the "top" of the demand curve, P_{AVE} is very large, Q_{AVE} is very small, so the term in the second parentheses is large. As we move down the demand curve, P_{AVE} becomes smaller and Q_{AVE} becomes larger, so the term in the second parentheses falls in value. The net result is that the absolute value of the price elasticity of demand falls as we move down the demand curve.

4) One of the most practical and important uses of the concept of price elasticity of demand is that it allows us to predict the *effect on total revenue* of a change in price. A fall in price will increase total revenue if demand is elastic, leave total revenue unchanged if demand is unit elastic, and decrease total revenue if demand is inelastic. Because price and quantity demanded always move in opposite directions along a demand curve, a fall in price will cause an increase in quantity demanded. Since total revenue equals price x quantity, the fall in price will tend to decrease total revenue, while the increase in quantity demanded will increase total revenue. The net effect depends on which of these individual effects is larger.

The concept of price elasticity of demand conveniently summarizes the net effect. For example, if demand is elastic, the percentage change in quantity demanded is greater than the percentage change in price. Hence, with a fall in price, the quantity effect dominates and total revenue will increase. If, however, demand is inelastic, the percentage change in quantity demanded is less than the percentage change in price. Hence, with a fall in price, the price effect dominates and total revenue will decrease.

5) Two other important elasticity concepts are the income elasticity of demand and the cross elasticity of demand.

Income Elasticity of Demand:

$$\eta_Y = \frac{\%\ \Delta \text{ Quantity Demanded}}{\%\ \Delta \text{ Income}}$$

$$= \left(\frac{\Delta Q}{Q_{AVE}}\right) \Big/ \left(\frac{\Delta Y}{Y_{AVE}}\right)$$

Cross Elasticity of Demand:

$$\eta_X = \frac{\%\ \Delta \text{ Quantity Demanded of Good } A}{\%\ \Delta \text{ Price of Good } B}$$

$$= \left(\frac{\Delta Q^A}{Q^A_{AVE}}\right) \Big/ \left(\frac{\Delta P^B}{P^B_{AVE}}\right)$$

Notice that these two elasticity formulae do *not* have absolute value signs and can take on either positive or negative values. While these, like all elasticity formulae measure responsiveness, both the magnitude *and the direction* of the response are important. In the case of income elasticity of demand, the response of quantity demanded to an increase in income will be positive for a normal good and negative for an inferior good. In the case of cross elasticity of demand, the response of the quantity demanded of good *A* to an increase in the price of good *B* will be positive if the goods are substitutes and negative if the goods are complements.

In calculating an income elasticity or a cross elasticity, be alert to the fact that the *price of the good in the numerator* of the formula *is assumed constant.* Income elasticity measures the quantity response to a change in income, *ceteris paribus.* Cross elasticity measures the quantity response of good *A* to a change in the price of good *B*, *ceteris paribus.* This means that we cannot simply read numerical values for calculating these elasticities from the equilibrium positions of a set of demand and supply curves. For example, when income increases, demand shifts right (for a normal good), and the new equilibrium quantity will also have a higher equilibrium price. To calculate income elasticity correctly, we compare the income and quantity demanded of the initial equilibrium with the new income and quantity demanded. To obtain the correct new quantity demanded, we must use the new demand curve, but we must calculate the quantity demanded that would have prevailed at the *initial*, unchanged price. (See problems 4 and 5 for examples).

Key Figures and Tables

Figure 5.2 Elasticity Along a Straight-Line Demand Curve, text page 108
While the slope of a straight-line demand curve is constant, the elasticity varies systematically as we move down it. The elasticity decreases as the price of the good falls and the quantity demanded rises. In the price range above the midpoint of a straight-line demand curve, demand is elastic, at the midpoint elasticity is 1 (demand is unit elastic), and in the price range below the midpoint, demand is inelastic.

Figure 5.3 Demand Curves with Constant Elasticity, text page 108
This figure illustrates three demand curves with constant price elasticity. The first, part (a), is a vertical demand curve which has zero elasticity since any price change will have no effect on quantity demanded. The demand curve in part (b) has constant unitary elasticity. The horizontal demand curve in part (c) is infinitely elastic since a small change in price will have an infinitely large effect on quantity demanded.

Figure 5.5 Income Elasticity of Demand, text page 113
The three graphs in this figure illustrate relationships between income (measured on the horizontal axis) and quantity demanded (measured on the vertical axis). Part (a) shows a relationship in which the quantity demanded increases as income increases, but the quantity demanded increases by a greater percentage than income. Thus the income elasticity is greater than 1. In part (b) quantity demanded and income again increase together but the percentage change in quantity demanded is less than the percentage change in income. The income elasticity is between zero and one. The first part of the relationship in part (c) is similar to that of part (b). However, as income continues to increase, eventually the quantity demanded reaches a maximum and thereafter decreases. At the point of maximum quantity demand, the income elasticity is zero and it is negative for higher levels of income.

Table 5.1 Calculating the Price Elasticity of Demand, text page 105
The price elasticity of demand is defined as the percentage change in the quantity demanded divided by the percentage change in the price. This table illustrates the procedure for calculating the price elasticity of demand between two points on a demand curve. You must master this table to be able to do problems involving any calculation of elasticity. Although this table only presents the procedure for calculating price elasticity of demand, the procedures for calculating all other elasticity concepts are very similar.

Table 5.6 A Compact Glossary of Elasticities of Demand, text page 115
Three kinds of elasticities of demand are presented in this chapter of the text: price elasticities, income elasticities, and cross elasticities of demand. The purpose of this table is to summarize the economic meaning of these measures as they assume values in alternative ranges. This table should serve as an excellent study device. You should understand and memorize all of the information contained in the table.

SELF-TEST

CONCEPT REVIEW

1) A units-free measure of the responsiveness of quantity demanded to price changes is given by the ______________ ______________ of demand.

2) The (price) elasticity of demand is calculated as the percentage change in the ______________ ______________ divided by the percentage change in the ______________.

3) If the (price) elasticity of demand is between 0 and 1, demand is said to be ______________ ; if it is greater than 1, demand is said to be ______________ ; if it is equal to 1, demand is said to be ______________ ______________.

4) A good that has many good substitutes is likely to have demand that is ______________. If only a small proportion of income is spent on a good, its demand will likely be ______________.

5) As time passes after a change in the price of a good, demand will tend to become more ______________.

6) If demand is elastic, an increase in the price implies that revenue (expenditures) will ______________.

7) A measure of the responsiveness of the quantity demanded of a good to changes in income is given by the ______________ ______________ of demand.

8) The income elasticity of demand is calculated as the percentage change in the ______________ ______________ divided by the percentage change in ______________.

9) The income elasticity is ______________ for inferior goods.

10) The responsiveness of the quantity demanded of one good to a change in the price of a complement or substitute is given by the ______________ ______________ of demand.

11) The cross elasticity of demand with respect to the price of a substitute is ______________. The cross elasticity of demand with respect to the price of a complement is ______________.

12) The elasticity of supply is a measure of the responsiveness of the ______________ ______________ to changes in ______________.

13) To illustrate the initial change in quantity supplied induced by a sudden change in price we use the ______________ supply curve. To illustrate the response of quantity supplied after all technologically possible long-run adjustments in the production process have been made we use the ______________ – ______________ supply curve.

14) The long-run supply curve will generally be more ______________ than a short-run supply curve, which will be more ______________ than the momentary supply curve.

TRUE OR FALSE

_____ 1) The price elasticity of demand measures how responsive prices are to changes in demand.

_____ 2) A horizontal demand curve is perfectly inelastic.

_____ 3) An increase in supply will increase revenue (expenditure) if demand is elastic.

_____ 4) The demand for gasoline is likely to become more inelastic with the passage of time after a price increase.

_____ 5) Price elasticity of demand is constant along a linear demand curve.

_____ 6) The more readily available are substitutes for a good, the more inelastic will be its demand.

_____ 7) If total revenue falls following an increase in price, demand must be inelastic.

_____ 8) If you like Pepsi Cola and Coca-Cola about the same, your demand for Pepsi is likely to be elastic.

_____ 9) If your expenditures on toothpaste are a small proportion of your total income, your demand for toothpaste is likely to be inelastic.

_____ 10) The more narrowly we define a good, the more elastic is its demand.

_____ 11) Long-run demand is more inelastic than short-run demand because there is more opportunity for substitution.

_____ 12) If the income elasticity of the demand for turnips is positive, then turnips are an inferior good.

_____ 13) The effect of the change in the price of one good on the quantity demanded of another good is measured by the cross elasticity of demand.

_____ 14) We would expect the cross elasticity of demand between hamburgers and hot dogs to be negative.

_____ 15) If a 10 percent increase in the price of widgets causes a 6 percent increase in the quantity of woozles demanded, then widgets and woozles must be complements.

_____ 16) If goods *A* and *B* are substitutes, then a decrease in the demand for *A* will lead to an decrease in the equilibrium price of *B*.

_____ 17) If a 3 percent decrease in price induces a 9 percent decrease in quantity supplied, then the supply curve is elastic.

_____ 18) Supply will generally be more inelastic in the long run than in the short run.

_____ 19) A vertical supply curve exhibits a supply elasticity of zero.

_____ 20) If a decrease in supply causes revenue to decrease, then demand must be inelastic.

_____ 21) For a linear demand curve, demand is more elastic at higher price ranges than at lower price ranges.

_____ 22) If a 10 percent increase in the price of good *A* causes a 6 percent decrease in the quantity of good *B* demanded, the cross elasticity of demand between *A* and *B* is 0.6.

_____ 23) If a 12 percent increase in income causes a 9 percent increase in quantity demanded, the income elasticity of demand is 1.33.

_____ 24) If a 10 percent decrease in income causes a 10 percent increase in quantity demanded, then the income elasticity of demand is 1.

_____ 25) If a 9 percent increase in price leads to a 5 percent decrease in quantity demanded, total revenue has decreased.

MULTIPLE-CHOICE

1) If price elasticity of demand is zero, then as the price falls,
a) total revenue does not change.
b) quantity demanded does not change.
c) quantity demanded falls to zero.
d) total revenue increases from zero.
e) none of the above occurs.

2) Two points on the demand curve for volleyballs are shown in Table 5.1.

Table 5.1

Price per volleyball	Quantity Demanded
$19	55
$21	45

What is the elasticity of demand between these two points?
a) 2.5
b) 2.0
c) 0.5
d) 0.4
e) none of the above

3) The fact that butter has margarine as a close substitute in consumption
a) makes the supply of butter more elastic.
b) makes the supply of butter less elastic.
c) makes the demand for butter more elastic.
d) makes the demand for butter less elastic.
e) does not affect butter's elasticity of supply or demand.

4) If the price elasticity of demand is 2, then a 1 percent decrease in price will
a) double the quantity demanded.
b) reduce the quantity demanded by half.
c) increase the quantity demanded by 2 percent.
d) reduce the quantity demanded by 2 percent.
e) increase the quantity demanded by 0.5 percent.

5) A given percentage increase in the price of a good is likely to cause a larger percentage decline in quantity demanded
a) the shorter the passage of time.
b) the larger the proportion of income spent on it.
c) the harder it is to obtain good substitutes.
d) when all of the above occur.
e) when none of the above occur.

6) A good will have a more price inelastic demand
a) the higher its price.
b) the larger the percentage of income spent on it.
c) the longer the time elapsed.
d) if it is a luxury good.
e) if it has no close substitutes.

7) A decrease in tuition fees will decrease the university's total revenue if the price elasticity of demand for university education is
a) negative.
b) greater than zero but less than one.
c) equal to one.
d) greater than one.
e) less than the price elasticity of supply.

8) If the demand for frozen orange juice is price elastic, then a severe frost which destroys large quantities of oranges will likely
a) reduce the equilibrium price of juice, but increase total consumer spending on it.
b) reduce the equilibrium quantity of juice as well as total consumer spending on it.
c) reduce both the equilibrium quantity and the price of juice.
d) increase the equilibrium price of juice as well as total consumer spending on it.
e) increase the equilibrium price of juice, but leave total consumer spending on it constant.

9) If a 4 percent rise in the price of peanut butter causes the total revenue from peanut butter sales to fall by 8 percent, then demand for peanut butter
a) is elastic.
b) is inelastic.
c) is unit elastic.
d) has an elasticity of 1/2.
e) has an elasticity of 2.

10) Tina and Brian work for the same recording company. Tina claims that they would be better off by increasing the price of their tapes, while Brian claims that they would be better off by decreasing the price. It can be concluded that
a) Tina thinks the demand for tapes has price elasticity of zero and Brian thinks price elasticity equals one.
b) Tina thinks the demand for tapes has price elasticity equal to one and Brian thinks price elasticity equals zero.
c) Tina thinks the demand for tapes is price elastic and Brian thinks it is price inelastic.
d) Tina thinks the demand for tapes is price inelastic and Brian thinks it is price elastic.
e) Tina and Brian should stick to singing and forget about economics.

11) A perfectly vertical demand curve has a price elasticity of
a) zero.
b) greater than zero but less than one.
c) one.
d) greater than one.
e) infinity.

12) Given the relationship shown in Figure 5.1 between total revenue from the sale of a good and the quantity of the good sold, then
a) this is an inferior good.
b) this is a normal good.
c) the elasticity of demand is zero.
d) the elasticity of demand is infinity.
e) the elasticity of demand is one.

Figure 5.1

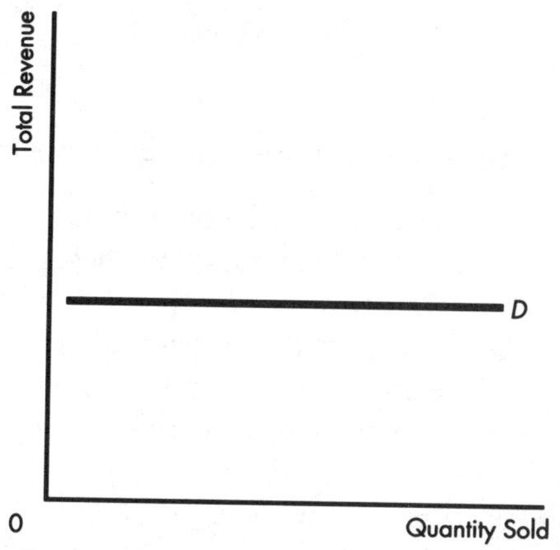

13) Preferences for brussel sprouts increase. The price of brussel sprouts will not change if the price elasticity of
a) demand is 0.
b) demand is 1.
c) supply is 0.
d) supply is 1.
e) supply is infinity.

14) If an increase in price causes a decrease in total revenue, then price elasticity of demand is
a) negative.
b) zero.
c) greater than zero but less than one.
d) equal to one.
e) greater than one.

15) If the Jets decrease ticket prices and find that total revenue does not change, then the price elasticity of demand for tickets is
a) zero.
b) greater than zero but less than one.
c) equal to one.
d) greater than one.
e) inferior.

16) If a 4 percent decrease in income (at a constant price) causes a 2 percent decrease in the consumption of dweedles, then
a) the income elasticity of demand for dweedles is negative.
b) dweedles are a necessity and a normal good.
c) dweedles are a luxury and a normal good.
d) dweedles are an inferior good.
e) both a) and d) are true.

17) Luxury goods tend to have income elasticities of demand which are
a) greater than one.
b) greater than zero but less than one.
c) positive.
d) negative.
e) first positive and then negative as income increases.

18) If a 10 percent increase in income causes a 10 percent decrease in the consumption of widgets (at a constant price), then
a) the price elasticity of demand for widgets equals 1.
b) the income elasticity of demand for widgets is negative.
c) the income elasticity of demand for widgets equals 1.
d) widgets are a normal good.
e) none of the above are true.

19) If a 10 percent increase in income causes a 5 percent increase in quantity demanded (at a constant price), what is the income elasticity of demand?
a) 0.5
b) –0.5
c) 2.0
d) –2.0
e) none of the above

20) The cross elasticity of the demand for white tennis balls with respect to the price of yellow tennis balls is probably
a) negative and high.
b) negative and low.
c) positive and high.
d) positive and low.
e) zero.

21) A decrease in the price of *X* from $6 to $4 causes an increase in the quantity of *Y* demanded (at the current price of *Y*) from 900 to 1,100 units. What is the cross elasticity of demand between *X* and *Y*?
a) 0.5
b) –0.5
c) 2
d) –2
e) both a) or b), depending on whether *X* and *Y* are substitutes or complements

22) When price goes from $1.50 to $2.50, quantity supplied increases from 9,000 to 11,000 units. What is the price elasticity of supply?
a) 0.4
b) 0.8
c) 2.5
d) 4.0
e) none of the above

23) A negative value for
a) price elasticity of supply implies an upward-sloping supply curve.
b) cross elasticity of demand implies complementary goods.
c) price elasticity of demand implies an inferior good.
d) income elasticity of demand implies a normal good.
e) income elasticity of demand implies an error in your calculation.

24) The magnitude of *both* the elasticity of demand and the elasticity of supply depend on
a) the ease of substitution between goods.
b) the proportion of income spent on a good.
c) the time elapsed since the price change.
d) the technological conditions of production.
e) none of the above factors.

25) The long-run supply curve is likely to be
a) more elastic than momentary supply but less elastic than short-run supply.
b) less elastic than momentary supply but more elastic than short-run supply.
c) less elastic than both momentary and short-run supply curves.
d) more elastic than both momentary and short-run supply curves.
e) vertical.

SHORT ANSWER

1) Why is elasticity superior to slope as a measure of the responsiveness of quantity demanded to changes in price?

2) In each of the following, compare the price elasticity of demand for each pair of goods and explain why the demand for one of the goods is more elastic than demand for the other.
a) IBM personal computers before the development of other "clone" personal computers versus IBM personal computers after the production of such clones
b) Television sets versus matches
c) Electricity just after an increase in its price versus electricity two years after the price increase
d) Acetaminophen versus Tylenol-brand acetaminophen

3) Why does demand tend to be more elastic in the long run?

4) Why does supply tend to be more elastic in the long run?

5) Which demand curve in Figure 5.2 (D_A or D_B) is more elastic in the price range P_1 to P_2? Explain why. [*Hint:* Use the formula for price elasticity of demand.]

Figure 5.2

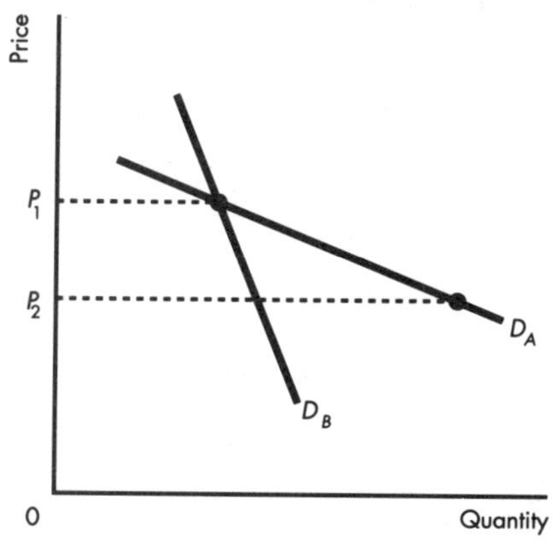

PROBLEMS

1) a) Given the demand curve in Figure 5.3, complete the second and third columns of Table 5.2: η (the price elasticity of demand) and ΔTR (the change in total revenue) as the price falls from the higher price to the lower price. Describe the relationship between elasticity and change in total revenue as price falls (moving down the demand curve).

Figure 5.3

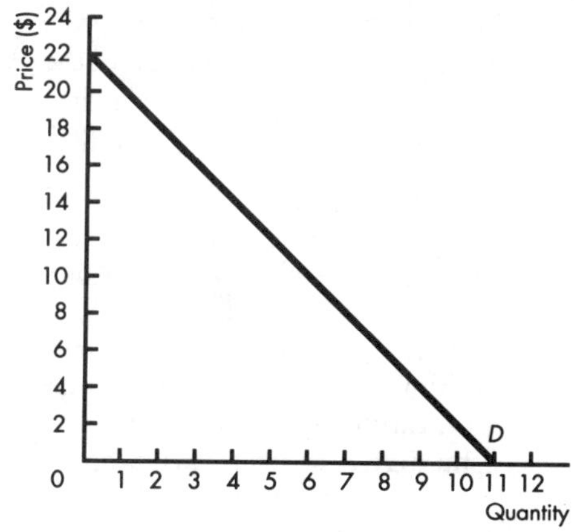

Table 5.2

ΔP($)	η	ΔTR ($)	η'	$\Delta TR'$ ($)
16 – 14				
14 – 12				
12 – 10				
10 – 8				
8 – 6				

b) Suppose income, which initially was $10,000, increases to $14,000, causing an increase in demand: at every price, quantity demanded increases by 2 units. Draw the new demand curve and label it D'. Use this new demand curve to complete the last two columns of Table 5.2 for η' (the new price elasticity of demand) and $\Delta TR'$ (the new change in total revenue).

c) Using the price range between $16 and $14, explain why D' is more inelastic than D.

d) Calculate the income elasticity of demand, assuming the price remains constant at $12. Is this a normal or inferior good? Explain why you could have answered the question even without calculating the income elasticity of demand.

2) The demand equation for woozles is $P = 60 - 2Q_D$. The supply equation for woozles is $P = 32 + 5Q_S$, where P is the price of a woozle in dollars, Q_D is the quantity of woozles demanded, and Q_S is the quantity of woozles supplied.

a) Calculate the price elasticity of demand for woozles between $Q_D = 4$ and $Q_D = 6$.

b) Initially, the woozle market is in equilibrium with $P^* = 52$ and $Q^* = 4$. Then, the supply curve shifts (the demand curve remains constant) yielding a new equilibrium price of $P^* = 48$.

Using all of the relevant information, show *two separate methods* for determining whether total revenue increases, decreases, or remains constant in moving from the initial equilibrium to the new equilibrium.

3) a) Suppose Jean loses his present job and his monthly income falls from $10,000 to $6,000, while his monthly purchases of grits increase from 200 to 400. Calculate his income elasticity of demand for grits.

b) Are grits a normal or an inferior good? Explain why.

4) The demand equation for tribbles is $P = 50 - 1Q_D$. The supply equation for tribbles is $P = 20 + 0.5Q_S$, where P is the price of a tribble in dollars, Q_D is the quantity of tribbles demanded, and Q_S is the quantity of tribbles supplied. The tribble market is initially in equilibrium, and income is $180.

a) What is the equilibrium quantity traded (Q^*) of tribbles?

b) What is the equilibrium price (P^*) of a tribble?

c) As a result of a decrease in income to $120, the demand curve for tribbles shifts (the supply curve remains the same). The new demand equation is:

$$P = 110 - 1Q_D$$

Use this information to calculate the following:

i) the new equilibrium quantity traded of tribbles

ii) the new equilibrium price of a tribble

d) Calculate the income elasticity of demand for tribbles. Are tribbles a normal or inferior good? [*Hint*: In your calculation be sure to: (1) use the information about the *initial* equilibrium conditions (initial equilibrium price, quantity, income), and (2) keep in mind that price is assumed *constant* in calculating income elasticity. Only income and quantity change.]

5) Table 5.3 gives the demand schedules for good *A* when the price of good *B* (P_B) is $8 and when the price of good *B* is $12. Complete the last column of the table by computing η_x, the cross elasticity of demand between goods *A* and *B* for each of the three prices of *A*. Are *A* and *B* complements or substitutes?

Table 5.3 Demand Schedules for Good A

	P_B = $8	P_B = $12	
P_A	Q_A	Q'_A	η_x
8	2,000	4,000	
7	4,000	6,000	
6	6,000	8,000	

ANSWERS

CONCEPT REVIEW

1) price elasticity
2) quantity demanded; price
3) inelastic; elastic; unit elastic
4) elastic; inelastic
5) elastic
6) decrease
7) income elasticity
8) quantity demanded; income
9) negative
10) cross elasticity
11) positive; negative
12) quantity supplied; price
13) momentary; long-run
14) elastic; elastic

TRUE OR FALSE

1) F	6) F	11) F	16) T	21) T
2) F	7) F	12) F	17) T	22) F
3) T	8) T	13) T	18) F	23) F
4) F	9) T	14) F	19) T	24) F
5) F	10) T	15) F	20) F	25) F

MULTIPLE-CHOICE

1) b	6) e	11) a	16) b	21) b
2) b	7) b	12) e	17) a	22) a
3) c	8) b	13) e	18) b	23) b
4) c	9) a	14) e	19) a	24) c
5) b	10) d	15) c	20) c	25) d

SHORT ANSWER

1) The slope of a demand curve tells us how much quantity demanded changes when price changes. However, the numerical value of the slope depends on the units we use to measure price and quantity, and will change if our unit of measure is changed even though demand is unchanged. For example, if we change our unit of measure for quantity from kilograms to grams, the new slope of the (same) demand curve will be 2,000 times the old slope. On the other hand, elasticity gives a units-free measure of the responsiveness of quantity demanded to price changes.

2) **a)** The demand for IBM personal computers will be more elastic after the production of clone personal computers since there would then be more readily available substitutes.
b) The demand for television sets will be more elastic since they will generally take a larger proportion of consumer income.
c) The demand for electricity after the passage of two years will be more elastic since consumers will have more time to find substitutes for electricity, for example, a gas stove.
d) The demand for Tylenol is more elastic. There are far more substitutes for Tylenol (other brands of acetaminophen) than there are for acetaminophen in general.

3) Demand is more responsive to price changes (more elastic) in the long run because more substitutes become available to consumers. Not only are new goods invented, but consumers also learn about and begin to use new substitutes.

4) Supply is more elastic in the long run because the passage of time allows producers to find better (more efficient) ways of producing that are not available in the short run. The responsiveness of production to an increase in price will increase as firms have time to discover and implement new technologies or to increase the scale of operation.

5) D_A is more elastic than D_B. To see why, look at the formula for price elasticity of demand:

$$\eta = \left| \frac{\%\ \Delta \text{ Quantity Demanded}}{\%\ \Delta \text{ Price}} \right|$$

The percentage change in price is the same for the two demand curves. But the percentage change in quantity is greater for D_A. At P_1, the initial quantity demanded is the same for both demand curves (Q_1). With the fall in price to P_2, the increase in quantity demanded is greater for D_A (to Q_{2A}) than for D_B (to Q_{2B}). Therefore, D_A is more elastic than D_B.

Figure 5.2 Solution

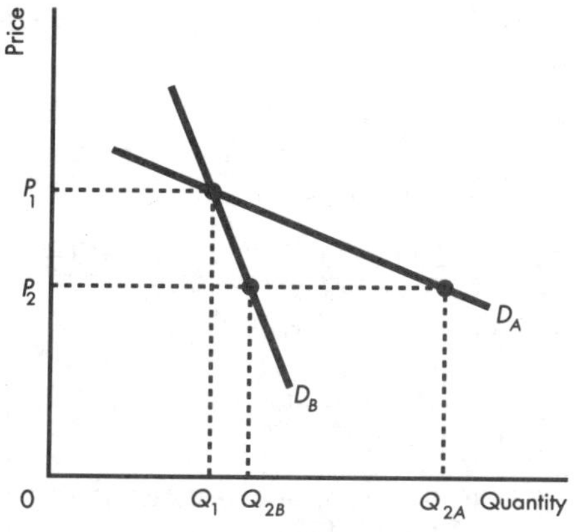

PROBLEMS

1) a) The completed columns of Table 5.2 are shown here. The second and third columns of the table show that as price falls, total revenue increases when demand is elastic; total revenue remains constant when demand is unit elastic; total revenue falls when demand is inelastic.

Table 5.2 Solution

ΔP($)	η	ΔTR($)	η'	$\Delta TR'$($)
16 – 14	2.14	+8	1.36	+4
14 – 12	1.44	+4	1.00	0
12 – 10	1.00	0	0.73	–4
10 – 8	0.69	–4	0.53	–8
8 – 6	0.47	–8	0.37	–12

b) The new demand curve is labelled D'. The last two columns of the table have been completed on the basis of the new demand curve shown in Figure 5.3 Solution.

Figure 5.3 Solution

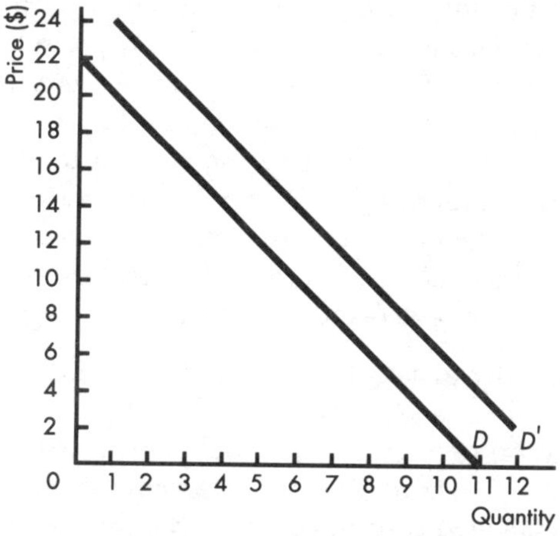

c) Since they are parallel, D' and D have exactly the same slope. Thus, we know that for a given change in price, the change in quantity demanded will be the same for the two curves. However, elasticity is determined by *percentage* changes, and the percentage change in quantity demanded is different for the two curves, although the percentage change in price will be the same. For a given percentage change in price, the percentage change in quantity demanded will always be less for D'. For example, as the price falls from \$16 to \$14 (a 13 percent change), the quantity demanded increases from 5 to 6 units along D' but from 3 to 4 along D. The percentage change in quantity demanded is only 18 percent along D' and 29 percent along D. Since the percentage change in price is the same for both curves, D' is more inelastic than D.

d) Income increases from \$10,000 to \$14,000. At a constant price of \$12, the increase in income, which shifts out the demand curve to D', increases the quantity consumers will demand from 5 units to 7 units. Substituting these numbers into the formula for the income elasticity of demand yields:

$$\eta_Y = \left(\frac{\Delta Q}{Q_{AVE}}\right) \Big/ \left(\frac{\Delta Y}{Y_{AVE}}\right)$$

$$= \left(\frac{2}{6}\right) \Big/ \left(\frac{4{,}000}{12{,}000}\right) = +1$$

The income elasticity of demand is a positive number, since both ΔQ and ΔY are positive. Therefore, this is a normal good. We already knew that from the information in part (b), which stated that the demand curve shifted out to the right with an increase in income. If this were an inferior good, the increase in income would have shifted the demand curve in to the left, and the income elasticity of demand would have been negative.

2) a) In order to calculate price elasticity of demand, we need to know two points (each point a combination of price and quantity demanded) on the demand curve. We only are given the quantity demanded co-ordinate of each point. By substituting $Q_D = 4$ and $Q_D = 6$ into the demand equation, we can solve for the two price co-ordinates:

At $Q_D = 4$; $P = 60 - 2(4) = 52$
At $Q_D = 6$; $P = 60 - 2(6) = 48$

These price and quantity demanded co-ordinates can now be substituted into the formula for the price elasticity of demand:

$$\eta = \left|\left(\frac{\Delta Q}{Q_{AVE}}\right) \Big/ \left(\frac{\Delta P}{P_{AVE}}\right)\right|$$

$$= \left|\left(\frac{-2}{5}\right) \Big/ \left(\frac{4}{50}\right)\right| = 5$$

b) One method is simply to compare total revenue ($P \times Q$) at each equilibrium.

Initial Equilibrium:
Total Revenue = $(P \times Q) = (52 \times 4) = 208$

New Equilibrium: If $P^* = 48$, Q^* can be calculated by substituting P^* into the demand equation:

$$48 = 60 - 2Q^*$$
$$2Q^* = 12$$
$$Q^* = 6$$

So total revenue = $(P \times Q) = (48 \times 6) = 288$.

In moving from the initial to the new equilibrium, total revenue has increased.

A second method is to use the information from part (a) on the price elasticity of demand. We know that between $Q_D = 4$ and $Q_D = 6$ on the demand curve, demand is elastic. These two points correspond to the initial equilibrium and, after the shift of the supply curve, the new equilibrium. Since demand here is elastic, we know that the fall in price from $P = 52$ to $P = 48$ will increase total revenue.

3) a) Using the formula for income elasticity of demand:

$$\eta_Y = \left(\frac{\Delta Q}{Q_{AVE}}\right) \Big/ \left(\frac{\Delta Y}{Y_{AVE}}\right)$$

$$= \left(\frac{200 - 400}{\frac{1}{2}(200 + 400)}\right) \Big/ \left(\frac{10{,}000 - 6{,}000}{\frac{1}{2}(10{,}000 + 6{,}000)}\right)$$

$$= \left(\frac{-200}{300}\right) \Big/ \left(\frac{4{,}000}{8{,}000}\right) = -\frac{4}{3}$$

b) Grits are an inferior good because the income elasticity of demand is negative

4) a) The initial equilibrium quantity traded (Q^*) of tribbles is \$20. [Refer back to *Study Guide* Chapter 4 if you need help in solving demand and supply equations.]

b) The initial equilibrium price (P^*) of a tribble is \$30. [Refer back to *Study Guide* Chapter 4 if you need help in solving demand and supply equations.]

c) i) The new equilibrium quantity traded of tribbles is 60.

ii) The new equilibrium price of a tribble is \$50.

d) At the initial income of \$180 and price of \$30, the quantity of tribbles demanded is 20. In order to find the new quantity demanded at income of \$120, we have to use the new demand equation. But, since *price* is assumed constant in calculating income elasticity, we have to substitute $P = 30$

into the new demand equation to find the appropriate new quantity. It would be *incorrect* to use the new equilibrium quantity, because that quantity corresponds to a *different price* ($50).

$$P = 110 - 1Q_D$$
$$30 = 110 - 1Q_D$$
$$Q_D = 80$$

We now have appropriate information about the initial quantity demanded (20) and income ($180), and about the new quantity demanded (80) and income ($120). Substituting this information into the formula for income elasticity of demand yields:

$$\eta_Y = \left(\frac{\Delta Q}{Q_{AVE}}\right) \bigg/ \left(\frac{\Delta Y}{Y_{AVE}}\right)$$
$$= \left(\frac{-60}{50}\right) \bigg/ \left(\frac{60}{150}\right) = -3$$

Since the income elasticity of demand for tribbles is negative, tribbles are an inferior good.

5) The cross elasticities of demand between *A* and *B* are listed in Table 5.3 Solution. Since the cross elasticities are positive, we know that *A* and *B* are substitutes.

Table 5.3 Solution: Demand Schedules for Good *A*

	P_B = $8	P_B = $12	
P_A	Q_A	Q'_A	η_X
8	2,000	4,000	1.67
7	4,000	6,000	1.00
6	6,000	8,000	0.71

Chapter 6 Markets in Action

Chapter in Perspective

Text Pages 125–150

This chapter extends the theory of demand and supply to three models that incorporate additional features of the economy. The first model analyzes the effects of government regulation of prices. In an attempt to control price fluctuations resulting from shifts in demand or supply, governments have introduced price ceilings (for example, rent controls) and price floors (for example, minimum wages). When prices are not allowed to adjust to restore equilibrium between demand and supply, the adjustment instead takes the form of search activity, black markets, or unemployment. The second model analyzes the effects of the uncertainty of future prices on supplier decisions. Suppliers must make production decisions today even though they are uncertain about the price at which their product will sell in the future. The demand and supply model can be used to forecast prices — to calculate a rational expectation of a future price. The third model analyzes the role of inventories in limiting price fluctuations when expectations turn out to be incorrect.

Learning Objectives

After studying this chapter, you will be able to:

- **Explain the short-run and long-run effects of a change in supply on price and the quantity traded.**
- **Explain the short-run and long-run effects of a change in demand on price and the quantity traded.**
- **Explain the effects of price controls.**
- **Explain why price controls can lead to black markets.**
- **Explain how people cope with uncertainty and make decisions in the face of unpredictable fluctuations in demand and supply.**
- **Explain how inventories and speculation limit price fluctuations.**

Helpful Hints

1) In the real world we frequently observe market regulation by governments in the form of price constraints of one form or another. It is thus important to study the effects of such regulation in its own right. Another significant benefit of exploring the effects of government regulation, however, is a clearer and deeper understanding of how markets work when, by contrast, the government does *not* affect the normal operation of markets.

   Whenever something happens to disturb an equilibrium in an unregulated (free) market, the desires of buyers and sellers are brought back into balance by price movements. If prices are controlled by government regulation, however, the price mechanism can no longer serve this purpose. Thus, *balance* must be restored in some other way. In the case of price ceilings, black markets are likely to arise. If black markets cannot develop because of strict enforcement of the price ceiling, then demanders will be forced to bear the costs of increased search activity, waiting in line, or something else.

2) This chapter focuses on government price constraints in two specific markets: rental housing and labour. It is important to realize that the principles raised in those two examples can be generalized to other markets.

   In any market with a legal price ceiling set below the market-clearing price, we will observe excess quantity demanded, because the price cannot increase to eliminate it. As a consequence, the value of the last unit of the good available will exceed the controlled price, and therefore, demanders are willing to engage in costly activities up to the value of that last unit (search activity, waiting lines, and black market activity) in order to obtain the good.

   Furthermore, if the price is allowed to increase in response to a decrease in supply or an increase in demand, there are incentive effects for suppliers to produce more and demanders to purchase less (movements along the supply and demand curves). Indeed, it is the response to these incentives that restores equilibrium in markets with freely adjusting prices. If, however, the price cannot adjust, these price-induced incentive effects do not have a chance to operate. Specifically, in the case of rent ceilings, we see that the inability of rents (price) to rise (after an earthquake, for example) means that: (1) there is no inducement to use the current stock of housing more intensively in the short run and (2) there is no incentive to construct new housing in the long run. Similarly, the effects on any market in which a minimum price (price floor) is set above the market-clearing (equilibrium) price will be similar to those discussed in the text for the labour market under a minimum wage.

3) In a market in which inventories are held, deviations of the current price from the rationally expected price will tend to be small. The reason is that if the current price deviates from its rational expectation, there is a potential for profits to be made by "buying low and selling high." For example, if the current price falls below the expected future price, there will be an incentive to buy at the current low price and sell later at the higher expected future price. Attempts to do so will drive the current price up until the profit opportunity is eliminated. In an efficient market, the current price is always equal to the expected future price. In such a market, if the market price changes, it does so because the expected future price has changed.

Key Figures

Figure 6.1 The San Francisco Housing Market in 1906, text page 129
In 1906, San Francisco was hit by a devastating earthquake that destroyed more than half the existing housing. This figure illustrates the response of the unregulated housing market in San Francisco. Part (a) of the figure gives the equilibrium situation before the earthquake. The short-run response of the market is illustrated in part (b). After the earthquake, the short-run supply of housing decreases and the short-run supply curve shifts from *SS* to SS_A. At the old equilibrium rent of $110 per month, there is a large shortage of housing, which drives rent up to the new equilibrium level of $120 per month. As the rent rises, the shortage is eliminated because existing housing is used more intensively (reflected in the movements along the *D* and SS_A curves). The increase in rent to $120 also provides a profit incentive to build more housing units. Since the current rent of $120 is higher than the long-run supply price of housing, new units will be built. This shifts the SS_A curve to the right until the rent has fallen back to $110 per month, as indicated in part (c).

Figure 6.2 A Rent Ceiling, text page 131
This figure illustrates what would have happened in the San Francisco housing market after the 1906 earthquake if a rent ceiling of $110 per month had been imposed. Since rent could not rise to clear the market, there would be no incentive to use existing housing more intensively or to construct additional housing in the long run. This means that the quantity of housing units supplied would remain

at 44,000. At this level the value of the last unit of housing is $130 per month. The difference between this value and the rent ceiling of $110 will be spent by individuals in the form of search time or other transactions costs.

Figure 6.3 A Market for Unskilled Labour, text page 133
This figure illustrates the consequences of a decrease in the demand for labour in an unregulated market for unskilled labour. Part (a) illustrates the market in an initial equilibrium at a wage rate of $4 per hour and employment of 30 million hours of labour per year. Then a labour-saving machine is invented which shifts the demand for labour curve to the left; from D to D_A in part (b). If the wage rate is allowed to adjust freely, it will fall to $3 per hour and employment will fall to 20 million hours in the short run. At the lower wage, some workers have the incentive to leave the unskilled labour market to seek training that qualifies them for higher paying jobs. This causes the short-run supply curve of labour to shift to the left; from SS to SS_A in part (c). As a result, the wage rate begins to rise and, as illustrated here, eventually returns to $4 per hour, while employment falls to 10 million hours per year.

Figure 6.4 The Minimum Wage and Unemployment, text page 136
Like Figure 6.3, this figure examines the consequences of a decrease in the demand for unskilled labour, but now a minimum wage of $4 per hour is imposed. In this case, the wage rate is not able to fall to $3 per hour to clear the market. Instead, the wage rate will remain at $4 per hour and employment will fall to 10 million hours. The quantity of labour supplied at $4 per hour is 30 million hours, but the quantity of labour demanded is only 10 million hours. Thus, 20 million hours of labour per year is unemployed as a result of the minimum wage.

Figure 6.6 Rational Expectation of Price, text page 139
The rational expectation of the price of a good is the price at which expected quantity demanded equals expected quantity supplied. Expected demand and expected supply are themselves the best forecasts available of the positions of the demand and supply curves. As illustrated in this figure, the rational expectation of a future price is given by the intersection of the expected demand and expected supply curves.

SELF-TEST

CONCEPT REVIEW

1) In an unregulated housing market, a sudden decrease in the supply of housing would cause rent to ______________ in the short run and thus create an incentive for the construction of new housing to ______________ in the long run.

2) A(n) ______________ ______________ is a regulation making it illegal to charge a rent higher than a specified level.

3) If a price ceiling is below the market clearing price, an excess quantity ______________ of the relevant good will exist. In such a situation two mechanisms will tend to arise in order to achieve equilibrium. We will observe an increase in ______________ activity as demanders spend more time trying to find a seller. In addition, illegal markets, called ______________ markets may arise in order to satisfy demand.

4) The invention of a new labour-saving technology will cause the demand curve for unskilled labour to shift to the ______________. If the labour market is unregulated, the wage rate will ______________.

5) Unemployment will be created if a legal minimum wage is established, which is ______________ the market clearing wage rate.

6) A forecast that is the best that can be made based on available relevant information is called a(n) ______________ expectation.

7) If the demand for corn is exactly as expected but the supply of corn is less than expected, then the price of corn will be ______________ than expected.

8) Goods that can be stored (held as inventories) will exhibit ______________ price fluctuations in the face of demand and supply fluctuations than goods that cannot be stored.

9) A market in which the actual price embodies all currently available relevant information is called a(n) ______________ market. In such a market the actual price is ______________ ______________ the expected future price.

10) The volatility of actual stock prices in the stock market is due to fluctuations in _______________ future stock prices.

TRUE OR FALSE

_____ 1) In an unregulated housing market, higher rents will result in an increase in the quantity of housing supplied.

_____ 2) When rents in an unregulated housing market rise due to a decrease in supply, people who are unable to pay the higher rents will not find housing.

_____ 3) In a housing market with rent ceilings, there will be a strong incentive to construct new housing.

_____ 4) If a rent ceiling exceeds people's willingness to pay, search activity and black markets will arise.

_____ 5) Search activity will tend to be greater in unregulated markets than in markets with price ceilings.

_____ 6) The black market price of a good is usually below the regulated price.

_____ 7) An increase in the minimum wage will reduce the number of workers employed.

_____ 8) In an unregulated labour market a decline in the demand for labour causes the wage rate to increase.

_____ 9) The impact of minimum wage laws on unemployment among young workers tends to be about the same as it is for older workers.

_____ 10) If demand is less than anticipated, price will be less than anticipated.

_____ 11) A rational expectation of the future price of corn is based largely on the current price of corn.

_____ 12) The rational expectation of price is the price at which expected demand equals expected supply.

_____ 13) A forecast based on rational expectations will be correct.

_____ 14) In order to form a rational expectation about the future price of corn, one must forecast the future price of soybeans, a substitute for corn.

_____ 15) Uncertainty about future household income implies uncertainty about the expected supply curve for peanut butter.

_____ 16) The expected market supply curve relates quantity supplied to next year's actual price.

_____ 17) Suppose the supply curve for corn fluctuates widely but the demand curve is stable. The price of corn will fluctuate more if demand is elastic rather than inelastic.

_____ 18) If actual demand is lower than expected demand, suppliers will have regrets, but if actual demand is greater than expected demand, suppliers will not have any regrets.

_____ 19) Buying goods to be put into inventory is equivalent to decreasing supply.

_____ 20) If the price is higher than an inventory holder's rational expectation, goods from inventory will be offered for sale.

_____ 21) The supply of a good that is held in inventory will be perfectly inelastic at the rationally expected price.

_____ 22) As long as future price expectations are stable, the existence of inventories means that price fluctuations will be much smaller than without inventories.

_____ 23) In an efficient market, the actual price would only rarely be equal to the expected future price.

_____ 24) Because rational expectations about future prices are stable, they will not change with changes in information.

_____ 25) If prices in an efficient market are volatile, it must be that expectations about future prices are volatile.

MULTIPLE-CHOICE

1) The short-run supply curve for rental housing is positively sloped because
   a) the supply of housing is fixed in the short run.
   b) the current stock of buildings will be used more intensively as rents rise.
   c) the cost of constructing a new building increases as the number of buildings increases.
   d) the cost of constructing a new building is about the same regardless of the number of buildings in existence.
   e) new buildings will be constructed as rents rise.

2) Rent ceilings imposed by governments
   a) keep rental prices below the unregulated market price.
   b) keep rental prices above the unregulated market price.
   c) keep rental prices equal to the unregulated market price.
   d) increase the stock of rental housing.
   e) increase the intensity of use of the current stock of rental housing.

3) Which of the following is *not* a likely outcome of rent ceilings?
   a) a black market for rent-controlled housing
   b) long waiting lists of potential renters of rent-controlled housing
   c) a short-run shortage of housing
   d) black market prices below the rent ceiling prices
   e) increased search activity for rent-controlled housing

4) In an unregulated market, which of the following is *not* a likely result of the sudden destruction of a large proportion of the stock of housing?
   a) higher rental prices
   b) a shortage of rental housing
   c) more basement apartments offered for rent
   d) more families sharing living quarters
   e) the construction of new rental housing

5) A price ceiling set below the equilibrium price will result in
   a) excess supply.
   b) excess demand.
   c) the equilibrium price.
   d) an increase in supply.
   e) a decrease in demand.

6) A price floor set below the equilibrium price results in
   a) excess supply.
   b) excess demand.
   c) the equilibrium price.
   d) an increase in supply.
   e) a decrease in demand.

7) If the miminum wage is set at $2 per hour in Figure 6.1, what is the level of unemployment in millions of hours?
   a) 50
   b) 40
   c) 20
   d) 10
   e) 0

Figure 6.1

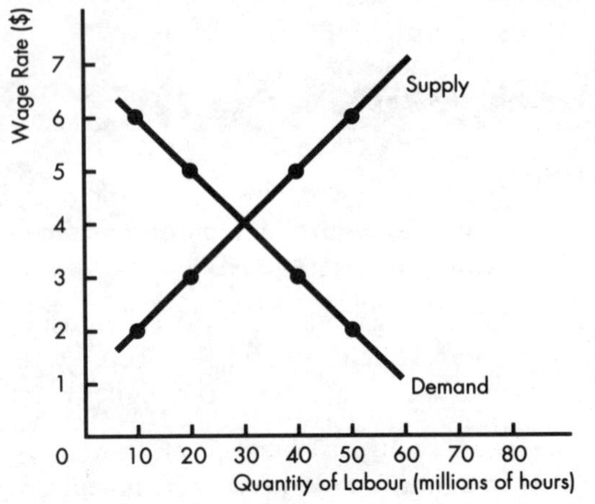

8) In Figure 6.1, if the minimum wage is set at $6 per hour, what is the level of unemployment in millions of hours?
   a) 50
   b) 40
   c) 20
   d) 10
   e) 0

9) Which of the following types of labour would be most significantly affected by an increase in the legal minimum wage?
   a) professional athletes
   b) young, unskilled labour
   c) skilled union workers
   d) university professors
   e) self-employed labour

10) Which of the following would *not* be considered a search activity?
   a) time spent moving from one job to another
   b) time spent looking for a new job
   c) reading a consumer magazine for information as you shop for a new stereo
   d) time spent looking for the best price of a particular chair
   e) using the *Yellow Pages* to compare prices

11) The expected demand (*ED*) for peanut butter depends on the expected values of all of the following *except*
   a) the prices of substitutes and complements in consumption for peanut butter.
   b) household income.
   c) costs of producing peanut butter.
   d) consumer preferences.
   e) population.

12) The expected supply (*ES*) of peanut butter depends on the expected values of
  a) prices of substitutes and complements in production for peanut butter.
  b) prices of inputs for making peanut butter.
  c) peanut butter technology.
  d) all of the above.
  e) a) and b) only.

13) In the case of no uncertainty about demand, but uncertainty about supply, which of the following combinations would generally yield the greatest price fluctuation?
  a) large supply fluctuations and inelastic demand
  b) large supply fluctuations and elastic demand
  c) large supply fluctuations and perfectly elastic demand
  d) small supply fluctuations and inelastic demand
  e) small supply fluctuations and elastic demand

14) A rational expectation of a price is *not*
  a) based on forecasts of expected demand (*ED*).
  b) based on forecasts of expected supply (*ES*).
  c) the price at which $ED = ES$.
  d) necessarily equal to actual price.
  e) a forecast that uses all relevant available information.

15) If demand is forecast correctly and the quantity produced is higher than its expected level, then
  a) the expected supply curve was not based on a rational expectation.
  b) the expected momentary supply curve was not based on a rational expectation.
  c) momentary supply is less than expected momentary supply.
  d) actual price is greater than the forecast price.
  e) actual price is less than the forecast price.

16) If supply is forecast correctly and actual demand is less than expected demand, then actual price is determined by the intersection of
  a) the momentary supply curve and the expected supply curve.
  b) the momentary supply curve and the actual demand curve.
  c) the expected supply curve and the expected demand curve.
  d) the expected supply curve and the actual demand curve.
  e) none of the above curves.

17) The existence of inventories will generally
  a) reduce price fluctuation but increase the fluctuation in quantity traded.
  b) reduce price fluctuation and reduce the fluctuation in quantity traded.
  c) increase price fluctuation and increase the fluctuation in quantity traded.
  d) increase price fluctuation but reduce the fluctuation in quantity traded.
  e) increase the market price.

18) Which of the following statements is *not* true?
  a) Buying goods to put into inventory is equivalent to decreasing the quantity supplied.
  b) Selling goods from inventory is equivalent to increasing the quantity supplied.
  c) In a market with inventories, producers' supply differs from market supply.
  d) Producers' supply is the sum of market supply and inventory supply.
  e) Inventory holders must forecast future prices.

19) Inventory holders
  a) sell goods from inventory when price is less than the expected future price.
  b) buy goods to put into inventory when price is greater than the expected future price.
  c) make the market supply curve perfectly elastic at the inventory holders' rational expectation of the price.
  d) do all of the above.
  e) do none of the above.

20) In an efficient market, which of the following statements is *not* true?
  a) The current price is equal to the expected future price.
  b) The current price embodies all available information.
  c) No predictable profit opportunities exist.
  d) Prices are stable, since holding stocks is holding inventories.
  e) Expectations are subject to fluctuations.

21) Stock market prices are volatile because
  a) expectations are irrational.
  b) expectations change frequently due to new information.
  c) stock markets are inefficient markets.
  d) holders of stock do not behave like inventory holders.
  e) all of the above statements are true.

SHORT ANSWER

1) a) Suppose there is a significant reduction in the supply of gasoline. Explain how an unregulated market adjusts.
   b) What is it that induces consumers to willingly reduce their consumption of gasoline?

2) Define a rational expectation and explain how to go about calculating the rational expectation of a future price.

3) Suppose demand for a good that can be stored is subject to unpredictable fluctuations. Explain how inventories help reduce the price variability of the good.

4) a) What is meant by an efficient market?
   b) Explain why the current market price will always be equal to the expected future price in an efficient market.

5) Why are stock market prices so volatile even though the stock market is an efficient market?

PROBLEMS

1) Suppose that the market for rental housing is initially in long-run equilibrium. Use graphs to answer the following.
   a) Explain how an unregulated market for rental housing would adjust if there is a sudden significant increase in demand. Consider what will happen to rent and the quantity of units rented in the short run and in the long run? Be sure to discuss the effect on incentives (in both the short run and the long run) as the market-determined price (rent) changes.
   b) Now explain how the market would adjust to the increase in demand if rent ceilings are established at the level of the initial equilibrium rent. What has happened to supplier incentives in this case?

2) Answer the following, given the information about the demand for and supply of gasoline in Table 6.1.
   a) What is the equilibrium price of gasoline and the equilibrium quantity of gasoline traded?
   b) Suppose that the quantity of gasoline supplied suddenly declines by 8 million litres per day at every price. Construct a new table of price, quantity demanded, and quantity supplied, and draw a graph of the demand curve and the initial and new supply curves. Assuming that the market for gasoline is unregulated, use either your table or graph to find the new equilibrium price of gasoline and the new equilibrium quantity of gasoline traded.

Table 6.1

Price (dollars per litre)	Quantity Demanded (millions of litres per day)	Quantity Supplied (millions of litres per day)
1.40	8	24
1.30	10	22
1.20	12	20
1.10	14	18
1.00	16	16
0.90	18	14

   c) How has the change in price affected the behaviour of demanders? the behaviour of suppliers?
   d) Suppose that the government imposes a price ceiling of $1 per litre of gasoline at the same time as the decrease in supply reported in part (b).
      i) What is the quantity of gasoline demanded?
      ii) What is the quantity of gasoline supplied?
      iii) What is the quantity of gasoline actually sold?
      iv) What is the excess quantity of gasoline demanded?
      v) What is the highest price demanders are willing to pay for the last litre of gasoline available?
      vi) Consider someone who values gasoline as in (d)(v). How long would that consumer be willing to sit in line to buy 10 litres of gasoline if the best alternative was to work at a wage rate of $8 per hour?

3) The expected demand for and supply of wheat are given in Table 6.2.

Table 6.2

Price (dollars per bushel)	Expected Quantity Demanded (millions of bushels per year)	Expected Quantity Supplied (millions of bushels per year)
4.00	140	350
3.50	180	320
3.00	220	290
2.50	260	260
2.00	300	230
1.50	340	200

a) If nothing happens to change expectations, what is the rational expectation of the
   i) price of a bushel of wheat?
   ii) quantity of wheat traded?
b) Suppose actual demand is exactly as expected but the weather turns out to be better than usual for growing wheat and actual wheat production (actual momentary supply) is 40 million bushels greater than the quantity expected.
   i) What is the quantity of wheat actually traded?
   ii) What is the actual price of a bushel of wheat?
   iii) How much wheat would farmers have supplied if they had accurately forecast the price?

4) Suppose the rational expectations of price and quantity traded in Table 6.2 remain unchanged. However, the actual quantity supplied (actual momentary supply) now turns out to be exactly as expected, but the demand for wheat is temporarily 40 million bushels greater (at every price) than expected.
   a) If wheat is not stored, what will be the new equilibrium price of wheat? the new quantity of wheat traded?
   b) Suppose now that wheat is stored and the rational expectation of future price has not been affected by the temporary increase in demand. Wheat is sold from inventories whenever the current price exceeds the expected future price and is purchased to be stored if the current price is less than the expected future price. In this case (a temporary increase in demand), what is the price of a bushel of wheat? What is the total quantity of wheat traded?

ANSWERS

CONCEPT REVIEW

1) increase; increase
2) rent ceiling
3) demanded; search; black
4) left; fall
5) above
6) rational
7) higher
8) smaller
9) efficient; equal to
10) expected

TRUE OR FALSE

1) T	6) F	11) F	16) F	21) F
2) T	7) T	12) T	17) F	22) T
3) F	8) F	13) F	18) F	23) F
4) F	9) F	14) T	19) T	24) F
5) F	10) T	15) F	20) T	25) T

MULTIPLE-CHOICE

1) b	4) b	7) e	10) a	13) a	16) b	19) c
2) a	5) b	8) b	11) c	14) d	17) a	20) d
3) d	6) c	9) b	12) d	15) e	18) d	21) b

SHORT ANSWER

1) a) If the market for gasoline is initially in equilibrium and there is a significant reduction in the supply of gasoline, there will be excess quantity demanded at the existing price. As a result, the price of gasoline will rise, which will cause movements along the new supply curve and the demand curve. As the price rises there will be a price-induced increase in quantity supplied and a price-induced decrease in quantity demanded. The price will continue to rise until the excess quantity demanded is eliminated.
   b) It is the price increase that causes consumers to reduce their desired consumption of gasoline.

2) A rational expectation is the forecast that uses all of the relevant information available about past and present events and has the least possible error. The rational expectation of a future price is the price at which expected quantity demanded equals expected quantity supplied.

   Thus, to calculate the rational expectation of a price, we must forecast, using all available and relevant information, the variables which determine the expected demand and expected supply curves.

   The forecast of expected demand depends on the expected values of the prices of substitutes and complements in consumption, income, population and preferences. The forecast of expected supply depends on the expected values of the prices of substitutes and complements in production, the prices of resource inputs, and technology.

3) Inventories are held to exploit any potential profit opportunities by selling goods from inventories if the current price is higher than the expected future price, which reduces the current price, or buying goods to be added to inventories if the current price is below the expected future price, which increases the current price. Selling, if the price is above, or buying, if the price is below the expected future price, means that the price will not deviate very far from the expected future price. Thus inventories help to reduce price fluctuations.

4) a) An efficient market is one in which the actual price embodies all available relevant information. The price will thus be equal to the rational expectation of the future price and there will be no predictable profit opportunities.

b) The current market price will always be equal to the expected future price in an efficient market because any deviation would immediately be eliminated, since it provides an expected profit opportunity. (See the discussion of the role of inventories in the answer to question 3 above.)

5) The stock market is an efficient market and so stock market prices are always equal to their expected future price. The volatility of stock prices, then, reflects the volatility of expected future stock prices. These expectations will change any time there is new information that is relevant for future stock prices. Such information becomes available frequently and so expectations are revised frequently. The consequence is frequent movements in stock market prices.

PROBLEMS

1) a) Figure 6.2 corresponds to an unregulated market for rental housing. The initial demand, short-run supply, and long-run supply curves are D_0, SS_0, and *LS* respectively. The market is initially in long-run equilibrium at point *a* corresponding to rent R_0 and quantity of rental units Q_0. Demand then increases to D_1, creating excess quantity demanded of $Q_2 - Q_0$ at the initial rent. In the short run, in an unregulated market, rent will rise to R_1 to clear the market and the equilibrium quantity of housing rented is Q_1 (point *b*). Note that as the rent rises, the quantity of rental housing supplied increases (a movement from point *a* to point *b* along supply curve SS_0), as the existing stock of housing is used more intensively. Also the quantity of housing demanded decreases (a movement from point *c* to point *b* along demand curve D_1). Together, these movements eliminate the excess quantity demanded. The higher rent also provides an incentive to construct new housing in the long run. This is illustrated by the shift in the supply curve from SS_0 to SS_1. Finally, a new long-run equilibrium is achieved at point *c*, with rent restored to its original level and the number of units rented equal to Q_2.

Figure 6.2

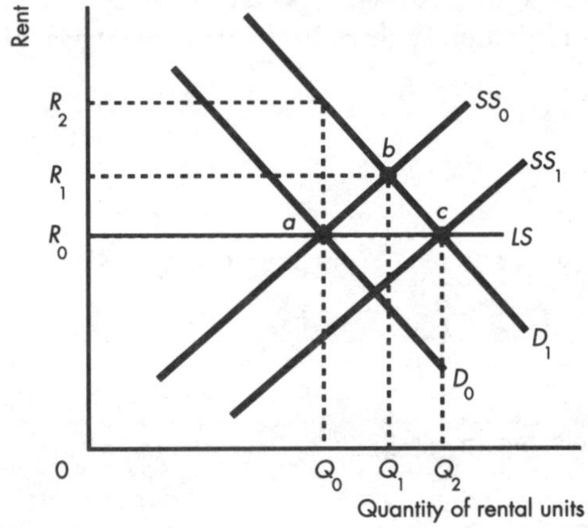

b) We now use the graph in Figure 6.2 to discuss the behaviour of a market with a rent ceiling set at R_0. Again we start in the same long-run equilibrium at point *a*. Once again we observe an increase in demand from D_0 to D_1. In this case, however, the rent cannot rise to restore equilibrium. There will be no incentive to use the existing stock of housing more intensively in the short run or to construct new housing in the long run. The quantity of rental housing supplied will remain at Q_0. Since the last unit of rental housing is valued at R_2, but rent is fixed at R_0, demanders of rental housing will be willing to bear additional costs up to $R_2 - R_0$ (in the form of additional search activity or illegal payments) in order to obtain rental housing.

2) a) The equilibrium price of gasoline is $1 per litre since, at that price, the quantity of gasoline demanded is equal to the quantity supplied (16 million litres per day). The equilibrium quantity of gasoline traded is 16 million litres of gasoline per day.

b) The new table and graph are shown in Table 6.3 and Figure 6.3.

Figure 6.3

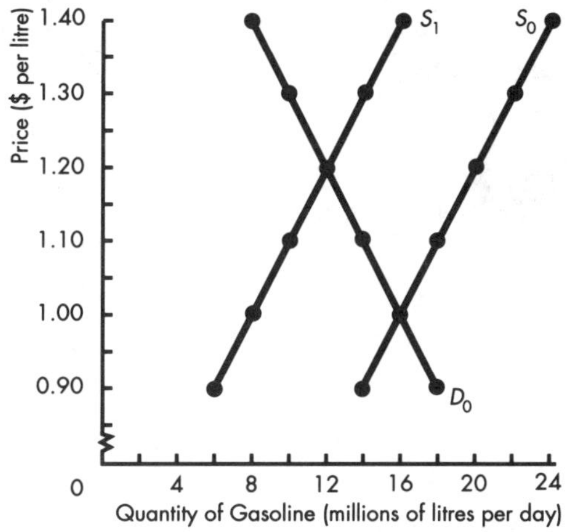

Table 6.3

Price (dollars per litre)	Quantity Demanded (millions of litres per day)	Quantity Supplied (millions of litres per day)
1.40	8	16
1.30	10	14
1.20	12	12
1.10	14	10
1.00	16	8
0.90	18	6

The new equilibrium price is $1.20 per litre since, at that price, the quantity of gasoline demanded equals the new quantity supplied (12 million litres per day). The new equilibrium quantity traded is 12 million litres of gasoline per day.

c) The increase in price has caused the quantity of gasoline demanded to decrease by 4 million litres per day (from 16 to 12 million). Given the new supply curve S_1, the increase in price from $1 to $1.20 per litre increases the quantity of gasoline supplied by 4 million litres per day (from 8 to 12 million).

d) i) At the ceiling price of $1, the quantity demanded is 16 million litres per day.

ii) The quantity supplied is 8 million litres per day.

iii) The quantity of gasoline actually sold is 8 million litres per day. When, at a given price, quantity demanded and quantity supplied differ, whichever quantity is *less* will determine the quantity actually sold.

iv) The excess quantity of gasoline demanded is 8 million litres per day.

v) The highest price consumers are willing to pay for the last unit of gasoline supplied (the 8 millionth litre per day) is $1.40. You can obtain this answer from your graph by imagining a vertical line from the quantity 8 million litres up to where it intersects the demand curve at $1.40. The demand curve shows the highest price consumers would be willing to pay for that last litre supplied.

vi) The regulated price of gasoline is $1 per litre, but the value to the consumer of the last litre is $1.40, so the consumer would be willing to bear costs of $4 above the regulated price of gasoline to obtain 10 litres ($0.40 x 10 litres). If the best alternative is to earn $8 per hour, the consumer would be willing to spend up to half an hour sitting in line to buy the 10 litres.

3) a) i) The rational expectation of the price of a bushel of wheat is $2.50 since, at that price, expected quantity demanded equals expected quantity supplied.

ii) The rational expectation of the quantity of wheat traded is 260 million bushels.

b) i) The actual momentary supply turns out to be 300 million bushels, 40 million bushels more than the 260 million expected. Thus the quantity of wheat traded is 300 million bushels.

ii) To clear the market of the 300 million bushels (where actual momentary supply intersects actual demand), the actual price of a bushel of wheat must be $2.

iii) If farmers had accurately forecast the price of $2 per bushel, they would have produced 230 million bushels of wheat. Thus, farmers would regret having produced too much wheat (300 million bushels instead of 230 million).

4) a) The new equilibrium price of wheat is $3 per bushel, since momentary supply is vertical at 260 million bushels and the quantity demanded has increased to 260 million bushels at $3 per bushel. The quantity of wheat traded is 260 million bushels.

b) The price will be equal to the expected future price of $2.50. At that price, given the temporary increase in demand, consumers demand 300 million bushels of wheat. The total quantity of wheat supplied by producers is 260 million bushels. Thus, 40 million bushels must be supplied from inventories for a total quantity of wheat traded of 300 bushels. Temporary demand fluctuations lead to fluctuations in the quantity traded and to fluctuations in the size of inventory holdings, but the price stays constant at the inventory holder's rational expectation of the future price.

Chapter 7 Utility and Demand

Chapter in Perspective

Text Pages 155–172

The fundamental economic concept of demand was introduced in Chapter 4. There we assumed that as the price of a good rises, the quantity demanded will decline. Assuming the law of demand, allowed us to draw a number of useful conclusions, and make predictions about the behaviour of prices and quantity traded. Because demand is such an important concept, our confidence in these results would be enhanced if it were not necessary to assume the law of demand — if the law of demand could be derived as a prediction of a more fundamental theory. This is the major task of this chapter. Not only is the law of demand derived as a prediction of the marginal utility theory, but other results that had previously been assumed, for example, a change in income causes a shift in demand, also turn out to be predictions.

This chapter, and the next, greatly deepen our understanding of the forces underlying the law of demand and associated concepts. It is difficult to overestimate the intellectual achievement of marginal utility theory in the development of modern economic thought.

Learning Objectives

After studying this chapter, you will be able to:

- **Explain the connection between individual demand and market demand.**
- **Define total utility and marginal utility.**
- **Explain the marginal utility theory of consumer choice.**
- **Use the marginal utility theory to predict the effects of changing prices.**
- **Use the marginal utility theory to predict the effects of changing income.**
- **Define and calculate consumer surplus.**
- **Explain the paradox of value.**

Helpful Hints

1) The concept of utility is an extremely useful abstract device, which allows us to think more clearly about consumer choice. Do not become confused by the fact that the units used to measure utility are arbitrary. The only thing that is important for marginal utility theory is that an individual is able to judge whether the additional satisfaction per dollar spent on good *X* is greater or less than the additional satisfaction per dollar spend on *Y*. If it is greater, then the decision is to consume an additional unit of *X*. How much greater is irrelevant, and perhaps meaningless, for the decision.

2) The marginal utility per dollar spent on good *X* can be written as MU_X/P_X where MU_X is the marginal utility of the last unit of *X* consumed and P_X is the price of a unit of good *X*. The consumer equilibrium (utility-maximizing) condition for goods *X* and *Y* can thus be written:

$$\frac{MU_X}{P_X} = \frac{MU_Y}{P_Y}$$

This implies that, in consumer equilibrium, the ratio of marginal utilities will equal the ratio of prices of the two goods:

$$\frac{MU_X}{MU_Y} = \frac{P_X}{P_Y}$$

This result is sometimes useful.

3) If an individual is not in consumer equilibrium, then the equation above is not satisfied. For example, consider spending all of one's income on a consumption plan where:

$$\frac{MU_X}{P_X} > \frac{MU_Y}{P_Y}$$

or, equivalently,

$$\frac{MU_X}{MU_Y} > \frac{P_X}{P_Y}$$

Since P_X and P_Y are given, this means that MU_X is "too large" and MU_Y is "too small." Utility can be increased by increasing consumption of *X* (and thereby decreasing MU_X due to the principle of diminishing marginal utility) and decreasing consumption of *Y* (and thereby increasing MU_Y due to diminishing marginal utility).

4) Table 7.7 in the text on page 167 is a good review device.

Key Figures and Table

Figure 7.1 Individual and Market Demand Curves, text page 157
The market demand curve is obtained by adding the quantities demanded at each price by each individual. This figure illustrates this in a market with two individuals. At each price, quantity demanded in the market is equal to the quantity demanded by Lisa plus the quantity demanded by Chuck. It is illustrated graphically and in a table.

Figure 7.2 Total Utility and Marginal Utility, text page 159
This figure shows (a) the total utility Lisa derives from consumption of movies as well as (b) the marginal (additional) utility resulting from each additional movie. The table shows that, as Lisa watches additional movies, her total utility increases but the marginal utility resulting from each additional movie is less than the marginal utility of the previous movie. Because of diminishing marginal utility, as Lisa watches additional movies, her total utility increases but at a diminishing rate. There is an explicit relationship between the increase in total utility in part (a) and marginal utility in part (b): between any two quantities, the slope of the total utility curve is equal to marginal utility. For example, between quantities 0 and 1, the slope of the total utility curve is 50/1, which is equal to the marginal utility in moving from 0 to 1 units consumed.

Figure 7.3 A Fall in the Price of Movies, text page 164
This figure illustrates the impact of a fall in the price of movies on Lisa's demand in two different markets. In the movie market (part (a)), the fall in price causes a movement down *along* her demand curve, increasing her *quantity demanded* of movies. In the pop market (part (b)), because pop and movies are considered to be substitutes, the fall in the price of movies causes a leftward *shift* in her demand curve for pop, decreasing Lisa's *demand* for pop.

Figure 7.4 A Rise in the Price of Pop, text page 165
This figure illustrates the impact of a rise in the price of pop on Lisa's demand in two different markets. In the pop market (part (a)), the rise in price causes a movement up *along* her demand curve, decreasing her *quantity demanded* of pop. In the movie market (part (b)), because pop and movies are considered to be substitutes, the rise in the price of pop causes a rightward *shift* in her demand curve for movies, increasing Lisa's *demand* for movies.

Figure 7.5 Consumer Surplus, text page 169
Consumer surplus is the difference between the most a person is willing to pay for a good (its value to that person) and its price (the amount actually paid). This figure illustrates the calculation of consumer surplus by examining Lisa's demand for movies. If the price of a movie is $3,

Lisa will see 5 movies per month. While the value of the fifth movie is $3 to Lisa, the values of the first through fourth movies are higher. Thus Lisa enjoys some consumer surplus. The value of the first movie is $7, but since the ticket price is $3, Lisa receives consumer surplus of $4 on it. Similarly, she receives $3 on the second, $2 on the third, and $1 on the fourth movie. Thus, her total consumer surplus is the sum of these: $10.

Table 7.7 Marginal Utility Theory, text page 167
This table summarizes the assumptions, implications, and predictions of marginal utility theory. Note particularly that the first prediction is the law of demand.

SELF-TEST

CONCEPT REVIEW

1) The ______________ demand curve is the sum of the quantities demanded by each individual at each ______________ .

2) The benefit or satisfaction a person receives from the consumption of a good or a service is called ______________ .

3) As consumption increases, utility ______________ .

4) The additional utility a person receives from consuming one more unit of a good is called ______________ ______________ .

5) As consumption increases, marginal utility ______________ . This is called the principle of ______________ marginal utility.

6) We assume that a household will choose quantities to consume so as to ______________ utility subject to its income and the prices it faces.

7) The marginal utility per dollar spent is the marginal utility of the last unit of a good consumed divided by its ______________ .

8) Utility will be maximized if the marginal utility per dollar spent is ______________ for all goods.

9) Marginal utility theory predicts that if the price of one good rises, ______________ of it will be consumed and ______________ of other goods will be consumed.

10) When the price of a good rises, the quantity demanded falls is an assumption of the consumer demand model of Chapter 4 but is a(n) ______________ of the marginal utility theory.

11) Marginal utility theory predicts that the higher household income is, the ______________ is the quantity consumed of all normal goods.

12) The difference between the value of a good and its price is called ______________ ______________ .

TRUE OR FALSE

_____ 1) Market demand is the sum of all individual demands.

_____ 2) The market demand curve is the sum of the price each individual is willing to pay for each quantity demanded.

_____ 3) Marginal utility theory was invented by Adam Smith.

_____ 4) Total utility equals the sum of the marginal utilities for all units consumed.

_____ 5) The principle of diminishing marginal utility means that as consumption of a good increases, total utility declines.

_____ 6) The principle of diminishing marginal utility means that as consumption of a good increases, total utility increases but at a decreasing rate.

_____ 7) The marginal utility theory assumes that as consumption increases, total utility declines, while marginal utility increases.

_____ 8) A consumer equilibrium exists when a consumer has allocated his/her income in a way that maximizes total utility.

_____ 9) Economists assume that households try to maximize their marginal utility per dollar spent.

_____ 10) A household will be maximizing utility if the marginal utility per dollar spent is equal for all goods and all its income is spent.

_____ 11) When the price of good *X* rises, the marginal utility from the consumption of *X* decreases.

_____ 12) If the marginal utilities from consuming two goods are not equal, then the consumer cannot be in equilibrium.

_____ 13) If the marginal utility per dollar spent on good *X* exceeds the marginal utility per dollar spent on good Y, total utility will increase by increasing consumption of X and decreasing consumption of Y.

_____ 14) Marginal utility theory predicts that if the price of a good falls, consumption of substitute goods will rise.

_____ 15) The price of a bat is \$2. The total utility of consuming 7 bats is 76, while the total utility of consuming 8 bats is 80. The marginal utility per dollar spent on bats is 2 if 8 units are consumed.

_____ 16) The quantity demanded of normal goods increases as income increases is an *assumption* of the marginal utility theory.

_____ 17) Utility cannot be observed or measured.

_____ 18) The fact that utility cannot be observed or measured makes the marginal utility theory essentially useless.

_____ 19) Marginal utility theory does *not* make predictions about the thought processes of consumers.

_____ 20) The value of a good is always the price of the good.

_____ 21) The principle of diminishing marginal utility guarantees that consumers will always make some consumer surplus.

_____ 22) Consumer surplus is the difference between the value of a good and its price.

_____ 23) Consumer surplus for relatively cheap goods like water will be relatively low.

_____ 24) If a shift in supply decreases the price of a good, consumer surplus increases.

_____ 25) The diamond–water paradox illustrates that relative prices actually reflect total utility rather than marginal utility.

MULTIPLE-CHOICE

1) Marginal utility equals
   a) total utility divided by price.
   b) total utility divided by the total number of units consumed.
   c) the slope of the total utility curve.
   d) the inverse of total utility.
   e) the area below the demand curve but above market price.

2) If Ms Petersen is maximizing her utility in the consumption of goods A and B, which of the following statements must be true?

   a) $MU_A = MU_B$
   b) $\frac{MU_A}{P_A} = \frac{MU_B}{P_B}$
   c) $\frac{MU_A}{P_B} = \frac{MU_B}{P_A}$
   d) $TU_A = TU_B$
   e) $\frac{TU_A}{P_A} = \frac{TU_B}{P_B}$

3) If a consumer is in equilibrium, then
   a) total utility is maximized given the consumer's income and the prices of goods.
   b) marginal utility is maximized given the consumer's income and the prices of goods.
   c) marginal utility per dollar spent is maximized given the consumer's income and the prices of goods.
   d) the marginal utility of the last unit of each good will be the same.
   e) none of the above is true.

4) Suppose that Arnie spends his entire income of \$10 on law books and silk ties. Law books cost \$2 and silk ties cost \$4. The marginal utility of each good shown in Table 7.1 is independent of the amount consumed of the other good.

Table 7.1

	Marginal Utility	
Quantity	Law Books	Silk Ties
1	12	16
2	10	12
3	8	8
4	6	4

If Arnie is maximizing his utility, how many silk ties does he buy?
   a) 0
   b) 1
   c) 2
   d) 3
   e) 4

5) If Soula is maximizing her utility and two goods have the same marginal utility then
   a) she will buy only one of them.
   b) she will buy equal quantities of them.
   c) she will be willing to pay the same price for each of them.
   d) she will get the same total utility from each of them.
   e) none of the above is true.

6) Shelley is maximizing her utility in her consumption of mink coats and Porsches. If the marginal utility of her last purchased mink coat is twice the marginal utility of her last purchased Porsche, then we know with certainty that
   a) Shelley buys twice as many mink coats as Porsches.
   b) Shelley buys twice as many Porsches as mink coats.
   c) Shelley buys more Porsches than mink coats, but we do not know how many more.
   d) the price of a mink coat is twice the price of a Porsche.
   e) the price of a Porsche is twice the price of a mink coat.

7) Total utility equals
   a) the sum of the marginal utilities of each unit consumed.
   b) the area below the demand curve but above the market price.
   c) the slope of the marginal utility curve.
   d) the marginal utility of the last unit divided by price.
   e) the marginal utility of the last unit consumed multiplied by the total number of units consumed.

8) Suppose that Madonna spends her entire income of $6 on purple nail polish and leather outfits. Nail polish costs $1/unit and outfits cost $2/unit. The marginal utility of each good, shown in Table 7.2 is independent of the amount consumed of the other good.

Table 7.2

	Marginal Utility	
Quantity	Nail Polish	Outfits
1	8	16
2	6	12
3	4	10
4	3	6

If Madonna is maximizing her utility, what is her *total* utility?
   a) 19
   b) 28
   c) 38
   d) 42
   e) none of the above

9) The relative prices of beer to backbacon are 2:1. If Bob's current consumption is at a level where $MU_{beer}/MU_{backbacon}$ is 1:2, then to achieve maximum utility Bob must
   a) consume more beer and less backbacon.
   b) not change his current consumption of beer and backbacon.
   c) consume less beer and more backbacon.
   d) increase the price of beer.
   e) consume twice as much beer and one-half as much backbacon.

10) Samir consumes apples and bananas and is in consumer equilibrium. The marginal utility of the last apple is 10 and the marginal utility of the last banana is 5. If the price of an apple is $0.50, then what is the price of a banana?
   a) $0.05
   b) $0.10
   c) $0.25
   d) $0.50
   e) $1

11) Sergio is maximizing his utility in his consumption of beer and bubblegum. If the price of beer is greater than the price of bubblegum, then we know with *certainty* that
   a) Sergio buys more beer than bubblegum.
   b) Sergio buys more bubblegum than beer.
   c) the marginal utility of the last purchased beer is greater than the marginal utility of the last purchased bubblegum.
   d) the marginal utility of the last purchased bubblegum is greater than the marginal utility of the last purchased beer.
   e) the marginal utilities of the last purchased beer and bubblegum are equal.

12) Chuck and Barry have identical preferences but Chuck has a much higher income. If each is maximizing his utility then
   a) they will have equal total utilities.
   b) Chuck will have lower total utility than Barry.
   c) Chuck will have lower marginal utility than Barry for most goods.
   d) Chuck will have higher marginal utility than Barry for most goods.
   e) they will have equal marginal utilities for most goods.

13) Which of the following is *not* a *prediction* of marginal utility theory?
   a) other things being equal, the higher the price of a good, the lower is the quantity demanded
   b) other things being equal, the higher the price of a good, the higher is the consumption of substitutes for that good
   c) other things being equal, the lower the price of a good, the lower is the consumption of substitutes for that good
   d) the law of demand
   e) decreasing marginal utility

14) Broomhilda is initially maximizing her utility in her consumption of goods X and Y. The price of good X doubles, *ceteris paribus*. For Broomhilda to once again maximize her utility, her *quantity of X consumed* must
a) rise until the marginal utility of X has doubled.
b) fall to one-half its previous level.
c) fall until the marginal utility of X has doubled.
d) fall until the marginal utility of X falls to one-half its previous level.
e) yield infinite bliss.

15) Squid costs $2/kilogram and octopus costs $1/kilogram. Jacques buys only octopus and gets 10 utils of satisfaction from the last kilogram he buys. Assuming that Jacques has maximized his utility, his marginal utility from the first kilogram of squid must be
a) more than 10 utils.
b) less than 10 utils.
c) more than 20 utils.
d) less than 20 utils.
e) zero utils.

16) A consumer maximizes his utility by purchasing 2 units of good X at $5/unit and 3 units of good Y at $7/unit. What is the ratio of the marginal utility of X to the marginal utility of Y?
a) 5/7
b) 7/5
c) 2/3
d) 3/2
e) 10/21

17) The value of a good is defined as the
a) market price.
b) average price paid by individuals in a market.
c) cost of producing the good.
d) highest price an individual is willing to pay.
e) total utility to an individual of all units of the good.

18) The difference between the value of a good and its price is known as
a) excess demand.
b) excess supply.
c) consumer surplus.
d) consumer excess.
e) marginal utility.

19) The demand schedule for marbles is shown in Table 7.3. If the actual price is $7, what is total consumer surplus?
a) $3
b) $4
c) $6
d) $12
e) $27

Table 7.3 Demand Schedule for Marbles

Price (per marble)	Quantity Demanded
$10	1
$ 9	2
$ 8	3
$ 7	4
$ 6	5

20) The high price of diamonds relative to the price of water reflects the fact that at typical levels of consumption
a) the total utility of water is relatively low.
b) the total utility of diamonds is relatively high.
c) the marginal utility of water is relatively high.
d) the marginal utility of diamonds is relatively low.
e) none of the above is true.

SHORT ANSWER

1) A consumer is initially maximizing utility in the consumption of goods A and B so that:

$$\frac{MU_A}{P_A} = \frac{MU_B}{P_B}$$

The price of A then rises as a result of the shift in supply shown in Figure 7.1.

Figure 7.1

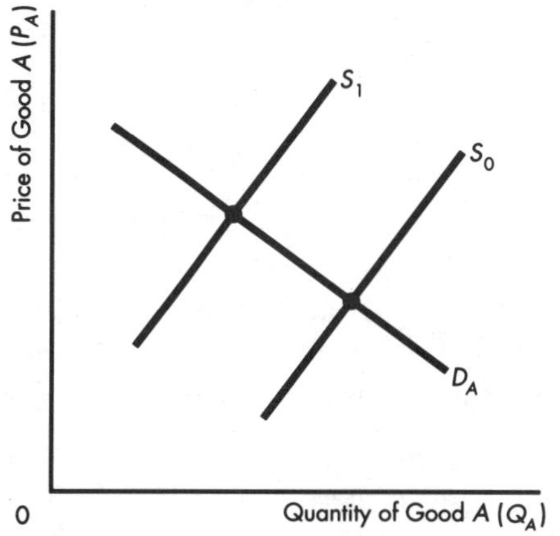

Use the conditions described for utility maximization to explain how the consumer will move to a new utility-maximizing equilibrium. Show the connection between your explanation and the change on the diagram.

2) Consider the following information relevant to a consumer who is trying to allocate her income between goods *X* and *Y* so as to maximize utility. The price of *X* is $2 and the price of *Y* is $1 per unit. When all income is spent, the marginal utility of the last unit of *X* is 20 and the marginal utility of the last unit of *Y* is 16.
   a) Why is the consumer not in equilibrium?
   b) To increase utility, which good should this consumer consume more of and which less?

3) Explain why the consumer equilibrium condition and the principle of diminishing marginal utility implies the law of demand.

4) How can marginal utility theory be useful even though utility cannot be measured?

5) How does marginal utility theory resolve the diamond–water paradox of value?

PROBLEMS

1) Table 7.4 gives the demand schedules for broccoli for three individuals: Tom, Jana, and Ted.

Table 7.4 Individual Demand for Broccoli

Price (per kilogram)	Quantity Demanded (kilograms per week)		
	Tom	Jana	Ted
$0.50	10	4	10
$0.75	9	2	7
$1.00	8	0	4
$1.25	7	0	1

   a) Calculate the market demand schedule.
   b) On a single diagram, draw the individual demand curves for Tom, Jana, and Ted, as well as the market demand curve.

2) Tables 7.5 and 7.6 give Amy's utility from the consumption of popcorn and candy bars during a week.
   a) Complete the tables.

Table 7.5 Amy's Utility from Popcorn

Bags of Popcorn	Total Utility	Marginal Utility
1	20	
2	36	
3	50	
4		12
5	72	
6	80	
7	86	

Table 7.6 Amy's Utility from Candy Bars

Number of Candy Bars	Total Utility	Marginal Utility
1	14	
2	26	
3		10
4	44	
5	51	
6	57	
7	61	

   b) Suppose the price of a bag of popcorn is $1 and the price of a candy bar is $0.50. Given the information in Tables 7.5 and 7.6, complete Table 7.7, where *MU/P* means marginal utility divided by price, which is equivalent to marginal utility per dollar spent.

Table 7.7

Bags of Popcorn	MU/P	Number of Candy Bars	MU/P
1		1	
2		2	
3		3	
4		4	
5		5	
6		6	

c) Amy's weekly allowance is $4. Answer the following if she spends her entire allowance on popcorn and candy.
   i) How much popcorn and how many candy bars will Amy consume each week if she maximizes her utility?
   ii) Show that the utility maximum condition is satisfied.
   iii) What is total utility?
   iv) If, instead, Amy consumed 3 bags of popcorn and 2 candy bars, explain why she would not be maximizing her utility using figures for both total utility and for the terms *MU/P*.

3) Suppose that Amy's preferences remain as they were in problem 2, but the price of a candy bar doubles to $1.
   a) Construct a new table (similar to Table 7.7 in problem 2(b)) of *MU/P* for popcorn and candy bars.
   b) Amy's allowance continues to be $4. After the price change, how much popcorn and how many candy bars will she consume each week?
   c) Are popcorn and candy bars substitutes or complements for Amy? Why?
   d) Based on the information you have obtained, draw Amy's demand curve for candy bars.
   e) Suppose that both bags of popcorn and candy bars continue to sell for $1 each, but now, Amy's allowance increases to $6 per week.
      i) How many candy bars and bags of popcorn will Amy choose to consume per week under the new situation?
      ii) Are popcorn and candy bars normal goods? Why or why not?

4) Suppose that John McEnroe spends his entire income of $8 on tennis rackets and books on creative cussing. The price of a book is $2 and the price of a tennis racket is $4. The marginal utility of each good, shown in Table 7.8, is independent of the amount consumed of the other good.

Table 7.8

Quantity	Marginal Utility: Books	Marginal Utility: Rackets
1	20	36
2	18	32
3	16	20
4	8	16

   a) If John is maximizing his utility, how many units of each good should he purchase?
   b) If John's income rises to $24, how many units of each good should he purchase?
   c) Using the information given, calculate John's income elasticity of demand for books.

5) Suppose that Igor maximizes his utility by spending his entire income on bats and lizards. The marginal utility of each good, shown in Table 7.9, is independent of the amount consumed of the other good.

Table 7.9

Quantity	Marginal Utility: Bats	Marginal Utility: Lizards
1	20	45
2	18	40
3	16	25
4	8	20

Igor's income is $16, the price of a bat is $2, and he buys 3 bats. If the marginal utility of the last lizard he buys is 40, calculate the price of a lizard using *two* separate methods.

6) Andy's weekly demand schedule for pizza is shown in Table 7.10. If the price of a pizza is $9, what is Andy's consumer surplus for the following number of pizzas he buys at that price?
   a) first pizza
   b) second pizza
   c) total number of pizzas

Table 7.10 Demand Schedule for Pizza

Price (per pizza)	Quantity Demanded
$15	1
$12	2
$10	3
$ 9	4
$ 8	5

ANSWERS

CONCEPT REVIEW

1) market; price
2) utility
3) increases
4) marginal utility
5) decreases; diminishing
6) maximize
7) price
8) equal
9) less; more
10) prediction
11) greater
12) consumer surplus

TRUE OR FALSE

1) T	6) T	11) F	16) F	21) T
2) F	7) F	12) F	17) T	22) T
3) F	8) T	13) T	18) F	23) F
4) T	9) F	14) F	19) T	24) T
5) F	10) T	15) T	20) F	25) F

MULTIPLE-CHOICE

1) c	5) c	9) c	13) e	17) d
2) b	6) d	10) c	14) c	18) c
3) a	7) a	11) c	15) d	19) c
4) b	8) d	12) c	16) a	20) e

SHORT ANSWER

1) When the price of *A* rises, *ceteris paribus*:

$$\frac{MU_A}{P_A} < \frac{MU_B}{P_B}$$

The consumer is no longer in equilibrium. In order to restore the equality in the equilibrium condition, the consumer must change his consumption to make MU_A rise and MU_B fall. (The consumer cannot change the prices of *A* and *B*.) Since marginal utility diminishes with increases in quantity consumed, the consumer must decrease consumption of *A* and increase consumption of *B*. Decreased consumption of *A* moves the consumer up to the left on the demand curve, from the initial intersection of *D* and S_0 to the new intersection of *D* and S_1. In the new consumer equilibrium, equality will be restored in the equilibrium condition.

2) a) This consumer is not in equilibrium because the marginal utility per dollar spent is not the same for goods *X* and *Y*. The marginal utility per dollar spent on *X* is $MU_X/P_X = 20/2 = 10$, which is less than the marginal utility per dollar spent on *Y*: $MU_Y/P_Y = 16$.

b) To equate the marginal utilities per dollar spent (and thus increase utility), this consumer should increase consumption of *Y* and decrease consumption of *X*. The principle of diminishing marginal utility implies that this will decrease the marginal utility of *Y* and increase the marginal utility of *X*.

3) Suppose we observe an individual in consumer equilibrium consuming X_0 units of good *X* and Y_0 units of good *Y* with the prices of *X* and *Y* given by P_X and P_Y, respectively. This means that at consumption levels X_0 and Y_0, the marginal utility per dollar spent on *X* equals the marginal utility per dollar spent on *Y*. Now let the price of *X* increase to $P_X{}^1$. This increase implies that the marginal utility per dollar spent on *X* declines and thus is now less than the marginal utility per dollar spent on *Y*. Therefore, to restore equilibrium, our consumer must increase the marginal utility of *X* and decrease the marginal utility of *Y*. From the principle of diminishing marginal utility we know that the only way to do this is to decrease the consumption of *X* and increase the consumption of *Y*. This demonstrates the law of demand since an increase in the price of *X* has been shown to require a decrease in the consumption of *X* to restore consumer equilibrium.

4) The fact that utility cannot be measured does not hinder us from deriving the law of demand and other useful results from marginal utility theory. All that is necessary are the assumptions that people derive utility (satisfaction) from the consumption of goods and services, that utility increases when people consume more, and that the principle of diminishing marginal utility holds. None of these requires an ability to measure utility.

5) The paradox of value is resolved by recognizing that while the total utility from consumption of water is large, the marginal utility from the last unit of water is small. Likewise, the total utility from the

consumption of diamonds is small, but the marginal utility of the last unit of diamonds is large. If consumers are in equilibrium, then the requirement that the marginal utility per dollar spent be the same for water and diamonds means that the price of water must be low and the price of diamonds must be high.

PROBLEMS

1) a) The market demand schedule in Table 7.11 is obtained by adding the quantities demanded by Tom, Jana, and Ted at each price.

Table 7.11 Market Demand Schedule for Broccoli

Price (per kilogram)	Quantity Demanded (kilograms per week)
$0.50	24
$0.75	18
$1.00	12
$1.25	8

b) Figure 7.2 illustrates the individual demand curves for Tom, Jana, and Ted as well as the market demand curve.

Figure 7.2

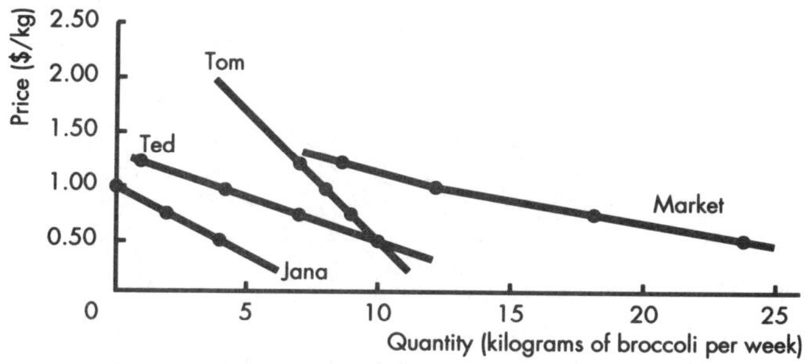

2) a) The tables are completed in Table 7.5 Solution and Table 7.6 Solution.

Table 7.5 Solution: Amy's Utility from Popcorn

Bags of Popcorn	Total Utility	Marginal Utility
1	20	20
2	36	16
3	50	14
4	62	12
5	72	10
6	80	8
7	86	6

Table 7.6 Solution: Amy's Utility from Candy Bars

Number of Candy Bars	Total Utility	Marginal Utility
1	14	14
2	26	12
3	36	10
4	44	8
5	51	7
6	57	6
7	61	4

b) The table is completed in Table 7.7 Solution.

Table 7.7 Solution

Bags of Popcorn	*MU/P*	Number of Candy Bars	*MU/P*
1	20	1	28
2	16	2	24
3	14	3	20
4	12	4	16
5	10	5	14
6	8	6	10

c) i) 2 bags of popcorn and 4 candy bars.
ii) The utility maximum condition is satisfied since Amy spends all of her income ($4) and the marginal utility per dollar spent is the same for popcorn and candy bars (16).
iii) Total utility is the utility from the consumption of 2 bags of popcorn (36) plus the utility from the consumption of 4 candy bars (44) = 80.
iv) If Amy consumed 3 bags of popcorn and 2 candy bars, total utility would be 76, which is less than 80, the total utility from the consumption of 2 bags of popcorn and 4 candy bars. For the combination of 3 bags of popcorn and 2 candy bars, *MU/P* for popcorn is 14, while *MU/P* for candy bars is 24. Since *MU/P* is not the same for both goods, this combination does not meet the condition for utility maximization.

3) a) Table 7.12 shows the completion.

Table 7.12

Bags of Popcorn	MU/P	Number of Candy Bars	MU/P
1	20	1	14
2	16	2	12
3	14	3	10
4	12	4	8
5	10	5	7
6	8	6	5

b) 3 bags of popcorn and 1 candy bar. Amy spends all of her income ($4) and the marginal utility per dollar spent is the same for popcorn and candy bars (14).
c) Popcorn and candy bars are substitutes for Amy, since an increase in the price of a candy bar causes an increase in the demand for popcorn.
d) Amy's demand curve for candy bars is given in Figure 7.3. Two points on the demand curve have been identified: when the price of a candy bar is $1, 1 candy bar will be demanded, and when the price is $0.50, 4 candy bars will be demanded. The demand curve is a line through these two points.

Figure 7.3 Amy's Demand Curve for Candy Bars

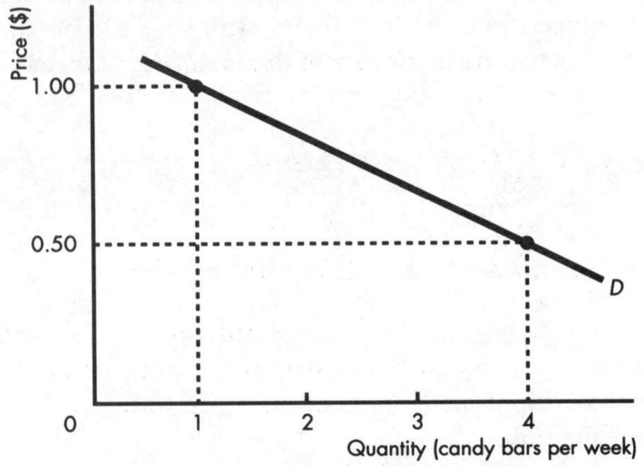

e) i) Now, Amy will choose to consume 4 bags of popcorn and 2 candy bars (instead of 3 bags of popcorn and 1 candy bar). Amy spends all of her income ($6) and the marginal utility per dollar spent is the same for popcorn and candy bars (12).
ii) Popcorn and candy bars are both normal goods for Amy since the increase in income (allowance) leads to increases in the demand for both goods.

4) a) The utility-maximizing combination of goods is shown in Table 7.13.

Table 7.13

Quantity	MU/P Books	MU/P Rackets
1	10	9
2	9	8
3	8	5
4	4	4

John should purchase 2 books and 1 racket. John spends all of his income ($8) and the marginal utility per dollar spent is the same for books and rackets (9).

b) John should purchase 4 books and 4 rackets. He spends all of his income ($24) and the marginal utility per dollar spent is the same for books and rackets (4).

c) The income elasticity of demand for books is:

$$\eta_Y = \frac{\frac{\Delta Q}{Q_{AVE}}}{\frac{\Delta Y}{Y_{AVE}}} = \frac{\frac{4-2}{\frac{1}{2}(4+2)}}{\frac{24-8}{\frac{1}{2}(24+8)}} = \frac{\frac{2}{3}}{\frac{16}{16}} = \frac{2}{3}$$

5) There are two methods for calculating the price of a lizard. One method is based on the fact that Igor spends all of his income on bats and lizards. This means that:

$$Y = P_B Q_B + P_L Q_L$$

where Y = income, P_B = the price of a bat, Q_B = the quantity of bats purchased, P_L = the price of a lizard, and Q_L = the quantity of lizards purchased. We know that $Y = 16$, $P_B = 2$, $Q_B = 3$, and if the marginal utility of the last lizard is 40, then $Q_L = 2$. Substituting in these values, we can solve for P_L.

$$16 = 2(3) + P_L(2)$$
$$10 = P_L(2)$$
$$5 = P_L$$

The second method uses the condition for utility maximization:

$$\frac{MU_B}{P_B} = \frac{MU_L}{P_L}$$

We know that $MU_L = 40$, $P_B = 2$, and if Igor buys 3 bats, $MU_B = 16$. Substituting in these values, we can solve for P_L.

$$\frac{16}{2} = \frac{40}{P_L}$$
$$80 = 16P_L$$
$$5 = P_L$$

6) a) The most Andy would be willing to pay for the first pizza is $15, but the price is only $9. Therefore, his consumer surplus is $6 ($15 – $9).

b) Andy's consumer surplus on the second pizza is the difference between the most he would be willing to pay ($12) and the price ($9). His consumer surplus is $3.

c) At a price of $9, Andy will buy 4 pizzas. He will receive consumer surplus on the first three pizzas in the amount of $6, $3, and $1, respectively. Thus, his total consumer surplus is $10.

Chapter 8 Possibilities, Preferences, and Choices

Chapter in Perspective

Text Pages 173–202

This chapter provides an alternative analysis of consumer choice and the law of demand that complements the marginal utility analysis of Chapter 7. Here, the analysis uses a model of consumer behaviour based on a budget equation which represents *possible choices* given a consumer's income and an indifference curve representation of *preferences.*

The model allows more systematic analysis of what happens to quantity demanded when the price of a good changes and when income changes, as well as more insight into the distinction between normal and inferior goods. Compared with the marginal utility analysis, the budget equation/indifference curve model has the advantage that it does not depend on the abstract notion of utility. Nonetheless, the two analyses of consumer choice have close parallels which are outlined in the appendix to the chapter on text pages 199–202.

Learning Objectives

After studying this chapter, you will be able to:

- **Calculate and graph a household's budget line.**
- **Work out how the budget line changes when prices and income change.**
- **Make a map of preferences by using indifference curves.**
- **Calculate a household's optimal consumption plan.**
- **Predict the effects of price and income changes on the pattern of consumption.**
- **Explain why the work week gets shorter as wages rise.**
- **Explain how budget lines and indifference curves can be used to understand all household choices.**

Helpful Hints

1) Although the analysis in this chapter may seem narrow and restrictive at first, it is helpful to maintain a broad view of the issues under investigation. From the most general economic perspective, the consumer's problem is to do the best given the constraints faced. These constraints, which limit the range of possible choices, depend on income and the prices of goods and are represented graphically by the budget line. Doing the best means finding the most preferred outcome consistent with those constraints. In this chapter, preferences are represented graphically by indifference curves. Thus, graphically, the consumer problem is to find the highest indifference curve attainable given the budget line. To make graphical analysis feasible, we restrict ourselves to choices between only two goods, but the same principles apply in the real world where the array of choices is much broader.

2) The budget equation for pop and movies that is calculated in the table of text Figure 8.1 on page 175 is as follows:

$$Q_p = \frac{y}{P_p} - \frac{P_m}{P_p} Q_m$$

This equation is in the form of a straight line equation ($y = a + bx$), which we discussed in *Study Guide*, Chapter 2. The only differences are that Q_p is the dependent variable (instead of y) and Q_m is the independent variable (instead of x). We can use the budget equation to graph the budget line by finding the Q_p-intercept (where the line intersects the vertical Q_p axis), finding the Q_m-intercept (where the line intersects the horizontal Q_m axis), and then connecting those two points with a straight line.

To find the Q_p-intercept, set $Q_m = 0$.

$$Q_p = \frac{y}{P_p} - \frac{P_m}{P_p}(0)$$

$$Q_p = \frac{y}{P_p}$$

To find the Q_m - intercept, set $Q_p = 0$.

$$0 = \frac{y}{P_p} - \frac{P_m}{P_p} Q_m$$

$$\frac{P_m}{P_p} Q_m = \frac{y}{P_p}$$

$$Q_m = \frac{y}{P_m}$$

The Q_p-intercept, $Q_p = y/P_p$, is the consumer's real income in terms of pop. It tells us how much pop could be purchased if the entire income was spent on pop. The Q_m-intercept, $Q_m = y/P_m$, is the consumer's real income in terms of movies. It tells us how many movies could be purchased if the entire income was spent on movies. These results gives us an easy method for drawing a budget line. Each of the two endpoints (the intercepts) is just income divided by the price of the good on that axis. Connecting those endpoints with a straight line yields the budget line.

The slope of the budget line provides additional information relevant for the consumer's choice between goods. The magnitude (absolute value) of the slope equals the relative price (or opportunity cost) of movies in terms of pop. To put it in different words, the magnitude of the slope equals the number of units of pop it takes to buy one movie. More generally, the magnitude of the slope of the budget line (P_X/P_Y) equals the relative price (or opportunity cost) of the good on the horizontal, x-axis in terms of the good on the vertical y-axis; or the number of units of vertical-axis goods it takes to buy one unit of the horizontal-axis good. See also the discussion of Table 8.1 on text page 177.

3) The marginal rate of substitution (*MRS*) is the rate at which a consumer gives up good Y for an additional unit of good X and still remains indifferent. The *MRS* equals the magnitude of the slope of the indifference curve, $\Delta Q_Y / \Delta Q_X$.

Because indifference curves are bowed towards the origin (convex), the magnitude of the slope and hence the *MRS* diminish as we move down an indifference curve. The diminishing *MRS* means that the consumer is willing to give up less of good Y for each additional unit of good X. As the consumer moves down an indifference curve, the consumer is coming to value good Y more and value good X less. This is easily explained by the principle of diminishing marginal utility, which underlies the following equation from the appendix to the chapter.

$$\text{Marginal rate of substitution} = \frac{MU_X}{MU_Y}$$

At the top of the indifference curve, the consumer is consuming little X and much Y, so the marginal utility of X (MU_X) is high and the marginal utility of Y (MU_Y) is low. Moving down the curve, as the quantity of X consumed increases, MU_X decreases; and as the quantity of Y consumed decreases, MU_Y increases. Thus, the principle of diminishing marginal utility provides an intuitive understanding of why the *MRS* diminishes as we move down an indifference curve.

4) At the consumer's best affordable point, the budget line is just tangent to the highest affordable indifference curve, so the magnitude of the slope of the budget line equals the magnitude of the slope of the indifference curve. Combining the information from *Hint 2* (the magnitude of the slope of the budget line equals P_X/P_Y) and *Hint 3* (the magnitude of the slope of the indifference curve equals MU_X/MU_Y) yields:

$$\frac{P_X}{P_Y} = \frac{MU_X}{MU_Y}$$

Rearranging terms yields:

$$\frac{MU_X}{P_X} = \frac{MU_Y}{P_Y}$$

This is the equation for utility maximization from Chapter 7. You can now see why the budget equation/indifference curve analysis of consumer choice developed here complements the marginal utility analysis of Chapter 7.

5) Understanding the distinction between the income and substitution effects of a change in the price of a good is sometimes a challenge for students. Consider a decrease in the price of good *A*. This has two effects which will influence the consumption of *A*. First, the decrease in the price of *A* will reduce the relative price of *A* and, second, it will increase real income. The substitution effect is the answer to the question: How much would the consumption of *A* change as a result of the relative price decline if we also (hypothetically) reduce income by enough to leave the consumer indifferent between the new and original situations? The income effect is the answer to the following question: How much more would the consumption of *A* change if we (hypothetically) restore the consumer's real income but leave relative prices at the new level?

Key Figures and Table

Figure 8.1 The Budget Line, text page 175
Household consumption is limited by the level of household income and the prices of goods and services. A budget line graphically represents those limits to consumption choices. This figure illustrates a budget line faced by Lisa who has a monthly income of $30 to be allocated between two goods: movies and pop. The price of a movie is $6 and the price of a six-pack of pop is $3. The table indicates six possible allocations of Lisa's income, given these prices. The budget line simply represents these points graphically. To locate the budget line, find the end points by asking how many six-packs of pop could be purchased if all income is spent on pop (the y-intercept) and how many movies could be seen if all income is spent on movies (the x-intercept). Then draw a straight line between the end points.

Figure 8.3 Mapping Preferences, text page 180
An indifference curve shows all the combinations of two goods among which an individual is indifferent. An indifference curve is thus a boundary between two areas: (1) combinations of the two goods that are preferred to any combination on the indifference curve and, (2) combinations that are inferior and so not preferred.

We start with Lisa consuming 2 movies and 6 six-packs per month, point *c* in part (a), and ask what other combinations of movies and pop would leave Lisa just as well off. By assumption, Lisa prefers more movies and pop to less, so the indifference curve must be negatively sloped. If we *reduce* her consumption of pop we must *increase* her consumption of movies in order to leave her just as well off. These tradeoffs to maintain indifference are the reason why the indifference curve cannot pass through the areas in part (b) of the figure labelled *Preferred* and *Not Preferred*. In the preferred area, Lisa can get more of at least one good without having to give up any of the other good. In the not preferred area, Lisa will get less of at least one good without getting any more of the other good. The indifference curve represented in part (c) gives the combinations of movies and pop consumed among which Lisa is indifferent; each combination leaves her just as well off as point *c*. All combinations of pop and movies represented by points above the indifference curve are preferred to point *c* and all combinations represented by points below the indifference curve are inferior to point *c*.

Figure 8.4 A Preference Map, text page 181
A preference map is a series of indifference curves for the same individual. This figure illustrates three indifference curves in Lisa's preference map. Along each indifference curve, Lisa is indifferent among the alternative consumption combinations; each would make her equally happy. However, higher indifference curves represent more preferred points. For example, all the movie and pop consumption combinations represented by points on the indifference curve labelled I_1 are preferred to those represented by points on the curve labelled I_0. Points on a higher indifference curve are preferred to points on a lower indifference curve.

Figure 8.7 The Best Affordable Point, text page 185
Points along the budget line represent maximum affordable combinations of consumption goods. Higher indifference curves represent more preferred consumption

points. The objective of the consumer is to obtain the best (most preferred) affordable consumption point possible. Graphically, this means that a consumer will choose the consumption point that is on the budget line and also on the highest indifference curve possible. The best affordable point will always be a point where the budget line is just tangent to (touches at one point only) the highest indifference curve possible. In this figure, this occurs at consumption point *c*. This is the best affordable consumption point because all other affordable points (on the budget line) intersect lower indifference curves. On the other hand, all points on higher indifference curves are not affordable.

Table 8.1 Calculating the Budget Equation, text page 177
This table derives the equation of Lisa's budget line, given her income and the prices of movies and pop. The procedure for deriving any budget line is similar. In the first part of the table, symbols are defined (on the left) and specific values for income and price for the example in the text are given (on the right). The second part of the table gives the general expression of the budget equation. It simply says that the amount spent on pop ($P_p \times Q_p$) plus the amount spent on movies ($P_m \times Q_m$) is equal to income (y). The third part of the table solves this equation for the quantity of pop (Q_p) and rearranges the equation so that Q_p is the dependent variable. The rearranged budget line equation is in the form of the equation of a straight line ($y = a + bx$) where the slope is equal to $- P_m/P_p$. The slope represents the *relative* price of the good on the horizontal axis (movies). In Lisa's case, the relative price of movies is 2 six-packs of pop (since P_m = \$6 and P_p = \$3).

SELF-TEST

CONCEPT REVIEW

1) A ______________ line describes the maximum amounts of consumption a household can undertake given its income and the prices of the goods it buys.

2) Real income is income expressed in units of ______________ .

3) The price of one good divided by the price of another is called a(n) ______________ price.

4) If the quantity of good *A* consumed is measured on the horizontal axis and the quantity of good *B* consumed is measured on the vertical axis, an increase in the price of good *A* will make the budget line ______________ . An increase in income will shift the budget line ______________ .

5) A(n) ______________ curve shows all combinations of goods that would leave a consumer indifferent.

6) Suppose we measure good *A* on the horizontal axis and good *B* on the vertical axis. The rate at which a person would give up good *B* to obtain more of good *A* is called the ______________ rate of ______________ . As the consumer increases consumption of good *A* (and decreases consumption of good *B* so as to remain indifferent), this rate ______________ .

7) The indifference curve for perfect complements will be ______________ .

8) The best affordable consumption point will be on both the ______________ line and on the highest attainable ______________ curve.

9) If the price of good *A* rises, the ______________ effect will always imply that less of *A* will be consumed, while the ______________ effect reinforces this only if *A* is a normal good.

10) If a decrease in income causes an increase in the consumption of good *B*, then *B* is a(n) ______________ good.

11) As the wage rate rises, the substitution effect encourages ______________ leisure and the income effect encourages ______________ leisure.

TRUE OR FALSE

_____ 1) At any point on the budget line, all income is spent.

_____ 2) The graph of a budget line will be bowed toward the origin.

_____ 3) An increase in the price of the good measured on the horizontal axis will make the budget line flatter.

_____ 4) *Ceteris paribus,* an increase in the price of goods means that real income falls.

_____ 5) The slope of the budget line depends on income while its position depends on the relative price of the goods.

_____ 6) An increase in income will cause an inward parallel shift of the budget line.

_____ 7) A decrease in income will decrease the magnitude of the slope of the budget line.

_____ 8) Preferences depend on income and the prices of goods.

_____ 9) We assume that more of any good is preferred to less of the good.

_____ 10) An indifference curve shows all combinations of two goods which the consumer can afford.

_____ 11) It is logically possible for indifference curves to intersect each other.

_____ 12) Higher indifference curves represent higher levels of income.

_____ 13) The principle of the diminishing marginal rate of substitution explains why indifference curves are bowed toward the origin.

_____ 14) The magnitude of the slope of an indifference curve is equal to the marginal rate of substitution.

_____ 15) The marginal rate of substitution falls as consumption of the good measured on the *y*-axis falls and consumption of the good measured on the *x*-axis rises.

_____ 16) Perfect substitutes will have L-shaped indifference curves.

_____ 17) At the best affordable consumption point, the slope of the budget line is equal to the slope of the indifference curve.

_____ 18) At the best affordable consumption point of movies and pop, the marginal rate of substitution equals the ratio of the price of movies to the price of pop.

_____ 19) For normal goods, a fall in the relative price of a good leads to increased consumption of that good.

_____ 20) When the relative price of a good falls, the substitution effect leads to less consumption of the good if it is inferior.

_____ 21) The law of demand can be derived from an indifference curve model by tracing the impact on quantity demanded of a decrease in income.

_____ 22) The theory of consumer choice claims that people actually compute marginal rates of substitution and set them equal to relative prices in order to make spending decisions.

MULTIPLE-CHOICE

1) Which of the following statements best describes a consumer's budget line?
   a) the amount of each good a consumer can purchase
   b) the limits to a consumer's set of affordable consumption choices
   c) the desired level of consumption for the consumer
   d) the consumption choices made by a consumer
   e) the set of all affordable consumption choices

2) The budget line depends on
   a) income.
   b) prices.
   c) income and prices.
   d) preferences.
   e) preferences and prices.

3) Which of the following statements about the budget line is *false*? The budget line
   a) divides affordable from unaffordable consumption points.
   b) is based on fixed prices.
   c) is based on fixed income.
   d) is based on fixed quantities.
   e) constrains consumer choices.

4) If the price of the good measured on the vertical axis increases, the budget line will
   a) become steeper.
   b) become flatter.
   c) shift inward but parallel to the original budget line.
   d) shift outward but parallel to the original budget line.
   e) shift inward and become steeper.

5) If income increases, the budget line will
   a) become steeper.
   b) become flatter.
   c) shift inward but parallel to the original budget line.
   d) shift outward but parallel to the original budget line.
   e) shift parallel but outward or inward depending on whether a good is normal or inferior.

6) The initial budget equation for pop and movies is $Q_p = 20 - 4Q_m$, and the price of pop (P_p) is \$5. If the price of pop falls to \$4, which of the following is the new budget equation?
   a) $Q_p = 25 - 2Q_m$
   b) $Q_p = 25 - 4Q_m$
   c) $Q_p = 25 - 5Q_m$
   d) $Q_p = 20 - 5Q_m$
   e) none of the above

7) A change in the price of the good measured on the horizontal (x) axis changes which aspect(s) of the budget equation?
   a) slope and y-intercept
   b) slope and x-intercept
   c) x- and y-intercepts but not slope
   d) slope only
   e) none of the above

8) A change in income changes which aspect(s) of the budget equation?
   a) slope and y-intercept
   b) slope and x-intercept
   c) x- and y-intercepts but not slope
   d) slope only
   e) none of the above

9) Bill consumes apples and bananas. Suppose Bill's income doubles and the prices of apples and bananas also double. Bill's budget line will
   a) shift in but not change slope.
   b) remain unchanged.
   c) shift out but not change slope.
   d) shift out and become steeper.
   e) shift out and become flatter.

10) Which of the following statements is *not* true?
   a) indifference curves are negatively sloped
   b) a preference map consists of a series of nonintersecting indifference curves
   c) indifference curves are bowed out from the origin
   d) the slope of an indifference curve is given by the marginal rate of substitution
   e) the marginal rate of substitution increases with movement up an indifference curve

11) Suppose good X is measured on the horizontal axis and good Y on the vertical axis. The marginal rate of substitution is best defined as the
   a) relative price of good X in terms of good Y.
   b) relative price of good Y in terms of good X.
   c) rate at which a consumer will give up good Y in order to obtain more of good X and remain indifferent.
   d) rate at which a consumer will give up good X in order to obtain more of good Y and remain indifferent.
   e) slope of the budget line.

12) In general, as a consumer moves down an indifference curve, increasing consumption of good X (measured on the horizontal axis),
   a) more of Y must be given up for each additional unit of X.
   b) a constant amount of Y must be given up for each additional unit of X.
   c) less of Y must be given up for each additional unit of X.
   d) the relative price of Y increases.
   e) the relative price of Y decreases.

13) If two goods are perfect substitutes then their
   a) indifference curves are positively-sloped straight lines.
   b) indifference curves are negatively-sloped straight lines.
   c) indifference curves are L-shaped.
   d) marginal rate of substitution is zero.
   e) marginal rate of substitution is infinity.

14) Consider the budget line and indifference curve in Figure 8.1. If the price of good X is \$2, what is the price of good Y?
   a) \$0.37
   b) \$0.67
   c) \$1.50
   d) \$2.67
   e) impossible to calculate without additional information

Figure 8.1

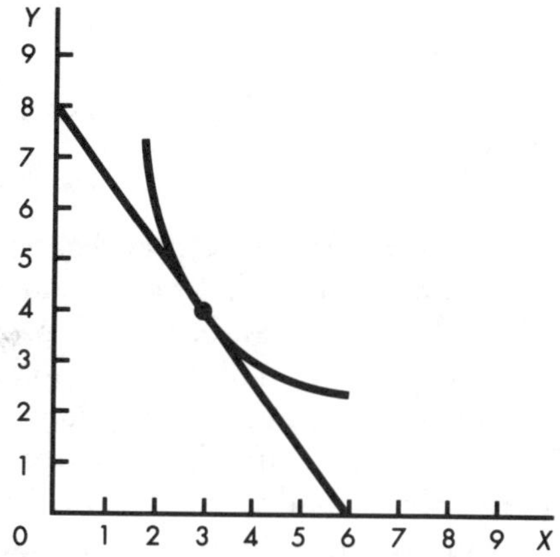

15) Which of the following statements about Figure 8.2 is / are *true*?
a) Point *s* is preferred to point *q*, but *s* is not affordable.
b) Points *q* and *r* yield the same utility, but point *q* is more affordable.
c) Point *t* is preferred to point *q*, but *t* is not affordable.
d) Points *q* and *s* cost the same, but *q* is preferred to *s*.
e) All of the above statements are true.

Figure 8.2

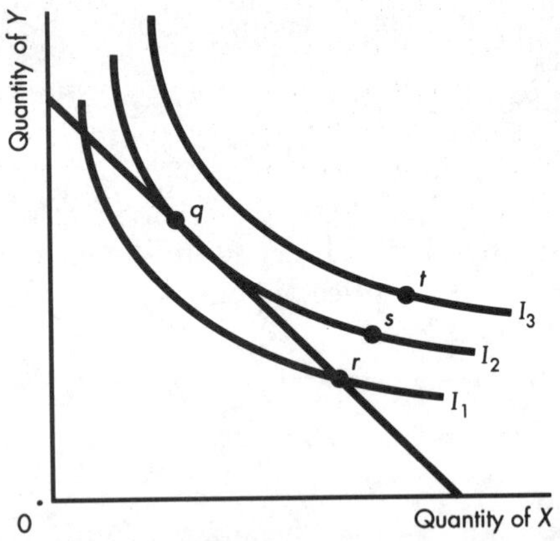

16) When the price of a good changes, the change in consumption that leaves the consumer indifferent is called the
a) utility effect.
b) substitution effect.
c) income effect.
d) price effect.
e) Giffen effect.

17) When the price of a normal good rises, the income effect
a) increases consumption of the good and the substitution effect decreases consumption.
b) decreases consumption of the good and the substitution effect increases consumption.
c) and the substitution effect both increase consumption of the good.
d) and the substitution effect both decrease consumption of the good.
e) is always larger than the substitution effect.

18) If the price of good *X* (measured on the horizontal axis) falls, the substitution effect is represented by a movement to a
a) higher indifference curve.
b) lower indifference curve.
c) steeper part of the same indifference curve.
d) flatter part of the same indifference curve.
e) flatter part of a higher indifference curve.

19) When the price of an inferior good falls, the
i) income and substitution effects both move quantity demanded in the same direction.
ii) income and substitution effects move quantity demanded in opposite directions.
iii) income effect is usually larger than the substitution effect.
iv) substitution effect is usually larger than the income effect.
a) i) and iii)
b) i) and iv)
c) ii) and iii)
d) ii) and iv)
e) none of the above

20) The initial budget line labelled *RS* in Figure 8.3 would shift to *RT* as a result of
a) an increase in the price of good *X*.
b) a decrease in the price of good *X*.
c) a decrease in preferences for good *X*.
d) an increase in the price of good *Y*.
e) an increase in real income.

Figure 8.3

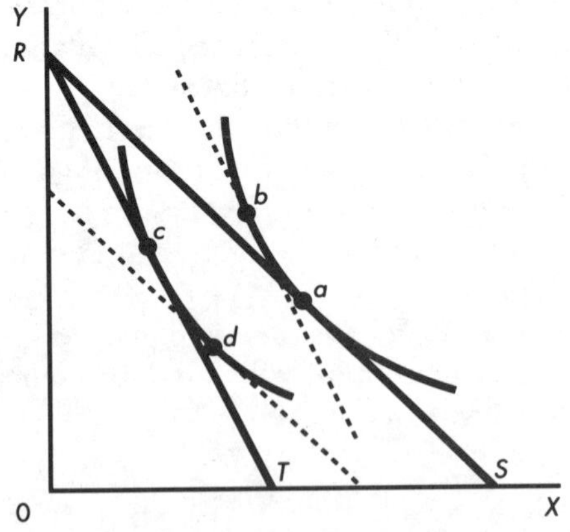

21) When the initial budget line labelled *RS* in Figure 8.3 shifts to *RT*, the substitution effect is illustrated by the move from point
   a) *a* to *b*.
   b) *a* to *c*.
   c) *a* to *d*.
   d) *b* to *d*.
   e) *d* to *c*.

22) When the initial budget line labelled *RS* in Figure 8.3 shifts to *RT*, the income effect is illustrated by the move from point
   a) *a* to *b*.
   b) *a* to *c*.
   c) *a* to *d*.
   d) *b* to *c*.
   e) *b* to *d*.

23) Over the last 100 years, the quantity of labour supplied has fallen as wages have increased. This indicates that the income effect
   a) and the substitution effect have both discouraged leisure.
   b) and the substitution effect have both encouraged leisure.
   c) discouraging leisure has been dominated by the substitution effect encouraging leisure.
   d) encouraging leisure has dominated the substitution effect discouraging leisure.
   e) has not affected the labour-leisure choice.

SHORT ANSWER

1) Why is an indifference curve negatively sloped?

2) Explain why it is logically impossible for indifference curves to intersect each other, by comparing points *a*, *b*, and *c* in Figure 8.4.

Figure 8.4

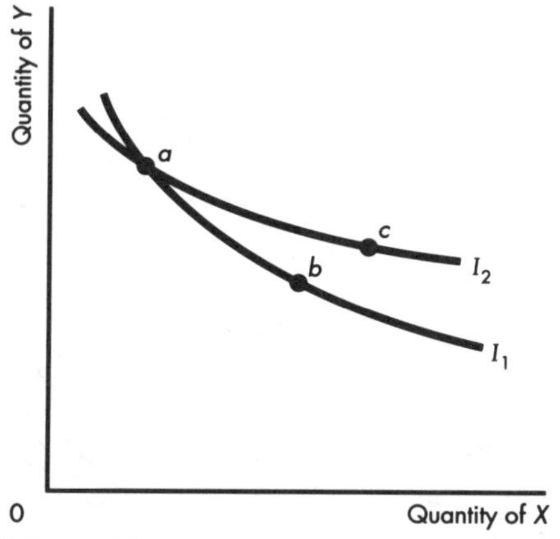

3) The appendix to Chapter 8 on text page 201 establishes that the

$$\text{Marginal rate of substitution} = \frac{\text{marginal utility of movies}}{\text{marginal utility of pop}}$$

As we move down an indifference curve, use the principle of diminishing marginal utility to explain why the marginal rate of substitution diminishes.

4) Suppose the price of a normal good falls. Without the use of graphs, distinguish between the income and substitution effects of this price decline.

5) For normal goods,
   a) an increase in income causes an *increase in demand* (demand curve shifts to the right).
   b) the income effect (due to a decrease in price) causes an *increase* in quantity demanded.

   Explain why these two statements are or are not contradictory. Be sure to define clearly any important concepts.

PROBLEMS

1) Jan and Dan both like bread and peanut butter and have the same income. Since they each face the same prices, they have identical budget lines. Currently, Jan and Dan consume exactly the same quantities of bread and peanut butter; they have the same best affordable consumption point. Jan, however, views bread and peanut butter as close (though not perfect) substitutes, while Dan considers bread and peanut butter to be quite (but not perfectly) complementary.
   a) On the same diagram, draw a budget line and representative indifference curves for Jan and Dan. (Measure the quantity of bread on the horizontal axis.)
   b) Now, suppose the price of bread declines. Graphically represent the substitution effects for Jan and Dan. For whom is the substitution effect greater?

2) Figure 8.5 on page 92 illustrates the indifference map for a consumer who consumes food and clothing.

Figure 8.5

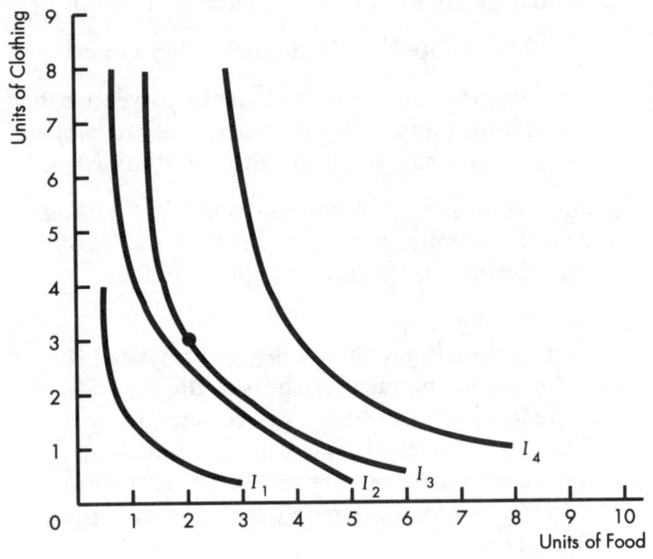

a) i) Initially, the price of a unit of clothing is $P_c = \$1$ and the price of a unit of food is $P_f = \$1.50$. If income is $y = \$9$, draw the consumer's budget line and label the best affordable point as point *a*. What is the quantity of food consumed?

ii) What is the equation of the budget line in terms of P_c, P_f and y? What is the equation of the budget line in numerical terms? Express the magnitude (absolute value) of the slope of the budget line as a ratio of P_c and P_f.

iii) At point *a*, what is the value of the marginal rate of substitution, or equivalently, MU_f / MU_c?

iv) Use your answers in parts (ii) and (iii) to derive the formula for utility maximization. Explain.

b) If P_f increases to \$3 per unit while income and P_c remain unchanged, draw the new budget line and label the new best affordable point as point *b*. What is the new quantity of food consumed?

c) If P_f increases again to \$4.50 per unit while income and P_c remain unchanged, draw the corresponding budget line and label the best affordable point as point *c*. What is the quantity of food consumed?

d) On a separate graph, plot and draw the demand curve for food which corresponds to points *a*, *b*, and *c*. Be sure to clearly label the axes.

e) i) Suppose prices remain at their initial values ($P_c = \$1$, $P_f = \$1.50$) but income falls to \$3. Draw the new budget line and label the best affordable point as point *z*. What is the quantity of food consumed? Is food a normal or inferior good? Explain.

ii) On your demand curve graph from part (d), plot point *z* and roughly sketch a demand curve corresponding to the new income level.

3) Figure 8.6 illustrates several indifference curves for Sharon who consumes goods *X* and *Y*. Initially the price of one unit of *X* is \$2, the price of a unit of *Y* is \$1, and Sharon's income is \$12.

a) How much of *X* and *Y* will Sharon initially consume at her best affordable point?

b) Suppose the price of *X* falls to \$1.

i) What will be the new quantities of *X* and *Y* consumed?

ii) What is the substitution effect, measured in terms of the change in the quantity consumed of *X*?

iii) What is the income effect, measured in terms of the change in the quantity consumed of *X*?

c) The price of *X* continues to be \$1 but Sharon's income now increases to \$14. How much of *X* and *Y* will now be consumed?

d) On a separate graph, plot two points on Sharon's demand curve for *X* and draw her straight line demand curve.

Figure 8.6

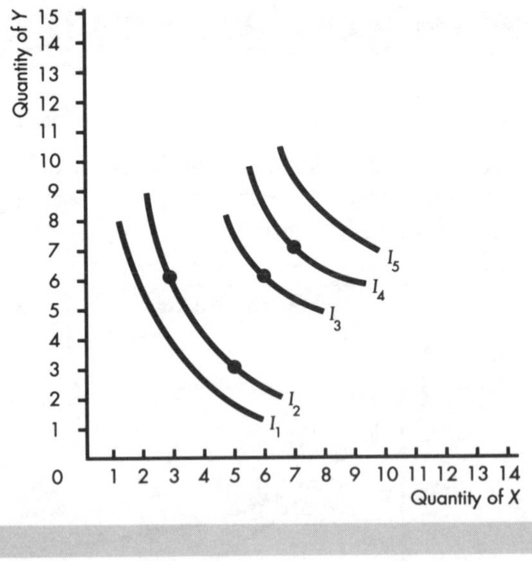

4) Ms Muffet consumes both curds and whey. The initial price of curds is \$1 per unit and the price of whey is \$1.50 per unit. Ms Muffet's initial income is \$12.

a) What is the relative price of curds?

b) Derive Ms Muffet's budget equation and draw her budget line on a graph. (Measure curds on the horizontal axis.)

c) On your graph, draw an indifference curve so that the best affordable point corresponds to 6 units of curds and 4 units of whey.
d) What is the marginal rate of substitution of curds for whey at this point?
e) Show that any other point on the budget line is inferior.

5) Given the initial situation described in problem 4, suppose Ms Muffet's income now increases.
a) Illustrate graphically, how the consumption of curds and whey are affected if both goods are normal. (Numerical answers are not necessary. Just show whether consumption increases or decreases.)
b) Draw a graph showing the effect of an increase in Ms Muffet's income if whey is an inferior good.

6) Return to the initial circumstances described in problem 4. Now, suppose the price of curds doubles to $2 a unit while the price of whey remains at $1.50 per unit and income remains at $12.
a) Draw the new budget line.
b) Why is the initial best affordable point (label it point *r*) no longer the best affordable point?
c) Using your graph, show the new best affordable point and label it *t*. What has happened to the consumption of curds?
d) Decompose the effect on the consumption of curds into the substitution effect and the income effect. On your graph, indicate the substitution effect as movement from point *r* to point *s* (which you must locate) and indicate the income effect as movement from point *s* to point *t*.

ANSWERS

CONCEPT REVIEW

1) budget
2) goods
3) relative
4) steeper; out
5) indifference
6) marginal; substitution; diminishes
7) L-shaped
8) budget; indifference
9) substitution; income
10) inferior
11) less; more

TRUE OR FALSE

1) T	7) F	13) T	19) T
2) F	8) F	14) T	20) F
3) F	9) T	15) T	21) F
4) T	10) F	16) F	22) F
5) F	11) F	17) T	
6) F	12) F	18) T	

MULTIPLE-CHOICE

1) b	7) b	13) b	19) d
2) c	8) c	14) c	20) a
3) d	9) b	15) c	21) a
4) b	10) c	16) b	22) d
5) d	11) c	17) d	23) d
6) c	12) c	18) d	

SHORT ANSWER

1) An indifference curve tells us how much the consumption of one good must change as the consumption of another good decreases in order to leave the consumer indifferent (no better or worse off). It is negatively sloped because the goods we measure on the axes are both desirable. This means that as we *decrease* the consumption of one good, in order to not be made worse off, consumption of the other good must *increase*. This implies a negative slope.

2) The explanation takes the form of a proof by contradiction. Since points *a* and *b* are on the same indifference curve (I_1), the consumer is indifferent between them. Since points *a* and *c* are on the same indifference curve (I_2), the consumer is also indifferent between them. If the consumer is indifferent between *a* and *b* and between *a* and *c*, this implies an indifference between *b* and *c*. But indifference between points *b* and *c* is logically impossible, because we assume that more of any good is preferred to less of that good. Since point *c* has more of both good *X* and good *Y* than point *b*, the consumer cannot be indifferent between *b* and *c*. Indifference between *b* and *c* contradicts the assumption that more is preferred to less. Hence, indifference curves cannot intersect.

3) As we move down an indifference curve such as in text Figure 8.3(c) on page 180 for pop and movies, we change the combination of goods consumed by

increasing the quantity of movies consumed and decreasing the quantity of pop consumed. As movie consumption increases, each additional movie yields lower marginal utility because of the principle of diminishing marginal utility. Thus the value of the numerator on the right-hand side of the equation below decreases.

$$\text{Marginal rate of substitution} = \frac{\text{marginal utility of movies}}{\text{marginal utility of pop}}$$

As pop consumption decreases, each previous pop consumed yields higher marginal utility. Thus, the value of the denominator on the right-hand side of the equation increases. The effect of both a decrease in the numerator and an increase in the denominator is that the ratio MU_{movies}/MU_{pop} falls as we move down an indifference curve, corresponding to a diminishing marginal rate of substitution on the left-hand side of the equation.

4) A decrease in the price of a good will have two effects on the consumption of the good. First, if all other prices remain constant, when the price of one good falls, real income increases. The substitution effect is the increase in consumption of the good resulting from the fall in its relative price accompanied by a hypothetical reduction in real income, which leaves the consumer indifferent between the new and initial situations. The income effect for a normal good is the further increase in consumption of the good when we hypothetically restore the consumer's real income but leave relative prices unchanged at the new level.

5) These statements appear to be contradictory because an increase in income leads, in the first statement, to a shift of the demand curve but, in the second statement, to a movement along the demand curve. The reason the statements are *not* contradictory has to do with a crucial distinction between *nominal* income and *real* income.

The first statement (an increase in income causes an increase in *demand* (demand curve shifts to the right)) describes how an increase in *nominal* income shifts the demand curve. *Nominal* income is measured in dollars.

The second statement (the income effect (due to a decrease in price) causes an increase in *quantity demanded*) describes how an increase in *real* income causes a movement along the stationary demand curve.

Real income is measured in purchasing power, or the quantities of goods that your nominal income can buy. When the price of a good decreases, your *real* income goes up because you can now purchase more of that good with the same, unchanged, *nominal* income. Because *nominal* income is unchanged in the second statement, the demand curve does not shift. But because *real* income has increased, the decrease in price leads to an increase in *quantity* demanded

PROBLEMS

1) a) Initially, Jan and Dan are at point *c* on the budget line labelled *AB* in Figure 8.7. Jan's indifference curve is illustrated by I_J. Note that her indifference curve is close to a straight line reflecting the fact that bread and peanut butter are close substitutes. On the other hand, since Dan considers bread and peanut butter to be complementary, his indifference curve, I_D, is more tightly curved.

Figure 8.7

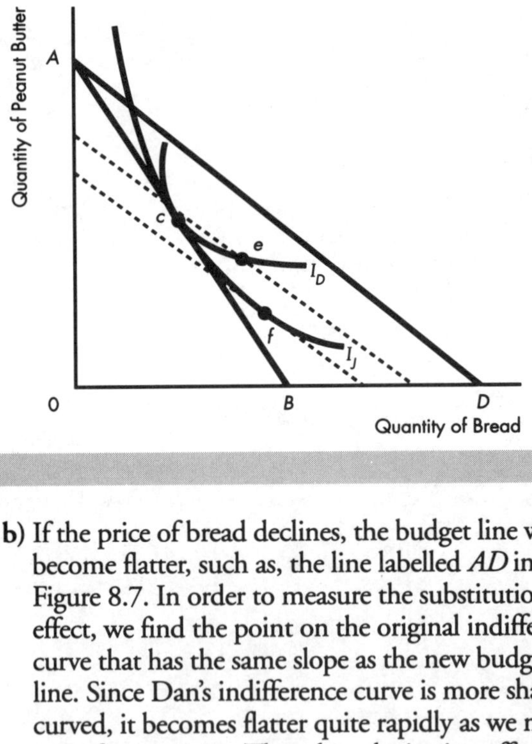

b) If the price of bread declines, the budget line will become flatter, such as, the line labelled *AD* in Figure 8.7. In order to measure the substitution effect, we find the point on the original indifference curve that has the same slope as the new budget line. Since Dan's indifference curve is more sharply curved, it becomes flatter quite rapidly as we move away from point *c*. Thus the substitution effect is quite small: from *c* to point *e*. Since Jan's indifference curve is almost a straight line, the substitution effect must be much larger: from *c* to point *f*.

2) The consumer's budget line is shown in Figure 8.5 Solution.

Figure 8.5 Solution

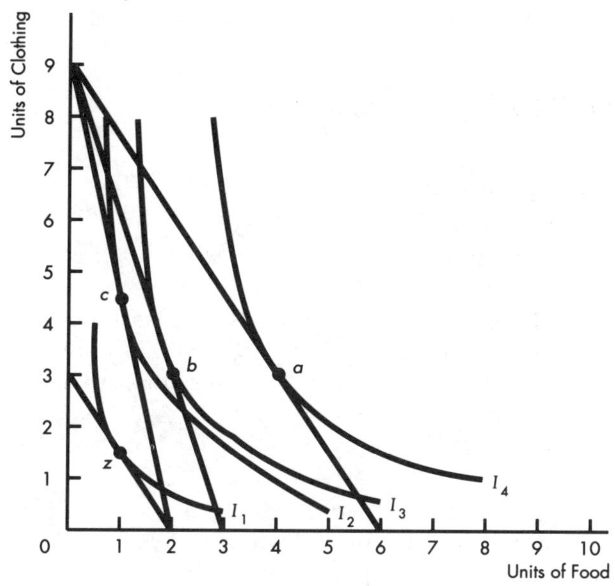

a) i) 4 units of food

ii) The consumer's budget is given by:

$$P_c Q_c + P_f Q_f = y$$

To obtain the budget equation, follow the calculation procedure in text Table 8.1 on page 177. Divide by P_c to obtain:

$$Q_c + \frac{P_f}{P_c} Q_f = \frac{y}{P_c}$$

Subtract $(P_f / P_c) Q_f$ from both sides to obtain:

$$Q_c = \frac{y}{P_c} - \frac{P_f}{P_c} Q_f$$

To obtain the budget equation in numerical terms, substitute in the values $P_c = \$1$, $P_f = \$1.50$ and $y = \$9$.

$$Q_c = \frac{9}{1} - \frac{1.50}{1} Q_f$$

$$Q_c = 9 - 3/2 Q_f$$

The magnitude (absolute value) of the slope of the budget line is 3/2, which is the ratio of P_f/P_c. Note that this price ratio cannot be read directly from the graph since the axes measure quantities, not prices.

iii) The marginal rate of substitution at point *a* is defined as the magnitude of the slope of the indifference curve at point *a*. Since the slope of the indifference curve at point *a* is equal to the slope of the tangent at *a*, and since the budget line is tangent at *a*, the magnitude of the slope of the indifference curve is 3/2. This magnitude is equivalent to MU_f/MU_c.

iv) The magnitude of the slope of the budget line is P_f/P_c and the magnitude of the slope of the indifference curve at *a* is MU_f/MU_c. Since the two magnitudes are equal, $P_f/P_c = MU_f/MU_c$ or $MU_f/P_f = MU_c/P_c$.

b) See Figure 8.5 Solution: 2 units of food

c) See Figure 8.5 Solution: 1 unit of food

d) The demand curve for food is shown in Figure 8.8.

e) i) See Figure 8.5 Solution: 1 unit of food. Food is a normal good because a *decrease* in income (with prices constant) causes a decrease in food consumption (from 4 units to 1 unit).

ii) See Figure 8.8.

Figure 8.8

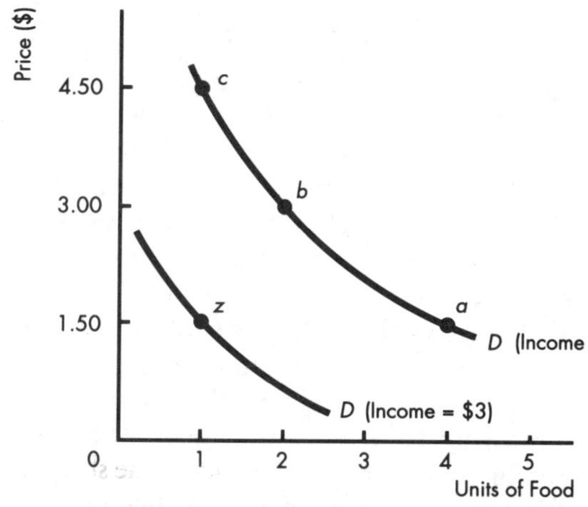

3) a) In order to find Sharon's best affordable point, draw the budget line on Figure 8.6 Solution given on page 96. The initial budget line is labelled *AB* and Sharon's best affordable point is point *c* on indifference curve I_2. Thus Sharon will consume 3 units of *X* and 6 units of *Y*.

Figure 8.6 Solution

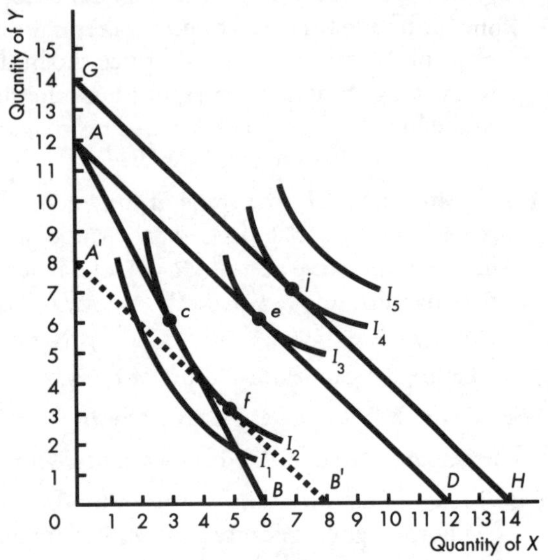

b) If the price of X falls to \$1, the budget line becomes AD.

i) Now Sharon's best affordable point is point e on indifference curve I_3. This corresponds to consumption of 6 units of X and 6 units of Y.

ii) To measure the substitution effect, first find the point on the initial indifference curve with the same slope as the new budget line. This is point f. The substitution effect of the decrease in the price of X is the movement from initial point c to point f, which is an increase in the quantity of X consumed of two units (from 3 units to 5 units).

iii) The income effect of the price decline is the movement from point f to point e, which is an increase in the quantity of X consumed of one unit (from 5 units to 6 units).

c) When income increases to \$14, the budget line shifts out to the line labelled GH. This allows Sharon to achieve her best affordable point at j, which corresponds to 7 units of X and 7 units of Y consumed.

d) From parts (a) and (b) we saw that holding income constant at \$12 and the price of Y constant at \$1, when the price of X is \$2, Sharon wants to purchase 3 units of X and when the price of X is \$1, Sharon wants to purchase 6 units of X. This gives us two points on Sharon's demand curve for X, which are labelled a and b in Figure 8.9. Drawing a line passing through these points allows us to obtain her straight line demand curve, labelled D.

Figure 8.9

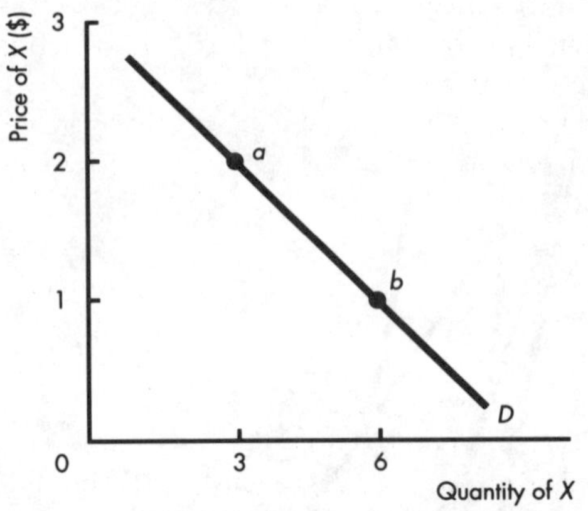

4) a) The relative price of curds is the price of curds divided by the price of whey:

$$\frac{\$1}{\$1.50} = \frac{2}{3}$$

b) Let P_c = the price of curds, P_w = the price of whey, Q_c = quantity of curds, Q_w = quantity of whey, and y = income. The budget equation, in general form, is:

$$Q_w = \frac{y}{P_w} - \frac{P_c}{P_w} Q_c$$

Since P_c = \$1, P_w = \$1.50, and y = \$12, Ms Muffet's budget equation is specifically given by:

$$Q_w = 8 - 2/3 Q_c$$

The graph of this budget equation, the budget line, is given by the line labelled AB in Figure 8.10.

Figure 8.10

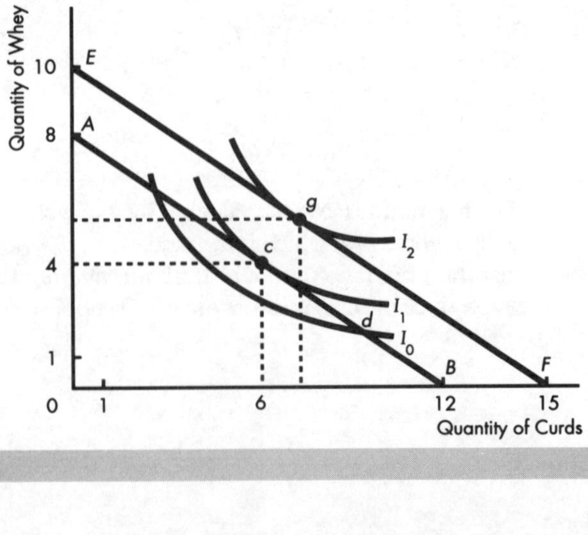

c) If the best affordable point corresponds to 6 units of curds and 4 units of whey, then the relevant indifference curve must be tangent to (just touches) the budget line *AB* at *c*, which is indifference curve I_1.

d) The marginal rate of substitution is given by the magnitude of the slope of the indifference curve at point *c*. We do not know the slope of the indifference curve directly but we can easily compute the slope of the budget line. Since, at point *c*, the indifference curve and the budget line have the same slope, we can obtain the marginal rate of substitution of curds for whey. Since the slope of the budget line is – 2/3, the marginal rate of substitution is 2/3. Ms Muffet is willing to give up 2 units of whey in order to receive 3 additional units of curds and still remain indifferent.

e) Since indifference curves cannot intersect each other and since indifference curve I_1 lies everywhere above the budget line (except at point *c*), we know that every other point on the budget line is on a lower indifference curve. For example, point *d* lies on indifference curve I_0. Thus every other point on the budget line is inferior to point *c*.

5) a) An increase in income will cause a parallel outward shift of the budget line, for example, to *EF* in Figure 8.10. If both curds and whey are normal goods, Ms Muffet will move to a point like *g* at which the consumption of both goods has increased.

Figure 8.11

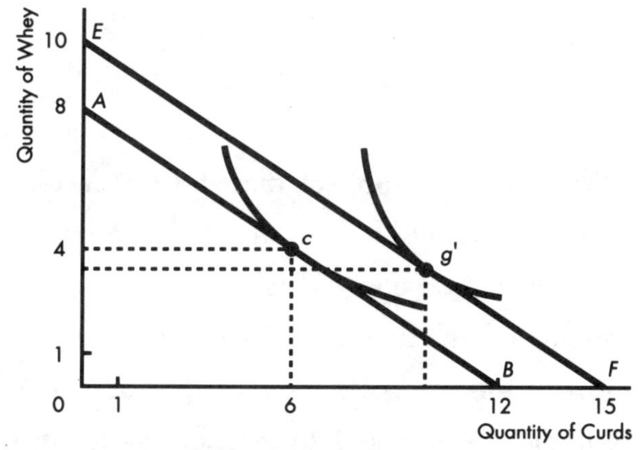

b) If whey is an inferior good, then its consumption will fall as income rises. This is illustrated in Figure 8.11. Once again the budget line shifts from *AB* to *EF*, but Ms Muffet's preferences are such that her new consumption point is given by a point like *g* ' where the consumption of whey has actually declined.

6) a) Ms Muffet's initial budget line is given by *AB* and the initial best affordable point by *r* in Figure 8.12. Note that point *r* in Figure 8.12 is the same as point *c* in Figure 8.10. The new budget line following an increase in the price of curds to $2 (income remains at $12) is represented by *AH*.

Figure 8.12

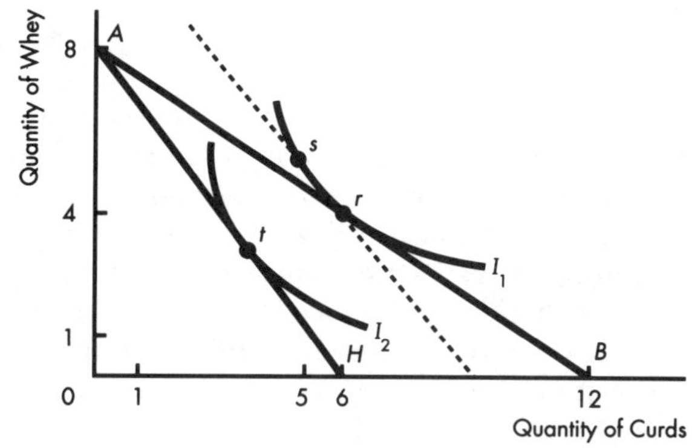

b) After the price increase, point *r* is no longer the best affordable point since it is no longer even affordable.

c) The new best affordable point (labelled *t* in Figure 8.12) indicates a decrease in the consumption of curds.

d) The substitution effect of the increase in the price of curds is indicated by the movement from *r* to *s* in Figure 8.12. This gives the effect of the change in relative prices while keeping Ms Muffet on the same indifference curve. The income effect is indicated by movement from *s* to *t*.

Chapter 9 Organizing Production

Chapter in Perspective

Text Pages 207–228

Chapter 1 of the text introduced economics as the science of choice; choice made necessary by the existence of scarcity. Chapters 7 and 8 examined consumer choice and the principles underlying demand. This chapter begins the analysis of firm choice and the principles underlying supply. The analysis here focuses on key differences that exist in how firms organize production.

The first difference relates to types of firms. While there are common characteristics shared by all firms, there are different forms of business organization, each with pros and cons. The second difference relates to types of business finance. Concepts you read about every day in the business press — bonds, stocks, present value, price–earnings ratios — are examined, as well as a difference between the accountant's and the economist's concepts of cost that depends crucially on opportunity cost. The third difference relates to the concepts of technological versus economic efficiency and the concepts of firm versus market co-ordination. The efficiency of firms (as an institution) make them a primary co-ordinating mechanism through which market economies tackle the problem of scarcity.

Learning Objectives

After studying this chapter, you will be able to:

- **Explain what a firm is, and describe the economic problems that all firms face.**
- **Describe and distinguish between different types of business organization.**
- **Explain how firms raise the money to finance their operations.**
- **Define present value and explain its use in a firm's financing decisions.**
- **Calculate and distinguish between a firm's historical costs and its opportunity costs.**
- **Define technological efficiency and economic efficiency and distinguish between them.**
- **Explain why firms solve some economic problems and markets solve others.**

Helpful Hints

1) The principal purpose of this chapter is to develop a fundamental understanding of why firms exist. Since it is obvious they do exist, it might seem better to simply begin with that fact and turn immediately to a study of their behaviour. Taking firms for granted, however, would eliminate an opportunity to acquire significant insights. As you consider the operation of firms in this and the next several chapters, ask yourself what it is that firms do and what are the alternative mechanisms for doing it. The example in the text of having a car repaired is a good place to start.

2) In spite of the somewhat abstract principal purpose of the chapter, it also presents a number of facts. Some of these consist mainly of institutional knowledge like the three main forms of business organization or the three types of stock. You will need to learn these facts, although common experience is likely to have made you aware of many of them.

3) The chapter defines several very important economic concepts.
   a) The concept of present value is fundamental in thinking about the value today of an investment or of future amounts of money. The intuition behind present value is that a dollar today is worth more than a dollar in the future because today's dollar can be invested to earn interest. To calculate the value *today* of a sum of money that will be paid in the future, we must discount that future sum to compensate for the forgone interest. The *present value* of a future sum of money is the amount that, if invested today, will grow as large as that future sum, taking into account the interest that it will earn.
   b) In this chapter, we again meet our old friend opportunity cost. Here we look at the costs firms face with a special emphasis on the differences between historical cost measures used by accountants and opportunity cost measures used by economists. Historical cost includes only explicit, out-of-pocket costs. Opportunity cost, which is the concept of cost relevant for economic decisions, includes *explicit costs and imputed costs.* Important examples of imputed costs include the owner's/investor's forgone interest, forgone rent, and forgone income. These differences in cost measures between accountants and economists lead to differences in profit measures as well, as outlined here.

   Accountants
   Historical costs = Explicit costs
   Accounting profits = Revenues – Explicit costs

   Economists
   Opportunity costs = Explicit costs + Imputed costs
   Economic profits = Revenues – (Explicit costs + Imputed costs)

   Imputed costs, which economists include but accountants exclude, are the key difference between accountants' and economists' measures of cost and profit.
   c) It is important to distinguish between technological efficiency and economic efficiency. The difference is critical since economic decisions will be made only on the basis of economic efficiency. Technological efficiency is an engineering concept and occurs when it is not possible to increase output without increasing inputs. There is no consideration of input costs. Economic efficiency occurs when the *cost* of producing a given output is at a minimum. All technologically efficient production methods are not economically efficient. But all economically efficient methods are also technologically efficient.

Key Tables

Table 9.1 Pros and Cons of Different Firm Types, text page 211
There are three main types of business organization: sole proprietorship, partnership, and corporation. This table presents some of the characteristics of these types of firms in the form of lists of advantages and disadvantages of each.

Table 9.4 Rocky's Mountain Bikes' Revenue, Cost, and Profit Statement, text page 221
Accounting costs and opportunity costs are usually *not* equal. As a result, accounting profit and economic profit will not be equal. This table illustrates the differences using the example of Rocky's Mountain Bikes. There are three key differences between accounting and economics costs in this statement — the opportunity cost of Rocky's time, the opportunity cost of Rocky's own investment in the firm, and the economic (opportunity-based) depreciation of the firm's assets. Be sure to look at the *Notes* at the bottom of the table which describe these key differences.

Table 9.6 Costs of Four Ways of Making 10 TV Sets per Day, text page 223
There are generally many technological methods available to produce a given quantity of a particular good, each of them using a different combination of inputs. The firm must choose which of these input combinations it will

use. For a given set of input prices, a profit-maximizing firm will choose the method (input combination) that has least cost. It will choose the economically efficient method. This table gives the costs associated with four different methods of producing 10 TV sets a day. Method *a* uses only 1 unit of labour and 1,000 units of capital (Table 9.5 on text page 222), while method *d* uses 1,000 units of labour and only 1 unit of capital. Method *b*, using 10 units of labour and 10 units of capital, is the economically efficient method of production since it produces TV sets at the lowest cost. Remember that the economically efficient method depends critically on input prices. Text Table 9.7 on page 223 shows that when input prices change, the economically efficient method can change.

SELF-TEST

CONCEPT REVIEW

1) An institution that organizes resources it has purchased or hired to produce and sell goods and services is called a(n) ______________ .

2) There are three main forms of business organization. The two simpler forms are a(n) ______________ (which has a single owner) and a(n) ______________ . In these two forms owners face ______________ liability. The third more complicated form is a(n) ______________ in which owners face ______________ liability.

3) Business corporations can raise money by selling ______________ , which are legal obligations to pay specified amounts at specified future dates. Corporations can also raise money by issuing shares of ______________ .

4) A dollar today is worth ______________ than a dollar in the future. Considering the fact that money can be invested to earn interest, the value today of a promise to receive some amount of money in the future is called the ______________ value of that future money.

5) The conversion of a future sum of money to its present value is called ______________ .

6) The ______________ – ______________ ratio is given by the current price of a stock divided by the current profit per shares.

7) In assessing costs, accountants measure ______________ cost, which values resources at the prices originally paid for them. Economists measure ______________ cost.

8) The change in the market price of a durable input over a given period is called economic ______________ .

9) ______________ efficiency is achieved when the cost of producing a given output is as low as possible. ______________ efficiency is achieved when no more output can be produced without increasing inputs.

10) Firms co-ordinate economic activity when they can do so more efficiently than ______________ .

11) The costs associated with finding a buyer, reaching agreement about exchange, and ensuring the fulfilment of the agreement are ______________ costs.

12) ______________ of ______________ exist when the cost of producing a unit of output falls as we produce more.

13) ______________ production occurs when a number of workers each perform specialized tasks in the production process.

TRUE OR FALSE

_____ 1) A firm purchases or hires factors of production and organizes production of goods and services.

_____ 2) A firm's residual claimant is the last individual or institution to loan money to the firm.

_____ 3) A partnership has joint unlimited liability.

_____ 4) The residual claimants of a corporation are its bond holders.

_____ 5) The income of a proprietorship is taxed twice; once as income to the firm and once as income to the owner.

_____ 6) The perpetual "life" of a corporation is an advantage over other forms of business organization when it comes to raising large sums of money.

_____ 7) A co-operative is a firm that has equal total costs and total revenue.

_____ 8) A Crown corporation is a firm that is publicly owned and operated under government supervision.

_____ 9) If the interest rate is 10 percent a year, then the present value of $100 in one year is $110.

_____ 10) The present value of a sequence of future money payments is the sum of the present values of the payments in each year.

_____ 11) In general, the price of a share of stock is the present value of its expected future dividends.

_____ 12) A low price–earnings ratio means current profits are low relative to expected future profits.

_____ 13) Historical cost is more likely to be the same as opportunity cost when firms use their own funds rather than borrowing.

_____ 14) In general, opportunity cost will be greater than historical cost.

_____ 15) When a firm produces using a machine it owns, its opportunity cost is lower than if it had rented the machine.

_____ 16) The opportunity cost of using inventories is the current replacement cost.

_____ 17) The opportunity cost of using inventories can be measured either by the "First In, First Out" or the "Last In, First Out" method.

_____ 18) A production process that is technologically efficient may become technologically inefficient if the relative prices of inputs change.

_____ 19) A production process that is economically efficient may become economically inefficient if the relative prices of inputs change.

_____ 20) Firms will co-ordinate economic activity in situations where there are economies of team production.

_____ 21) Markets will co-ordinate economic activity in situations where there are economies of scale.

_____ 22) The higher the interest rate, the greater is the present value of a given future sum of money.

MULTIPLE-CHOICE

1) Which of the following statements is *not* true of firms?
   a) Firms are like markets in that they are an institution for co-ordinating economic activity.
   b) Firms organize factors of production in order to produce goods and services.
   c) Firms sell goods and services.
   d) Technologically efficient firms can eliminate scarcity.
   e) Firms include Crown corporations.

2) What is a firm called that has two or more owners with joint unlimited liability?
   a) a proprietorship
   b) a partnership
   c) a conglomerate
   d) a corporation
   e) none of the above

3) Which of the following types of firms issue(s) shares of stock?
   a) proprietorship
   b) partnership
   c) corporation
   d) not-for-profit
   e) all of the above

4) Which of the following groups is the residual claimant of a corporation?
   a) stockholders
   b) bondholders
   c) banks and other creditors
   d) government taxing agencies
   e) managers

5) What is a *disadvantage of a corporation* relative to a proprietorship or partnership?
   a) owners have unlimited liability
   b) profits are taxed as corporate profits and as dividend income to stockholders
   c) there is difficulty in raising money
   d) perpetual life
   e) none of the above

6) Most firms are
   a) proprietorships.
   b) partnerships.
   c) corporations.
   d) not-for-profit firms.
   e) Crown corporations.

7) The owner's stake in a business is called
   a) present value.
   b) redemption value.
   c) historical cost.
   d) equity capital.
   e) preferred stock.

8) A bond
   a) represents a right to share in the profits of a corporation.
   b) allows the holder to vote for corporate directors.
   c) is a promise to pay a corporation given amounts of money on specified future dates.
   d) cannot be issued by a corporation.
   e) is none of the above.

9) The present value of a future payment of money will be higher, the
   a) higher the interest rate, or the further in the future the payment.
   b) lower the interest rate, or the further in the future the payment.
   c) higher the interest rate, or the nearer the date of the future payment.
   d) lower the interest rate, or the nearer the date of the future payment.
   e) lower the interest rate and independent of the date of the future payment.

10) If the rate of interest is 10 percent per year, what is the present value of $100 one year from now?
   a) $90.00
   b) $90.91
   c) $95.45
   d) $100.00
   e) $110.00

11) If the interest rate is 10 percent per year, what is the present value of $100 *two* years from now?
   a) $80.00
   b) $82.64
   c) $90.91
   d) $120.00
   e) $121.00

12) If the present value of $500 one year from now is $463, what is the annual interest rate?
   a) 5 percent
   b) 8 percent
   c) 10 percent
   d) 20.8 percent
   e) 37 percent

13) Which of the following gives the holder the right to vote at stockholders' meetings?
   a) corporate bonds
   b) convertible stock
   c) preferred stock
   d) common stock
   e) all of the above

14) XYZ Corporation is expected to pay a dividend of $5 a share every year into the indefinite future. If the interest rate is 5 percent per year, what is the market price of a share of XYZ stock?
   a) $4.76
   b) $5.00
   c) $5.25
   d) $50.00
   e) $100.00

15) Historical cost calculates the value of resources at the
   a) original purchase price.
   b) original purchase price minus depreciation.
   c) original purchase price minus economic depreciation.
   d) current market price.
   e) value of the best forgone alternative.

16) The construction cost of a building is $100,000. The conventional depreciation allowance is 5 percent per year. At the end of the first year the market value of the building is $80,000. For the first year, the depreciation cost is
   a) $20,000 to an accountant or an economist.
   b) $5,000 to an accountant or an economist.
   c) $5,000 to an accountant but $20,000 to an economist.
   d) $20,000 to an accountant but $5,000 to an economist.
   e) none of the above.

17) John operates his own business and pays himself a salary of $20,000 per year. He was offered a job that pays $30,000 per year. What is the opportunity cost of John's time in the business?
   a) $10,000
   b) $20,000
   c) $30,000
   d) $50,000
   e) zero

18) In general,
i) opportunity cost is greater than historical cost.
ii) opportunity cost is less than historical cost.
iii) economic profit is greater than accounting profit.
iv) economic profit is less than accounting profit.
a) i) only
b) i) and iii)
c) i) and iv)
d) ii) and iii)
e) ii) and iv)

19) The rate of interest is 10 per cent per year. If you invest $50,000 of your own money in a business and earn *accounting* profits of $20,000 after one year, what are your *economic* profits?
a) $20,000
b) $15,000
c) $5,000
d) $2,000
e) – $15,000

20) Which of the following statements is *true*?
a) All technologically efficient methods are also economically efficient.
b) All economically efficient methods are also technologically efficient.
c) Technological efficiency changes with changes in relative input prices.
d) Technologically efficient firms will be more likely to survive than economically efficient firms.
e) None of the above statements is true.

21) Firms will be more efficient than the market as a co-ordinator of economic activity when firms have
a) lower transactions costs.
b) lower monitoring costs.
c) economies of scale.
d) economies of team production.
e) all of the above.

22) Economies of scale exist when
a) transactions costs are high.
b) transactions costs are low.
c) hiring additional inputs does not increase the price of inputs.
d) the cost of producing a unit of output falls as the output rate increases.
e) the firm is too large and too diversified.

SHORT ANSWER

1) Give the meaning of present value by explaining (in words) why $110 one year from now has a present value of $100 if the interest rate is 10 percent per year.

2) Why do stock prices tend to rise when the interest rate falls?

3) Compare the historical cost and opportunity cost approaches in each of the following cases:
a) depreciation cost
b) the firm borrows money to finance its operation
c) the firm uses its own funds rather than borrowing

4) Distinguish between technological efficiency and economic efficiency.

5) Markets and firms are alternative ways of co-ordinating economic activity that arise because of scarcity. Why is it that both firms and markets exist?

PROBLEMS

1) Complete Table 9.1 by computing the present value of each of three future payment sequences, first assuming the interest rate to be 10 percent per year ($i = 0.1$) and then assuming the interest rate to be 5 percent per year ($i = 0.05$). The three future payment sequences are:
A: $100 paid after one year.
B: $100 paid after two years.
C: A 2-year, $1,000 bond with a coupon payment of $100 per year. For example, the bondholder will receive a $100 coupon payment at the end of one year and again at the end of two years. At the end of two years, the bondholder will also receive $1,000 (the face value of the bond).

Table 9.1

Future Payment Sequence	Present Value ($) $i = 0.1$	Present Value ($) $i = 0.05$
A		
B		
C		

2) Bonds *A* and *B* are described as follows.
A: Pays $220 after two years.
B: Pays $110 after one year and $110 after two years.
For which of these bonds would you be willing to pay more? Why? [*Hint*: You do not need to know the interest rate to answer this question. Think of the $220 payment of bond *A* as two $110 payments, each paid after two years.]

3) A share of stock in the PDQ Corporation is expected to pay a dividend of $10 per share per year forever. What is the value of a share of stock in the PDQ Corporation if the rate of interest is 10 percent per year?

4) Frank was a bricklayer, but a year ago, he decided to start his own business as a doll furniture manufacturer. Frank has two sisters; Angela is an accountant and Edith is an economist. (Both sisters are good with numbers, but Edith doesn't have enough personality to be an accountant.) Each of the sisters computes Frank's cost and profit for the first year using the following information:
   i) Frank took no income from the firm. He has a standing offer to return to work as a bricklayer for $30,000 a year.
   ii) Frank rents the machinery he uses from an equipment rental firm. His annual rent is $9,000.
   iii) Frank owns the garage in which he produces but could rent it out at $3,000 per year.
   iv) To start the business, Frank used $10,000 of his own money and borrowed another $30,000 at the market rate of interest of 10 percent per year.
   v) Frank hires one employee at an annual salary of $20,000.
   vi) The cost of materials during the first year is $40,000.
   vii) End of year inventory is zero.
   viii) Frank's revenue for his first year is $100,000.
   a) Set up a table indicating how Angela and Edith would compute Frank's cost. What is Frank's cost as computed by Angela? by Edith?
   b) What is Frank's profit (or loss) as computed by Angela? by Edith?

5) Your roommate has said that it is always more economically efficient to produce wheat using some machinery than using only labour. Suppose that there are two technologically efficient methods of producing one tonne of wheat.

   Method 1 requires 20 machine hours plus 20 human hours.

   Method 2 requires 100 human hours.

   Country *A* has a highly developed industrial economy, while country *B* is less developed. In country *A* the price of an hour of human labour (the wage rate) is $8, while the wage rate in country *B* is $4. The price of a machine hour is $20 in both countries. Which method is economically efficient in country *A*? in country *B*? Explain.

6) Consider countries *A* and *B* described in problem 5.
   a) What wage rate in country *B* would make the two methods equally efficient in country *B*?
   b) What price of a machine hour would make the two methods be equally efficient in country *A*?

ANSWERS

CONCEPT REVIEW

1) firm
2) proprietorship; partnership; unlimited; corporation; limited
3) bonds; stock
4) more; present
5) discounting
6) price; earnings
7) historical; opportunity
8) depreciation
9) Economic; Technological
10) markets
11) transactions
12) Economies; scale
13) Team

TRUE OR FALSE

1) T	7) F	13) F	19) T
2) F	8) T	14) T	20) T
3) T	9) F	15) F	21) F
4) F	10) T	16) T	22) F
5) F	11) T	17) F	
6) T	12) F	18) F	

MULTIPLE-CHOICE

1) d	7) d	13) d	19) b
2) b	8) e	14) e	20) b
3) c	9) d	15) a	21) e
4) a	10) b	16) c	22) d
5) b	11) b	17) c	
6) a	12) b	18) c	

SHORT ANSWER

1) The present value of $110 one year from now is the amount which, invested today at the market rate of interest, would grow to be $110 in one year. Since the interest rate is 10 percent, $100 invested today at 10 percent would grow to be $110 in one year. Thus, $100 is the present value of $110 in one year.

2) When the interest rate falls, the present value of fixed future amounts of money will rise. Since the price of a share of stock is the present value of expected future dividends, that present value will decline as the interest rate rises (holding the amounts of expected future dividends constant).

3) a) From the historical cost approach, depreciation cost is computed as a prespecified percentage of the original purchase price of the capital good, with no reference to current market value. The opportunity cost approach measures economic depreciation cost as the change in the market value of the capital good over the period in question.
   b) If a firm borrows money, the historical and opportunity cost approaches will be the same; both will include the explicit interest payments.
   c) If a firm uses its own funds rather than borrowing, the historical and opportunity cost approaches will differ. The historical cost will be zero since there are no explicit interest payments. The opportunity cost approach recognizes that those funds could have been loaned out and thus the (imputed) interest income forgone is the opportunity cost.

4) A method is technologically efficient if it is not possible to increase output without increasing inputs. A method is economically efficient if the cost of producing a given level of output is as low as possible. Technological efficiency is independent of prices, while economic efficiency depends on the prices of inputs. An economically efficient method of production is always technologically efficient, but a technologically efficient method is not necessarily economically efficient.

5) As we saw in the text example on page 224, car repair can be co-ordinated by the market or by a firm. The institution (market or firm), which actually co-ordinates in any given case, will be the one which is more efficient. In cases where there are significant transaction costs, economies of scale, or economies of team production, firms are likely to be more efficient, and we will see firms dominate the co-ordination of economic activity. But the efficiency of firms is limited and there are many circumstances in which we observe market co-ordination of economic activity because it is more efficient.

PROBLEMS

1) The completed table is shown here as Table 9.1 Solution. While each answer is a straightforward application of the present value formula, here are details for computing the present value of future payment sequence C when $i = 0.05$. Payment sequence C is best thought of as a two-part promise: (1) $100 after one year and (2) $1,100 after two years (the sum of value of the bond and the second coupon payment). The present value is then the sum of the present values of the two parts. The present value of (1) is $\$100/1.05 = \$95.24$, and the present value of (2) is $\$1{,}100/(1.05)^2 = \$997.73$. Therefore, the present value of the two-year bond is the sum $\$95.24 + \$997.73 = \$1{,}092.97$.

Table 9.1 Solution

Future Payment Sequence	Present Value ($) $i = 0.1$	$i = 0.05$
A	90.91	95.24
B	82.64	90.70
C	1,000.00	1,092.97

2) A bond-holder would be willing to pay more for bond *B* than bond *A* because bond *B* has a higher present value. While both bonds pay the same total dollar amount over two years, bond *B* pays half of that amount after only one year. A holder of bond *A*, however, must wait two years for the full amount.

If we think of the $220 payment of bond *A* as two $110 payments, each paid after two years, each payment is discounted by (divided by) $(1 + i)^2$. The second $110 payment of bond *B* is also paid after two years and is also discounted by $(1 + i)^2$. So one $110 payment from bond *A* and one $110 payment from bond *B* have equal present values. But the first $110 payment of bond *B* is paid after one year and is therefore only discounted by $(1 + i)$, which is a smaller number than the discount of $(1 + i)^2$, and this applies to the other \$110 payment of bond *A*. Since this discount factor is in the denominator of the present value formula, the smaller denominator for the bond *B* calculation means a higher present value than for the bond *A* calculation. This result is shown in the following expression comparing the present values of bond *A* (PV_A) and bond *B* (PV_B).

$$PV_B = \frac{100}{1+i} + \frac{110}{(1+i)^2} \text{ is greater than}$$

$$PV_A = \frac{110}{(1+i)^2} + \frac{110}{(1+i)^2} = \frac{220}{(1+i)^2}$$

3) The value of a share of PDQ stock is the present value of the expected future dividends. The present value of \$10 per year forever is the amount which, if invested today at the market rate of interest, would yield \$10 per year forever. The formula for calculating the present value of \$*A* per year forever at an interest rate of *i* per year is $PV = A/i$. Therefore, A/i = \$10/0.1, and the present value of the expected future dividends, the value of the stock, is \$100.

4) a) Table 9.2 gives the cost as computed by Angela and Edith. The item numbers correspond to the item numbers in the problem.

Table 9.2

Item Number	Angela's Accounting Computation (Historical Cost)	Edith's Economic Computation (Opportunity Cost)
i)	\$0	\$ 30,000
ii)	9,000	9,000
iii)	0	3,000
iv)	3,000	4,000
v)	20,000	20,000
vi)	40,000	40,000
vii)	0	0
Total Cost	\$72,000	\$106,000

b) Revenue is \$100,000. Angela's accounting computation of profit uses this formula:

Accounting profits = Revenues – Historical costs
= \$100,000 – \$72,000
= \$28,000

Edith's economic computation of profit uses the formula:

Economic profits = Revenues – Opportunity costs
= \$100,000 – \$106,000
= – \$6,000 (an economic loss)

5) Both production methods are technologically efficient. To find the economically efficient production method we want to know which of the methods has the lower cost of producing a tonne of wheat. In country *A*, the price of an hour of labour is \$8 and the price of a machine hour is \$20. Thus, the cost of producing a tonne of wheat is \$560 using method 1 and \$800 using method 2. Therefore method 1 is economically efficient for country *A*.

The price of an hour of labour is \$4 in country *B* and thus it will face different costs of producing a tonne of wheat. Under method 1, the cost will be \$480 but under method 2 which uses only labour, the cost will be \$400. So method 2 is economically efficient for country *B*.

The reason for this difference is that economic efficiency means producing at lowest cost. If the relative prices of inputs are different in two countries, there will be differences in the relative costs of production using alternative methods. Therefore, your roommate is wrong.

6) a) If the wage rate in country *B* were to increase to \$5 an hour, then production of a tonne of wheat would be \$500 under either method. How did we obtain this answer? Express the cost under method 1 (C_1) and the cost under method 2 (C_2) as follows:

$$C_1 = 20\,P_m + 20\,P_h$$
$$C_2 = 100\,P_h$$

where P_m is the price of a machine hour and P_h is the price of a human hour (the wage rate). We are given that P_m = \$20 and asked to find the value of P_h that makes the two methods equally efficient; the value of P_h that makes $C_1 = C_2$. Thus, we solve the following equation for P_h:

$$20P_m + 20P_h = 100P_h$$
$$20(\$20) + 20P_h = 100P_h$$
$$\$400 = 80P_h$$
$$\$5 = P_h$$

b) If the price of a machine hour is \$32, production of a tonne of wheat would be \$800 under either method in country *A*. This question asks: Given the wage rate of \$8 (P_h) in country *A*, what value of P_m makes $C_1 = C_2$? Thus, we solve the following equation for P_m:

$$20P_m + 20P_h = 100P_h$$
$$20P_m + 20(\$8) = 100(\$8)$$
$$20P_m = \$640$$
$$P_m = \$32$$

Chapter 10 **Output and Costs**

Chapter in Perspective

Text Pages 257–276

In a modern market economy, goods and services are produced primarily by firms. In Chapter 9 we saw that firms exist because they provide economically efficient ways of organizing factors of production for producing and selling goods and services. Economic efficiency means producing at the least possible cost. In this chapter we begin to analyze the production and cost constraints that firms face, and thus, how efficiency is pursued.

What kinds of costs do firms face? How do these costs change as a firm's planning horizon changes? How will a firm, motivated by the desire to maximize profit, decide how much output to produce? When will a firm hire more labour? When will it increase its plant size? This chapter begins to answer these questions, which are of fundamental importance in exploring the nature of cost and supply.

Learning Objectives

After studying this chapter, you will be able to:

- **Explain the objective of a firm.**
- **Explain what limits a firm's profitability.**
- **Explain the relationship between a firm's output and its costs.**
- **Derive a firm's short-run cost curves.**
- **Explain how cost changes when a firm's plant size changes.**
- **Explain long-run cost and derive a firm's long-run average cost curve.**
- **Explain why some firms operate with excess capacity and others overutilize their plants.**

Helpful Hints

1) This chapter introduces many new concepts and graphs and may at first appear overwhelming. Don't get lost among the trees and lose sight of the forest. There is a simple and fundamental relationship between production functions and cost functions.

The chapter begins with the short-run production function and the concepts of total product, marginal product, and average product. This is followed by the short-run cost function and the concepts of total cost, marginal cost, average variable cost, and average total cost.

All of these seemingly disparate concepts are related to the law of diminishing returns. The law states that as a firm uses additional units of a variable input, while holding constant the quantity of fixed inputs, the marginal product of the variable input will eventually diminish. This law explains why the marginal product and average product curves eventually fall, and why the total product curve becomes flatter. When productivity falls, costs increase, and the law explains the eventual upward slope of the marginal cost curve. The marginal cost curve, in turn, explains the U-shape of the average variable cost and average total cost curves. When the marginal cost curve is below the average variable (or total) cost curve, the average variable (or total) cost curve is falling. When marginal cost is above the average variable (or total) cost curve, the average variable (or total) cost curve is rising. The marginal cost curve intersects the average variable (or total) cost curve at the minimum point on the average variable (or total) cost curve.

Use the law of diminishing returns as the key to understanding the relationships between the many short-run concepts and graphs in the chapter. But all concepts and graphs are not equally important. Pay most attention to the unit cost concepts and graphs — especially marginal cost, average variable cost, and average total cost — because these will be used the most in later chapters to analyze the behaviour of firms. Be sure to thoroughly understand text Figure 10.4(b) on page 238. It is the most important figure in the entire chapter.

2) You will probably draw the unit cost graph with the marginal cost, average variable cost, and average total cost curves at least one hundred times in this course. Here are some hints on drawing the graph quickly and easily.

a) Be sure to label the axes; quantity of output (Q) on the horizontal axis and average cost on the vertical axis.

b) Draw an upward-sloping marginal cost curve , as shown here in Figure 10.1. The marginal cost curve can have a small downward-sloping section at first, but this is not important for subsequent analysis. Draw a shallow U-shaped curve that falls until it intersects the marginal cost curve and then rises. Then pick a point further up the marginal cost curve. Draw another shallow U-shaped curve whose minimum point passes through your second point. Finally, label the curves.

c) Any time a test question (including those in the Self-Test) asks about these curves, *draw a graph* before you answer.

Figure 10.1

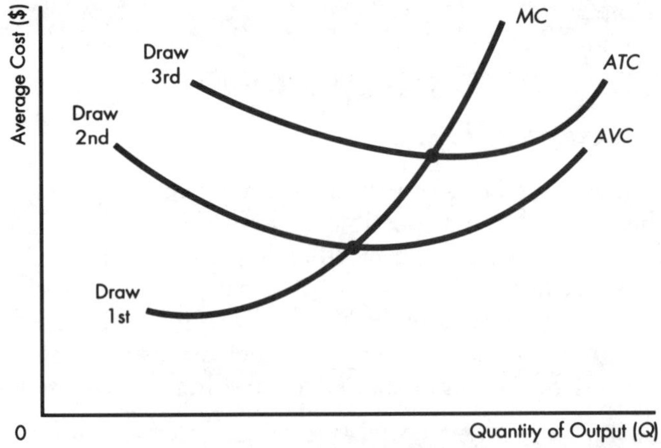

3) Be sure to understand how economists use the terms *short run* and *long run.* These terms do not refer to any notion of calendar time. They are better thought of as planning horizons. The short run is a planning horizon short enough that, while some inputs are variable, at least one input cannot be varied but is fixed. The long run refers to a planning horizon that is long enough that all inputs can be varied.

4) The later sections of the chapter explain the long-run production function and cost function when plant size is variable. While diminishing returns was the key for understanding short-run costs, the concept of returns to scale is the key for understanding long-run costs. Returns to scale are the increase in output relative to the increase in inputs when *all inputs* are increased by the same percentage. Returns to scale can be increasing, constant, or decreasing, and correspond to the downward-sloping, horizontal and upward-sloping sections of the long-run average cost curve.

Key Figures and Table

Figure 10.2 Total Product and Marginal Product, text page 234

This figure illustrates how to calculate marginal product from total product. Marginal product of labour is the increase in total product resulting from the use of an additional unit of labour. The table calculates the marginal product of labour as the change in total product when additional units of labour are used. Part (a) illustrates the total product curve and indicates the addition to total product associated with each additional unit of labour. Notice that the slope of the total product curve, $\Delta TP / \Delta L$, is equal to marginal product. Thus, if you know the total product curve, you can always derive the marginal product curve.

When graphing the marginal product curve, as in part (b), notice that marginal product is plotted *midway* between the corresponding units of labour, emphasizing that marginal product is the result of *changing* inputs. For example, the marginal product of changing from 0 to 1 labourer is 4 sweaters, and the value 4 is plotted midway between 0 and 1 labourers.

Figure 10.3 Total, Marginal, and Average Product, text page 235

This figure uses the same data as Figure 10.2, and simply adds the calculation of average product. Average product is defined as *TP/L*, and is computed in the table. Graphically, as shown in part (a), average product can be measured by the slope of a straight line from the origin to a point on the total product curve. Thus, if you know the total product curve, you can always derive the average product curve. As the quantity of labour increases, notice that the slope of the line from the origin to the corresponding point on the total product curve first increases, reaches a maximum, and then decreases.

Part (b) simply represents the average product graphically. The concept of average product does not involve any idea of changing inputs, it measures the average product of a *fixed* number of labourers. Hence, values for average product are plotted directly above the corresponding units of labour. For example, the average product of 3 workers is 4.33 sweaters, and the value 4.33 is plotted directly above 3 labourers. Notice the relationship between the average product and marginal product curves. The marginal product curve is above the average product curve when average product is increasing and below the average product curve when average product is decreasing. The marginal product curve intersects the average product curve when average product is at a maximum.

Figure 10.4 Short-Run Costs, text page 238

In the short run, total cost (*TC*) is divided into total fixed cost (*TFC*) and total variable cost (*TVC*). The left half of the table lists these costs for Swanky, Inc. Part (a) illustrates graphically the corresponding total cost, total fixed cost, and total variable cost curves. Since $TC = TFC + TVC$, the vertical distance between the *TC* and *TVC* curves is equal to *TFC*, which by definition is constant (fixed).

The graph in part (b) is one of the most important graphs in all of microeconomics, and you must understand it thoroughly. The curves for average total cost (*ATC*), average fixed cost (*AFC*), and average variable cost (*AVC*) are derived by taking the values for *TC*, *TFC*, and *TVC* and dividing by quantity of output. Since these are average values for a fixed quantity of output, they are plotted directly above the corresponding units of output. On the other hand, marginal cost (*MC*) is the *change* in total cost (or equivalently, in total variable cost) resulting from a one unit increase in output. It is plotted in the graph in part (b) *midway* between the corresponding units of output. The *ATC*, *AVC*, and *MC* curves are crucially important. The *ATC* and *AVC* curves are both U-shaped. The *MC* curve is also U-shaped and intersects the *ATC* and *AVC* curves at their minimum points. The *MC* curve is below the *ATC* and *AVC* curves when *ATC* and *AVC* are falling, and above the *ATC* and *AVC* curves when they are rising. The less important *AFC* curve falls continuously as output increases. See *Helpful Hint 2* for tips on how to draw the crucially important curves.

Figure 10.8 Short-Run and Long-Run Costs, text page 246

In the short run, capital inputs are fixed, while in the long run all inputs are variable. This figure illustrates the relationship between short-run and long-run costs for Swanky, Inc. Four different plants are considered: one for each of one through four units of capital (knitting machines). Given a choice of plant, Swanky, Inc. is then in the short run. For example, if Swanky chooses to buy 2 knitting machines, it has chosen to operate plant *b* in the short run and thus faces average total cost curve given by ATC_b in the graph in part (a). The costs for each plant are given in the table on text page 247 and the corresponding *ATC* curves are illustrated in part (a). In the long run, Swanky's will choose the plant which minimizes the *ATC* of producing the desired level of output. The construction of the long-run average cost (*LRAC*) curve is illustrated in part (b). The *LRAC* traces the lowest *ATC* possible for each level of output.

Figure 10.9 Returns to Scale, text page 248

This figure uses the *LRAC* curve from Figure 10.8 on text page 246 to illustrate the ranges over which the *LRAC* curve exhibits alternative returns to scale. When the *LRAC* curve is negatively sloped (up to output of 15 sweaters per day), there are increasing returns to scale or economies of scale. When the *LRAC* curve is positively sloped (output levels above 15 sweaters per day), there are decreasing returns to scale or diseconomies of scale. See Figure 10.10 on text page 249 for an illustration of constant returns to scale.

Table 10.2 A Compact Glossary on Product and Cost, text page 240
Numerous new total, average, and marginal concepts of product and cost are introduced in this chapter. This table brings them together in a convenient summary form, and is an excellent study tool. It includes the term, the symbol used, the equation form of the definition, and a verbal definition. You must know and *understand* all of the equations in this table in order to do well on tests and examinations.

SELF-TEST

CONCEPT REVIEW

1) The profits of a firm are limited by two types of constraints: ______________ constraints, which are conditions under which the firm can buy its inputs and sell its output, and ______________ constraints, which limit the feasible ways in which inputs can be converted into output.

2) A production process that uses large amounts of capital relative to labour is called a(n) ______________ – ______________ technique while a(an) ______________ – ______________ technique uses a large amount of labour relative to capital.

3) The term economists use for a period of time in which the quantities of some inputs are fixed, while others can be varied, is the ______________ ______________. The period of time in which all inputs are variable is the ______________ ______________.

4) The total product curve is a graph of the maximum output attainable at each level of a ______________ input, given the amount of fixed inputs. The change in total product resulting from a one-unit increase in labour input, holding the quantity of capital constant, is called the ______________ ______________ of labour. The average product of labour is ______________ ______________ divided by the units of ______________.

5) If marginal product is greater than average product, then average product must be ______________. Marginal product ______________ average product when average product reaches a maximum.

6) The shape of the marginal product curve can be described as follows: it first ______________, reaches a ______________ and then ______________ as labour inputs increase.

7) Increasing marginal returns occur when the marginal product of an additional worker is ______________ than the marginal product of the previous workers. As more of a variable input is used, holding other inputs fixed, the marginal product of the variable input begins to decline. This is a statement of the law of ______________ ______________.

8) $TC = FC +$ ______________.

9) Marginal cost is the increase in total cost resulting from a one-unit increase in ______________.

10) If the average variable cost curve is decreasing, then the marginal cost curve must be ______________ the average variable cost curve.

11) The output at which a plant's average total cost is a minimum is called the ______________ of the plant.

12) If output increases by 20 percent when all inputs are increased by 10 percent, the production process is said to display ______________ ______________ to ______________.

13) If a firm is experiencing constant returns to scale, a 10 percent increase in inputs will result in a ______________ percent ______________ in output. When the long-run average cost curve rises, there are ______________ returns to scale.

14) A technological advance will tend to ______________ product curves and ______________ cost curves.

TRUE OR FALSE

_____ 1) Limitations on the feasible ways in which inputs can be converted into outputs is an example of a market constraint on firm profitability.

_____ 2) All economically efficient production methods are also technologically efficient.

_____ 3) The short run is a time period in which there is at least one fixed input and at least one variable input.

_____ 4) All inputs are fixed in the long run.

_____ 5) Marginal product is given by the slope of the total product curve.

_____ 6) Given a fixed quantity of capital, if 2 additional labourers produce 15 additional units of output, the marginal product of labour is 15 units of output.

_____ 7) Average product can be measured as the slope of a line drawn from the origin to a point on the total product curve.

_____ 8) The average product curve cuts the marginal product curve from above at the maximum point on the marginal product curve.

_____ 9) The law of diminishing returns implies that eventually the marginal product curve will be negatively sloped as the variable input increases.

_____ 10) The law of diminishing returns implies that we will not observe a range of increasing marginal returns.

_____ 11) In the short run, marginal variable cost and marginal total costs are always identical.

_____ 12) Average total cost, average variable cost, and average fixed cost are all U-shaped.

_____ 13) Average variable cost reaches its minimum at the same level of output at which average product is a maximum.

_____ 14) In the real world, marginal cost curves are rarely upward sloping.

_____ 15) If average variable cost is decreasing then marginal cost must be decreasing.

_____ 16) A firm producing on the downward-sloping part of its average total cost curve is said to have excess capacity.

_____ 17) By capacity, economists mean the physical limits of production.

_____ 18) If average total cost is greater than marginal cost, then average total cost must be increasing.

_____ 19) No part of any short-run average total cost curve can lie below the long-run average cost curve.

_____ 20) Increasing returns to scale means that the long-run average cost curve is negatively sloped.

_____ 21) With some fixed inputs, if a 20% increase in variable inputs yields a 20% increase in output, then there are constant returns to scale.

_____ 22) In the long run, the total cost and total variable cost curves are the same.

_____ 23) If the price of inputs falls, the average variable cost and average total cost curves will shift up.

_____ 24) A firm facing highly variable demand for its output would want to increase plant size only if it was persistently operating on the upward-sloping part of its short-run average total cost curve.

MULTIPLE-CHOICE

1) In economics, the short run is a time period
   a) of one year or less.
   b) in which all inputs are variable.
   c) in which all inputs are fixed.
   d) in which there is at least one fixed input and at least one variable input.
   e) in which all inputs are variable but the technology is fixed.

2) A profit maximizing firm is constrained by all of the following *except*
   a) limited demand for a product.
   b) limited input supplies.
   c) limited number of technologically efficient production methods.
   d) limited competition from other firms.
   e) the length of the planning period.

3) The total product represents the
   a) sum of the average and marginal product curves.
   b) maximum output attainable for each quantity of a variable input at each price of the variable input.
   c) maximum output attainable for each quantity of a variable input given the amount of other inputs.
   d) total output divided by the quantity of the fixed input.
   e) slope of the marginal product curve.

4) The average product of labour can be measured as the
   a) slope of a straight line from the origin to a point on the total product curve.
   b) slope of the total product curve.
   c) slope of a straight line from the origin to a point on the marginal product curve.
   d) slope of the marginal product curve.
   e) change in output divided by the change in labour input.

5) A field of ripe corn is waiting to be harvested. Labour is the only variable input, and the total product (in bushels) of various numbers of labourers is given in Table 10.1.

Table 10.1

Number of Labourers	Total Product
0	0
1	3
2	7
3	10
4	12

Diminishing returns *begin* when you add which labourer?
a) 1st labourer
b) 2nd labourer
c) 3rd labourer
d) 4th labourer
e) there are no diminishing returns since total product always rises

6) When the marginal product of labour is less than the average product of labour,
a) the average product of labour is increasing.
b) the marginal product of labour is increasing.
c) the total product curve is negatively sloped.
d) the firm is experiencing diminishing returns.
e) none of the above is true.

7) According to the law of diminishing returns,
i) marginal productivity eventually rises.
ii) marginal productivity eventually falls.
iii) marginal cost eventually rises.
iv) marginal cost eventually falls.
a) i) and iii)
b) i) and iv)
c) ii) and iii)
d) ii) and iv)
e) iv) only

8) The vertical distance between the *TC* and *TVC* curves is
a) decreasing as output increases.
b) increasing as output increases.
c) equal to *AFC*.
d) equal to *TFC*.
e) equal to *MC*.

9) The marginal cost (*MC*) curve intersects the
a) *ATC*, *AVC*, and *AFC* curves at their minimum points.
b) *ATC* and *AFC* curves at their minimum points.
c) *AVC* and *AFC* curves at their minimum points.
d) *ATC* and *AVC* curves at their minimum points.
e) *TC* and *TVC* curves at their minimum points.

10) Marginal cost is the amount that
a) total cost increases when one more labourer is hired.
b) fixed cost increases when one more labourer is hired.
c) variable cost increases when one more labourer is hired.
d) total cost increases when one more unit of output is produced.
e) fixed cost increases when one more unit of output is produced.

11) Total cost is $20 at 4 units of output and $36 at 6 units of output. Between 4 and 6 units of output, marginal cost
a) is less than average total cost.
b) is equal to average total cost.
c) is equal to average variable cost.
d) is greater than average total cost.
e) cannot be compared with any average cost without additional information.

12) A firm's fixed costs are $100. If total costs are $200 for one unit of output and $310 for two units, what is the marginal cost of the second unit?
a) $100
b) $110
c) $200
d) $210
e) $310

13) If *ATC* is falling then *MC* must be
a) rising.
b) falling.
c) equal to *ATC*.
d) above *ATC*.
e) below *ATC*.

14) In the long run,
a) only the scale of plant is fixed.
b) all inputs are variable.
c) all inputs are fixed.
d) a firm must experience decreasing returns to scale.
e) none of the above is true.

15) The problem of a firm in the long run is to
a) derive the long-run average cost curve.
b) choose the scale of plant that has minimum average cost of producing the desired level of output.
c) choose the amount of labour that has minimum average cost of producing the desired level of output, given the scale of plant.
d) produce the largest amount of output possible.
e) operate on the increasing returns to scale range of the *LRAC* curve.

16) When a firm is producing at capacity, it is
a) maximizing profit.
b) producing at its physical limits.
c) producing the level of output at which marginal cost equals average total cost.
d) producing on the upward-sloping part of its *LRAC* curve.
e) producing at the minimum point of its *LRAC* curve.

17) If all inputs are increased by 10 percent and output increases by less than 10 percent, it must be the case that
a) average total cost is decreasing.
b) average total cost is increasing.
c) the *LRAC* curve is negatively sloped.
d) there are increasing returns to scale.
e) there are decreasing returns to scale.

18) The marginal cost curve slopes upwards because of
a) diminishing marginal utility.
b) diminishing returns.
c) technological inefficiency.
d) economic inefficiency.
e) none of the above statements.

19) Constant returns to scale means that as all inputs are increased,
a) total output remains constant.
b) average total cost remains constant.
c) average total cost increases at the same rate as inputs.
d) long-run average cost remains constant.
e) long-run average cost rises at the same rate as inputs.

20) The long-run average cost curve
a) shifts up when fixed costs increase.
b) shifts down when fixed costs increase.
c) is the short-run average total cost curve with the lowest cost.
d) traces the minimum points on all the short-run average total cost curves for each scale of plant.
e) traces the minimum short-run average total cost for each output.

21) A technological advance will shift
i) *TP*, *AP*, and *MP* curves up.
ii) *TP*, *AP*, and *MP* curves down.
iii) *TC*, *ATC*, and *MC* curves up.
iv) *TC*, *ATC*, and *MC* curves down.
a) i) and iii)
b) i) and iv)
c) ii) and iii)
d) ii) and iv)
e) none of the above

22) A firm will want to increase its scale of plant if
a) it persistently produces on the upward-sloping part of its short-run average total cost curve.
b) it persistently produces on the downward-sloping part of its short-run average total cost curve.
c) it is producing below capacity.
d) marginal cost is below average total cost.
e) marginal cost is below average variable cost.

23) The average variable cost curve will shift up if
a) there is an increase in fixed costs.
b) there is a technological advance.
c) the price of variable input decreases.
d) the price of output increases.
e) none of the above occurs.

24) A rise in the price of a fixed input will cause a firm's
a) average variable cost curve to shift up.
b) average total cost curve to shift up.
c) average total cost curve to shift down.
d) marginal cost curve to shift up.
e) marginal cost curve to shift down.

SHORT ANSWER

1) What market constraints does a firm face on its ability to make profits?

2) Why does a steeper slope of the total product curve imply a higher level of the marginal product curve?

3) Why is it the case that the marginal product curve must intersect the average product curve at its maximum point?

4) What is the difference, if any, between diminishing returns and decreasing returns to scale?

5) How is the long-run average cost curve obtained and how does it differ from Jacob Viner's mistaken conception of it?

PROBLEMS

1) For a given scale of plant, Table 10.2 gives the total monthly output of golf carts attainable using varying quantities of labour.

Table 10.2 Monthly Golf Cart Production

Labourers (per month)	Output (units per month)	Marginal Product	Average Product
0	0		
1	1		
2	3		
3	6		
4	12		
5	17		
6	20		
7	22		
8	23		

a) Complete the table for the marginal product and average product of labour. (Note that marginal product should be entered *midway* between rows to emphasize that it is the result of *changing* inputs — moving from one row to the next. Average product corresponds to a *fixed* quantity of labour and should be entered on the appropriate row.)

b) Label the axes and draw a graph of the total product curve (*TP*).

c) On a separate piece of paper, label the axes and draw a graph of both marginal product (*MP*) and average product (*AP*). (Marginal product should be plotted *midway* between the corresponding units of labour, as in text Figure 10.2 on page 234, while average product should be plotted directly above the corresponding units of labour, as in text Figure 10.3(b) on page 235.)

2) Now let's examine the short-run costs of golf cart production. The first two columns of Table 10.2 are reproduced in the first two columns of Table 10.3. The cost of 1 labourer (the only variable input) is $2,000 per month. Total fixed cost is $2,000 per month.

Table 10.3 Short-run Costs (Monthly)

Labourers (per month)	Output (units per month)	*TFC* ($)	*TVC* ($)	*TC* ($)	*MC* ($)	*AFC* ($)	*AVC* ($)	*ATC* ($)
0	0	2,000						
1	1							
2	3							
3	6							
4	12							
5	17							
6	20							
7	22							
8	23							

a) Given this information, complete Table 10.3 by computing total fixed cost (*TFC*), total variable cost (*TVC*), total cost (*TC*), marginal cost (*MC*), average fixed cost (*AFC*), average variable cost (*AVC*), and average total cost (*ATC*). Your completed table should look like the table in text Figure 10.4 on page 238, with marginal cost entered *midway* between the rows.

b) Label the axes and draw the *TC*, *TVC*, and *TFC* curves on a single graph.

c) Label the axes and draw the *MC*, *ATC*, *AVC*, and *AFC* curves on a single graph. Be sure to plot *MC midway* between the corresponding units of output.

d) Now suppose that the price of a labourer increases to $2,500 per month. Construct a table for the new *MC* and *ATC* curves (output, *MC*, *ATC*). Label the axes and draw a graph of the new *MC* and *ATC* curves. What is the effect of the increase in the price of the variable input on these curves?

3) Return to the original price of labour of $2,000 per month. Now suppose that we double the quantity of fixed inputs so that total fixed costs also double to $4,000 per month. This increases the monthly output of golf carts for each quantity of labour as indicated in Table 10.4.

a) Construct a table for the new *MC* and *ATC* curves (output, *MC*, *ATC*). Label the axes and draw a graph of the new *MC* and *ATC* curves.

Table 10.4 New Monthly Production of Golf Carts

Labourers (per month)	Output (units per month)
0	0
1	1
2	4
3	10
4	19
5	26
6	31
7	34
8	36

b) What is the effect on these curves compared to the original *MC* and *ATC* curves in problem 2(c) of an increase in "plant size?" Are there economies of scale?

c) Draw the long-run average cost (*LRAC*) curve if these are the only two plant sizes available.

4) Figure 10.2 gives a sequence of short-run *ATC* curves numbered 1 through 7 corresponding to seven different plant sizes.

Figure 10.2

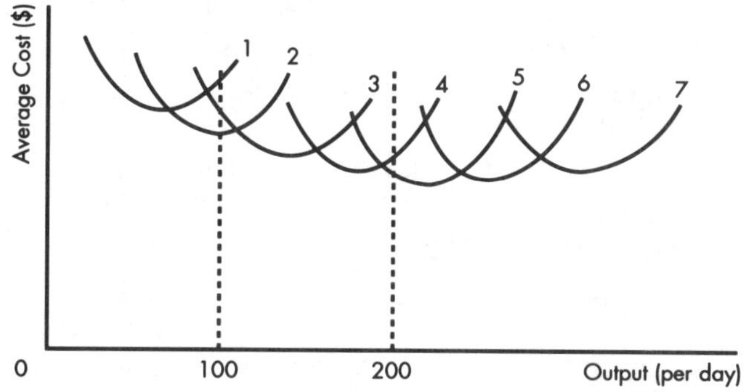

a) Draw the long-run average cost curve on Figure 10.2.

b) If the desired level of output is 100 units per day, what is the best plant size? (Give the number of the associated short-run *ATC* curve.)

c) If the desired level of output is 200 units per day, what is the best plant size?

ANSWERS

CONCEPT REVIEW

1) market; technological
2) capital-intensive; labour-intensive
3) short run; long run
4) variable; marginal product; total product (output); labour
5) rising; equals
6) increases; maximum; decreases
7) greater; diminishing returns
8) VC
9) output
10) below
11) capacity
12) increasing returns; scale
13) 10; increase; decreasing
14) raise; lower

TRUE OR FALSE

1) F	7) T	13) T	19) T
2) T	8) F	14) F	20) T
3) T	9) T	15) F	21) F
4) F	10) F	16) T	22) T
5) T	11) T	17) F	23) F
6) F	12) F	18) F	24) T

MULTIPLE-CHOICE

1) d	7) c	13) e	19) d
2) d	8) d	14) b	20) e
3) c	9) d	15) b	21) b
4) a	10) d	16) c	22) a
5) c	11) d	17) e	23) e
6) d	12) b	18) b	24) b

SHORT ANSWER

1) Every firm is constrained by the supply of inputs it uses and by the demand for the output it produces. Because of the law of supply, firms, in general, can obtain more inputs only if they are willing to pay more for them. On the other hand, given the law of demand, firms in general, can sell more of their output only if they are willing to drop the price.

2) Marginal product is equal to the slope of the total product curve since it is defined as the change in total product resulting from an increase in the variable input. Since a steeper slope means a larger slope, it also means a higher marginal product.

3) Since the average product curve first rises and then falls, when average product is rising, marginal product must be greater than average product, and when average product is falling, marginal product must be less than average product. If this is the case, then the marginal product curve intersects the average product curve at its maximum point. In order for average product to increase, it must have been *pulled up* by a larger increase in product from the last unit of input. Therefore, the marginal product is higher than average product. Similarly, when average product is falling, it must be that it has been *pulled down* by a lower marginal product. When average product is at its maximum, it is neither rising nor falling, so marginal product cannot be higher or lower than average product. Therefore, the marginal product must be equal to average product.

4) The law of diminishing returns states that as a firm uses additional units of a variable input, *while holding constant the quantity of fixed inputs*, the marginal product of the variable input will eventually diminish. Decreasing returns to scale occur when a firm increases *all of its inputs by an equal percentage*, and this results in a lower percentage increase in output. Diminishing (marginal) returns is a short-run concept since there must be a fixed input. Decreasing returns to scale is a long-run concept since all inputs must be variable.

5) Any given level of output can be produced using alternative scales of plant, but for each level of output, one scale of plant will result in the lowest value of short-run average total cost. The scale of plant can be varied in the long run, and the long-run average cost curve traces out the lowest short-run average total cost at each level of output. Jacob Viner's mistaken conception of the long-run average cost curve was that (a) it must pass through the *minimum point* of each of the short-run average cost curves (which is incorrect) and, (b) it must not be above any short-run cost curve at any point (which is correct). The mistake is that these two properties cannot be satisfied simultaneously. Indeed, the long-run average cost curve does *not* pass through the minimum point of each of the short-run average cost curves.

PROBLEMS

1) a) Completed Table 10.2 is shown here.

Table 10.2 Solution: Monthly Golf Cart Production

Labourers (per month)	Output (units per month)	Marginal Product	Average Product
0	0		0
		1	
1	1		1.00
		2	
2	3		1.50
		3	
3	6		2.00
		6	
4	12		3.00
		5	
5	17		3.40
		3	
6	20		3.33
		2	
7	22		3.14
		1	
8	23		2.88

b) Figure 10.3 gives the graph of the total product curve.

Figure 10.3

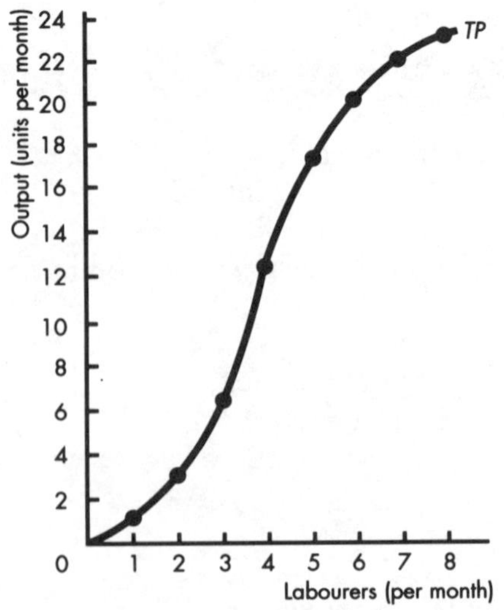

c) Figure 10.4 gives the graphs of marginal product and average product.

Figure 10.4

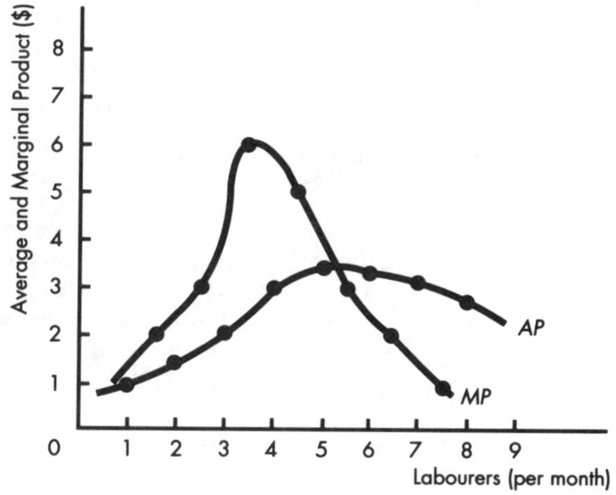

2) a) Completed Table 10.3 is given here.

Table 10.3 Solution: Short-run Costs (Monthly)

Labourers (per month)	Output (units per month)	*TFC* ($)	*TVC* ($)	*TC* ($)	*MC* ($)	*AFC* ($)	*AVC* ($)	*ATC* ($)
0	0	2,000	0	2,000		—	—	—
1	1	2,000	2,000	4,000	2,000	2,000	2,000	4,000
2	3	2,000	4,000	6,000	1,000	667	1,333	2,000
3	6	2,000	6,000	8,000	667	333	1,000	1,333
4	12	2,000	8,000	10,000	333	167	667	833
5	17	2,000	10,000	12,000	400	118	588	706
6	20	2,000	12,000	14,000	667	100	600	700
7	22	2,000	14,000	16,000	1,000	91	636	727
8	23	2,000	16,000	18,000	2,000	87	696	783

b) The *TC*, *TVC*, and *TFC* curves are graphed in Figure 10.5.

Figure 10.5

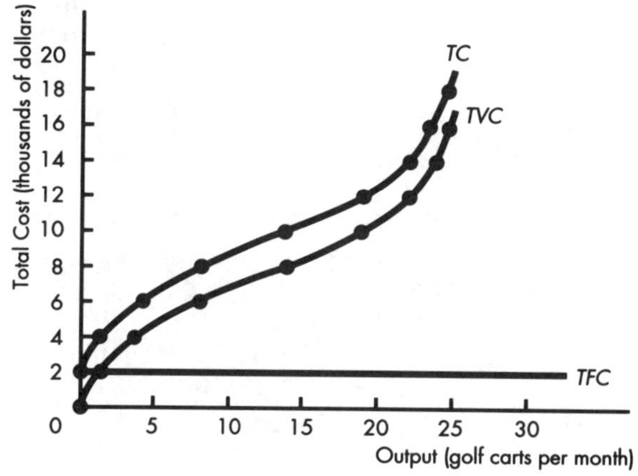

c) The *MC*, *ATC*, *AVC*, and *AFC* curves are graphed in Figure 10.6.

Figure 10.6

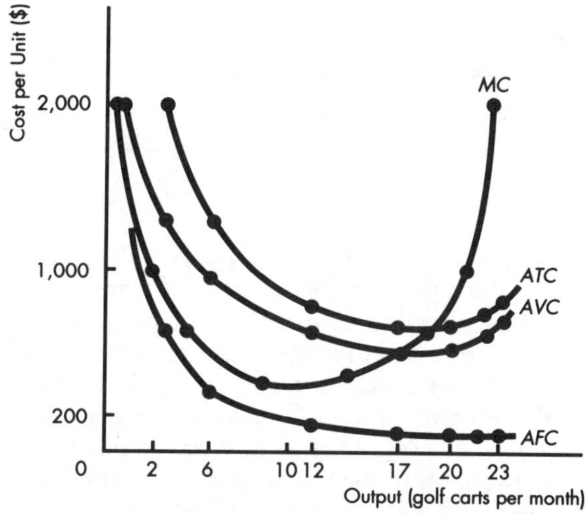

d) The new *MC* and *ATC* curves (and the associated table) are given in Figure 10.7. The original curves, MC_1 and ATC_1, are indicated for reference. The new curves are labelled MC_2 and ATC_2. Both curves have shifted up as a result of an increase in the price of labour.

Figure 10.7

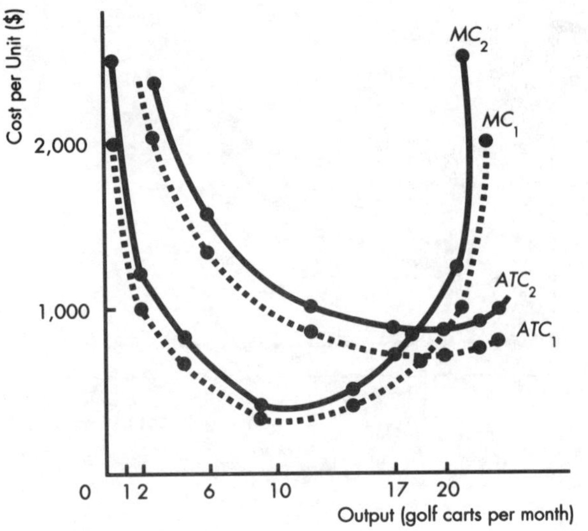

Output	MC ($)	ATC ($)
0		0
	2,500	
1		4,500
	1,250	
3		2,333
	833	
6		1,583
	417	
12		1,000
	500	
17		853
	833	
20		850
	1,250	
22		886
	2,500	
23		957

Figure 10.8

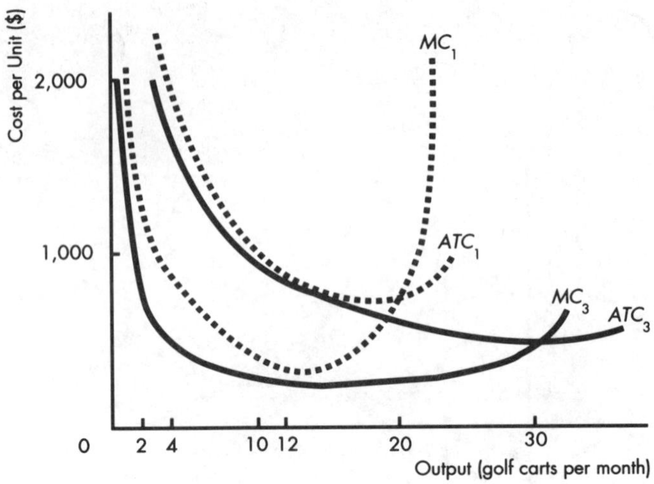

Output	MC ($)	ATC ($)
0		0
	2,000	
1		6,000
	667	
4		2,000
	333	
10		1,000
	222	
19		632
	286	
26		538
	400	
31		516
	667	
34		529

3) a) The new *MC* and *ATC* curves (and the associated table) are given in Figure 10.8. The new curves are labelled MC_3 and ATC_3. The original curves, MC_1 and ATC_1, are indicated for reference.

b) The curves have shifted (generally) down and to the right as a result of increasing the plant size. There are economies of scale (increasing returns to scale) up to the level of output at which MC_3 intersects ATC_3 (approximately 32 units).

c) The long-run average cost curve is indicated in Figure 10.8 by the heavy line tracing out the lowest short-run average total cost of producing each level of output. In this example, that happens to correspond entirely to ATC_3.

4) a) The long-run average cost curve is indicated in Figure 10.2 Solution by the heavy line tracing out the lowest short-run average total cost of producing each level of output.

b) If the desired level of output is 100 units, the best plant size is the one associated with short-run average total cost curve 2.

Figure 10.2 Solution

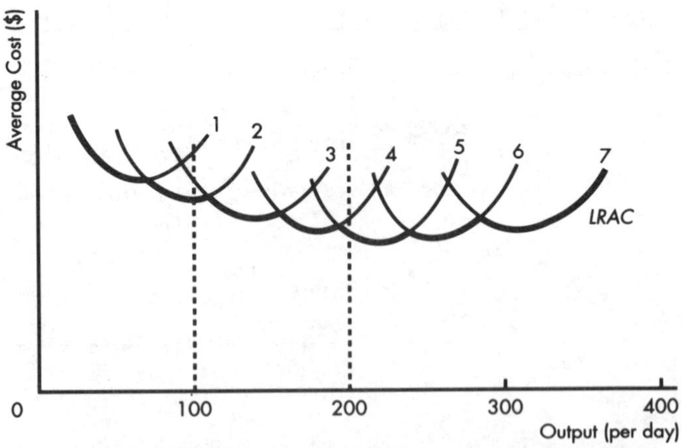

c) If the desired level of output is 200 units, the best plant size is the one associated with short-run average total cost curve 5.

Chapter 11 Producing at Least Cost

Chapter in Perspective

Text Pages 257–276

There are usually numerous ways to produce any good. Some methods for producing a given quantity of a particular good use relatively more labour and others use relatively more capital. Given this array of possible production techniques, how should a firm choose the best combination of inputs? This chapter addresses that question. We find that a firm should choose the combination of inputs that allows it to produce at least cost. This is certainly not a surprising result, but the conditions that must exist to assure least-cost production provide important insights which allow us to predict how production techniques will change when input prices change and to explain why different industries and different countries frequently use very different combinations of inputs.

Learning Objectives

After studying this chapter, you will be able to:

- **Define and calculate the marginal rate of substitution between two inputs.**
- **Explain what an isoquant measures.**
- **Explain what an isocost line measures.**
- **Calculate the least-cost technique of production.**
- **Predict the effect of a change in input prices on the least-cost technique.**
- **Explain variations in capital intensity across industries and countries.**

Helpful Hints

1) The principle of substitution plays a pervasive role in economics. In previous chapters, consumers substituted one good for another in consumption. Indeed that is the likely response to a change in relative prices. This chapter emphasizes that substitution also takes place in the production process. Firms substitute one input for another in response to a change in the relative prices of inputs.

2) You have probably noticed the clear parallels between the analysis in this chapter of the choices facing the firm and the analysis in Chapter 8 of the choices facing the consumer. The parallels extend from the shapes of the curves, to the technical definitions and even to the adjustment processes to equilibrium. If you have mastered the analysis in Chapter 8, you will find this chapter much easier than it first appears.

   Consider first the parallel between isoquants and indifference curves. An isoquant describes the different combinations of inputs that yield the same output for the firm; an indifference curve describes the different combinations of goods that yield the same utility for the consumer.

   A similar parallel exists between isocost lines and budget lines. An isocost line describes the different combinations of inputs that the firm can purchase for a fixed total cost; a budget line describes the different combinations of goods that the consumer can purchase with a fixed income. While both the firm and the consumer are assumed to be optimizing — doing the best that they can with their scarce resources — there is a slight difference in their respective objectives.

   Graphically, the firm is seeking the lowest total cost (isocost line) for producing a given output, while the consumer is seeking the highest level of utility given a fixed income (budget line). In the language of optimizing, *the firm is minimizing cost subject to a given output constraint,* while the *consumer is maximizing utility subject to a given budget constraint.* Despite this slight difference, the graphical analyses of the firm and the consumer have remarkable parallels.

   Similar parallels exist for technical definitions. The marginal rate of substitution of capital for labour is the decrease in capital per unit increase in labour that keeps the firm's output constant. The marginal rate of substitution is the rate at which a consumer gives up good *Y* per additional unit of good *X* and still remains indifferent (constant utility). The marginal rate of substitution of capital for labour equals the magnitude of the slope of the isoquant, and decreases as we move down the isoquant. The consumer's marginal rate of substitution equals the magnitude of the slope of the indifference curve, and decreases as we move down the indifference curve. Similarly, the magnitude of the slope of the isocost line equals the relative price of the input (labour) on the horizontal axis in terms of the input (capital) on the vertical axis. The magnitude of the slope of the budget line equals the relative price of the good on the horizontal axis in terms of the good on the vertical axis.

   The firm's (cost-minimizing) optimum occurs when an isocost line is just tangent to an isoquant so that both have equal slopes, yielding the equation:

$$\begin{aligned} MRS &= MP_L/MP_K \\ &= P_L/P_K \end{aligned}$$

   This equation can be rearranged as follows:

$$MP_L/P_L = MP_K/P_K$$

   This least-cost condition says that the extra output (MP_L) from the last dollar spent on labour must equal the extra output (MP_K) from the last dollar spent on capital. If this condition is not met, for example, if

$$MP_L/P_L > MP_K/P_K$$

   then the firm can decrease costs by hiring more labour, (which yields higher marginal productivity per dollar) and less capital. The increased use of labour lowers the MP_L and the decreased use of capital raises the MP_K. This restores equality to the least-cost equation. Notice that the firm cannot affect the prices of inputs (P_L and P_K), but by adjusting its choice of technique, it can increase productivity and hence decrease cost.

   The consumer's (utility-maximizing) optimum occurs when a budget line is just tangent to an indifference curve so that both have equal slopes, yielding the equation:

$$\begin{aligned} MRS &= MU_x/MU_y \\ &= P_x/P_y \end{aligned}$$

   This equation can be rearranged as follows:

$$MU_x/P_x = MU_y/P_y$$

   This utility-maximizing condition says that the extra utility (MU_x) from the last dollar spent on good *X* must equal the extra utility (MU_y) from the last dollar spent on good *Y*. If this condition is not met, for example, if

$$MU_x/P_x > MU_y/P_y$$

   then the consumer can increase utility by consuming more of good *X* (which yields higher marginal utility per dollar) and less of good *Y*. The increased consumption of good *X* lowers the MU_x and the decreased consumption of good *Y* raises the MU_y. This restores equality to the utility-maximizing equation. Notice that the consumer cannot affect the prices of goods (P_x and P_y), but by adjusting consumption choices, the consumer can increase utility.

3) A production function involving two inputs, for example, labour and capital is a three-dimensional relationship (among output and the two inputs). The production function for sweaters faced by Swanky, Inc., is illustrated in the "three-dimensional" graph of text Figure 11.1 on page 259. Since three-dimensional graphs are difficult to work with, it is useful to reduce the problem to two dimensions. An isoquant map does just that by holding the quantity of output fixed for each isoquant. The two-dimensional isoquant in text Figure 11.2, on page 261 is derived from the three-dimensional production function in Figure 11.1 on page 259.

Key Figures and Tables

Figure 11.1 Swanky's Production Function, text page 259
A production function shows the maximum output that can be obtained using alternative combinations of inputs. This figure illustrates the production function for sweaters faced by Swanky, Inc. The output is sweaters and the inputs are labour and capital. Representing these three dimensions, the figure shows the maximum quantity of sweaters that can be produced for alternative combinations of labour and capital. Note that there is more than one combination of inputs which can produce almost any quantity of output. For example, 15 sweaters can be produced using three alternative input combinations: 1 unit of labour and 4 units of capital, 2 units of labour and 2 units of capital, and 4 units of labour and 1 unit of capital.

Figure 11.2 An Isoquant, text page 261
An isoquant shows the different input combinations that can be used to produce a given quantity of output. This figure illustrates the isoquant corresponding to 15 sweaters for Swanky, Inc. From Figure 11.1 in the previous paragraph we know that there are at least three ways to produce 15 sweaters. These combinations of labour and capital are labelled points *a*, *b*, and *c*. A curve is then fitted between the points to indicate intermediate input combinations which can produce 15 sweaters (assuming that fractional units of inputs can be used).

Figure 11.4 An Isoquant Map, text page 263
An isoquant map is a series of isoquants, each corresponding to a different level of output. Part (a) of this figure illustrates an isoquant map for sweater production by Swanky, Inc. It reflects information from the production function of Figure 11.1 on text page 259, which is represented in a slightly different way in part (b) of this figure. Swanky's isoquant map is a two-dimensional representation of the three-dimensional production function. (See *Helpful Hint 3.*) In this example, the isoquants for 10, 15, and 21 sweaters a day are shown.

Figure 11.5 Swanky's Input Possibilities, text page 264
This figure illustrates the isocost line which faces Swanky corresponding to $100. An isocost line shows the alternative combinations of inputs that can be purchased (the input possibilities) for a *given* total cost, given the prices of inputs. The magnitude of the slope of the isocost line equals the relative price of labour in terms of capital; the ratio of the price of labour (the input measured on the horizontal axis) to the price of capital (the input measured on the vertical axis). The higher the price of labour relative to the price of capital, the steeper the isocost line. In the example, the prices of labour and capital are both $25 per day, so the absolute value of the slope of the isocost line is 1.

Figure 11.7 An Isocost Map, text page 266
An isocost map is a series of isocost lines, each corresponding to a different level of total cost. This isocost map contains three isocost lines, corresponding to total cost amounts of $75, $100, and $125. The position of the isocost line depends on the amount of total cost. An isocost line associated with a higher total cost has the same slope but lies above (and to the right) of a lower-cost isocost line. There are other isocost lines corresponding to other levels of total cost, but these are not shown. The isocost lines in an isocost map all have the same slope and are parallel because input prices are given.

Figure 11.8 The Least-Cost Technique of Production, text page 267
This is the most important figure in the chapter for understanding how firms choose the least-cost production technique, which occurs when the relevant isoquant is tangent to an isocost line. The least-cost technique (input combination) for 15 sweaters per day in this figure is at point *b* corresponding to 2 units of labour and 2 units of capital. The minimum cost of production is $100. Fifteen sweaters could also be produced using any other input combinations on the isoquant, but each of these would be on a higher isocost line and thus require greater total cost to produce the same amount of output. For example, 15 sweaters a day could also be produced using 1 unit of labour and 4 units of capital (point *a*) but the total cost would be $125.

Table 11.2 Calculating an Isocost Equation, text page 264
This table derives Swanky's isocost equation, given total cost and the prices of labour and capital inputs. The procedure for deriving any isocost equation is similar.

In the first part of the table, symbols are defined (on the left) and specific values for total cost and inputs prices for the example in the text are given (on the right).

The second part of the table gives the firm's total cost equation. It simply says that the amount spent on labour ($P_L \times L$) plus the amount spent on capital ($P_K \times K$) is equal to total cost (TC).

The third part of the table solves this equation for the quantity of capital (K) and rearranges the equation so that K is the dependent variable. After rearranging, we have an isocost equation which is in the form of the equation of a straight line ($y = a + bx$) where the slope b is equal to $-P_L/P_K$. The magnitude of the slope represents the relative price of labour (the input on the horizontal axis) in terms of capital. In Swanky's case, the relative price of labour is 1 unit of capital since P_L = \$25 and P_K = \$25.

Table 11.3 The Least-Cost Technique, text page 272
This table develops notation and then offers several equivalent conditions that must be satisfied if a firm is using the least-cost technique. Part (a) introduces some "short-hand" notation and part (b) gives expressions for the slopes of the isoquant and the isocost line. Then three alternative equivalent conditions are stated which characterize a least-cost technique. *Helpful Hint 2,* discussed previously, gives some of these in further detail.

SELF-TEST

CONCEPT REVIEW

1) The ratio of capital to labour used in a production process is called capital _______________ .

2) The additional output from an additional unit of capital is called the _______________ _______________ of capital.

3) The decrease in capital needed as we increase labour by one unit in order to keep output constant is called the _______________ _______________ _______________ _______________ of capital for labour.

4) The law of diminishing marginal rate of substitution states that the marginal rate of substitution of capital for labour _______________ as the amount of capital decreases and the amount of _______________ increases.

5) A curve that shows the different combinations of labour and capital required to produce a given quantity of output is called a(n) _______________ . The marginal rate of substitution is given by the _______________ of the _______________ of this curve.

6) All combinations of capital and labour that can be bought for the same total cost are represented by a(n) _______________ line. If we measure capital on the vertical axis, the higher the relative cost of labour, the _______________ is the slope of this line.

7) The production process using the combination of inputs which minimizes total cost is called the _______________ – _______________ technique. When a firm is using this technique, the marginal rate of substitution between the inputs _______________ their relative price.

8) If the relative price of labour rises, the efficient production process will use relatively less _______________ and relatively more _______________ .

9) The marginal rate of substitution of capital for labour is equal to the marginal product of _______________ divided by the marginal product of _______________ .

TRUE OR FALSE

_____ 1) If increasing labour inputs by 2 units requires reducing the number of machines used by 1 unit, in order to maintain the same level of output, the marginal rate of substitution of capital for labour is 2.

_____ 2) As more labour and less capital are used, the marginal rate of substitution of capital for labour will decrease.

_____ 3) An isoquant is a curve that shows the different levels of output that can be produced by a given quantity of labour and capital.

_____ 4) The marginal rate of substitution equals the slope of the isoquant.

_____ 5) As labour (measured on the horizontal axis) increases and capital decreases, the isoquant becomes flatter.

_____ 6) Isoquants are bowed away from the origin.

_____ 7) An isoquant map consists of a series of isoquants, each for a different set of input prices.

_____ 8) The isocost line shows all combinations of capital and labour that can be bought for a given total cost.

_____ 9) If capital is measured on the vertical axis and the relative price of capital increases, the magnitude of the slope of the isocost equation will increase.

_____ 10) The variables (the firm's choices) in the total cost equation are the quantities of inputs employed.

_____ 11) When a firm is using the least-cost technique, the marginal rate of substitution is equal to the relative price of the inputs.

_____ 12) If a firm is using the least-cost technique, an increase in the price of labour with no change in the price of capital means that the firm will hire more labour and less capital.

_____ 13) The marginal rate of substitution of capital for labour is the marginal product of labour divided by the marginal product of capital.

_____ 14) Using the least-cost technique, the marginal product per dollar spent on an input will be equal across all inputs.

_____ 15) A least-cost technique is both economically efficient and technologically efficient.

_____ 16) If the relative price of labour increases, the isoquant will become steeper.

_____ 17) Differences in capital intensity across industries within a country are explained mainly by differences in input prices across industries.

_____ 18) Differences in capital intensity across countries are explained mainly by differences in wages.

_____ 19) If the relative price of labour rises, capital intensity will increase.

_____ 20) If capital and labour are close substitutes in production, the isoquants will curve tightly (sharply).

_____ 21) If input contributions to marginal cost differ, the firm will increase the use of the input with the lower contribution to marginal cost.

MULTIPLE-CHOICE

1) The marginal rate of substitution of capital for labour measures the
   a) increase in capital per unit increase in labour to keep output constant.
   b) decrease in capital per unit increase in labour to keep output constant.
   c) price of labour relative to the price of capital.
   d) price of capital relative to the price of labour.
   e) slope of the isocost line.

2) Which of the following reflects the law of diminishing marginal rate of substitution? As we continually increase labour one unit at a time,
   a) the addition to output will become larger, if capital is held constant.
   b) the addition to output will become smaller, if capital is held constant.
   c) larger reductions in capital will be required to keep output constant.
   d) smaller reductions in capital will be required to keep output constant.
   e) none of the above occurs.

3) Figure 11.1 shows a series of isoquants. Which of the following combinations of labour and capital could *not* produce 30 units of output?
   a) 8 units of labour and 1 unit of capital
   b) 7 units of labour and 2 units of capital
   c) 5 units of labour and 3 units of capital
   d) 2 units of labour and 6 units of capital
   e) 1 unit of labour and 8 units of capital

Figure 11.1

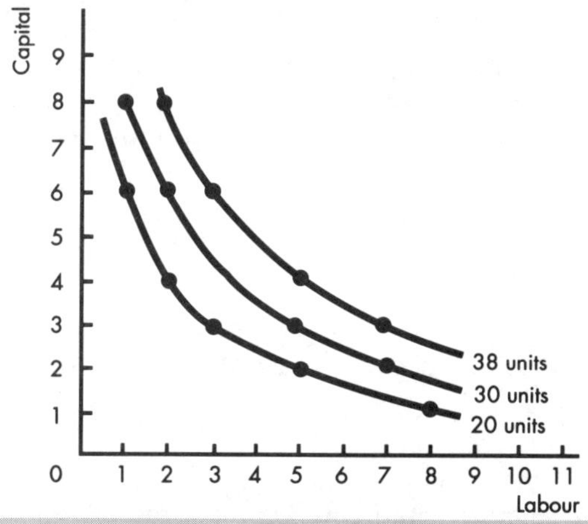

4) In Figure 11.1, what is the marginal rate of substitution of capital for labour as labour is increased from 2 to 3 units if output is being kept constant at 38 units?
a) 1/2
b) 1
c) 2
d) 3
e) 6

5) In Figure 11.1, 6 units of capital and 2 units of labour are currently in use. What is the marginal product of an additional unit of labour?
a) 6
b) 8
c) 10
d) 18
e) cannot be determined without additional information

6) What characteristic of the isoquants in Figure 11.1 reflects the law of diminishing marginal rate of substitution?
a) the isoquants are negatively sloped
b) the isoquants become flatter as labour input increases
c) the isoquants further to the right correspond to larger output
d) output increases by a smaller amount as isoquants continually shift to the right
e) as labour is added to a fixed quantity of capital, the marginal product of labour diminishes

7) Figure 11.1 is an example of
a) an isoquant map.
b) an isocost map.
c) a preference map.
d) a shifting production function.
e) the least-cost technique.

8) The absolute value of the slope of an isocost line (with labour measured on the horizontal axis) is the ratio of
a) the marginal product of labour to the marginal product of capital.
b) the marginal product of capital to the marginal product of labour.
c) the price of labour to the price of capital.
d) the price of capital to the price of labour.
e) none of the above.

9) Figure 11.2 shows an isocost line. Which of the following combinations of capital and labour could *not* be bought for $240?
a) 0 units of labour and 6 units of capital
b) 3 units of labour and 5 units of capital
c) 4 units of labour and 3 units of capital
d) 5 units of labour and 2 units of capital
e) 8 units of labour and 0 units of capital

Figure 11.2

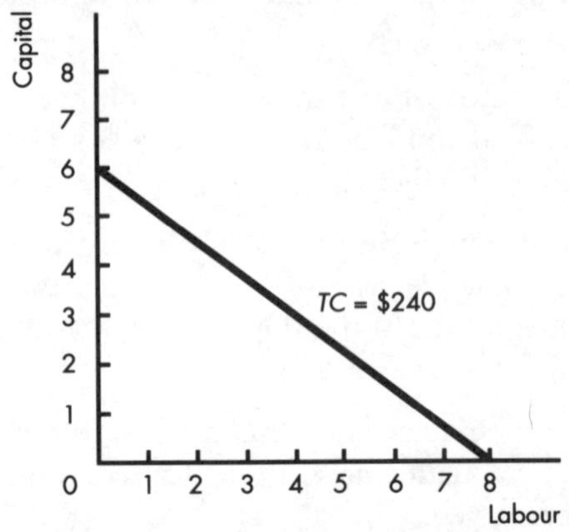

10) What is the price of a unit of capital in Figure 11.2?
a) $10
b) $20
c) $30
d) $40
e) none of the above

11) If the price of labour rises, the isocost line in Figure 11.2 will
a) become steeper.
b) become flatter.
c) shift inward but parallel to the original isocost line.
d) shift outward but parallel to the original isocost line.
e) shift inward and become flatter.

12) Which of the following is *not* a characteristic of the least-cost technique of production?
a) The marginal rate of substitution of capital for labour equals the ratio of the price of labour to the price of capital.
b) The slope of the isoquant equals the slope of the isocost line.
c) The isocost line is tangent to the isoquant.
d) The marginal product of labour equals the marginal product of capital.
e) All inputs have the same impact on marginal cost.

13) Figure 11.3 gives isoquants and isocost lines for a firm. What combination of labour and capital give the least-cost technique for producing 20 units of output?
a) 1 unit of labour and 8 units of capital
b) 3 units of labour and 4 units of capital
c) 4 units of labour and 5 units of capital
d) 6 units of labour and 2 units of capital
e) none of the above

Figure 11.3

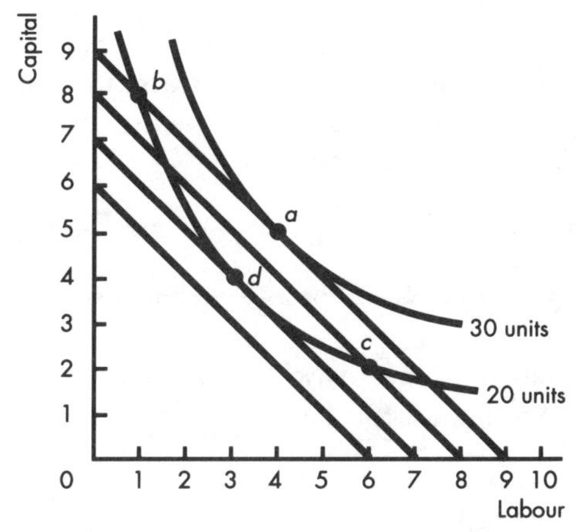

14) At point *a* in Figure 11.3, what is the marginal rate of substitution of capital for labour?
a) 1
b) 5/4
c) 4/5
d) 1/9
e) 9

15) Refer to Figure 11.3. If the price of a unit of capital is $20, what is the least cost required to produce 30 units of output?
a) $80
b) $100
c) $140
d) $180
e) $360

16) Which of the following is true at point *c* in Figure 11.3?
a) Total cost is the same as at point *b*.
b) Total cost is less than at point *d*.
c) The marginal product of labour per dollar spent on labour is equal to the marginal product of capital per dollar spent on capital.
d) The marginal product of labour per dollar spent on labour is greater than the marginal product of capital per dollar spent on capital.
e) None of the above is true.

17) Suppose the price of capital falls. If capital is measured on the vertical axis, the isocost curve will become
a) steeper and production will become more capital intensive.
b) steeper and production will become less capital intensive.
c) flatter and production will become more capital intensive.
d) flatter and production will become less capital intensive.
e) flatter and production will become less efficient.

18) For a firm using the least-cost production technique, the marginal product of capital is 5, the price of a unit of capital is $20, and the price of a unit of labour is $8. What is the marginal product of labour?
a) 0.5
b) 2.0
c) 5.0
d) 12.5
e) 32.0

19) If the ratio of the marginal product of labour to the marginal product of capital is greater than the ratio of the price of labour to the price of capital, a firm can produce
a) more only if it increases total cost.
b) more at the same total cost only if the price of capital falls.
c) more at the same total cost only if the price of labour falls.
d) the same amount at lower cost if it decreases labour and increases capital.
e) the same amount at lower cost if it increases labour and decreases capital.

20) The main reason for variations in capital intensity across different industries in a single country is/are differences in
a) the price of labour.
b) the slope of isocost lines.
c) production functions.
d) access to technology.
e) both a) and b).

SHORT ANSWER

1) Explain why the law of diminishing marginal rate of substitution implies that isoquants must be bowed toward the origin.

2) Explain what a cost-minimizing firm should do if it finds that, for the technique it is currently using, the ratio of the marginal product of labour (MP_L) to the marginal product of capital (MP_K) is greater than the ratio of the price of labour (P_L) to the price of capital (P_K).

3) How does the least-cost technique change when the price of labour rises?

4) Why are there variations in capital intensity across industries in a given country?

5) What is the principal explanation of the differences in capital intensity across countries?

PROBLEMS

1) Figure 11.4 gives the production function for an earmuff firm. It shows the number of earmuffs that can be produced in a day using various combinations of labour and capital. The number of units of labour (from 1 to 6) is given on the horizontal axis and the number of units of capital (from 1 to 6) is given on the vertical axis. For example, if 2 units of labour and 3 units of capital are used, the firm can produce 37 earmuffs per day.

Figure 11.4 The Production Function for Earmuffs

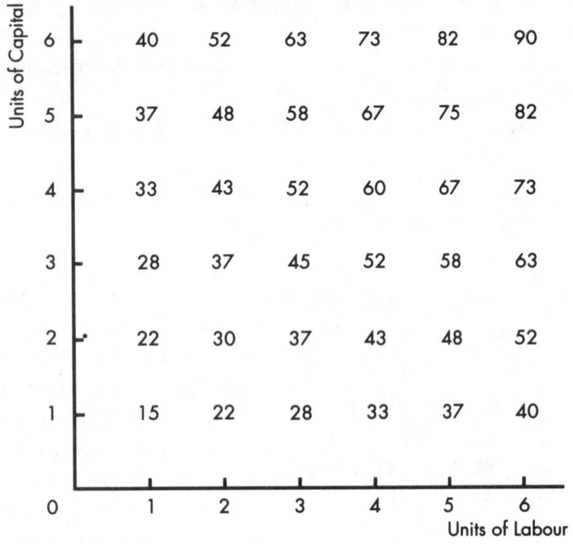

a) On a graph, identify 4 points on the isoquant for 37 earmuffs and 4 points on the isoquant for 52 earmuffs. Using these points, sketch the two isoquants.
b) Assuming that output is kept at 37 earmuffs per day, calculate the marginal rate of substitution of capital for labour if labour increases from
   i) 1 to 2 units.
   ii) 2 to 3 units.
   iii) 3 to 5 units.
c) Is this consistent with the law of diminishing marginal rate of substitution?

2) Suppose that the price of labour (P_L) is \$8 per unit and the price of capital (P_K) is \$12 per unit.
a) What is the absolute value of the slope of an isocost line?
b) Table 11.1 gives the combinations of labour and capital that produce 37 earmuffs per day. They are the 4 points indicated on the relevant isoquant in problem 1. Compute the total cost of producing 37 earmuffs for each combination and then complete the column labelled *Total Cost I* assuming the prices given are P_L = \$8, P_K = \$12. Which combination of labour and capital provides the least-cost technique for producing 37 earmuffs per day?

Table 11.1 Input Combinations for Producing 37 Earmuffs

Earmuffs (units)	Labour (units)	Capital (units)	Total Cost I (\$)	Total Cost II (\$)	Total Cost III (\$)
37	1	5			
37	2	3			
37	3	2			
37	5	1			

3) Now, suppose the price of labour increases to \$12 per unit and the price of capital decreases to \$8 per unit.
a) What is the absolute value of the slope of a new isocost line? How does this compare to the slope of an isocost line in Problem 2?
b) Compute the total cost of producing 37 earmuffs using these new prices and complete the column of Figure 11.5 labelled *Total Cost II.*
c) Which combination of labour and capital now provides the least-cost technique for producing 37 earmuffs per day? How does this compare with your answer to problem 2(b)?

4) Finally, suppose the prices of labour and capital both double to P_L = \$24 per unit and P_K = \$16 per unit.
a) What is the absolute value of the slope of an isocost line? How does this compare to the slope of an isocost line in problem 3?
b) Compute the total cost of producing 37 earmuffs using these prices and complete the column of Table 11.1 labelled *Total Cost III.*
c) Which combination of labour and capital provides the least-cost technique for producing 37 earmuffs per day? How does this compare with your answer to 3(c)?

5) In country *A* the price of labour is \$8 per unit and the price of capital is \$8 per unit. In country *B*, the price of labour is \$4 per unit and the price of capital is \$8. Country *B* is a "low-wage" country. Consider the production problem faced by two firms, one in each

country, which produce the same good. Firm 1 is in country *A* and firm 2 is in country *B*. Both firms have access to the same production technology, and therefore, they have the same production function.

a) Draw a graph of an isoquant and isocost line for firm 1 which illustrates the least-cost production technique for some level of output.
b) Now consider firm 2. Since both firms have the same production function, their isoquants are identical. On the same graph as in part (a), illustrate the least-cost production technique for firm 2 producing the same level of output.
c) Using the graph you have constructed, show that the combination of labour and capital used by
   i) firm 1 is more expensive than the combination used by firm 2 when the price of labour is as in country *B*.
   ii) firm 2 is more expensive than the combination used by firm 1 when the price of labour is as in country *A*.

ANSWERS

CONCEPT REVIEW

1) intensity
2) marginal product
3) marginal rate of substitution
4) falls; labour
5) isoquant; magnitude; slope
6) isocost; steeper
7) least-cost; equals
8) labour; capital
9) labour; capital

TRUE OR FALSE

1) F	7) F	13) T	19) T
2) T	8) T	14) T	20) F
3) F	9) F	15) T	21) T
4) F	10) T	16) F	
5) T	11) T	17) F	
6) F	12) F	18) T	

MULTIPLE-CHOICE

1) b	6) b	11) a	16) e
2) d	7) a	12) d	17) a
3) a	8) c	13) b	18) b
4) c	9) b	14) a	19) d
5) b	10) d	15) d	20) c

SHORT ANSWER

1) The law of diminishing marginal rate of substitution states that the marginal rate of substitution of capital for labour will decrease as the quantity of capital decreases and the quantity of labour increases. This means that as we move down an isoquant, the magnitude of the decline in capital for each unit increase in labour will decrease. In other words, the isoquant will become flatter and flatter as capital decreases and labour increases. Thus the isoquant will be bowed toward the origin.

2) If $MP_L/MP_K > P_L/P_K$, we know that MP_L/MP_K is too large to minimize cost. This implies that a firm should increase the quantity of labour it uses and reduce the quantity of capital. Since the marginal product of an input declines as the quantity of the input increases, the increase in labour will decrease MP_L and the decrease in capital will increase MP_K. This means that MP_L/MP_K will decline, which is the desired result in order to make the ratio of marginal products equal to the ratio of prices.

3) If a firm is using its least-cost production technique and the price of labour rises, the firm will engage in input substitution. The rise in the price of labour makes $MP_L/MP_K < P_L/P_K$. Thus, the firm will decrease the use of labour (since its price has increased) and increase the use of capital. This will increase the marginal product of labour and decrease the marginal product of capital so that the ratio MP_L/MP_K will increase until it equals P_L/P_K.

4) Capital intensity, the ratio of capital to labour is determined by the isoquant curves and isocost lines. Different industries in a given country are likely to face the same prices for inputs so isocost lines will be the same. However, the production functions for different products will generally be different, which means that isoquants and input combinations (capital intensity) will vary across industries.

5) In general, the same industry in different countries has the same technologies available to it and so the isoquants will be similar. However, the price of labour (wages) varies widely across countries. Thus, isocost lines will be flatter in "low-wage" countries, which means that such countries will use less capital-intensive production techniques.

PROBLEMS

1) a) Figure 11.5 represents the isoquants for 37 and 52 earmuffs per day. The points from Figure 11.4 on page 126 are indicated on each curve.

Figure 11.5

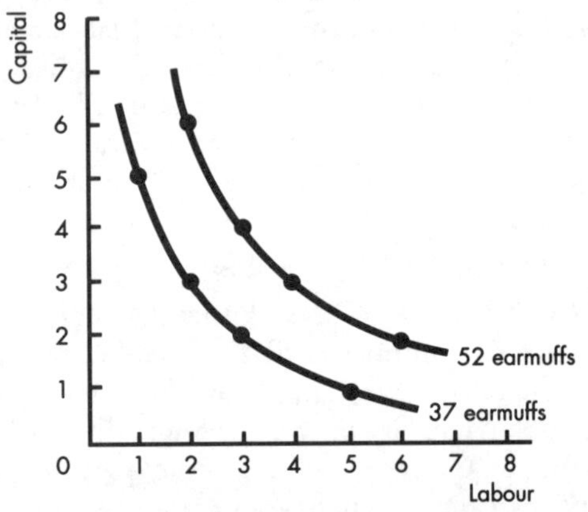

b) The marginal rate of substitution of capital for labour is the decrease in capital needed per unit increase in labour in order to keep output constant at 37 earmuffs per day.

i) If labour increases from 1 to 2 units, capital must decrease from 5 to 3 units. Thus, the marginal rate of substitution of capital for labour is 2.

ii) If labour increases from 2 to 3 units, capital must decrease from 3 to 2 units. Thus, the marginal rate of substitution of capital for labour is 1.

iii) If labour increases from 3 to 5 units, capital must decrease from 2 to 1 unit. Thus, the marginal rate of substitution of capital for labour is 1/2.

c) Since the marginal rate of substitution of capital for labour falls as capital decreases and labour increases (moving down the isoquant), this is consistent with the law of diminishing marginal rate of substitution.

2) a) The absolute value of the slope of the isocost line is the ratio of the price of labour to the price of capital, which is 2/3.

b) The column labelled *Total Cost I* is shown completed here. The total cost is given by $TC = \$8 \times L + \$12 \times K$ evaluated at each combination of L and K. The least-cost technique uses 3 units of labour and 2 units of capital for a total cost of $48.

Table 11.1 Solution: Input Combinations for Producing 37 Earmuffs

Earmuffs (units)	Labour (units)	Capital (units)	Total Cost I ($)	Total Cost II ($)	Total Cost III ($)
37	1	5	68	52	104
37	2	3	52	48	96
37	3	2	48	52	104
37	5	1	52	68	136

3) a) The absolute value of the slope of the new isocost line is given by $P_L/P_K = 3/2$. Since the relative price of labour has risen, the isocost line has become steeper.

b) The column labelled *Total Cost II* is completed in Table 11.1 Solution.

c) As can be readily ascertained by looking at the *Total Cost II* column in Table 11.1 Solution, the least-cost technique is the one using 2 units of labour and 3 units of capital. Total cost is $48.

4) a) The absolute value of the slope of an isocost line is given by $P_L/P_K = 3/2$. Doubling both prices leaves the relative price unchanged. Thus the isocost line's slope remains unchanged.

b) The column labelled *Total Cost III* is completed in Table 11.1 Solution.

c) Looking at the *Total Cost III* column in Table 11.1 Solution tells us that the least-cost technique uses 2 units of labour and 3 units of capital. While the input combination remains unchanged, total cost has doubled to $96. This illustrates that the least-cost combination of inputs depends on the *relative* prices of inputs, not on their absolute prices.

5) a) See Figure 11.6 shown here. The isoquant for the chosen level of output is given by the curve labelled *Q*. Since firm 1 is in country *A*, where the price of labour and capital are the same ($8 per unit), the slope of isocost lines is 1 in absolute value. The least-cost isocost line for firm 1 is given by the line labelled *AA*, which is tangent to the isoquant at point *a*. Thus, for firm 1, the least-cost input combination is L_1 units of labour and K_1 units of capital.

Figure 11.6

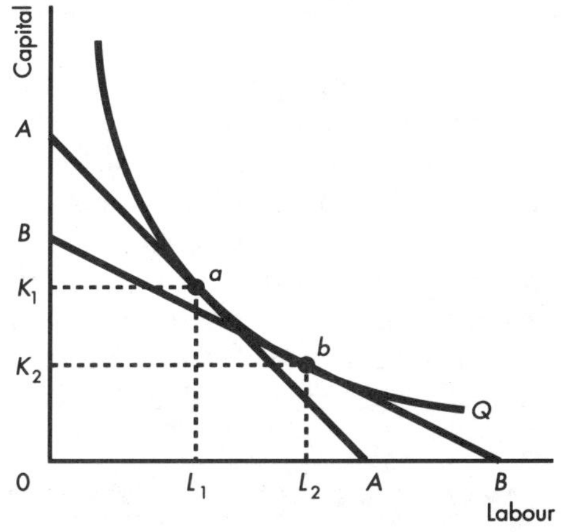

b) See Figure 11.6. The isoquant for firm 2 is the same as for firm 1 and is the curve labelled *Q*. Since firm 2 is in country *B*, where the price of labour ($4 per unit) is one half of the price of capital ($8 per unit), the slope of its isocost lines is 1/2 in absolute value. The least-cost isocost for firm 2 is given by the line labelled *BB*, which is tangent to the isocost at point *b*. Thus, for firm 2, the least-cost combination is L_2 units of labour and K_2 units of capital.

c) i) We know that when input prices are as in country *B*, all isocost lines will have the absolute value of the slope equal to 1/2 and be parallel to line *BB*. Note that point *a*, corresponding to the input combination used by firm 1 lies above the *BB* isocost line and therefore must lie on a higher isocost line. This means that the input combination represented by point *a* is more costly than the input combination represented by point *b*.

ii) The argument here is essentially the same except that now all relevant isocost lines will have a slope in absolute value of 1 and be parallel to line *AA*. Point *b* lies above the *AA* isocost line and therefore must lie on a higher isocost line. This means that the input combination represented by point *b* is more costly than the input combination represented by point *a*.

Chapter 12 **Competition**

Chapter in Perspective

Text Pages 281–314

This chapter combines the cost information of Chapters 9 and 10 with new revenue information in order to analyze the profit-maximization decision of firms in a perfectly competitive market. The analysis includes derivations of both the individual firm supply curve and industry supply curve. While we have previously simply assumed that supply curves are upward sloping, this chapter derives upward-sloping supply curves as a prediction of the theory of perfect competition. The theory also allows us to make precise predictions about the behaviour of firms and their responses to changes in market conditions. Although perfect competition does not occur frequently in the real world, the theory allows us to isolate the effects of competitive forces, which are at work in *all* markets, even in those that do not match the assumptions of the theory of perfect competition.

Learning Objectives

After studying this chapter, you will be able to:

- **Define perfect competition.**
- **Explain why a perfectly competitive firm cannot influence the market price.**
- **Explain how a competitive industry's output changes when price changes.**
- **Explain why firms sometimes shut down temporarily and lay off workers.**
- **Explain why firms enter and leave an industry.**
- **Predict the effects on an industry and on a typical firm of a change in demand and of a technological advance.**
- **Explain why farmers have had such a bad time in recent years.**
- **Explain why perfect competition is efficient.**

Helpful Hints

1) Although perfectly competitive markets are quite rare in the real world, there are three important reasons to develop a thorough understanding of their behaviour.

First, many markets quite closely approximate perfectly competitive markets. Thus, the analysis developed in this chapter gives direct and useful insights into the behaviour of these markets.

Second, the theory of perfect competition allows us to isolate the effects of competitive forces, which are at work in *all* markets, even in those that do not match the assumptions of perfect competition.

Third, the perfectly competitive model serves as a useful benchmark against which to evaluate relative allocative efficiency.

2) In the short run, a perfectly competitive firm cannot change the scale of its plant — it has fixed inputs. The firm also is a price, taker; it always sells at the market price which it cannot influence. Thus, the only variable that the firm controls is its level of output. The short-run condition for profit maximization is to choose the level of output at which marginal revenue equals marginal cost. This is a general condition which, as we will see in subsequent chapters, applies to other market structures such as monopoly and monopolistic competition. Since, for the perfectly competitive firm, marginal revenue is equal to price, this profit-maximizing condition takes a particular form; choose the level of output at which price is equal to marginal cost ($P = MC$).

3) Many students have trouble understanding why a firm continues to operate at the breakeven point, where economic profits are zero. The key to understanding lies in the definition of which costs are included in the average total cost curve. Recall from Chapter 9 that a firm's total costs are defined by the economist as *opportunity costs*, which include both explicit costs and *imputed costs*.

Imputed costs include the owners'/investors' forgone interest, forgone rent, and forgone income. Therefore, at the breakeven point where total revenue equals total cost (or, equivalently, average revenue equals average total cost), the owners/investors of the firm are earning a return on their investment, which is equal to the best return that they could earn elsewhere. That is the definition of opportunity cost — the best alternative forgone. Economists sometimes refer to these imputed costs or best alternative return on investment as "normal profits." As the phrase implies, these are profits that could normally be earned in any other industry. At the breakeven point, the firm is earning "normal profits" even though its economic profits (sometimes called "extra-normal profits") are zero. In earning "normal profits," the firm is earning just as much profit as it could anywhere else, and is therefore totally content to continue producing in this industry.

4) When the price of output falls below the breakeven point, but is above the shutdown point, the firm will continue to produce even though it is making economic losses. In this price range, the firm is no longer earning "normal profits" and theoretically could earn more by switching to another industry. Nonetheless, the firm will continue to operate in this industry in the short run because switching has costs. In order to switch industries, the firm must shut down, which entails losing its total fixed costs.

As long as the price is above the shutdown point (minimum average variable cost), however, a firm will decide to produce since it will be covering total variable cost and part of total fixed cost. Thus its loss will be less if it continues to produce at the output where $P = MC$ than if it shuts down.

If the price falls below the shutdown point, a firm which produces output will not only lose its total fixed costs, it will lose additional money on every unit of output produced, since average revenue is less than average variable cost. Thus, when the price is less than average variable cost, the firm will choose to minimize its loss by shutting down.

5) In the long run, fixed costs disappear and the firm can switch between industries and change scale of plant without cost. Economic profits serve as the signal for the movement or reallocation of firm resources until long-run equilibrium is achieved. Firms will move out of industries with negative economic profits and into industries with positive economic profits. Only when economic profits are zero will there be no tendency for firms to exit or enter industries.

The fact that there are no restrictions on entry into the industry is what assures that economic profits will be zero and that firms will be producing at the minimum of their long-run average cost curves in long-run equilibrium.

6) In long-run equilibrium, three conditions are satisfied for each firm in an industry:
   i) $MR = P = MC$. This implies that profits are maximized for each firm.
   ii) $P = ATC$. This implies that economic profits are zero and each firm is just earning "normal profits."
   iii) $P =$ minimum $LRAC$. This implies that production takes place at the point of minimum long-run average cost.

Key Figures

Figure 12.2 Total Revenue, Total Cost, and Profit, text page 288
Profit is defined as total revenue minus total cost. In part (a) of this figure, the total revenue and total cost curves are both illustrated. Profit is the vertical distance between them; a positive profit when total revenue lies above total cost and a loss when total revenue lies below total cost. This difference is plotted against output as the profit curve in the graph in part (b). It is easy to see that, in the example, profit is a maximum when 9 sweaters are produced.

Figure 12.3 Marginal Revenue, Marginal Cost, and Profit-Maximizing Output, text page 289
This figure illustrates the alternative profit maximizing condition: marginal revenue (*MR*) equals marginal cost (*MC*). Producing and selling one more unit of a good (sweaters in the example) adds both to revenue and to cost. If the addition to revenue (*MR*) is greater than the addition to cost (*MC*), then profit will increase and the additional unit should be produced.

If, on the other hand, marginal revenue is less than marginal cost, profit will decrease and the additional unit should not be produced. Therefore, a profit-maximizing firm should produce each unit up to the point at which marginal revenue equals marginal cost.

This is illustrated with a table and corresponding graph for the example of Swanky, Inc. Producing each of the first up to the ninth sweater adds to profit ($MR > MC$) but the tenth sweater decreases profit ($MR < MC$). Nine sweaters is the profit-maximizing output at which the profit-maximizing condition, $MR = MC$, holds. Since, for a perfectly competitive firm, $MR = P$, the profit maximizing condition can also be expressed as the output at which $P = MC$.

Figure 12.5 Swanky's Supply Curve, text page 293
Part (a) of the figure derives Swanky's supply curve by asking: How much will Swanky, a profit-maximizing firm, produce at given prices? This, of course is exactly what a supply curve tells us.

Since the profit maximizing condition is $P = MC$, Swanky's supply curve is the same as its marginal cost curve as long as the price is above minimum average variable cost. For any price below minimum average variable cost, Swanky will minimize its losses by shutting down and producing nothing. As a result, the firm's supply curve becomes vertical at zero output for prices below minimum average variable cost.

When drawing graphs we usually ignore this vertical section of the supply curve. The most important section of the supply curve is the upward-sloping section corresponding to the portion of the marginal cost curve above minimum average variable cost.

Figure 12.6 Firm and Industry Supply Curves, text page 294
The relationship between the firm and industry supply curves is straightforward. The industry supply curve is obtained by summing horizontally the individual supply curves of all of the firms in the industry. For a given price, this means moving horizontally to each individual firm's supply curve, reading off the quantity supplied, and summing these quantities. In the case of an industry where all firms are identical, this is equivalent to reading off one firm's quantity supplied and multiplying by the number of firms to get the industry's quantity supplied.

Since the individual firm supply curve is the same as its marginal cost curve above minimum average variable cost, the industry supply curve is the horizontal sum of these marginal cost curves. Below minimum average variable cost, the industry supply curve is vertical at an output of zero. As in text Figure 12.5 on page 293, the upward-sloping section of the supply curve is most important, and we usually ignore the vertical section.

Figure 12.13 Long-Run Price and Quantity Changes, text page 302
This figure illustrates three alternative relationships between price and quantity supplied in the long-run. Starting in long-run equilibrium, suppose there is an increase in demand. The question here is: In the long run, does the price of the good rise, fall, or remain the same?

In the short run, as industry demand increases, the price will rise and profit maximizing firms will employ more variable inputs and increase output. Thus, the industry short-run supply curve is positively sloped since it is the horizontal sum of positively-sloped firm supply curves (firm *MC* curves). But, the increase in price will cause profits to increase, and thus new firms will be attracted into the industry. This will shift the industry supply curve to the right.

When long-run equilibrium is restored (zero economic profits), the question becomes: Is the intersection of the new demand and new supply curves at a price that is higher, lower, or equal to the original price?

In industries where costs increase as output increases (external diseconomies), the long-run price will be higher. In industries where costs decrease as output increases (external economies), the long-run price will be lower. And in industries where costs remain unchanged as output increases (no external economies or diseconomies), the long-run price will remain unchanged.

Figure 12.16 Allocative Efficiency, text page 308
Allocative efficiency is achieved when marginal social benefit (*MSB*) equals marginal social cost (*MSC*). Additional output adds both to social benefit and social cost.

If the addition to social benefit (*MSB*) is greater than the addition to social cost (*MSC*), the additional unit should be produced.

If the marginal social benefit of an additional unit of output is less than the marginal social cost, it should not be produced. Allocative efficiency occurs at output Q^*, where $MSB = MSC$.

If there are no external costs or benefits, the perfectly competitive industry supply curve is the marginal social cost curve and the industry demand curve is the marginal social benefit curve. Thus the competitive market equilibrium will achieve allocative efficiency.

SELF-TEST

CONCEPT REVIEW

1) Perfect competition occurs in a market under the following conditions.
   a) There are _______________ firms, each selling a(n) _______________ product.
   b) There are _______________ buyers.
   c) There are no restrictions on _______________ into the industry.

2) A firm in a perfectly competitive market is said to be a price _______________ since it cannot influence the price of the good it produces. Such a firm faces a demand curve that is perfectly _______________.

3) We assume that the firm's single objective is to maximize its _______________.

4) Total revenue divided by the total quantity sold is called _______________ _______________. The change in revenue resulting from a one-unit increase in the quantity sold is called _______________ _______________.

5) In the case of perfect competition, average revenue and marginal revenue are both equal to _______________.

6) An output at which total cost equals total revenue is called a _______________ point. The point at which a firm's maximum profit (minimum loss) is the same regardless of whether the firm produces any output or not is called the _______________ point.

7) Profit is maximized when marginal revenue equals _______________ _______________.

8) Market price is determined by _______________ demand and _______________ supply.

9) In the range of prices greater than the minimum average variable cost, a perfectly competitive firm's supply curve is the same as its _______________ _______________ curve. At prices below minimum average variable cost, the firm will produce _______________ and make a loss equal to its _______________ _______________ _______________.

10) New firms will enter a perfectly competitive industry if firms in the industry are making economic _______________. As new firms enter the industry, the price will _______________. If economic _______________ are being made, firms will tend to exit the industry.

11) Long-run equilibrium occurs in a perfectly competitive industry when economic profits are _______________. Each firm will also be producing at the _______________ point of its long-run average cost curve.

12) Factors beyond the control of an individual firm that lower its cost as industry output increases are called _______________ _______________. Factors beyond the control of an individual firm that raise its costs as industry output increases are called _______________ _______________.

13) _______________ _______________ occurs when no one can be made better off without making someone else worse off.

14) Costs that are not borne by the producer but are borne by other members of society are called _______________ _______________. Benefits which accrue to people other than the buyer of a good are called _______________ _______________.

TRUE OR FALSE

_____ 1) In a perfectly competitive industry no single firm can exert a significant effect on the market price of a good.

_____ 2) In a perfectly competitive industry there are no restrictions on entry into the industry.

_____ 3) The demand curve facing a firm in a perfectly competitive industry is essentially perfectly inelastic.

_____ 4) The industry demand curve in a perfectly competitive industry is horizontal.

_____ 5) The objective of firms in a competitive industry is to maximize revenue.

_____ 6) The average revenue curve and marginal revenue curve are the same as the firm's demand curve in a perfectly competitive industry.

_____ 7) If marginal revenue is greater than marginal cost, a firm can increase profit by decreasing output.

_____ 8) Firms can make losses in the long run but not the short run.

_____ 9) A firm is breaking even if its economic profit is zero.

_____ 10) If the price is below the minimum average total cost, a firm will shut down.

_____ 11) In the price range above minimum average variable cost, the perfectly competitive firm's supply curve is the same as the marginal revenue curve.

_____ 12) The supply curve of a perfectly competitive firm gives the quantities of output supplied at alternative prices as long as the firm earns economic profits.

_____ 13) All firms in a competitive market will be maximizing profit in short-run equilibrium.

_____ 14) The short-run industry supply curve is obtained as the horizontal sum of the supply curves of the individual firms.

_____ 15) In long-run equilibrium, each firm in a perfectly competitive industry will be making zero economic profit.

_____ 16) The entry of new firms into an industry will increase the price and increase the profit of each firm.

_____ 17) In long-run equilibrium, each firm in a perfectly competitive industry will choose the scale of plant associated with the minimum long-run average cost.

_____ 18) If, in a competitive industry, there are external economies, the long-run industry supply curve will be positively sloped.

_____ 19) Suppose a competitive industry is in long-run equilibrium when a new technology is invented. During the adjustment to a new long-run equilibrium, some firms will be making economic profits while others will be experiencing economic losses.

_____ 20) Suppose a competitive industry is in long-run equilibrium when there is a substantial increase in total fixed costs. All firms will now be making economic losses and some firms will go out of business.

_____ 21) If a firm is economically efficient, then it must be allocatively efficient.

_____ 22) A firm is economically efficient if it is maximizing profit.

_____ 23) When the quantity of a good bought by a consumer at a given price is a point on the demand curve, consumer efficiency has occurred.

_____ 24) Allocative efficiency occurs when marginal social benefit is greater than marginal social cost.

_____ 25) A perfectly competitive industry will achieve allocative efficiency if there are no external costs or external benefits.

MULTIPLE-CHOICE

1) Which of the following is *not* a characteristic of a perfectly competitive industry?
   a) downward-sloping industry demand curve
   b) perfectly elastic demand curve for each individual firm
   c) each firm decides its quantity of output
   d) slightly differentiated products
   e) many firms each supplying a small fraction of industry supply

2) If a firm faces a perfectly elastic demand for its product, then
   a) it is not a price taker.
   b) it will want to lower its price to increase sales.
   c) it will want to raise its price to increase total revenue.
   d) its marginal revenue curve is equal to the price of the product.
   e) it will always earn zero economic profits.

3) A perfectly competitive firm is maximizing profit if
   a) marginal cost equals price and price is above minimum average variable cost.
   b) marginal cost equals price and price is above minimum average fixed cost.
   c) total revenue is at a maximum.
   d) average variable cost is at a minimum.
   e) average total cost is at a minimum.

4) Mugs can be produced from labour alone. Table 12.1 shows two output/input combinations.

Table 12.1

Mugs	Labour-Hours
25	4
27	5

If the price of a mug is $100 and labour costs $50/hour, what is the marginal cost of production in this range of output?
a) $25
b) $40
c) $50
d) $100
e) none of the above

5) In which of the following situations will a perfectly competitive firm earn economic profits?
a) $MR > AVC$
b) $MR > ATC$
c) $ATC > MC$
d) $ATC > AR$
e) $AR > AVC$

6) The maximum loss a firm will experience in the short run is equal to
a) zero.
b) total costs.
c) total variable costs.
d) total fixed costs.
e) none of the above.

7) In the price range below minimum average variable cost, a perfectly competitive firm's supply curve is
a) horizontal at the market price.
b) vertical at zero output.
c) the same as its marginal cost curve.
d) the same as its average variable cost curve.
e) none of the above.

8) The short-run industry supply curve is
a) the horizontal sum of the individual firm's supply curves.
b) the vertical sum of the individual firm's supply curves.
c) vertical at the total level of output being produced by all firms.
d) horizontal at the current market price.
e) none of the above.

9) If profits are being made by firms in a competitive industry, new firms will enter. This will initially shift
a) the industry demand curve to the left, causing market price to fall.
b) the industry demand curve to the right, causing market price to rise.
c) the industry supply curve to the left, causing market price to rise.
d) the industry supply curve to the right, causing market price to fall.
e) none of the above curves.

10) The supply curve for an individual firm in a perfectly competitive industry is $P = 1 + 2Q_S$. If the industry consists of 100 identical firms, then what is industry supply when $P = 7$?
a) 300
b) 400
c) 600
d) 800
e) none of the above

11) If a perfectly competitive firm in the short run is able to pay its variable costs and part, but not all, of its fixed costs, then it is operating in the range on its marginal cost curve that is
a) above the breakeven point.
b) below the breakeven point.
c) above the shutdown point.
d) below the shutdown point.
e) between the shutdown and breakeven points.

12) In a perfectly competitive industry of 100 firms, the demand curve facing the individual firm
a) has unitary elasticity.
b) is identical to the industry demand curve.
c) is 1/100 of the industry demand curve.
d) is one where $AR = MR$.
e) is none of the above.

13) In a perfectly competitive industry, the market price is $10. An individual firm is producing the output at which $MC = ATC = \$15$. AVC at that output is $10. What should the firm do to maximize its short-run profits?
a) shut down
b) expand output
c) contract output
d) leave output unchanged
e) insufficient information to answer

14) In a perfectly competitive industry, the market price is $5. An individual firm is producing the level of output at which marginal cost is $5 and is increasing, and average total cost is $25. What should the firm do to maximize its short-run profits?
a) shut down
b) expand output
c) contract output
d) leave output unchanged
e) insufficient information to answer

15) If a profit maximizing firm in perfect competition is earning economic profits, then it must be producing a level of output where
a) price is greater than marginal cost.
b) price is greater than marginal revenue.
c) marginal cost is greater than marginal revenue.
d) marginal cost is greater than average total cost.
e) average total cost is greater than marginal cost.

16) A firm in a perfectly competitive industry is maximizing its short-run profits by producing 500 units of output. At 500 units of output, which of the following *must be false*?
a) $MC < AVC$
b) $MC < ATC$
c) $MC > ATC$
d) $AR < ATC$
e) $AR > AVC$

17) The maximum loss a firm will experience in long-run equilibrium is
a) zero.
b) its total cost.
c) its total variable cost.
d) its average total cost.
e) none of the above.

18) When economic profits are zero,
a) the product will not be produced in the short run.
b) the product will not be produced in the long run.
c) firms will leave the industry.
d) revenues are not covering imputed costs.
e) none of the above will occur.

19) For a perfectly competitive firm in long-run equilibrium, which of the following is *not* equal to price?
a) short-run average total cost
b) short-run average variable cost
c) short-run marginal cost
d) long-run average cost
e) average revenue

20) A perfectly competitive industry is in short-run equilibrium with price below average total cost. Which of the following is *not* a prediction of the long-run consequences of such a situation?
a) Price will increase.
b) The output of the industry will increase.
c) Firms will leave the industry.
d) The output of each existing firm will increase.
e) Economic profits will be zero.

21) The long-run competitive industry supply curve will be positively sloped if there are
a) external economies.
b) external diseconomies.
c) no external economies or diseconomies.
d) external costs.
e) external benefits.

22) Which of the following is *not* true of a new long-run equilibrium resulting from a new technology in a perfectly competitive industry?
a) Price will be lower.
b) Industry output will be greater.
c) Firm profits will be greater.
d) All firms in the industry will be using the new technology.
e) Average total cost will be lower.

23) If an industry experiences external economies as the industry expands in the long run, the long-run industry supply curve will
a) be perfectly inelastic.
b) be perfectly elastic.
c) have a positive slope.
d) have a negative slope.
e) have allocative inefficiency.

24) Under which of the following circumstances would a long-run equilibrium in a perfectly competitive industry *not* be allocatively efficient?
a) firms are price takers
b) new technologies are developed
c) external economies or external diseconomies are present
d) external costs or external benefits are present
e) free entry to the industry

SHORT ANSWER

1) Why will a firm in a perfectly competitive industry choose *not* to charge a price either above or below the market price?

2) Why is the perfectly competitive firm's supply curve the same as the marginal cost curve above minimum average variable cost?

3) Why will economic profits be zero in long-run equilibrium in a perfectly competitive industry?

4) Suppose we observe a perfectly competitive industry in a long-run equilibrium when there is a permanent *decrease* in demand for the product produced by the industry. Assume that there are no external economies or diseconomies. How does the industry adjust to a new long-run equilibrium? What happens to price, industry quantity traded, firm profits, and the number of firms during the adjustment process?

5) Suppose output is at a level such that marginal social benefit is greater than marginal social cost. Explain why this level of output is allocatively *inefficient.*

PROBLEMS

1) a) Table 12.2 gives the total cost structure for one of many identical firms in a perfectly competitive industry. Complete the table by computing total variable cost, average total cost, average variable cost, and marginal cost at each level of output. (Remember, as in the problems in *Study Guide*, Chapter 10, marginal cost should be entered midway between rows.)

Table 12.2

Quantity (units per day)	Total Cost (dollars)	Total Variable Cost (dollars)	Average Total Cost (dollars)	Average Variable Cost (dollars)	Marginal Cost (dollars)
0	12				
					...
1	24				
					...
2	32				
					...
3	42				
					...
4	54				
					...
5	68				
					...
6	84				

b) Complete Table 12.3 by computing the profit (per day) for the firm at each level of output if the price of output is $9, $11, or $15.

c) Consider the profit-maximizing output decision of the firm at alternative prices. How much will the firm produce if the price of output is $9? $11? $15? Explain each of your answers.

Table 12.3

Quantity (units per day)	Profit $P = \$9$	Profit $P = \$11$	Profit $P = \$15$
0			
1			
2			
3			
4			
5			
6			

2) A firm will maximize profit if it produces every unit of output for which marginal revenue exceeds marginal cost. This is sometimes called the marginal approach to profit maximization. Using the marginal approach, determine the profit-maximizing level of output for the firm of problem 1 when the price of output is $15. How does your answer here compare with your answer in 1(c)?

3) This problem concerns a hypothetical pottery manufacturing firm that produces ceramic mugs for sale in a purely competitive market. With a plant of given size, the firm can turn out the quantities of ceramic mugs shown in Table 12.4, by varying the amount it uses of a single variable input, labour.

Table 12.4

Number of Mugs	Labour-Hours (per day)
20	6.50
40	11.50
60	14.50
80	17.50
100	20.50
120	23.75
140	27.50
160	32.00
180	37.50
200	44.50
220	53.50
240	65.00
260	79.50
280	97.50

Suppose the firm can hire all the labour it would ever want at the going wage of $8 per labour-hour. The firm's total fixed costs are $64 per day.

a) Draw a table showing output, total variable cost (*TVC*), total cost (*TC*), average variable cost (*AVC*), average total cost (*ATC*), and marginal cost (*MC*). (Remember that marginal cost should be entered midway between rows of output.)

b) On a graph with *Mugs (per day)* on the horizontal axis, draw the three "per-unit" cost curves, *AVC*, *ATC*, and *MC*. (Note that the marginal cost values from your table should be plotted on the graph *midway* between the corresponding units of output.)

c) Consider (separately) the following alternative market prices that the firm might face: $P = \$3.20$, $P = \$2$, $P = \$1.65$, $P = \$1.40$. Assuming that the firm wants to maximize its profit, for *each* of the above prices, answer the following:
   i) Approximately how many mugs per day would the firm produce? How do you know?
   ii) Is the firm making a profit at that price? And if so, approximately how much?

d) Suppose that the ceramic pottery mug industry consists of 60 firms, each identical to the single firm discussed above. On another graph, draw the industry short-run supply curve.

e) The industry demand schedule for ceramic pottery mugs is given by the equation

$$P = 7.36 - 0.0004Q_D$$

where P is the price of a mug in dollars and Q_D is the quantity demanded per day. Table 12.5 represents some points on the demand schedule.

Table 12.5

Price (dollars)	Q_D
1.00	15,900
1.60	14,400
2.20	12,900
2.80	11,400
3.40	9,900
4.00	8,400
4.60	6,900
5.20	5,400
5.80	3,900
6.40	2,400
7.00	900

   i) Plot the industry demand curve on the same graph as the industry supply curve of part (d).
   ii) What is the short-run equilibrium price of ceramic pottery mugs?
   iii) Is the ceramic pottery mug industry in long-run equilibrium? Explain your answer.

4) A perfectly competitive industry has 100 identical firms in the short run, each of which has the short-run cost curves (costs in dollars) listed in Table 12.6.

Table 12.6

Output (units)	Average Total Cost (dollars)	Average Variable Cost (dollars)	Marginal Cost (dollars)
11	20.5	13.1	
			... 12
12	19.8	13.0	
			... 14
13	19.3	13.1	
			... 16
14	19.1	13.3	
			... 18
15	19.0	13.6	
			... 20
16	19.1	14.0	
			... 22
17	19.2	14.5	
			... 24
18	19.5	15.0	
			... 26
19	19.8	15.6	
			... 28
20	20.3	16.2	
			... 30
21	20.7	16.9	

This short-run average total cost curve touches the long-run average cost curve at the minimum point on the long run average cost curve as in text Figure 12.10 on page 298. The industry demand schedule in the long and the short run is given by the equation $P = 43 - 0.01Q_D$ where P is the price of output in dollars and Q_D is the quantity demanded in the relevant time period. Table 12.7 represents some points on the demand schedule.

Table 12.7

Price (dollars)	Q_D
11	3,200
13	3,000
15	2,800
17	2,600
19	2,400
21	2,200
23	2,000
25	1,800
27	1,600
29	1,400
31	1,200

a) What is the quantity of output corresponding to the firm's breakeven point? the shutdown point? Explain your answers.
b) What is the short-run equilibrium price in this market? Show how you found your answer.
c) What amount of profit or loss is being made by each firm at the short-run equilibrium price? Is this industry in long-run equilibrium at its present size? Why or why not?
d) Exactly how many firms will exist in this industry in the long run? Explain your answer. How much economic profit will each firm earn in the long run?
e) Return to the original short-run situation with 100 firms in the industry. The 100 firms now form an output-restriction cartel that imposes an upper limit of 14 units on the production of every firm. What will now be the market price, and what will be the profit or loss made by each firm? Is the cartel-imposed outcome likely to persist for any length of time? Why or why not?

5) a) Consider a perfectly competitive industry in long-run equilibrium. All the firms in the industry are identical. Draw a two-part graph illustrating the long-run equilibrium for the industry (part (a) on the left) and for the typical firm (part (b) on the right). The graph of the firm should include the *MC*, *ATC*, *MR*, and *LRAC* curves. Assume that the *LRAC* curve is U-shaped as it is in text Figure 12.10 on page 298. Label the equilibrium price P_0, the equilibrium industry quantity traded Q_0, and the output of the firm q_0.
b) Now, suppose there is a decline in industry demand. Using your graphs from part (a),
i) show what happens to market price, firm output, firm profits, and industry quantity traded in the short run. (Assume that the shutdown point is not reached.)
ii) show what happens to market price, firm output, firm profits, and industry quantity traded in the long run (assume that there are no external economies or diseconomies.) What has happened to the number of firms?

ANSWERS

CONCEPT REVIEW

1) many; identical; many; entry
2) taker; elastic (or horizontal)
3) profit
4) average revenue; marginal revenue
5) price
6) breakeven; shutdown
7) marginal cost
8) industry; industry
9) marginal cost; nothing; total fixed cost
10) profits; fall; losses
11) zero; minimum
12) external economies; external diseconomies
13) Allocative efficiency
14) external costs; external benefits

TRUE OR FALSE

1) T	6) T	11) F	16) F	21) F
2) T	7) F	12) F	17) T	22) T
3) F	8) F	13) T	18) F	23) T
4) F	9) T	14) T	19) T	24) F
5) F	10) F	15) T	20) T	25) T

MULTIPLE-CHOICE

1) d	7) b	13) c	19) b
2) d	8) a	14) e	20) b
3) a	9) d	15) d	21) b
4) a	10) a	16) a	22) c
5) b	11) e	17) a	23) d
6) d	12) d	18) e	24) d

SHORT ANSWER

1) If a firm in a perfectly competitive industry charged a price even slightly higher than the market price, it would lose all of its sales. Thus, it will not charge a price above the market price. Since it can sell all it wants at the market price, it would not be able to increase sales by lowering its price. Thus, it would not charge a price below the market price since this would decrease total revenue and hence profits.

2) A perfectly competitive firm will want to supply the quantity that will maximize profit. This is done by equating marginal revenue and marginal cost. Since marginal revenue is equal to price for a perfectly

competitive firm, the firm will produce the level of output at which price equals marginal cost. Since this is true for each price above minimum *AVC*, the firm's supply curve is the same as its marginal cost curve above minimum *AVC*. For prices below minimum *AVC*, the firm will maximize profit (actually minimize loss) by shutting down. The loss from shutting down will be equal to total fixed cost. If the firm continued to produce at a price below minimum *AVC*, its loss would exceed total fixed cost.

3) In a perfectly competitive industry, the existence of positive economic profits will attract the entry of new firms, which will shift the industry supply curve to the right, causing the market price to fall and firm profits to decline. This tendency will exist so long as there are positive economic profits. Similarly, the existence of economic losses will cause firms to exit from the industry, which will shift the industry supply curve to the left, causing the market price to rise and firm profits to rise (losses to decline). This tendency will exist as long as losses are being made. Thus, the only point of rest in the long run (the only equilibrium) is one in which economic profits are zero.

4) The decrease in market demand will cause the market price to fall. Since, in the initial long-run equilibrium, each firm was earning zero economic profit, the fall in price means that profits will fall and so firms will now be making losses. Since the decrease in demand is permanent, these losses will induce some firms to leave the industry. This will shift the industry supply curve to the left, causing an increase in market price. The increasing price will cause profits to increase for the remaining firms which means that their losses will decline. The exit of firms will continue until the losses are eliminated. If there are no external economies or diseconomies, since costs have not been affected by the decrease in demand, the price must continue rising until it reaches its original level in the new long-run equilibrium. The output of each firm will also equal its original level but the quantity traded at the industry level will be less because the number of firms has declined.

5) A level of output at which marginal social benefit is greater than marginal social cost is allocatively inefficient, because some people can be made better off without making anyone worse off if more is produced. Since the production of an additional unit of output will add more to social benefit than to social cost, those who bear the additional costs can be compensated out of the additional benefits (and thus be left no worse off) with some additional benefits left over (making those who receive the additional benefits better off).

PROBLEMS

1) a) Completed Table 12.2 is shown here as Table 12.2 Solution.

Table 12.2 Solution

Quantity (units per day)	Total Cost (dollars)	Total Variable Cost (dollars)	Average Total Cost (dollars)	Average Variable Cost (dollars)	Marginal Cost (dollars)
0	12	0	—	—	
					... 12
1	24	12	24.00	12.00	
					... 8
2	32	20	16.00	10.00	
					... 10
3	42	30	14.00	10.00	
					... 12
4	54	42	13.50	10.50	
					... 14
5	68	56	13.60	11.20	
					... 16
6	84	72	14.00	12.00	

b) Completed Table 12.3 is given here as Table 12.3 Solution. The values for profit are computed as total revenue minus total cost, where total revenue is price times quantity and total cost is given in Table 12.1.

Table 12.3 Solution

Quantity (units per day)	Profit P = \$9	Profit P = \$11	Profit P = \$15
0	−12	−12	−12
1	−15	−13	−9
2	−14	−10	−2
3	−15	−9	3
4	−18	−10	6
5	−23	−13	7
6	−30	−18	6

c) If the price is \$9, profit is maximized (actually loss is minimized) when the firm shuts down and produces zero units. If the firm chooses to produce, its loss will be at least \$14, which is greater than the fixed cost loss of \$12. Therefore the firm will minimize losses by shutting down. If the price is $11, the firm is still unable to make a positive economic profit. The loss is minimized (at $9) if the firm produces 3 units. At this price, all of variable cost and part of fixed cost can be recovered. At a price of $15, the firm will maximize profit (at $7) at an output of 5 units per day.

2) The marginal approach to profit maximization states that the firm should produce all units of output for which marginal revenue exceeds marginal cost. For a perfectly competitive firm, marginal revenue equals price, so the approach states (equivalently) that the firm should produce every unit for which price exceeds marginal cost. If the price of output is $15, we can see from Table 12.2 Solution that the firm should produce 5 units. Since the marginal cost of moving from the 4th to the 5th unit ($14) is less than price ($15), the 5th unit should be produced. The marginal cost of moving to the 6th unit ($16), however, is greater than price. It should not be produced. The answer obtained here is the same as the answer obtained in 1(c).

3) a) With only one variable input (labour), *TVC* (for any level of output) = (labour hours × wage rate). The requested table is Table 12.8.

Table 12.8

Output (per day)	*TVC* ($)	*TC* ($)	*AVC* ($)	*ATC* ($)	*MC* ($)
0	0	64	—	—	
20	52	116	2.60	5.80	... 2.60
40	92	156	2.30	3.90	... 2.00
60	116	180	1.93	3.00	... 1.20
80	140	204	1.75	2.55	... 1.20
100	104	228	1.64	2.28	... 1.20
120	190	254	1.58	2.12	... 1.30
140	220	284	1.57	2.03	... 1.50
160	256	320	1.60	2.00	... 1.80
180	300	364	1.67	2.02	... 2.20
200	356	420	1.78	2.10	... 2.80
220	428	492	1.95	2.24	... 3.60
240	520	584	2.17	2.43	... 4.60
260	636	700	2.45	2.69	... 5.80
280	780	844	2.79	3.01	... 7.20

b) The graph appears in Figure 12.1. It also illustrates the answers to part (c).

Figure 12.1

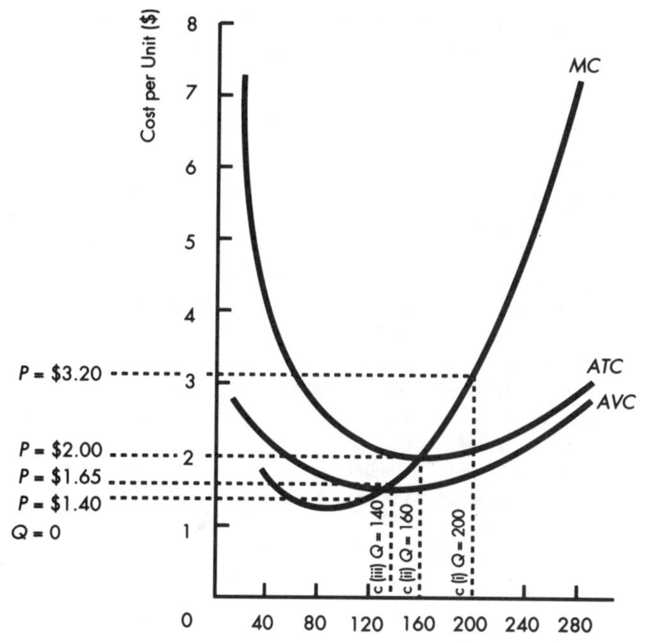

c) In every case, the output at which profit is a maximum is the output at which marginal revenue (which, for a price-taking firm in a perfectly competitive market, is the same as market price) is equal to marginal cost, provided that price is greater than average variable cost.

Profit "per unit of output" is the difference between average revenue (price) and average total cost at the level of output. Total profit is "per unit profit" × number of units of output. Economic profit might be zero or negative (a loss) and still be the best the firm can attain in the short run. The calculations of total profit at each price appear in Table 12.9 on page 142.

Table 12.9

Price ($)	Output Chosen	Per Unit Profit ($)	Total Profit ($)
3.20	200	1.10	220.00
2.00	160	0	0
1.65	140	−0.38	−53.20
1.40	0	0	−64.00

Note the following:

1. Marginal cost is \$3.20 at approximately 200 units.
2. The per unit profit is *P* − *ATC*.
3. An output of 160 units is the "breakeven" level of output, where *MC* = minimum *ATC* and the firm is just covering all its opportunity costs.
4. At an output of 140 units, the firm continues to produce in the short run because it can more than cover its variable costs. If it produced zero units, its loss would be greater, \$64, which is the amount of its fixed costs.
5. Any positive output increases losses when the price is below the shutdown price, which here is about \$1.57. When price is less than minimum *AVC*, the firm not only loses its fixed costs, it would also lose additional money on every unit it produced.

d) There are 60 identical price-taking firms. For every possible price (above minimum *AVC* of *approximately* about \$1.57), each firm will supply the quantity at which *P* = *MC*. We can derive (in Table 12.10) the industry supply schedule from the *MC* curve of an individual firm.

Table 12.10

Price ($)	Quantity Supplied by 1 Firm	Quantity Supplied by 60 Firms
1.57	134	8,040
1.80	150	9,000
2.20	170	10,200
2.80	190	11,400
3.60	210	12,600
4.60	230	13,800
5.80	250	15,000
7.20	270	16,200

The graph of the industry supply curve appears in Figure 12.2, along with the industry demand curve from part (e).

e) i) See Figure 12.2.

ii) The short-run equilibrium price is \$2.80 (where a total of 11,400 mugs per day are supplied and sold; or 190 mugs per day supplied by each firm at *MC* of \$2.80).

iii) At a price of \$2.80 and output of 190, for each firm, *P* > *ATC* where *ATC* = \$2.06. So all existing firms are making economic profits after covering *all* opportunity costs including a "normal" profit. (See *Helpful Hint 3*.) The industry will attract new entrants because it offers more than normal profits. Therefore, even though the industry is in short-run equilibrium it is *not* in long-run equilibrium because the number of firms has not "stabilized." New firms will enter the industry, the industry supply curve will shift to the right, and price will fall until no firm is making economic profits.

Figure 12.2

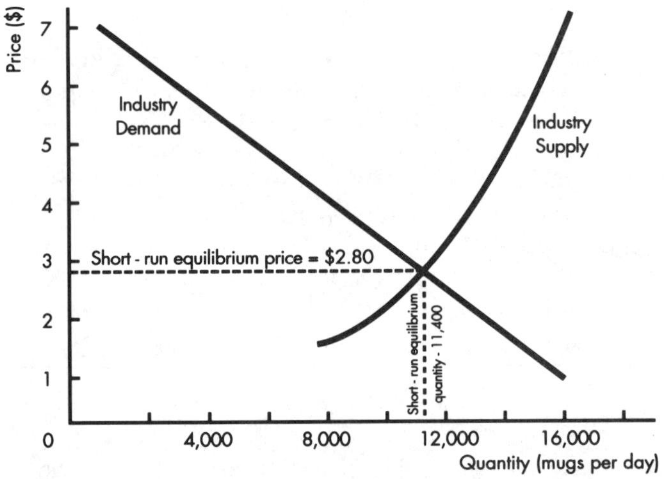

4) a) The breakeven point occurs at 15 units of output. At this level of output, *ATC* is at its minimum (\$19) and is equal to *MC*. Since the *MC* of moving from the 14th to the 15th unit is \$18, and the *MC* of moving from the 15th to the 16th units is \$20, we can interpolate the *MC* exactly at 15 units as midway between \$18 and \$20, or as \$19. The shutdown point occurs at 12 units of output. At this level of output, *AVC* is at its minimum (\$13) and is equal to *MC*. The interpolated value of *MC* at exactly 12 units of output is midway between \$12 and \$14, or is \$13.

b) The short-run equilibrium price is \$25. This is the price at which industry quantity supplied equals quantity demanded as shown in Table 12.11.

Table 12.11

P = MC ($)	Quantity Supplied by 1 Firm	Quantity Supplied by 100 Firms	Quantity Demanded
13	12	1,200	3,000
15	13	1,300	2,800
17	14	1,400	2,600
19	15	1,500	2,400
21	16	1,600	2,200
23	17	1,700	2,000
25	18	1,800	1,800
27	19	1,900	1,600
29	20	2,000	1,400

c) At a price of $25, each firm produces 18 units of output. At 18 units, *ATC* is $19.50, so economic profits are being earned. The amount of profit is ($25 – $19.50) per unit = $5.50 per unit. Total economic profit per *firm* is $5.50/unit X 18 units = $99. This means that new entrants will be attracted to the industry. We conclude that the industry is *not* in long-run equilibrium.

d) Entry continues until economic profits are competed away, and all firms are operating at the minimum point of the *LRAC* curve (which, in this problem, is also the minimum point of the given short-run average total cost curve).

Minimum *ATC* for each firm occurs at 15 units of output, when *ATC* = *MC* = $19, so price in the long run *must* be $19. At a price of $19, consumers demand 2,400 units (from Table 12.11). It follows that when the industry is in long-run equilibrium, there must be 2,400 units/15 units per firm = 160 firms in the industry, each producing 15 units of output, at *zero economic profit.*

e) Quantity supplied is fixed at a maximum of 14 units per firm, or a total of 1,400 units for the 100 firms. Firms are no longer just "price takers and quantity adjusters." With the given demand schedule, 1,400 units can find willing buyers at a price of $29. So long as total output is restricted to 1,400 units, the price stays at $29. Each firm, producing 14 units, has *ATC* = $19.10, so its profit per unit is ($29 – $19.10) = $9.90. Total profit per firm is $9.90/unit × 14 units = $138.60 (larger than in part (c)).

However, the cartel is likely to be unstable unless it has "police power" to enforce the quota. Otherwise there is an incentive to cheat — to violate the quota. For example, with the cartel-induced price of $29, if any one firm increases output to 20 units (*ATC* at 20 units = $20.30), it can get average revenue of (virtually) $29, and total profit = 20 units × (profit per unit of $29 – $20.30 = $174.00). This profit is better than if it stuck to the quota restriction.

But if there is an incentive for *one* firm to cheat, there is an equal incentive for *all* to cheat. If all firms increased output to 20 units per firm, total industry output would be 2,000 units, price would fall to $23, and profit per firm would fall to 20 units × (profit per unit of $23– $20.30 = $54). This profit is less than in part (c).

Even if the cartel can "police" output in the short run, it would also have to have the power to prohibit new entry. Otherwise the high profits would attract new entry and compete away the economic profits. In the most fundamental sense, it is freedom of entry that keeps a perfectly competitive industry competitive.

5) a) A long-run equilibrium in a perfectly competitive industry is illustrated in Figure 12.3.

Part (a) illustrates industry equilibrium at the intersection of industry demand (D_0) and industry supply (S_0): point *a*. The equilibrium industry quantity traded is labelled Q_0 and the equilibrium market price is labelled P_0.

Part (b) illustrates the situation for a single firm in long-run equilibrium. The firm is at point *a'*, the minimum point of both the short-run average total cost curve (*ATC*) and the long-run average cost curve (*LRAC*). The firm is producing the output labelled q_0 and earning zero economic profit.

Figure 12.3

(a) Industry

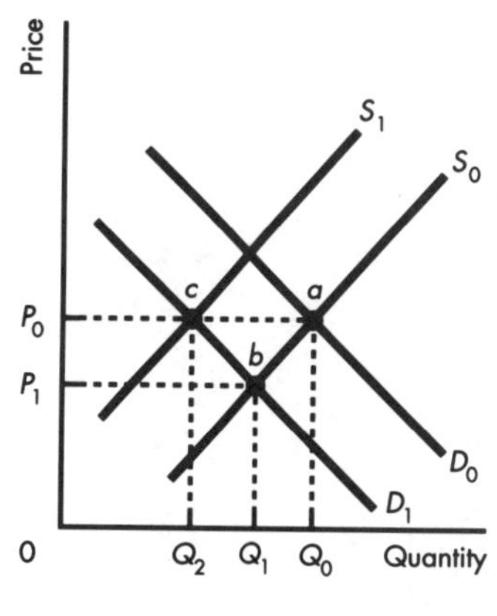

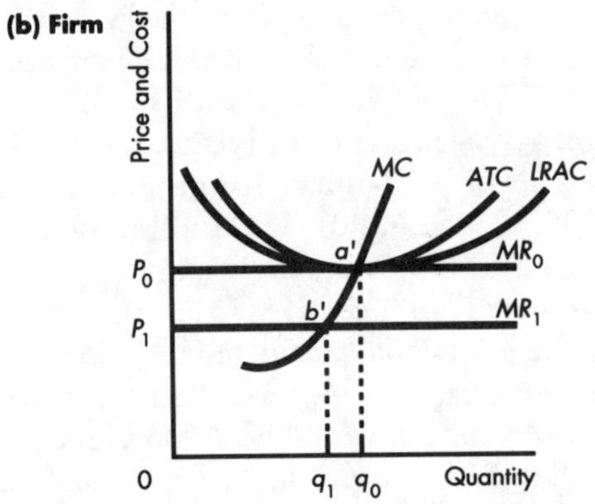

b) i) The new short-run equilibrium is also illustrated in Figure 12.3. The decrease in demand shifts the market demand curve to the left, from D_0 to D_1. The new market equilibrium is at point *b*. The price has fallen from P_0 to P_1 and the industry quantity traded has fallen from Q_0 to Q_1. The fall in price induces firms to reduce output as shown by the move from point *a*' to point *b*' on the *MC* curve in part (b). Since P_1 is less than minimum *ATC*, firms are making losses in the new short-run equilibrium.

ii) The new long-run equilibrium is also illustrated in Figure 12.3. Since losses are experienced in short-run equilibrium, firms will exit from the industry in the long run.

This will cause the industry supply curve to shift to the left causing the price to rise and thus reducing losses. Firms will continue to leave until the industry supply curve has shifted enough to eliminate losses, from S_0 to S_1. This gives a new long-run industry equilibrium at point *c* and the price has returned to its initial level, P_0, but industry quantity traded has fallen to Q_2.

As firms exit and the market price rises, remaining firms will increase their output (moving up the *MC* curve from point *b*' to point *a*') and their losses will be reduced. When sufficient firms have left the industry, the price will have risen (returned) to P_0 and firms will have returned to point *a*' in part (b). At this point, each firm is again earning zero economic profit and firm output has returned to q_0. But, since there are now fewer firms, industry quantity traded is less.

Chapter 13 **Monopoly**

Chapter in Perspective

Text Pages 315–342

The perfectly competitive firms of Chapter 12 are price takers. Each firm is so small relative to the size of the industry that its output decision cannot influence the product price. At the opposite extreme are industries in which there is a single firm, a monopoly. Unlike a perfectly competitive firm, a monopoly's output decision has a direct effect on price; it cannot sell more output unless it drops its price.

This chapter pursues the answers to numerous questions about monopoly: Why does monopoly exist? How does a monopoly choose how much to produce? What constraints on behaviour does a monopoly face? How much profit will a monopoly make? When will a monopoly charge different prices to different customers for the same good or service? How does a monopoly compare with perfect competition in terms of efficiency? Is monopoly always "bad?"

Learning Objectives

After studying this chapter, you will be able to:

- **Define monopoly.**
- **Explain the conditions under which monopoly arises.**
- **Distinguish between legal monopoly and natural monopoly.**
- **Explain how a monopoly determines its price and output.**
- **Define price discrimination.**
- **Explain why price discrimination leads to a bigger profit.**
- **Compare the performance of a competitive and monopolistic industry.**
- **Define rent seeking and explain why it arises.**
- **Explain the conditions under which monopoly is more efficient than competition.**

Helpful Hints

1) The opposite extreme of perfect competition is monopoly. In perfect competition there are many firms which can decide only on quantity produced but not on price, whereas a monopoly is a single firm with the ability to set both quantity and price. These differences create differences in the revenue situation facing the monopoly. The cost curves for the two market structures are assumed to be the same.

   Because there is only one firm, the industry demand curve is also the firm demand curve. In order to sell additional output, the monopoly must lower the price. A single-price monopoly must lower the price on all units of output, not just the additional unit. As the explanation for Figure 13.1 states, this means that marginal revenue is less than price. Combining this new revenue situation with our familiar cost curves from Chapter 10 yields the following important diagram:

Figure 13.1

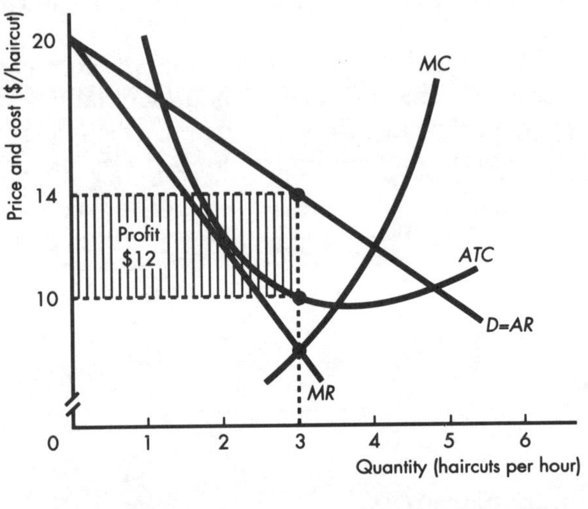

Notice the following points about this diagram.

i) The rule for profit maximization is to find the quantity of output where $MR = MC$. This is the same rule that applies to a perfectly competitive firm.

   For a perfectly competitive firm MR is also equal to price, so the intersection of MR and MC yields the profit-maximizing output and price. This is not true for the monopolist. MR is not equal to price, and once the profit-maximizing output is identified, the monopolist still has to set the price.

ii) To find the profit-maximizing price, draw an imaginary vertical line up to the demand curve from the intersection of MR and MC. Then draw an imaginary horizontal line to the price axis to read the price.

iii) Understanding what the vertical and horizontal distances of the total profit area represent will make you less likely to make mistakes in drawing that area. The vertical distance is between the demand (or average revenue) curve and the average total cost curve. That distance measures average revenue minus average total cost, which equals average profit, or profit per unit. The horizontal distance is just the number of units produced. So the area of the rectangle (vertical distance × horizontal distance) = profit per unit × number of units = total profit. Do *not* make the mistake of drawing the vertical distance down to the intersection of MC and MR. That intersection has no economic meaning for the calculation of total profit.

2) There is an easy trick for drawing the marginal revenue curve corresponding to any linear demand curve. The price intercept (where $Q = 0$) is the same as for the demand curve, and the quantity intercept (where $P = 0$) is exactly *half* of the output of the demand curve. The marginal revenue curve is, therefore, a downward-sloping straight line whose slope is twice as steep as the slope of the demand curve.

Key Figures

Figure 13.1 Demand and Marginal Revenue for a Single-Price Monopoly, text page 320

In a monopoly industry there is a single firm facing the industry (market) demand. Thus the firm has some control over the price it will charge. A single-price monopolist charges the same price to all customers. This figure illustrates the relationship between the demand and marginal revenue curves for a single-price monopolist using the example of Bobbie's Barbershop.

Because the firm faces a negatively-sloped demand curve, if it wants to sell one more unit of output, it must lower its price. This has two effects on revenue. First, the sale of an additional unit will increase revenue by the amount of the price. However, since the firm must also *drop the price on previous units*, revenue on these will decrease. The net change in revenue, the marginal revenue, will thus be less than price, and the marginal revenue curve will lie below the demand curve.

Figure 13.2 A Single-Price Monopoly's Revenue Curves, text page 321
This figure illustrates the relationship between a single-price monopolist's revenue curves and the elasticity of demand. Recall (from Chapter 5) that a straight-line demand curve is elastic (elasticity > 1) above its midpoint, unit elastic (elasticity equal to 1) at its midpoint, and inelastic (elasticity < 1) below its midpoint. Recall also, that in the elastic range of the demand curve, a drop in price will increase total revenue, so marginal revenue will be positive. When the demand curve is unit elastic, a drop in price will leave total revenue unchanged so marginal revenue will be zero. In the inelastic range of the demand curve, a drop in price will decrease total revenue so marginal revenue will be negative. These relationships are combined and shown graphically in part (a) of the figure. The corresponding ranges of increasing total revenue, maximum total revenue, and decreasing total revenue are shown in part (b).

Figure 13.3 A Single-Price Monopoly's Profit-Maximizing Output and Price, text page 322
Since profit is the difference between total revenue and total cost, the determination of the profit-maximizing output and price requires cost as well as revenue information. The table associated with this figure reports the revenues and costs for Bobbie's Barbershop. This information is used to illustrate how a single-price monopoly will choose the profit-maximizing output and price.

Part (a) of the figure shows the total revenue and total cost curves facing the firm. Profit is a maximum when the vertical amount by which total revenue exceeds total cost is a maximum. For Bobbie's Barbershop, this turns out to be 3 haircuts per hour.

Part (b) shows the total profit curve itself; it is derived from the figure in part (a) by taking the difference between total revenue and total cost at each level of output. Profit is maximized when this curve reaches its maximum.

Part (c) shows that profit is a maximum at the quantity where marginal revenue is equal to marginal cost. The price the monopoly will charge for this quantity is the highest possible corresponding point on the demand curve. In the case of Bobbie's Barbershop, the profit-maximizing output is 3 haircuts per hour, the price is \$14 per haircut, and total profit is \$12 per hour. The diagram of marginal cost and marginal revenue in part (c) is the most important and useful of the three diagrams.

Figure 13.7 Monopoly and Competition Compared, text page 334
This figure compares the price and quantity results in a monopoly industry with the price and quantity results if the same industry were competitive.

Imagine that a competitive industry with a large number of firms is taken over by a single monopoly. The competitive industry will produce at the intersection of the industry supply and demand curves (labelled *S* and *D* in the figure). Thus, a competitive industry will produce the quantity *C* and charge the price P_C.

If the same industry became a single-price monopoly, its marginal cost curve would be the supply curve of the competitive industry. (Recall that the competitive industry supply curve is just the horizontal sum of the competitive firms' marginal cost curves.) A profit-maximizing single-price monopoly will produce the output level at which marginal revenue equals marginal cost. Thus the monopoly will produce the quantity *M* and charge the price P_M. The single-price monopoly output is lower than for a competitive industry and the price is higher than the competitive price. A perfectly price-discriminating monopoly produces the competitive output *C* and charges a different price (all above P_C) for each unit sold.

SELF-TEST

CONCEPT REVIEW

1) A firm that is the single supplier of a good in an industry is called a(n) ______________ . The key feature of such an industry is the existence of ______________ preventing the entry of new firms.

2) A monopoly that charges the same price for every unit of output it sells is called a(n) ______________ - ______________ monopoly.

3) The demand curve facing a monopoly firm is the ______________ demand curve.

4) For a monopoly charging a single price, the average revenue curve is the ______________ curve and the marginal revenue curve is ______________ the average revenue curve.

5) The output range over which total revenue is rising is the same as that over which marginal revenue is ______________ . This is the same range of output over which the (price) elasticity of demand is ______________ than 1. If elasticity of demand is ______________ than 1, marginal revenue is ______________ . This implies that a profit-maximizing monopoly will never produce an output in the ______________ range of its demand curve.

6) Unlike a perfectly competitive firm, a monopoly's decision to produce more or less of a good will affect the ______________ of the good.

7) A profit-maximizing monopoly will want to produce less if, at the current level of output, marginal ______________ is greater than marginal ______________ .

8) Unlike a perfectly competitive firm, a monopoly can be making positive economic ______________ in the long run.

9) The practice of charging some customers a higher price than others for exactly the same good is called ______________ ______________. This kind of pricing policy can be seen as an attempt by the monopoly to capture all or part of the consumer ______________.

10) Charging different prices to different groups of customers will increase the profits of a monopoly only if the groups of customers have different ______________ of demand for the product. A monopoly that charges different prices to different groups of customers will produce ______________ than would a monopoly that charges a single price.

11) If a perfectly competitive industry is taken over by a single monopoly firm, output will ______________ and the price will ______________. The reduction in consumer and producer surplus resulting from this new monopoly is called the ______________ loss.

12) The activity of creating monopoly is called ______________ ______________. If there are no barriers to such activity, the value of the resources used up in the process will, in equilibrium, be ______________ ______________ the monopoly's profit.

13) A firm that has a decrease in average total cost when it increases the number of different goods it produces is said to have economies of ______________.

TRUE OR FALSE

_____ 1) An essential difference between a perfectly competitive firm and a monopoly is that the monopolist's output decisions can affect the price of output.

_____ 2) Natural monopoly can arise because of economies of scale.

_____ 3) For a single-price monopoly, average revenue always equals price.

_____ 4) Over the output range where total revenue is decreasing, marginal revenue is positive.

_____ 5) The marginal revenue curve lies below the demand curve for a single-price monopoly because, when the price is lowered to sell additional units of output, it must be lowered on all units of output.

_____ 6) A profit-maximizing, single-price monopoly will produce only in the elastic range of its demand curve.

_____ 7) The supply curve of a monopoly firm is its marginal cost curve.

_____ 8) For a single-price monopoly, price will be less than marginal revenue at the profit-maximizing output.

_____ 9) A monopoly will always make economic profits.

_____ 10) Price discrimination occurs when a firm charges one group of customers more than another or when a firm gives quantity discounts.

_____ 11) A monopoly can acquire all of the consumer surplus for itself if it practises perfect price discrimination.

_____ 12) A price-discriminating monopoly will charge a higher price to the consumer group with the more elastic demand.

_____ 13) Price discrimination is an attempt by a monopolist to capture the producer surplus.

_____ 14) A perfect price-discriminating monopolist produces the level of output at which the marginal cost curve intersects the demand curve.

_____ 15) For a perfect price-discriminating monopolist, the demand curve is also the marginal revenue curve.

_____ 16) Price discrimination only works for goods that can be readily resold.

_____ 17) A perfectly price-discriminating monopolist achieves the same allocative efficiency as perfect competition.

_____ 18) In moving from perfect competition to single-price monopoly, all of the surplus lost by consumers is captured by the monopoly.

_____ 19) In moving from perfect competition to single-price monopoly, part of the deadweight loss is due to a reduction in producer surplus.

_____ 20) No deadweight loss results from a perfect price-discriminating monopoly because the monopoly gains everything the consumer loses.

_____ 21) Because of the existence of rent seeking, the social cost of monopoly is smaller than the deadweight loss.

_____ 22) When rent seeking is taken into account, economic profits from monopoly are guaranteed in the long run.

_____ 23) If there is no barrier to rent seeking, the resources used up in rent seeking equal the monopoly profits.

_____ 24) A monopoly industry with large economies of scale and scope may produce more output and charge a lower price than does a perfectly competitive industry.

MULTIPLE-CHOICE

1) Which of the following is a *natural* barrier to the entry of new firms in an industry?
   a) licensing of professions
   b) economies of scale
   c) issuing a patent
   d) a public franchise
   e) all of the above

2) In order to increase sales from 7 units to 8 units, a single-price monopolist must drop the price from $7/unit to $6/unit. What is marginal revenue in this range?
   a) $48
   b) $6
   c) $1
   d) –$1
   e) none of the above

3) If marginal revenue is negative at a particular output, then
   a) price must be negative.
   b) the monopolist should increase output.
   c) the elasticity of demand is less than 1 at that output.
   d) demand must be elastic at that output.
   e) the monopolist should shut down.

4) A single-price monopolist will maximize profits if it produces the output where
   a) price equals marginal cost.
   b) price equals marginal revenue.
   c) marginal revenue equals marginal cost.
   d) average revenue equals marginal cost.
   e) average revenue equals marginal revenue.

5) A profit-maximizing monopoly will never produce at an output level
   a) at which it would make economic losses.
   b) where marginal revenue is less than price.
   c) at which average cost is greater than marginal cost.
   d) in the inelastic range of its demand curve.
   e) in the inelastic range of its marginal revenue curve.

6) For a single-price monopolist, which of the following is *false*?
   a) There is no unique one-to-one relationship between price and quantity supplied.
   b) For any output greater than zero, $MR < AR$.
   c) The industry demand curve is the monopolist's demand curve.
   d) The intersection of *MR* and *MC* provides all information necessary for identifying the profit-maximizing quantity and price.
   e) Total revenue is at a maximum where $MR = 0$.

7) If a profit-maximizing monopoly is producing at an output at which marginal cost exceeds marginal revenue, it
   a) should raise price and lower output.
   b) should lower price and raise output.
   c) should lower price and lower output.
   d) is making losses.
   e) is maximizing profit.

8) A monopoly will go out of business in the short run if
   a) it is making an economic loss.
   b) *MR* is less than *AVC*.
   c) the price is less than *AVC*.
   d) the profit-maximizing level of output is in the elastic range of the demand curve.
   e) *MR* is less than *AR*.

9) A single-price monopoly never operates
   a) on an elastic portion of the demand curve.
   b) on a portion of the demand curve that is unit elastic.
   c) on an inelastic portion of the demand curve.
   d) at a quantity where marginal revenue is positive since total revenue is not at a maximum.
   e) under any of the above conditions.

10) If a single-price monopoly has shut down, then at the level of output where marginal cost and marginal revenue intersect, it *must* be true that
   a) marginal revenue is less than average variable cost.
   b) marginal cost is less than average variable cost.
   c) price is less than average variable cost.
   d) total revenue is less than total cost.
   e) all of the above are correct.

11) The supply curve for a single-price monopoly is
   a) its marginal cost curve.
   b) its marginal cost curve above minimum average variable cost.
   c) its average variable cost curve.
   d) its marginal revenue curve.
   e) none of the above.

12) For the single-price monopoly depicted in Figure 13.2, when profit is maximized, quantity is
a) 3 and price is $3.
b) 3 and price is $6.
c) 4 and price is $4.
d) 4 and price is $5.
e) 5 and price is $4.

Figure 13.2

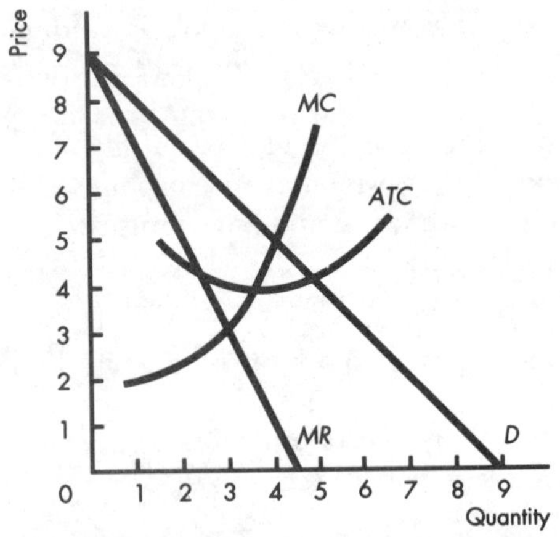

13) If the monopoly depicted in Figure 13.2 is maximizing profit, what is the total profit?
a) $3
b) $4
c) $6
d) $9
e) none of the above

14) A perfect price-discriminating monopoly
a) has a demand curve which is also its average revenue curve.
b) will maximize revenue.
c) is assured of making a profit.
d) will produce the quantity at which the marginal cost curve intersects the demand curve.
e) will be allocatively inefficient.

15) When perfect price discrimination occurs, which of the following statements is *false*?
a) Buyers cannot resell the product.
b) The firm can distinguish between buyers.
c) The firm sets prices.
d) The firm captures consumer surplus.
e) Allocative efficiency is worse than with single-price monopoly.

16) A successful price-discriminating firm must be able to
a) prevent consumer resale.
b) differentiate consumers with high price elasticity of demand and charge them low prices.
c) differentiate consumers with low price elasticity of demand and charge them high prices.
d) do all of the above.
e) do none of the above.

17) The output of a (not perfect) price-discriminating monopoly will be
a) less than a single-price monopoly.
b) more than a single-price monopoly, but less than a perfectly competitive industry.
c) the same amount as a perfectly competitive industry.
d) more than a perfectly competitive industry.
e) none of the above.

18) Table 13.1 lists marginal costs for the XYZ firm. If XYZ sells 3 units at a price of $6 each, what is its producer surplus?
a) $2
b) $6
c) $7
d) $9
e) $12

Table 13.1

Quantity	Marginal Cost
1	2
2	3
3	4
4	5

19) Consider the industry demand curve in Figure 13.3. Which area in the diagram indicates the deadweight loss from a single-price monopoly?
a) *eacf*
b) *acd*
c) *abd*
d) *bcd*
e) none of the above

Figure 13.3

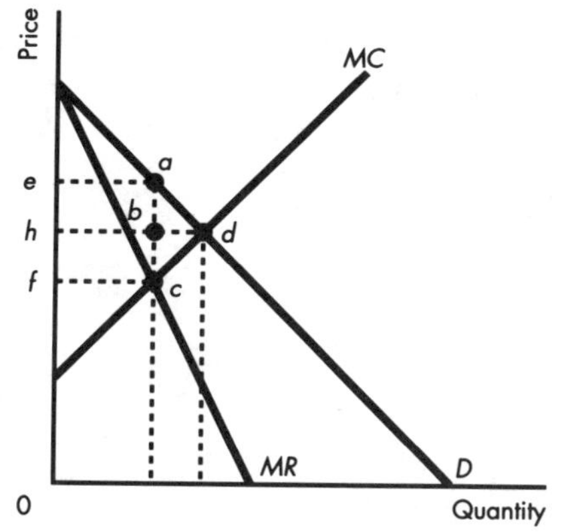

20) Which area in Figure 13.3 indicates the deadweight loss from a perfect price-discriminating monopoly?
   a) *eacf*
   b) *acd*
   c) *abd*
   d) *bcd*
   e) none of the above

21) Which of the following is true for a producing single-price monopolist but not for a producing perfect competitor?
   a) The firm maximizes profit by setting marginal cost equal to marginal revenue.
   b) The firm is a price-taker.
   c) The firm can sell any level of output at any price it sets.
   d) The firm's marginal cost is less than average revenue.
   e) None of the above statements is true.

22) Why is the quantity of output produced by a single-price monopolist allocatively inefficient?
   a) Average social cost exceeds average social benefit.
   b) Marginal social cost exceeds marginal social benefit.
   c) Average social benefit exceeds average social cost.
   d) Marginal social benefit exceeds marginal social cost.
   e) None of the above statements is true.

23) Activity for the purpose of creating monopoly is
   a) called rent seeking.
   b) illegal in Canada.
   c) called price discrimination.
   d) called legal monopoly.
   e) costless.

24) A monopoly has economies of scope if
   a) average total cost declines as the firm's scale increases.
   b) average total cost declines as output increases.
   c) total profit declines as output increases.
   d) average total cost declines as the number of different goods produced increases.
   e) total profit declines as the number of different goods produced increases.

SHORT ANSWER

1) Why is marginal revenue less than price for a single-price monopoly?

2) Does a single-price monopoly produce in the elastic or inelastic range of its demand curve? Why?

3) Explain why the output of a competitive industry will always be greater than the output of the *same* industry under single-price monopoly.

4) The price of the last unit sold and the quantity sold are exactly the same in an industry under perfect competition and under a perfect price discriminating monopoly. Are consumers therefore indifferent between the two? Explain.

5) Under what circumstances would a monopoly be more efficient than a large number of competitive firms? Illustrate graphically such a situation where a monopoly produces more and charges a lower price than would be the case if the industry consisted of a large number of perfectly competitive firms.

PROBLEMS

1) a) A single-price monopoly is the only seller of skyhooks in the Canadian market. The firm's total fixed cost is $112 per day. Its total variable costs and total costs (both in dollars per day) are shown in Table 13.2. Complete the table by computing marginal cost, average variable cost, and average total cost. (Remember that marginal cost should be entered midway between rows of output.)

Table 13.2

Quantity	Total Variable Cost (*TVC*)	Total Cost (*TC*)	Marginal Cost (*MC*)	Average Variable Cost (*AVC*)	Average Total Cost (*ATC*)
9	135	247			
10	144	256			
11	155	267			
12	168	280			
13	183	295			
14	200	312			
15	219	331			
16	240	352			
17	263	375			
18	288	400			
19	315	427			
20	344	456			
21	375	487			

b) The firm has determined that it faces the demand curve given by the equation $P = 66 - 1Q_D$ (where P is the price of a skyhook in dollars and Q_D is the quantity demanded per day). Table 13.3 lists some points on the demand schedule, as well as the total cost information from part (a). Complete the table by copying your values for marginal cost from Table 13.2 and by computing total revenue, marginal revenue, and profit. (Remember that marginal revenue, like marginal cost, should be entered midway between rows of output.)

Table 13.3

Price (*P*)	Quantity Demanded (*Q*)	Total Revenue (*RTR*)	Marginal Revenue (*MR*)	Total Cost (*TC*)	Marginal Cost (*MC*)	Profit
57	9			247		
56	10			256		
55	11			267		
54	12			280		
53	13			295		
52	14			312		
51	15			331		
50	16			352		
49	17			375		
48	18			400		
47	19			427		
46	20			456		
45	21			487		

What is the firm's profit-maximizing quantity of output? At what price will it sell skyhooks? What will be its total profit? Explain your answers.

c) On the graph in Figure 13.4, plot the demand curve and the *MR*, *AVC*, *ATC*, and *MC* curves corresponding to the data in parts (a) and (b). Show the equilibrium output and the *area* of profit on your diagram.

Figure 13.4

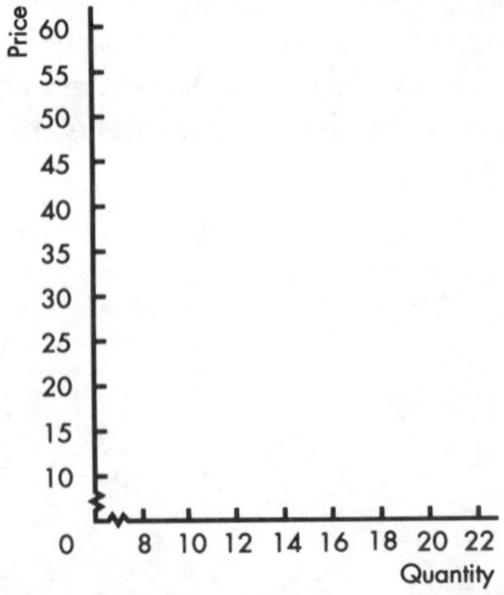

d) The firm's cost curves are unchanged, but now consumer demand shifts so that the new demand curve is given by the equation $P = 29 - 1/2Q_D$. Table 13.4 lists some points on the new demand schedule, as well as the total cost information from part (a). Complete the table by copying your values for marginal cost from Table 13.2, and by computing the new values for total revenue, marginal revenue, and profit.

Table 13.4

Price (*P*)	Quantity Demanded (*Q*)	Total Revenue (*TR*)	Marginal Revenue (*MR*)	Total Cost (*TC*)	Marginal Cost (*MC*)	Profit
24.50	9			247		
24.00	10			256		
23.50	11			267		
23.00	12			280		
22.50	13			295		
22.00	14			312		
21.50	15			331		
21.00	16			352		
20.50	17			375		
20.00	18			400		
19.50	19			427		
19.00	20			456		
18.50	21			487		

What is the firm's new profit-maximizing quantity of output? At what price will it now sell skyhooks? What will be its total profit? Explain your answers.

e) On the graph in Figure 13.5 , plot the new demand curve and *MR* curve. Copy the *AVC*, *ATC*, and *MC* curves from Figure 13.4. Show the new equilibrium output and the *area* of profit on your diagram.

Figure 13.5

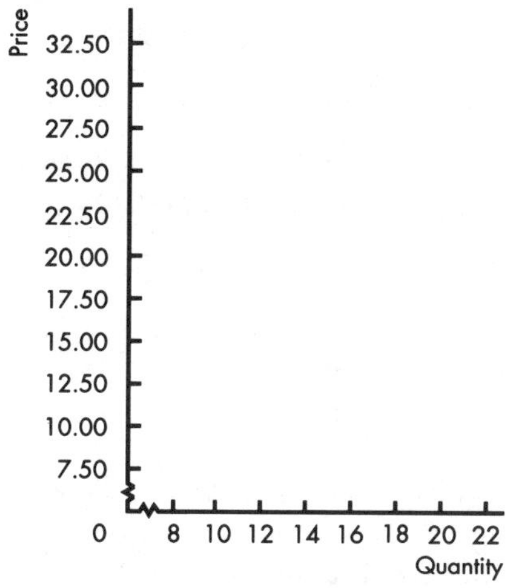

f) Suppose demand falls even further so that the new demand equation is $P = 19 - 1/2Q_D$. On the graph in Figure 13.6, plot this demand curve and copy the *AVC* curve from Figure 13.4. Explain why the monopolist will shut down in the short run.

Figure 13.6

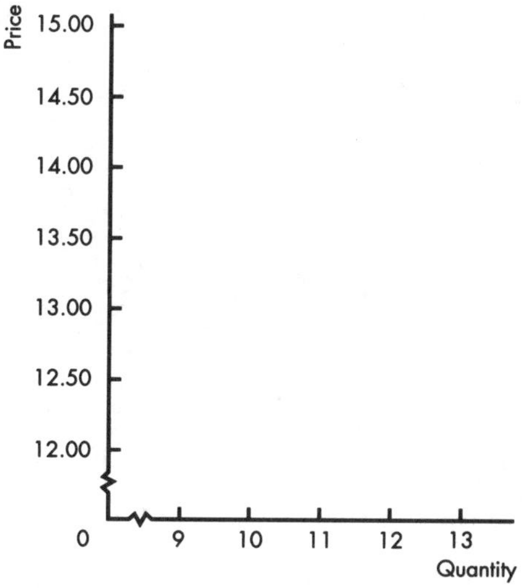

2) You are given the following information about an industry consisting of 100 identical firms.
The demand curve facing the industry is:

$$P = 36 - 0.01Q$$

The marginal revenue curve facing the industry is:

$$MR = 36 - 0.02Q$$

The marginal cost curve of an individual firm is:

$$MC = -12 + 2Q$$

The horizontal sum of the marginal cost curves of all of the firms in the industry is:

$$MC = -12 + 0.02Q$$

Use this information to answer the following questions.

a) Suppose all 100 firms are controlled by a single-price monopolist.
   i) Calculate the profit-maximizing quantity of output for the monopolist.
   ii) Calculate the price per unit of output that the monopolist will charge.
b) Suppose instead that the 100 firms operate independently as a perfectly competitive industry.
   i) Calculate the short-run equilibrium quantity of output for the industry as a whole.
   ii) Calculate the short-run equilibrium price for the industry.
   iii) *Without* using your answer to part (b)i), calculate the short-run equilibrium output per firm.
c) Compare the monopoly price and quantity outcomes with the perfect competition price and quantity outcomes.

3) Keith's Lunch has two kinds of customers for lunch: stock brokers and retired senior citizens. The demand schedules for lunches for the two groups are given in Table 13.5.

Keith has decided to price discriminate between the two groups by treating each demand separately and charging the price that maximizes profit in each of the two sub-markets. Marginal cost and average total cost are equal and constant at $2 per lunch.

a) Complete Table 13.5 by computing the total and marginal revenue associated with stock broker demand (TR_{SB} and MR_{SB}) as well as the total and marginal revenue associated with senior citizen demand (TR_{SC} and MR_{SC}). (Remember that marginal revenue should be entered midway between rows.)
b) What are the profit-maximizing output and price for stock brokers?
c) What are the profit-maximizing output and price for senior citizens?
d) What is total profit?
e) Show that the total profit in part (d) is the maximum by comparing it with total profit if instead Keith served
   i) 1 additional lunch *each* to stockbrokers and senior citizens.
   ii) 1 less lunch *each* to stockbrokers and senior citizens.

Table 13.5

	Stock Brokers			Senior Citizens		
Price (P)	Quantity Demanded (Q_D)	Total Revenue (TR_{SB})	Marginal Revenue (MR_{SB})	Quantity Demanded (Q_D)	Total Revenue (TR_{SC})	Marginal Revenue (MR_{SC})
8	0			0		
7	1			0		
6	2			0		
5	3			1		
4	4			2		
3	5			3		
2	6			4		
1	7			5		
0	8			6		

4) Figure 13.7 gives the demand, marginal revenue, and marginal cost curves for a certain industry. In this problem we consider how consumer and producer surplus are distributed under each of four ways of organizing the industry. In each case redraw any relevant part of Figure 13.7 and then (1) indicate the region of the graph corresponding to consumer surplus by drawing horizontal lines through it; (2) indicate the region corresponding to producer surplus by drawing vertical lines through it, and (3) indicate the region (if any) corresponding to deadweight loss by putting dots in the area.
   a) The industry consists of many perfectly competitive firms.
   b) The industry is a single-price monopoly.
   c) The industry is a price-discriminating monopoly charging two prices: P_1 and P_3.
   d) The industry is a perfect price-discriminating monopoly.

Figure 13.7

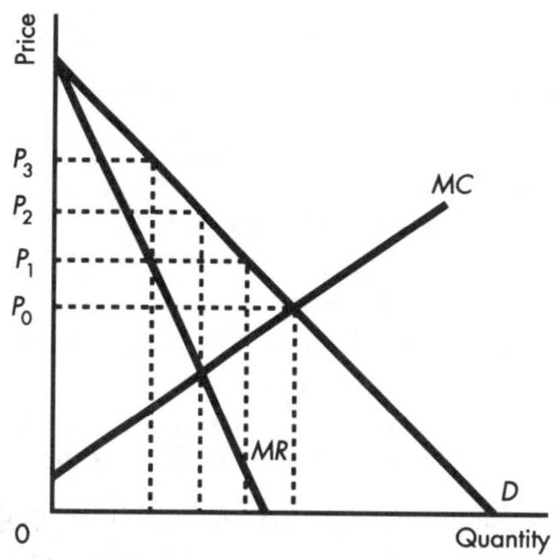

ANSWERS

CONCEPT REVIEW

1) monopoly; barriers
2) single-price
3) industry
4) demand; below
5) positive; greater; less; negative; inelastic
6) price
7) cost; revenue
8) profits
9) price discrimination; surplus
10) elasticities; more
11) decrease; increase; deadweight
12) rent seeking; equal to
13) scope

TRUE OR FALSE

1) T	7) F	13) F	19) T
2) T	8) F	14) T	20) T
3) T	9) F	15) T	21) F
4) F	10) T	16) F	22) F
5) T	11) T	17) T	23) T
6) T	12) F	18) F	24) T

MULTIPLE-CHOICE

1) b	7) a	13) c	19) b
2) d	8) c	14) d	20) e
3) c	9) c	15) e	21) d
4) c	10) c	16) d	22) d
5) d	11) e	17) b	23) a
6) d	12) b	18) d	24) d

SHORT ANSWER

1) In order to sell an additional unit of output, a monopoly must drop the price. This has two effects on revenue, one positive and equal to price, and the other negative. Marginal revenue is the net effect, which must be less than price. First, the additional unit sold at the new lower price adds an amount to revenue equal to the price. But, a single-price monopoly must also lower the price to previous customers who would have paid more. The net effect on marginal revenue is equal to the price minus the loss of revenue from lowering the price to previous customers. This difference must necessarily be less than price.

2) A single-price monopoly will always produce in the *elastic* range of the demand curve. The reason is straightforward. Marginal cost is always positive. Thus the profit maximizing condition that marginal cost equals marginal revenue, must be satisfied over the range of output for which marginal revenue is positive, the elastic range.

3) A competitive industry will produce the level of output at which the industry marginal cost curve intersects the demand curve facing the industry. A single-price monopoly will produce at the level of output at which the industry marginal cost curve intersects the monopoly marginal revenue curve. Since the marginal revenue curve lies below the demand curve, this implies a lower level of output in the monopoly industry.

4) While the quantity sold and the price charged to the last customer are the same in the cases of perfect competition and a perfect price discriminator, the distribution of consumer surplus is not the same. Since a perfect price discriminator charges each customer the most he/she is willing to pay, they have no consumer surplus. Any consumer surplus that would have occurred under perfect competition now accrues to the monopoly. Consumers would like to obtain more consumer surplus, and therefore pay less for the same amount. Consequently, consumers prefer perfect competition.

5) A monopoly would be more efficient than perfect competition if the monopoly has sufficient economies of scale and/or scope. Those economies must be large enough that the monopoly produces more than the competitive industry and sells it at a lower price. Figure 13.8 illustrates such a situation. The important feature is that the marginal cost curve for the monopoly must not only be lower than the supply curve of the competitive industry, but it must be sufficiently lower so that it intersects the *MR* curve at an output greater than *C* (the competitive output). Such a situation could arise if there are extensive economies of scale and/or scope.

Figure 13.8

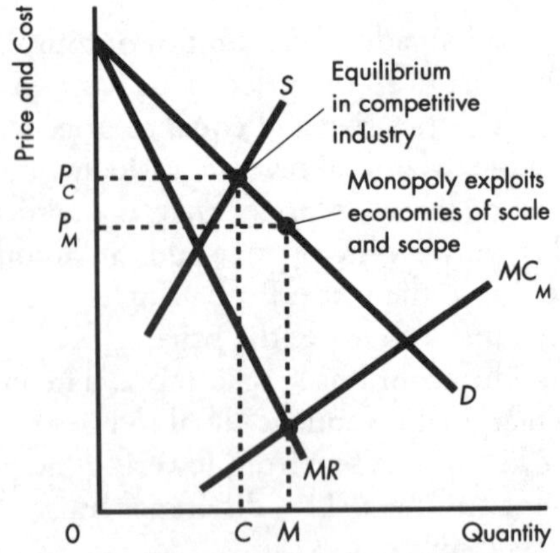

PROBLEMS

1) a) Completed Table 13.2 is given here as Table 13.2 Solution.

Table 13.2 Solution

Quantity	Total Variable Cost (*TVC*)	Total Cost (*TC*)	Marginal Cost (*MC*)	Average Variable Cost (*AVC*)	Average Total Cost (*ATC*)
9	135	247		15.00	27.44
			9		
10	144	256		14.40	25.60
			11		
11	155	267		14.09	24.27
			13		
12	168	280		14.00	23.33
			15		
13	183	295		14.08	22.69
			17		
14	200	312		14.29	22.29
			19		
15	219	331		14.60	22.07
			21		
16	240	352		15.00	22.00
			23		
17	263	375		15.47	22.06
			25		
18	288	400		16.00	22.22
			27		
19	315	427		16.58	22.47
			29		
20	344	456		17.20	22.80
			31		
21	375	487		17.86	23.19

b) Completed Table 13.3 is shown on page 156 as Table 13.3 Solution.

Table 13.3 Solution

Price (*P*)	Quantity Demanded (*Q*)	Total Revenue (*TR*)	Marginal Revenue (*MR*)	Total Cost (*TC*)	Marginal Cost (*MC*)	Profit
57	9	513		247		266
			47		 9	
56	10	560		256		304
			45		11	
55	11	605		267		338
			43		13	
54	12	648		280		368
			41		15	
53	13	689		295		394
			39		17	
52	14	728		312		416
			37		19	
51	15	765		331		434
			35		21	
50	16	800		352		448
			33		23	
49	17	833		375		458
			31		25	
48	18	864		400		464
			29		27	
47	**19**	**893**		**427**		**466**
			27		29	
46	20	920		456		464
			25		31	
45	21	945		487		458

Equilibrium output occurs where *MC* = *MR* = 28, *Q* = 19, *P* = 47, profit = $4.66.

The profit-maximizing quantity of output occurs where marginal cost equals marginal revenue, at 19 units. The maximum price the firm can charge and still sell 19 units is $47. This combination of quantity and price yields a total profit of $466, which, as can be seen from the table, is the maximum possible profit.

c) The requested diagram appears in Figure 13.4 Solution.

Figure 13.4 Solution

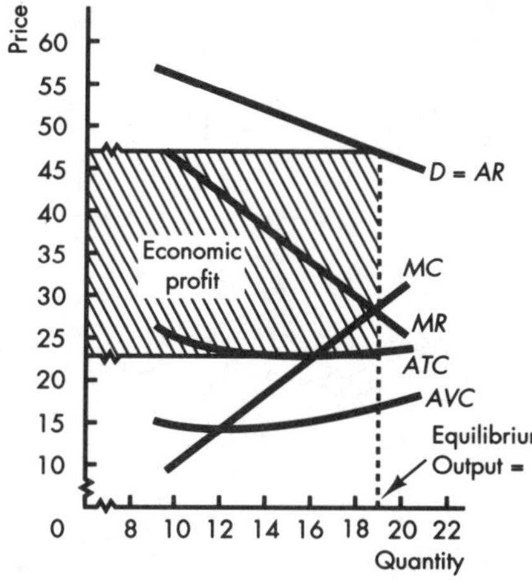

d) Completed Table 13.4 is given here as Table 13.4 Solution.

Table 13.4 Solution

Price (*P*)	Quantity Demanded (*Q*)	Total Revenue (*TR*)	Marginal Revenue (*MR*)	Total Cost (*TC*)	Marginal Cost (*MC*)	Profit
24.50	9	220.50		247		–26.50
			....19.50		 9	
24.00	10	240.00		256		–16.00
			....18.50		11	
23.50	11	258.50		267		–8.50
			....17.50		13	
23.00	12	276.00		280		–4.00
			....16.50		15	
22.50	13	292.50		295		–2.50
			....15.50		17	
22.00	14	308.00		312		–4.00
			....14.50		19	
21.50	15	322.50		331		–8.50
			....13.50		21	
21.00	16	336.00		352		–16.00
			....12.50		23	
20.50	17	348.50		375		–26.50
			....11.50		25	
20.00	18	360.00		400		–40.00
			....10.50		27	
19.50	19	370.50		427		–56.50
			....9.50		29	
19.00	20	380.00		456		–76.00
			....8.50		31	
18.50	21	388.50		487		–98.50

Equilibrium output occurs where *MC* = *MR* = 16, *Q* = 13, *P* = 22.50, profit = –$2.50.

The profit-maximizing quantity of output occurs where marginal cost equals marginal revenue, now at 13 units. The maximum price the firm can charge and still sell 13 units is $22.50. This combination of quantity and price yields a total profit of –$2.50 (a loss). As can be seen from the table, this is the minimum possible loss. The firm will continue to produce in the short run because this loss is less than its shut-down loss, which would be $112, the amount of its fixed cost.

e) The requested diagram appears in Figure 13.5 Solution on page 158.

Figure 13.5 Solution

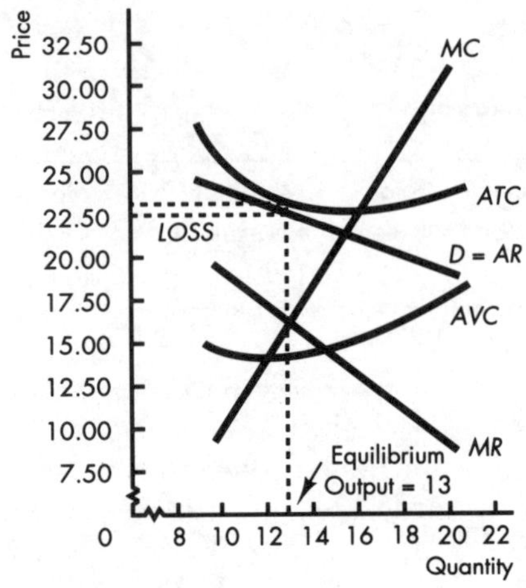

f) The requested diagram appears in Figure 13.6 Solution. Since the demand curve is everywhere below the *AVC* curve, no matter what quantity of output the firm might produce, price will be less than *AVC*. This means that the firm will lose money on every unit produced in addition to losing its total fixed cost. The monopolist will minimize loss in this case by shutting down and losing just its fixed cost ($112).

Figure 13.6 Solution

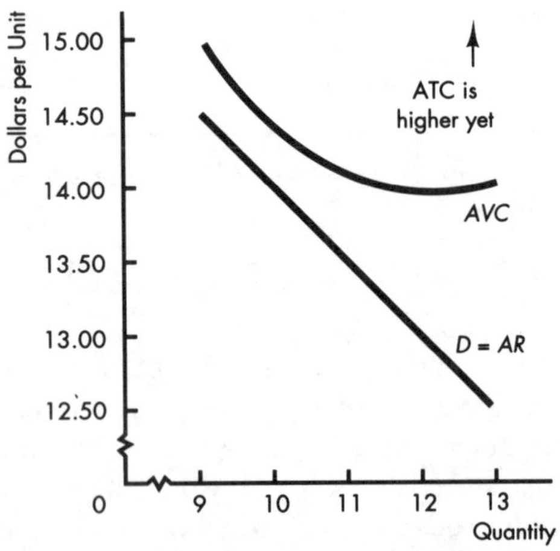

2) a) i) The monopolist will choose the quantity of output where marginal revenue equals marginal cost. To calculate this quantity, set the equation for marginal revenue equal to the equation for *industry* marginal cost (since the monopolist controls all of the firms).

$$36 - 0.02Q = -12 + 0.02Q$$
$$48 = 0.04Q$$
$$1{,}200 = Q$$

ii) To calculate the price that the monopolist will charge, substitute the quantity 1,200 into the demand equation. This is the mathematical equivalent of graphically, after finding the quantity corresponding to the intersection of *MC* and *MR*, moving your eye up vertically to the demand curve to read the price.

$$P = 36 - 0.01Q$$
$$P = 36 - 0.01(1{,}200)$$
$$P = 36 - 12$$
$$P = 24$$

b) i) The perfectly competitive industry's short-run equilibrium quantity of output occurs where industry demand intersects industry supply. Set the industry demand equation equal to the industry supply equation, which is the horizontal sum of the marginal cost curves of all the firms in the industry.

$$36 - 0.01Q = -12 + 0.02Q$$
$$48 = 0.03Q$$
$$1{,}600 = Q$$

ii) To calculate the short-run equilibrium price for the industry, we can substitute the quantity 1,600 into either the industry demand equation or the industry supply equation.
Using the industry demand equation yields:

$$P = 36 - 0.01Q$$
$$P = 36 - 0.01(1{,}600)$$
$$P = 36 - 16$$
$$P = 20$$

Using the industry supply equations yields the same result:

$$P = -12 + 0.02Q$$
$$P = -12 + 0.02(1{,}600)$$
$$P = -12 + 32$$
$$P = 20$$

iii) If industry output is 1,600 units and there are 100 identical firms, then the output per firm is 1,600 units/100 firms or 16 units/firm. But the question specifically asks you *not* to use the information about industry output.

The other way to calculate the short-run equilibrium output per firm is to substitute the equilibrium price of 20 into the individual firm's marginal cost curve, which is also its short-run supply curve.

$$P = -12 + 2Q$$
$$20 = -12 + 2Q$$
$$32 = 2Q$$
$$16 = Q$$

c) The monopoly price (24) is higher than the perfect competition price (20) and the monopoly quantity of output (1,200) is lower than the perfect competition quantity of output (1,600).

3) a) The completed table is given in Table 13.5 Solution.

b) The profit-maximizing output for stock brokers occurs when $MC = \$2 = MR_{SB}$. This is at 3 lunches and the price is \$5 per lunch to stock brokers.

c) The profit-maximizing output for senior citizens occurs when $MC = \$2 = MR_{SC}$. This occurs at 2 lunches and the price to senior citizens is \$4 per lunch.

d) Since average total cost is also \$2 per lunch, the total cost is \$2 × 5 lunches = \$10. Total revenue is \$15 from stock brokers and \$8 from senior citizens, or \$23. Thus total profit is \$13.

e) i) If Keith served 1 additional lunch each to stock brokers and senior citizens, that would make 4 lunches for stock brokers (at \$4/lunch) and 3 lunches for senior citizens (at \$3/lunch). Since average total cost is \$2 per lunch, the total cost is \$2 × 7 lunches = \$14. Total revenue is \$16 from stock brokers and \$9 from senior citizens, or \$25. Thus total profit is \$11, less than the \$13 in part (d).

Table 13.5 Solution

	Stock Brokers			Senior Citizens		
Price (P)	Quantity Demanded (Q_D)	Total Revenue (TR_{SB})	Marginal Revenue (MR_{SB})	Quantity Demanded (Q_D)	Total Revenue (TR_{SC})	Marginal Revenue (MR_{SC})
8	0	0		0	0	
			7			0
7	1	7		0	0	
			5			0
6	2	12		0	0	
			3			0
5	3	15		1	5	
			1			3
4	4	16		2	8	
			-1			1
3	5	15		3	9	
			3			-1
2	6	12		4	8	
			-5			-3
1	7	7		5	5	
			-7			-5
0	8	0		6	0	

For stock brokers, equilibrium output occurs where $MC = MR = 2$, $Q_{SB} = 3$, $P_{SB} = 5$.
For senior citizens, equilibrium output occurs where $MC = MR = 2$, $Q_{SC} = 2$, $P_{SC} = 4$.

ii) If Keith served 1 less lunch each to stock brokers and senior citizens, that would make 2 lunches for stock brokers (at $6/lunch) and 1 lunch for senior citizens (at $5/lunch). Since average total cost is $2 per lunch, the total cost is $2 × 3 lunches = $6. Total revenue is $12 from stock brokers and $5 from senior citizens, or $17. Thus total profit is $11, less than the $13 in part (d).

4) a) Under perfect competition, price equals marginal cost. The amount of consumer surplus is given by the area under the demand curve but above the price (P_0), while the amount of producer surplus is given by the area above the *MC* curve but below the price; see Figure 13.7 Solution (a).

b) If the industry is a single-price monopoly, price will be greater than *MC* and output will be less than under competition. Consumer surplus is still given by the area under the demand curve but above the price (P_2), while producer surplus is given by the area above the *MC* curve but below the price up to the monopoly level of output. The remaining part of the large triangle is a deadweight loss since it is the amount of surplus under competition that is lost under a single-price monopoly; see Figure 13.7 Solution (b).

c) Similar reasoning allows us to establish regions in Figure 13.7 Solution (c) corresponding to consumer surplus, producer surplus, and deadweight loss.

d) Under perfect price discrimination, all of the potential surplus is captured by the producer and there is no deadweight loss (or consumer surplus). See Figure 13.7 Solution (d).

Figure 13.7 Solution

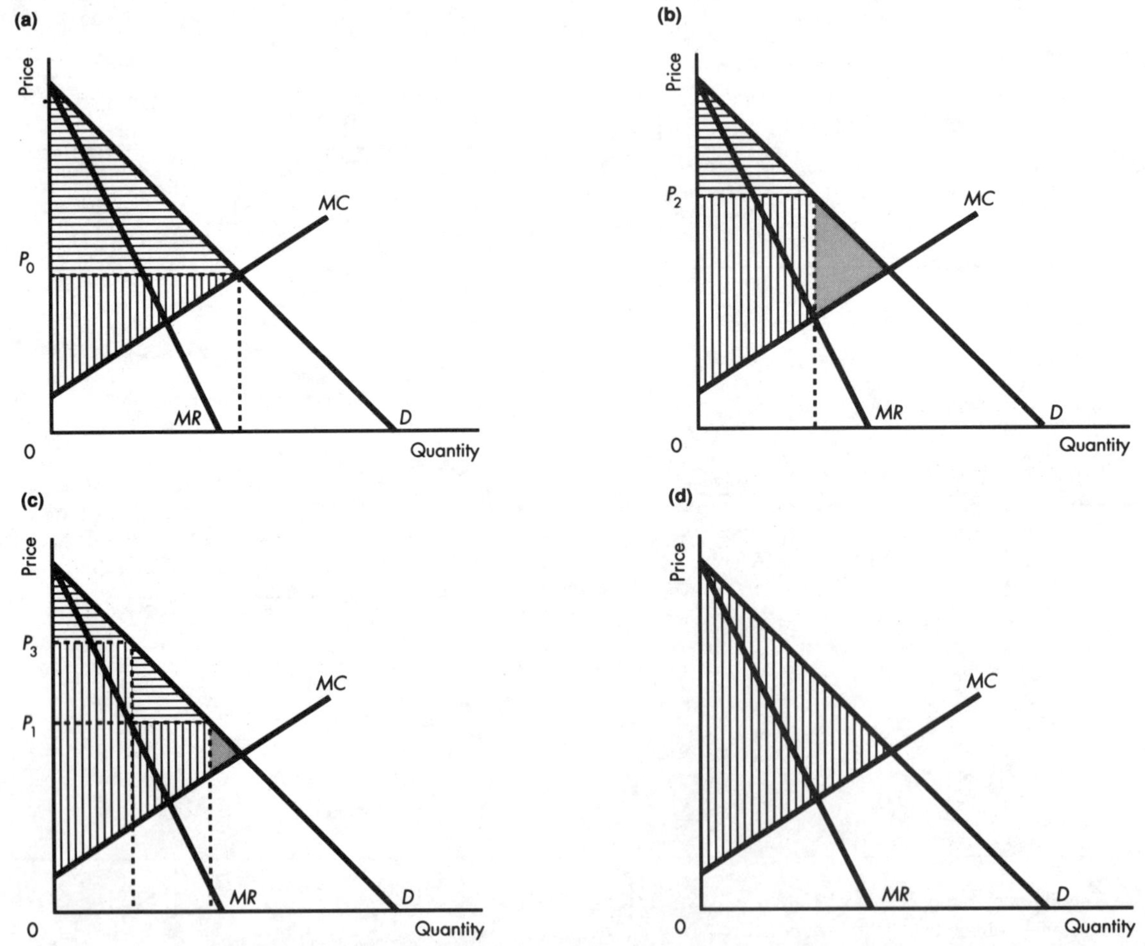

Chapter 14 Monopolistic Competition and Oligopoly

Chapter in Perspective

Text Pages 343–374

In Chapter 12 we examined the output and price decisions facing firms in a perfectly competitive industry, and in Chapter 13 we investigated the output and price decisions of a monopoly.

A perfectly competitive industry is characterized by a large number of firms, each of which produces a homogeneous product and has no control over the price of the good it sells — it is a price taker.

Monopoly represents the other extreme of market structure. A monopoly is the only firm in an industry with barriers to entry and it produces a good with no close substitutes. It faces a downward-sloping demand curve and thus can choose its price.

Our analysis of the behaviour of firms in these two extreme forms of market structure yielded some very useful principles. However, perfect competition and strict monopoly are actually quite rare. Most firms that we observe seem to lie somewhere between these two polar cases.

This chapter explores the behaviour of the in-between firms that populate the real world. We will discover that the tools of analysis developed in the previous two chapters will take us a long way.

Learning Objectives

After studying this chapter, you will be able to:

- **Describe and distinguish among market structures that lie between perfect competition and monopoly.**
- **Define monopolistic competition.**
- **Explain how price and output are determined in a monopolistically competitive industry.**
- **Define oligopoly and duopoly.**
- **Explain what game theory is.**
- **Explain the prisoner's dilemma game.**
- **Explain duopoly and oligopoly as games that firms play.**
- **Predict the price and output behaviour of duopolists.**
- **Make predictions about price wars and competition among small numbers of firms.**

Helpful Hints

1) Most industries are neither perfectly competitive nor pure monopolies; they lie somewhere between these two extremes. This does not mean that the last two chapters have been wasted.

   Indeed, because we have examined firms under these extreme market structures, we are able to spend a single chapter discussing the range of industries between them. It is important not only to know the different key characteristics of the alternative forms of market structure, but to understand how these characteristics explain differences in firm behaviour. See text Table 14.2 on page 347 for a review.

2) We continue to assume that all firms are profit-maximizers. In spite of this common objective, the equilibrium price and level of output will be different for each of the market structures. This is due to differences in the nature of constraints faced by firms in each of the four types of market structure. For example, except in the case of perfect competition, firms face downward-sloping demand curves and thus have some control over the price of the good they sell. In these cases, profit-maximizing firms will (typically) produce less than would have been produced in the competitive case and will charge a price higher than the competitive price.

3) In graphing a monopolistically competitive firm in long-run equilibrium, be sure that the *ATC* curve is tangent to the demand curve at the same level of output at which the *MC* and *MR* curves intersect. Also, be sure that the *MC* curve intersects the *ATC* curve at the minimum point on the *ATC* curve.

4) This chapter explains the use of elementary game theory to help understand oligopoly. Be sure to thoroughly understand the prisoner's dilemma game because it illustrates, simply, the most important game theory concepts (rules, strategies, payoffs), which are then used in more complex game theory models like those of repeated games.

   Understand the incentives faced by the players and why a particular outcome is an equilibrium. The key to finding the equilibrium of a simple game is to carefully construct and examine the payoff matrix.

Key Figures and Tables

Figure 14.1 Monopolistic Competition, text page 349
This figure illustrates the output and pricing decisions of a monopolistically competitive firm in both the short run and the long run. Such a firm is similar to a monopoly since it faces a downward-sloping demand curve. It maximizes profit by producing the level of output at which marginal revenue (*MR*) is equal to marginal cost (*MC*) and charges the highest possible price (P_S), which is determined by the height of the demand curve.

In the short run, the firm can make either a positive profit, as illustrated in part (a) of the figure, or a loss. A monopolistically competitive firm is also like a competitive firm since there are many firms and free entry into the industry.

When firms are making profits, new firms will enter, causing the demand curves of existing firms to shift to the left. Prices and firm profits will fall. Entry will continue as long as profit opportunities remain. Similarly, if firms are making losses in the short run, some will leave the industry, which will increase prices and profits (reduce losses).

In long-run equilibrium, illustrated in part (b) of the figure, firms will be making zero profits and there will be no more tendency for firms to either exit or enter the industry.

Figure 14.2 Costs and Demand, text page 359
If there are no barriers to entry, an industry will be characterized by duopoly if costs and industry demand are such that only two firms can survive in the long run. This figure illustrates such an industry using the example of two firms: Trick and Gear.

The firms have identical costs, which are shown in part (a). The minimum *ATC* of $6,000 occurs at the quantity of 3,000 switchgears per firm per week. Since, at a price of $6,000, the total quantity demanded in the industry is 6,000 switchgears per week, only two firms can survive in the long run.

Figure 14.3 Colluding to Make Monopoly Profits, text page 360
The two firms of a duopoly industry obtain maximum total profit by colluding. This is illustrated in this figure once again using the example of Trick and Gear.

In order to maximize total profit, the firms will, together, behave as a single monopolist by producing the output at which *industry* marginal cost is equal to *industry* marginal revenue.

The individual (identical) firm cost curves are given in part (a) of the figure. The industry marginal cost curve is the horizontal sum of the two firms' marginal cost curves and is given in part (b). The industry marginal revenue curve is also given there.

The firms will produce the quantity at which the *MC* and *MR* curves intersect (4,000 units) and charge the monopoly price obtained from the industry demand curve ($9,000). The firms then divide the production and the profits. As seen in part (a), each firm produces 2,000 switchgears per week and earns a profit of $2 million per week.

Figure 14.5 Both Firms Cheat, text page 362
After the firms of a duopoly enter into a collusive agreement, each firm can either abide by the agreement or cheat by increasing output and reducing price.

Each firm has an incentive to cheat since it can increase its profit (at the expense of the noncheating firm) by doing so. The case of both firms cheating is illustrated for Trick and Gear in this figure. The limit to the breakdown of the agreement is the competitive equilibrium. The limit for each firm is shown in part (a) and for the industry in part (b).

Once the collusive agreement has broken down by the cheating of the firms, successively lower prices will result until the price has fallen to the competitive level and both firms are making zero profit as seen in part (a). The industry output and price will be those associated with the competitive equilibrium, at the intersection of the industry marginal cost curve and the industry demand curve.

Table 14.2 Market Structure, text page 347
This table summarizes the characteristics of the four market structures that have been discussed in this and previous chapters. These are, from most competitive to least competitive: perfect competition, monopolistic competition, oligopoly, and monopoly. These are compared on the basis of the number of firms in the industry, the kind of product, the nature of any barriers to entry, the firm's control over price, and the concentration ratio. The table also provides examples of each market structure. This table is an excellent study tool.

Table 14.4 Duopoly Payoff Matrix, page 363
One way to analyze the interactive behaviour of firms in an oligopoly is to use game theory and construct a payoff matrix. A payoff matrix indicates the payoffs associated with the alternative strategy combinations of the players of the game. The payoff matrix for Trick and Gear is illustrated in this table.

These two firms of a duopoly industry have entered into a collusive agreement with the intent of maximizing total profit. Once the agreement has been established, each firm has two possible strategies: to cheat on the agreement or to comply. The payoff matrix indicates the profit for each firm, which results from each of the four possible strategy pairs. Each firm then chooses its best strategy.

For example, Trick will consider it's best strategy under each choice that Gear might make. If Gear cheats, Trick is better off by cheating (zero profit is better than a $1 million loss). If Gear complies, Trick is also better off by cheating (a $4.5 million profit is better than a $2 million profit). Thus Trick's dominant strategy is to cheat. The same analysis leads Gear to decide to cheat also. The result is a Nash equilibrium in which both firms cheat.

SELF-TEST

CONCEPT REVIEW

1) The most commonly used measure of concentration is called the four-firm ______________ ______________. This is the percentage of ______________ accounted for by the largest four firms in the industry.

2) The market structure characterized by a large number of firms that compete with each other by making similar but slightly different products is called ______________ ______________. The market structure characterized by a small number of producers competing with each other is called ______________.

3) When profits are being made in a monopolistically competitive industry, firms will ______________. If losses are being made, firms will ______________. As a result, in a monopolistically competitive industry, in long-run equilibrium, each firm will make a(n) ______________ economic profit and will have ______________ capacity.

4) The modern approach to understanding oligopoly uses ______________ theory, a method of analyzing strategic interaction invented by John von Neumann. In such a theory all the possible actions of each player are called ______________ and the score of each player is called the ______________.

5) A market structure in which only two producers of a commodity compete with each other is called ______________.

6) The table that shows the payoffs for every possible action by each player for every possible action by the other player is called a(n) ______________ ______________.

7) The equilibrium of a game like the prisoner's dilemma is called a(n) ______________ equilibrium. A special case of such an equilibrium occurs when the best strategy for each player is the same regardless of the action taken by the other player. This is called a(n) ______________ ______________ equilibrium.

8) A group of firms that has entered into a collusive agreement to restrict output and increase price and profits is called a(n) ______________ . Each firm in the group can pursue one of two strategies: it can either comply or ______________ .

9) In a repeated game, the strategy in which a player begins by co-operating and then cheats only if the other player cheated the previous time the game was played is called a(n) ______________ - ______________ - ______________ strategy.

10) In a repeated game, the strategy in which a player co-operates if the other player co-operates, but plays the Nash equilibrium strategy forever thereafter if the other player cheats is called a ______________ ______________ .

11) The equilibrium which results from each player responding rationally to a credible threat of a heavy penalty from the other player if the agreement is broken, is called a(n) ______________ equilibrium.

TRUE OR FALSE

_____ 1) A low concentration ratio indicates a low degree of competition.

_____ 2) A high concentration ratio guarantees a low degree of competition.

_____ 3) In a monopolistically competitive industry, each firm faces a downward-sloping demand curve.

_____ 4) Product differentiation is what gives a monopolistically competitive firm some monopoly power.

_____ 5) A critical difference between monopoly and monopolistic competition is that in the latter case there is free entry.

_____ 6) Free entry is the key characteristic of monopolistic competition that produces excess capacity.

_____ 7) We use game theory to analyze monopolistic competition because the behaviour of any one firm will have a significant influence on other firms.

_____ 8) If firms in a monopolistically competitive industry are making profits, we can expect to see their demand curves shift to the left as new firms enter.

_____ 9) When a monopolistically competitive industry is in long-run equilibrium, economic profits are zero and price equals minimum average total cost.

_____ 10) In long-run equilibrium, a monopolistically competitive firm will produce more output than that associated with the minimum point on it's average total cost curve.

_____ 11) Advertising by monopolistic competitors will always be allocatively inefficient.

_____ 12) An oligopolist will consider the reaction of other firms before it decides to cut its price.

_____ 13) In the prisoner's dilemma, the choices of confessing or denying, which are available to each player, are called strategies.

_____ 14) A Nash equilibrium occurs when *A* takes the best possible action, given the action of *B*, and *B* takes the best possible action, given the action of *A*.

_____ 15) If two players in a game face the same choices, there cannot be a dominant strategy equilibrium.

_____ 16) If duopolists agree to collude, they can (jointly) make as much profit as a single monopoly.

_____ 17) A member of a cartel could increase its profit if it increased its output, and all other members of the cartel produced their agreed level of output.

_____ 18) In the case of colluding duopolists in a nonrepeated game, the dominant strategy equilibrium is for both firms to cheat.

_____ 19) More than one equilibrium is possible if the game described in question 18 is repeated indefinitely.

_____ 20) In a cartel with several firms, if a single firm cuts its price, the best strategy for the other firms is to maintain the agreed upon price.

_____ 21) A situation in which both firms cheat could not be a Nash equilibrium.

MULTIPLE-CHOICE

1) The four-firm concentration ratio measures the share of the largest four firms in total industry
   a) profits
   b) sales
   c) cost
   d) capital
   e) none of the above

2) Which of the following is *not* a problem with concentration ratios as a measure of industry competitiveness?
   a) Concentration ratios are national measures, but firms in some industries operate in regional markets.
   b) Concentration ratios are national measures, but firms in some industries operate in international markets.
   c) Concentration ratios tell us nothing about the severity of barriers to entry in the industry.
   d) Concentration ratios tell us nothing about how cost varies among firms in the industry.
   e) Concentration ratios have difficulty classifying multiproduct firms by industry.

3) Under monopolistic competition, long-run economic profits tend toward zero *because of*
   a) product differentiation.
   b) the lack of barriers to entry.
   c) excess capacity.
   d) inefficiency.
   e) the downward-sloping demand curve facing each firm.

4) In the long run, the firm in monopolistic competition will
   a) face a perfectly elastic demand curve.
   b) produce more than the quantity that minimizes *ATC*.
   c) produce less than the quantity that minimizes *ATC*.
   d) produce the quantity that minimizes *ATC*.
   e) earn economic profits.

5) Figure 14.1 represents a monopolistically competitive firm in short-run equilibrium. What is the firm's level of output?
   a) Q_1
   b) Q_2
   c) Q_3
   d) Q_4
   e) zero

Figure 14.1

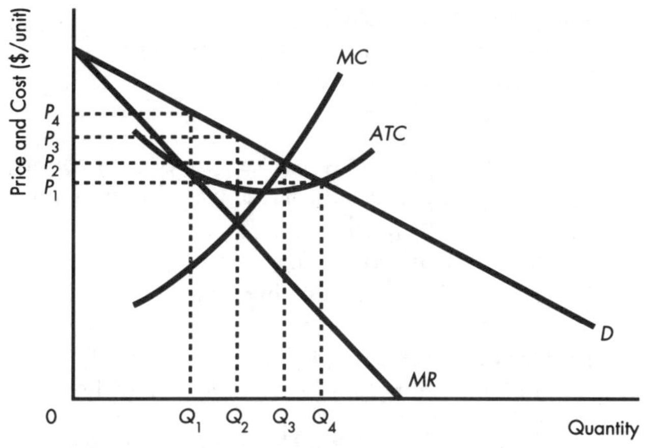

6) What will be the price charged by the monopolistic competitor of Figure 14.1?
   a) P_1
   b) P_2
   c) P_3
   d) P_4
   e) zero, since the firm has shut down

7) Refer again to the short-run situation illustrated in Figure 14.1. We know, in the long run,
   a) there will be entry of new firms and each existing firm's demand will shift to the left.
   b) there will be entry of new firms and each existing firm's demand will shift to the right.
   c) existing firms will leave and each remaining firm's demand will shift to the left.
   d) existing firms will leave and each remaining firm's demand will shift to the right.
   e) there will be no change from the short run.

8) In the long run, a monopolistically competitive firm will produce the output at which price equals
   a) marginal cost.
   b) marginal revenue.
   c) average variable cost.
   d) average total cost.
   e) both b) and d).

9) Which of the following characteristics is *not* shared by single-price monopoly and monopolistic competition?
   a) firms face a downward-sloping demand curve
   b) profit-maximizing quantity where $MC = MR$
   c) $P = AR$
   d) positive long-run economic profits
   e) positive long-run normal profits

10) In the long run, a monopolistically competitive firm will earn the same economic profits as
a) a monopolistically competitive firm in the short run.
b) a member of a cartel.
c) a pure price-discriminating monopolist.
d) a perfectly competitive firm.
e) none of the above.

11) Which of the following is true for perfect competition, monopolistic competition, and single-price monopoly?
a) homogeneous product
b) zero long-run economic profits
c) short-run profit maximizing quantity where $MC = MR$
d) easy entry and exit
e) none of the above

12) Each of the following is a characteristic of monopolistic competition. Which of them is *not* also a characteristic of oligopoly?
a) Each firm faces a downward-sloping demand curve.
b) Firms are profit-maximizers.
c) The sales of one firm will not have a significant effect on other firms.
d) There is more than one firm in the industry.
e) Firms set prices.

13) The kinked demand curve theory
a) suggests that price will remain constant even with fluctuations in demand.
b) suggests how the current price is determined.
c) assumes that marginal revenue sometimes increases with output.
d) assumes that competitors will match price cuts and ignore price increases.
e) suggests none of the above.

14) Which of the following is *not* an aspect common to all games?
a) rules
b) collusion
c) strategies
d) payoffs
e) the analysis of strategic interaction

15) In the prisoner's dilemma with players Alf and Bob, each prisoner would be best off if
a) both prisoners confess.
b) both prisoners deny.
c) Alf denies and Bob confesses.
d) Bob denies and Alf confesses.
e) none of the above is done.

16) In the prisoner's dilemma with players Alf and Bob, the dominant strategy equilibrium is
a) both prisoners confess.
b) both prisoners deny.
c) Alf denies and Bob confesses.
d) Bob denies and Alf confesses.
e) indeterminate.

17) If a duopoly with collusion maximizes profit,
a) each firm must produce the same amount.
b) each firm must produce its maximum output possible.
c) industry marginal revenue must equal industry marginal cost at the level of total output.
d) industry demand must equal industry marginal cost at the level of total output.
e) total output will be greater than without collusion.

18) The firms Trick and Gear form a cartel to collude to maximize profit. If this game is nonrepeated, the dominant strategy equilibrium is
a) both firms cheat on the agreement.
b) both firms comply with the agreement.
c) Trick cheats while Gear complies with the agreement.
d) Gear cheats while Trick complies with the agreement.
e) indeterminate.

19) Consider the same cartel consisting of Trick and Gear. Now, however, the game is repeated indefinitely and each firm employs a tit-for-tat strategy. The equilibrium is
a) both firms cheat on the agreement.
b) both firms comply with the agreement.
c) Trick cheats while Gear complies with the agreement.
d) Gear cheats while Trick complies with the agreement.
e) indeterminate.

20) The name of the equilibrium in question 19 is called a
a) credible strategy equilibrium.
b) dominant player equilibrium.
c) duopoly equilibrium.
d) trigger strategy equilibrium.
e) co-operative equilibrium.

21) Table 14.1 gives the payoff matrix in terms of profit for firms *A* and *B* when there are two strategies facing each firm: (1) charge a low price or (2) charge a high price. The equilibrium in this game (played once) is a dominant strategy equilibrium since
a) firm *B* will reduce profit by more than *A* if both charge a lower price.
b) firm *B* is the dominant firm.
c) the best strategy for each firm does not depend on the strategy chosen by the other.
d) there is no credible threat by either firm to punish the other if it breaks the agreement.
e) all of the above are true.

Table 14.1

		Firm B: Low Price	Firm B: High Price
Firm A	Low Price	A: $2 B: $5	A: $20 B: –$15
Firm A	High Price	A: -$10 B: $25	A: $10 B: $20

22) Refer again to the nonrepeated game in Table 14.1. In equilibrium, what are firm *A*'s profits?
a) –$10
b) $2
c) $10
d) $20
e) indeterminate

SHORT ANSWER

1) a) Considering the geographical scope of markets, how might concentration ratios *understate* the degree of competitiveness in an industry?
b) How might they *overstate* the degree of competitiveness in an industry?

2) Why will a firm in a monopolistically competitive industry always have excess capacity in long-run equilibrium?

3) Compare the advantages and disadvantages of perfect competition and monopolistic competition in terms of allocative efficiency.

4) Consider the case of two colluding duopolists in a nonrepeated game. Why will both firms cheat on the agreement in equilibrium?

5) How can a price war which eliminates profits be explained using game theory?

PROBLEMS

1) Consider a single firm in a monopolistically competitive industry in the short run. On a grid similar to the grid shown in Figure 14.2, draw a new graph for each of the following situations.

Figure 14.2

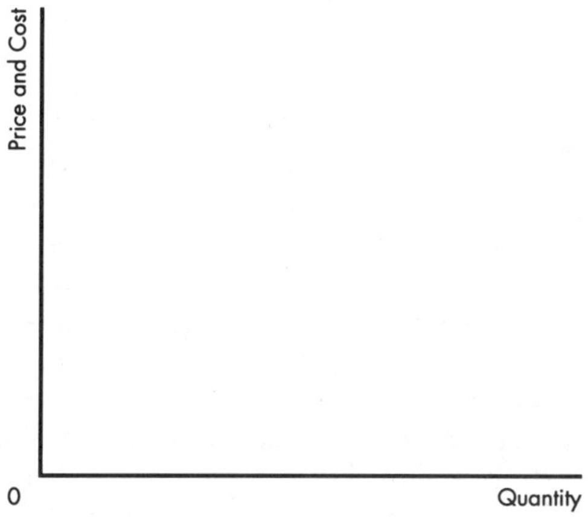

a) The firm is making a profit.
b) The firm is making a loss that will cause shutdown.
c) The firm is making a loss but is still producing.
d) Starting from the situation in part (c), explain what will happen in this industry and how your graph in part (c) will be affected? (No new graph is required.)
e) The firm is in long-run equilibrium.

2) Consider a monopolistically competitive industry in long-run equilibrium. Firm *A* in this industry decides to attempt to increase profits by advertising.
   a) On the grid in Figure 14.3, show graphically, and briefly discuss what will happen in the short run as a result of the decision to advertise.

Figure 14.3

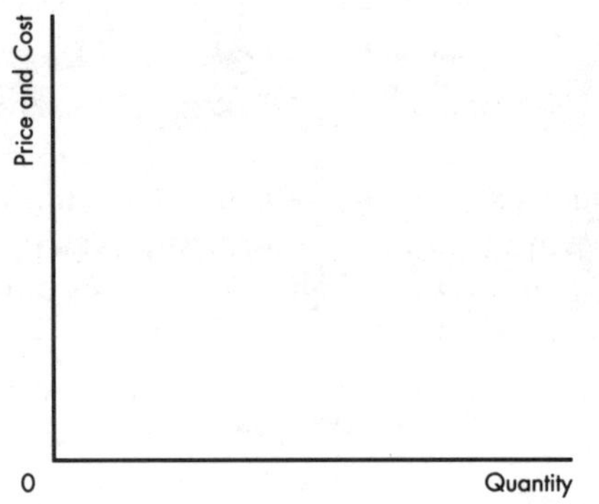

   b) If the firm is successful in raising profits in the short run, what will happen in the long run?

3) A duopoly industry with no collusion consists of firms *A* and *B*, which are essentially identical. Currently, neither firm is advertising and each is making a profit of $5 million per year. If *A* advertises and *B* does not, *A* will make an annual profit of $12 million while *B* will make a loss of $5 million.
   On the other hand, if *B* advertises and *A* does not, *B* will make a $12 million profit and *A* will make a loss of $5 million. If both advertise, each will make a zero profit.
   a) Represent this duopoly as a game by identifying the players, strategies, and possible outcomes.
   b) Construct the payoff matrix.
   c) What is the equilibrium outcome? Explain.

4) Use the graphs given in Figure 14.4 to answer this question. Figure 14.4 (a) gives the average total cost (*ATC*)curve for each of two identical firms (call them *A* and *B*) in a duopoly. Figure 14.4 (b) gives the market demand curve and the firms' joint marginal cost curve. Suppose these firms collude to maximize profit and agree to divide output equally *for a single year.*
   a) How much will each firm produce by the agreement and what price will they charge?
   b) What is each firm's average total cost and profit?

Figure 14.4

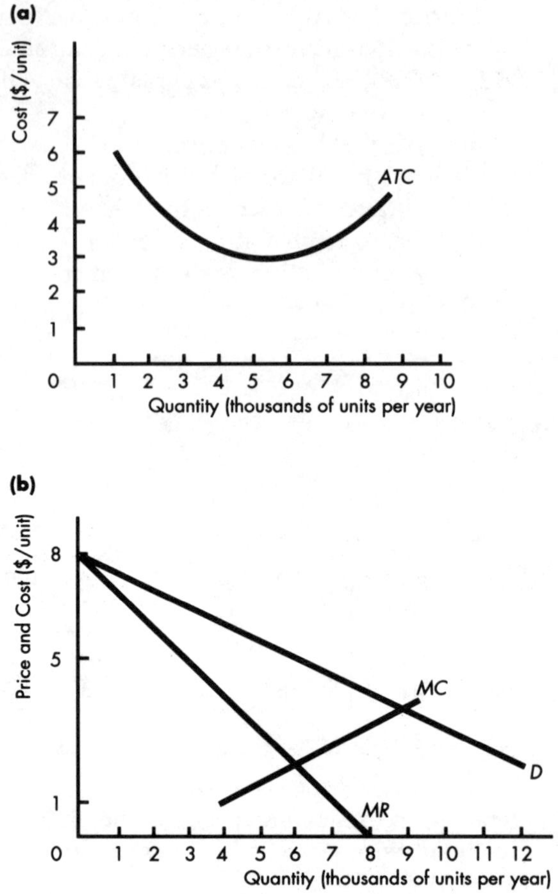

   c) Now suppose that firm *B* convinces *A* that demand has decreased and they must reduce their price by $1 per unit in order to sell their agreed upon quantity. Of course, demand has ***not*** decreased but *A* produces its agreed amount and charges $1 less per unit. Firm *B*, the cheater, also charges $1 less than the original agreement price but increases output sufficiently to satisfy the rest of demand at this price.
      i) How much does *B* produce?
      ii) What is firm *A*'s average total cost and profit?
      iii) What is firm *B*'s average total cost and profit?
   d) Return to the initial situation. The firms are preparing to enter into a *long-term* agreement but before they do, firm *A* assures firm *B* (credibly) that if firm *B* cheats, it will undercut *B*'s price as soon as the cheating is discovered. Would *B* want to cheat now? Why or why not?

ANSWERS

CONCEPT REVIEW

1) concentration ratio; sales
2) monopolistic competition; oligopoly
3) enter; leave; zero; excess
4) game; strategies; payoff
5) duopoly
6) payoff matrix
7) Nash; dominant strategy
8) cartel; cheat
9) tit-for-tat
10) trigger strategy
11) co-operative

TRUE OR FALSE

1) F	8) T	15) F
2) F	9) F	16) T
3) T	10) F	17) T
4) T	11) F	18) T
5) T	12) T	19) T
6) F	13) T	20) F
7) F	14) T	21) F

MULTIPLE-CHOICE

1) b	6) c	11) c	16) a	21) c
2) d	7) a	12) c	17) c	22) b
3) b	8) d	13) d	18) a	
4) c	9) d	14) b	19) b	
5) b	10) d	15) b	20) e	

SHORT ANSWER

1) a) Since concentration ratios are calculated from a national perspective, if the actual geographical scope of the market is not national, the concentration ratio is likely to misstate the degree of competitiveness in an industry. For example, if the actual market is global, the concentration ratio will understate the degree of competitiveness, and it will be too high. It is possible for a firm to have a concentration ratio of 100 because it is the only producer in the nation, but faces a great deal of international competition.

b) Similarly, when the scope of the market is regional, the degree of competitiveness is likely to be less than would be indicated by the simple concentration ratio.

2) A firm is defined to have excess capacity if it is producing in the negatively-sloped portion of its average total cost curve. At the long-run equilibrium level of output (sales) in a monopolistically competitive industry, each firm will be earning zero profit and its average total cost curve will be tangent to its demand curve. Since the demand curve of a monopolistic competitor is downward sloping, so is the average total cost curve at that level of output. Therefore, the monopolistically competitive firm will have excess capacity in long-run equilibrium.

3) The advantage of perfect competition is that it leads to production at minimum average total cost, while monopolistic competition leads to a higher average total cost with reduced output.

The advantage of monopolistic competition is that it leads to greater product variety, which consumers value, while in a perfectly competitive industry there is a single, identical product produced by all firms. Thus, the loss in allocative efficiency (higher *ATC*) that occurs in monopolistic competition has to be weighed against the gain of greater product variety.

4) Each firm's best strategy is to cheat regardless of the strategy of the other firm. Call the firms *A* and *B*. Firm *A* knows that if firm *B* follows the collusive agreement, *A* can increase its profit by cheating. If firm *B* cheats, then firm *A* knows that it must also cheat to minimize its loss of profit. Thus cheating is the dominant strategy for firm *A*. Accordingly, it is also the dominant strategy for firm *B*.

5) Game theory explains price wars as the consequence of firms in a colluding industry responding to the cheating of a firm. If one firm cheats by cutting its price, then all other firms will cut their prices, and a price war will ensue. Once the price has fallen sufficiently, (perhaps to the zero profit level), the firms will again have a strong incentive to rebuild their collusion.

PROBLEMS

1) a) Figure 14.2 Solution (a) illustrates a monopolistically competitive firm making a profit in the short run. The important feature of the graph is that at the profit-maximizing output, price is greater than average total cost. Profit is given by the shaded area in the graph.

Figure 14.2 Solution

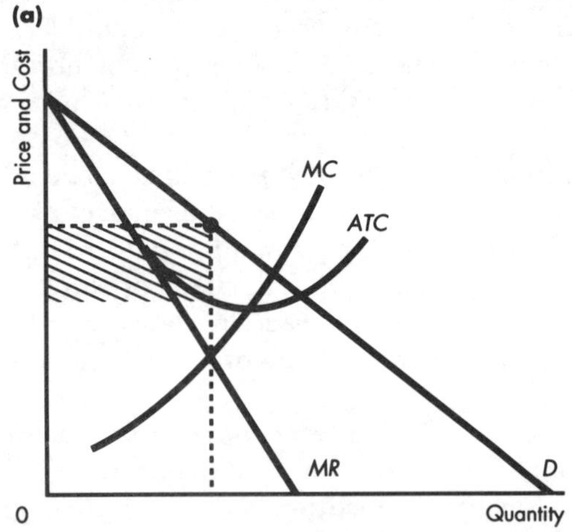

b) Figure 14.2 Solution (b) illustrates a firm that will shut down in the short run since price is less than average variable cost at the profit maximizing (loss minimizing) level of output.

Figure 14.2 Solution

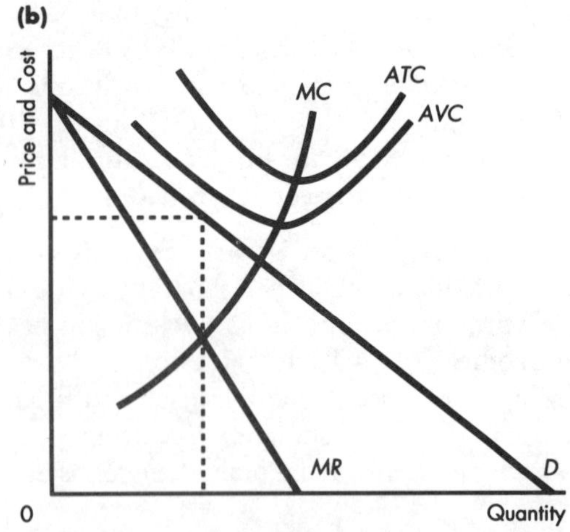

c) Figure 14.2 Solution (c) illustrates a firm making a loss but continuing to produce. The loss is given by the shaded area in the graph. Note that, at the profit maximizing output, price is less than *ATC* but greater than *AVC*.

Figure 14.2 Solution

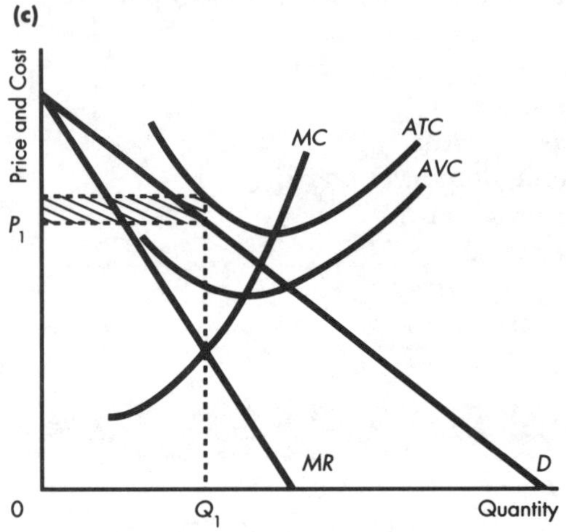

d) Since firms are typically experiencing a loss, firms will leave the industry. This means that the demand curves facing each of the remaining firms will begin to shift out as they each attract some of the customers of the departing firms. As the firm demand curves shift out, losses are reduced. Firms will continue to have an incentive to leave until losses have been eliminated. Thus, firm demand curves will continue to shift out until they are tangent to the *ATC* curve.

e) Figure 14.2 Solution (e) on page 171 illustrates a typical monopolistically competitive firm in long-run equilibrium. The key feature is that the demand curve facing the firm is tangent to the *ATC* curve at the profit maximizing output. Thus the firm is making a zero profit.

Figure 14.2 Solution

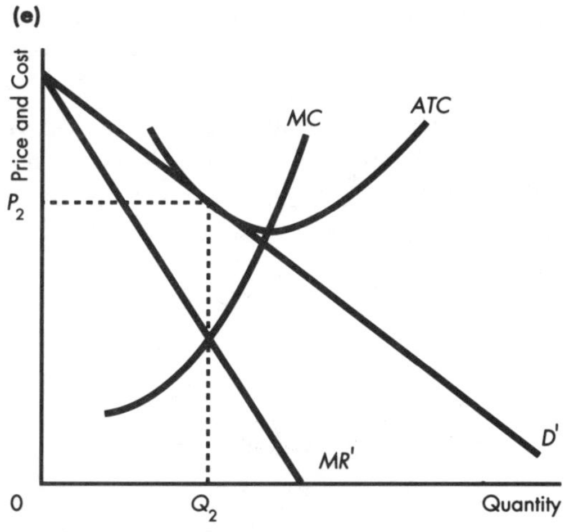

2) a) Advertising will increase firm *A*'s cost but also increase demand (it hopes). If the increase in demand (revenue) is greater than the increase in cost, then firm *A* will have increased its profit. Figure 14.3 Solution illustrates this situation. The initial curves are given by D_0, ATC_0, MR_0.

Initially the firm is producing Q_0 and selling at price P_0 and making zero profit. Advertising, which is a fixed cost, raises the *ATC* curve to ATC_1 (*MC* does not shift), but also increases the demand and marginal revenue curves to D_1 and MR_1, respectively. The shift in the demand curve is sufficiently great that there is now a positive profit at the new profit-maximizing level of output (Q_1). The profit is indicated by the shaded area of the graph.

Figure 14.3 Solution

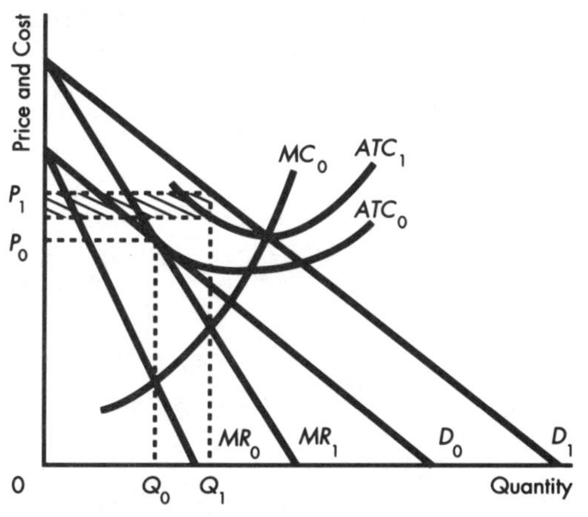

b) No doubt other firms will also begin to advertise in an attempt to increase their profit (or recover lost profit). As all other firms advertise, the demand curve for our firm will shift back to the left as it loses some of the customers it has gained. In the long run, once again, all firms will be making zero profit even after advertising.

3) a) The players are firms *A* and *B*. Each firm has two strategies: to advertise or not to advertise. There are four possible outcomes: (1) both firms advertise, (2) firm *A* advertises but firm *B* does not, (3) firm *B* advertises but firm *A* does not, and (4) neither firm advertises.

b) The payoff matrix is given in Table 14.2. The entries give the profit earned by firms *A* and *B* under each of the four possible outcomes.

Table 14.2

		Firm B: Advertise	Firm B: Not Advertise
Firm A	Advertise	A: 0 B: 0	A: \$12 million B: –\$5 million
	Not Advertise	A: –\$5 million B: \$12 million	A: \$5 million B: \$5 million

c) First consider how firm *A* decides which strategy to pursue. If *B* advertises, *A* can advertise and make zero profit or not advertise and make a \$5 million loss. Thus firm *A* will want to advertise if firm *B* does.

If *B* does not advertise, *A* can advertise and make a \$12 million profit or not advertise and make a \$5 million profit. Therefore, firm *A* will want to advertise whether firm *B* advertises or not. Firm *B* will come to the same conclusion. Thus, the dominant strategy equilibrium is that both firms advertise.

4) a) The firms will agree to produce 3,000 units each and sell at a price of \$5 per unit. We determine this by noticing (Figure 14.2 (b)) that the profit-maximizing (monopoly) output is 6,000 units for the industry (*MR* = *MC* at 6,000) at a price of \$5. Since the firms have agreed to divide output equally, each will produce 3,000 units.

b) From Figure 14.2 (a) we determine that, at 3,000 units, each firm's average total cost is \$4 per unit. Since price is $5, profit will be $3,000 for each firm.

c) i) At the new price of $4, the total quantity demanded is 8,000 units. Since *A* continues to produce 3,000 units, this means that firm *B* will produce the remaining 5,000 units demanded.

ii) Since firm *A* continues to produce 3,000 units, its average total cost continues to be $4 per unit. With the new price also at $4, firm *A* will make a zero profit.

iii) Firm B has increased output to 5,000 units, which implies average total cost of $3 per unit. Thus, given a price of $4, firm B's profit will be $5,000.

d) Given that the agreement is longterm, firm B would almost surely not cheat. The reason is that, while firm B could increase short-term profit by cheating, it would lose much more future profit (in terms of present value) if firm A retaliates.

The basic point to be understood is that firm *B*'s behaviour changes, not because cost or demand have changed, but rather because firm *A*'s behaviour is different. Thus, the best strategy for any firm will depend on the behaviour of other firms.

Chapter 15 Pricing and Allocating Factors of Production

Chapter in Perspective

Text Pages 379–404

In Chapters 9 through 11 we examined the output decisions that firms make. We explored the nature of costs and how firms bring together factors of production to produce output. For convenience and to allow us to focus directly on the issues at hand, we assumed there that the prices of the factors of production were given and constant.

In this chapter we explain how those factor prices are determined. As with the prices of outputs of goods and services, the prices of productive inputs are determined in markets — markets for factors of production. These markets have many of the same characteristics as the markets for goods and services we have examined in Chapters 12 through 14. Here we take a broad first look at markets for factors of production, leaving more detailed discussion of specific markets to later chapters.

Learning Objectives

After studying this chapter, you will be able to:

- **Explain how firms choose the quantities of labour, capital, and land to employ in their production activities.**
- **Explain how households choose the quantities of labour, capital, and land to supply.**
- **Explain how wages, interest, and land rent are determined in competitive factor markets.**
- **Explain the concept of economic rent.**
- **Distinguish between economic rent and transfer earnings.**

Helpful Hints

1) The purpose of this chapter is to give a broad overview of the characteristics that are common to the markets for all factors of production. For example, the assumption that firms are profit-maximizers implies that they will hire each factor of production up to the point where marginal revenue product is equal to the marginal cost of the factor, regardless of whether the factor of production is labour, land, or capital.

2) Be sure to distinguish carefully between the marginal revenue product of a factor of production and the marginal revenue of a unit of output. As noted in the text, the marginal revenue product of a factor of production can be calculated by multiplying marginal revenue and marginal product ($MRP = MR \times MP$). We can think of this intuitively as follows: marginal product tells us how much more output we receive from using more of a factor, and marginal revenue tells us how much more revenue we receive from each unit of that additional output. Therefore, *MP* times *MR* tells us how much more revenue we receive from using more of the factor (the *MRP*).

Key Figures and Tables

Figure 15.1 Demand and Supply in a Factor Market, text page 382
Factor prices are determined in factor markets. The demand and supply curves for factors of production have the same properties as the demand and supply curves for goods.

The quantity of a factor demanded decreases as the price of the factor increases and the quantity of a factor supplied increases as the price of the factor increases.

This figure depicts the market for a factor of production. Equilibrium occurs at the intersection of the demand and supply curves. The amount of total factor income is given by the area of the blue rectangle which is the price of a unit of the factor (*PF*) times the quantity of factors hired (*QF*).

Figure 15.4 Marginal Revenue Product and the Demand for Labour at Max's Wash 'n' Wax, text page 387
A firm's demand for labour curve is the same as it's marginal revenue product curve of labour. This is illustrated in the figure using the example of Max's Wash 'n' Wax.

Part (a) of the figure shows the average revenue product curve (*ARP*) and the corresponding marginal revenue product curve (*MRP*). These curves plot the values reported in Table 15.1 on text page 385.

Notice that the values for *MRP* are plotted midway between the labour inputs used in their calculation. For example, the *MRP* of moving from 0 to 1 labourer is 20, so the value of 20 on the *MRP* curve is plotted midway between 0 and 1 labourers.

Part (b) constructs Max's demand for labour by asking how much labour Max would be willing to hire at alternative wage rates. Since Max is a profit-maximizer, he will want to hire labour up to the point where the marginal revenue product of labour is equal to the wage rate. For example, if the wage rate is $10 per hour, Max will hire 3 workers since marginal revenue product is $10 when 3 workers are hired. Other points on the labour demand curve can be obtained in similar fashion. The result, as seen in part (b), is that the labour demand curve is the same as the *MRP* curve.

Figure 15.8 Labour Market Equilibrium, text page 396
This figure shows equilibrium in two different labour markets. Part (a) illustrates the labour market for news anchors. News anchors are portrayed as having a very high marginal revenue product (as indicated by the height of the demand curve). Since the supply of news anchors is low, the equilibrium wage rate for news anchors is very high ($500 per hour).

Part (b) illustrates the labour market for fast-food servers. The marginal revenue product of servers is relatively low and the supply is large. As a result, the wage rate for servers is quite low ($2 an hour).

Figure 15.9 Capital Market Equilibrium, text 397
Two markets for capital are shown here. Part (a) illustrates the market for capital in the steel industry and part (b) illustrates the market for capital in the computer industry. In both cases, the demand curves for capital are downward-sloping, like the demand curves for other factors of production. Also, in both industries, the long-run supply of capital is perfectly elastic at interest rate *R*.

In the short run, however, the supply of steel-making capital equipment actually in place is fixed at Q_1, and the short-run equilibrium interest rate earned by owners of capital in the steel industry is R_1.

The short-run supply of computer-making capital equipment actually in place is fixed at Q_3, and the short-run equilibrium interest rate earned by owners of capital in the computer industry is R_2. Since the short-run return on capital is higher in the computer industry than in the steel industry ($R_2 > R_1$), there will be an incentive to transfer capital from the steel industry to the computer industry.

Over time, this will reduce the short-run supply of capital equipment in the steel industry and increase the short-run supply of capital equipment in the computer industry. As a result, the interest rate on capital in the steel industry will rise and the interest rate on capital in the computer industry will fall. This transfer of capital will continue until the short-run interest rates in both capital markets are equal to *R*, which will then be a long-run equilibrium.

Figure 15.10 Land Market Equilibrium, text page 398
This figure illustrates factors that determine whether equilibrium rent in specific land markets will be high or low. Part (a) illustrates a market in which the marginal revenue product of land is high but there is a very limited fixed supply. Note that the quantity of land is measured in square metres. This market is for well-located urban land: Toronto's Yorkville district. The combination of high marginal revenue product (high demand) and low supply yields an equilibrium annual land rent which is very high: $1,000 per square metre.

Part (b) illustrates a market in which the marginal revenue product of land is not so high and the fixed supply is large. Note that the quantity of land is measured in hectares. This is the market for Manitoba farmland. The resulting equilibrium annual land rent is rather low: $500 per hectare.

Figure 15.11 Economic Rent and Transfer Earnings, text page 399
Total income received by the owners of a factor of production can be divided into two components: economic rent and transfer earnings. This figure illustrates the division.

It shows the demand and supply curves for a factor of production. The total income received by the factor owners is given by the price of the factor (*PF*) times the quantity of the factor hired (*QF*), which is the area of the blue and yellow rectangle in the figure.

Transfer earnings are the part of income that is required to induce the supply of the factor. They are measured by the part of the income rectangle that lies below the supply curve, shown in yellow in the figure. Economic rent is the part of factor income that exceeds transfer earnings, shown in blue in the figure.

Table 15.2 Compact Glossary of Factor Market Terms, text page 386
While this chapter discusses a variety of specific factor markets, there are some important general terms that are used when discussing any factor markets. These terms are reviewed in this table, providing a handy resource for reference and review.

Table 15.3 Two Conditions for Maximum Profit, text page 388
Output and input decisions are guided by the firm's desire to maximize profit. In previous chapters we learned that a profit-maximizing firm will choose the level of output at which marginal revenue equals marginal cost ($MR = MC$). In this chapter, we have seen that a profit-maximizing firm will hire a factor up to the level at which marginal revenue product equals the price of the factor ($MRP = PF$). This table demonstrates that these two profit maximization conditions are equivalent.

Table 15.4 A Firm's Demand for Labour, text page 389
This table summarizes the law of demand as it applies to labour. The quantity of labour demanded is negatively related to the price of labour (the wage rate) along a given demand for labour curve. The table also indicates the *ceteris paribus* assumptions that, if changed, cause the demand for labour curve to shift.

SELF-TEST

CONCEPT REVIEW

1) Owners of factors of production receive income from firms for the use of those factors of production. The payment for labour is called _______________, the payment for capital is called _______________, and the payment for land is called _______________.

2) An increase in the demand for a factor of production will _______________ that factor's income. If the supply curve for a factor of production is very elastic, the resulting change in quantity traded will be _______________ and the change in price will be _______________.

3) The demand for a factor as an input in the productive process rather than for its own sake is called a(n) _______________ demand.

4) The change in total revenue resulting from _______________ an additional unit of _______________ is called the marginal revenue product of labour. If a profit-maximizing firm finds that the marginal revenue product of labour exceeds the wage, the firm should _______________ the quantity of labour it hires.

5) The law of diminishing returns implies that the marginal revenue product curve will be _______________ sloped. A firm's demand for labour curve will be based on its _______________ _______________ _______________ curve.

6) If the price of the good produced by firm *A* increases, the demand curve for labour hired by firm *A* will shift to the ______________ . A technological change that increases the marginal product of labour will shift the demand curve for labour to the ______________ .

7) Other things being equal, the higher the elasticity of demand for a product, the ______________ is the elasticity of demand for the labour that produces it. The more readily capital can be substituted for labour in production, the ______________ elastic is the long-run elasticity of demand for labour.

8) The lowest wage for which a household will supply labour to the market is called its ______________ wage.

9) An increase in the wage will have two effects on the quantity of labour supplied by a household. The income effect will lead to a(n) ______________ in the quantity of labour supplied and the substitution effect will lead to a(n) ______________ in the quantity of labour supplied.

10) The amount of saving by households will determine the supply of ______________ . Other things being equal, as the interest rate rises, households will ______________ the amount they save.

11) The income received by the owner of a factor of production, which exceeds the amount just necessary to induce the owner to offer the factor for use, is called ______________ ______________ .
The income required to induce the supply of the factor is called ______________ earnings.

TRUE OR FALSE

_____ 1) When the elasticity of demand for labour is greater than 1, an increase in the supply of labour will lead to a decrease in labour income.

_____ 2) As long as the labour supply curve is positively sloped, an increase in the demand for labour will increase total labour income.

_____ 3) A profit-maximizing firm will hire the quantity of a factor of production for which the marginal revenue product equals the marginal cost of the factor.

_____ 4) Marginal revenue product can be calculated as marginal revenue times average product.

_____ 5) The firm's demand for labour curve is the same as the average revenue product curve.

_____ 6) The market demand curve for labour is the horizontal sum of the individual firms' marginal revenue product of labour curves.

_____ 7) When discussing the short-run demand for labour, labour is considered to be the only variable input.

_____ 8) If the production of good *A* is labour intensive, the demand for labour used in the production of good *A* is likely to be rather inelastic.

_____ 9) The steeper the marginal product curve for labour, the less elastic is the firm's demand for labour.

_____ 10) The marginal revenue product of labour diminishes as more workers are hired because of the principle of diminishing marginal utility.

_____ 11) The short-run elasticity of demand for labour depends on the substitutability of capital for labour in the production process.

_____ 12) If the wage rate increases, the substitution effect results in the household increasing the time spent in market activities and decreasing the time spent in nonmarket activities.

_____ 13) A household supplies no labour at wage rates below its reservation wage.

_____ 14) If the wage rate increases, the income effect results in the household increasing its demand for leisure.

_____ 15) A backward-bending supply curve for labour will arise if the substitution effect dominates the income effect.

_____ 16) If a household has current income that is low when compared with its expected future income, it will save very little.

_____ 17) The household supply curve for capital shows the relationship between the interest rate and the quantity of capital supplied.

_____ 18) The market supply curve of capital is likely to be quite inelastic.

_____ 19) The market supply of a particular piece of land is perfectly elastic.

_____ 20) In the long run, the equilibrium interest rate on capital will be the same in all industries.

_____ 21) If the supply of a factor of production is perfectly inelastic, its entire income is transfer earnings.

_____ 22) If Lloyd Robertson would be willing to read the news for $100,000 per year, and he is paid $2,100,000 per year to do so, he is earning economic rent of $2,000,000.

MULTIPLE-CHOICE

1) The income received by owners of factors of production are wages paid for labour,
   a) profit paid for capital, and interest paid for money.
   b) dividends paid for capital, and interest paid for money.
   c) dividends paid for capital, and rent paid for land.
   d) interest paid for capital, and rent paid for land.
   e) profit paid for capital, and rent paid for land.

2) Suppose that the supply of a factor of production is very elastic. Then an increase in the demand for that factor will result in a
   a) large increase in the quantity supplied of the factor and a small increase in its price.
   b) small increase in the quantity supplied of the factor and a large increase in its price.
   c) large increase in the supply of the factor and a small increase in its price.
   d) small increase in the supply of the factor and a large increase in its price.
   e) small increase in the supply of the factor and a small increase in its price.

3) An increase in the supply of a factor of production will
   a) increase the factor's income if the elasticity of factor demand is less than 1.
   b) decrease the factor's income if the elasticity of factor demand is less than 1.
   c) increase the factor's income if the elasticity of factor supply is less than 1.
   d) decrease the factor's income if the elasticity of factor supply is less than 1.
   e) always decrease the factor's income.

4) An example of derived demand is the demand for
   a) sweaters derived by an economics student.
   b) sweaters produced by labour and capital.
   c) labour used in the production of sweaters.
   d) sweater brushes.
   e) none of the above.

5) The change in total revenue resulting from employing an additional unit of capital is the
   a) marginal product of capital.
   b) marginal revenue of capital.
   c) marginal revenue cost of capital.
   d) marginal revenue product of capital.
   e) average revenue product of capital.

6) When a firm is a price-taker in the labour market, its marginal revenue product of labour curve is also its
   a) marginal cost curve for labour.
   b) demand curve for labour.
   c) supply curve of labour.
   d) supply curve of output.
   e) average revenue curve.

7) Which of the following will *not* be true in a profit-maximizing equilibrium?
   a) Marginal revenue equals marginal product.
   b) Marginal revenue equals marginal cost.
   c) Marginal revenue times marginal product of a factor equals marginal factor cost.
   d) Marginal revenue product of a factor equals marginal factor cost.
   e) Marginal revenue product of a factor divided by marginal factor cost equals marginal product of a factor.

8) A profit-maximizing firm will continue to hire units of a variable factor of production until the
   a) marginal cost of the factor equals its marginal product.
   b) marginal cost of the factor equals its average revenue product.
   c) average cost of the factor equals its marginal revenue product.
   d) marginal cost of the factor equals its marginal revenue product.
   e) factor's marginal revenue product equals zero.

9) Suppose a profit-maximizing firm hires labour in a competitive labour market. If the marginal revenue product of labour is greater than the wage, the firm should
   a) increase the wage rate.
   b) decrease the wage rate.
   c) increase the quantity of labour it hires.
   d) decrease the quantity of labour it hires.
   e) shift to a more labour-intensive production process.

10) The demand curve for a factor of production will shift to the right as a result of
   a) a decrease in the price of the factor.
   b) an increase in the price of the factor.
   c) a decrease in the price of a substitute factor.
   d) an increase in the price of a substitute factor.
   e) a decrease in the price of output.

11) If the price of its output falls, a perfectly competitive firm will hire
   a) less labour, causing the wage to fall.
   b) less labour, causing the marginal product of labour to rise.
   c) less labour, causing the marginal product of labour to fall.
   d) more labour, causing the marginal product of labour to rise.
   e) more labour, causing the marginal product of labour to fall.

12) A technological change that causes an increase in the marginal product of labour will shift
  a) the labour demand curve to the left.
  b) the labour demand curve to the right.
  c) the labour supply curve to the left.
  d) the labour supply curve to the right.
  e) both b) and d).

13) Other things being equal, the larger the proportion of total cost coming from labour, the
  a) more elastic is the demand for labour.
  b) less elastic is the demand for labour.
  c) more elastic is the supply of labour.
  d) less elastic is the supply of labour.
  e) lower is the demand for labour.

14) Which of the following statements about the short-run demand for labour, *ceteris paribus*, is true?
  a) The larger the elasticity of demand is for the product, the less elastic is the demand for labour.
  b) The higher the labour intensity of the production process is, the less elastic is the demand for labour.
  c) The steeper is the marginal product of labour curve, the less elastic is the demand for labour.
  d) All of the above are true.
  e) None of the above is true.

15) If the wage rate increases, the *substitution* effect will give a household an incentive to
  a) raise its reservation wage.
  b) increase its nonmarket activity and decrease its market activity.
  c) increase its market activity and decrease its nonmarket activity.
  d) increase both market and nonmarket activity.
  e) decrease both market and nonmarket activity.

16) If the wage rate increases, the *income* effect will give a household an incentive to
  a) raise its reservation wage.
  b) increase its nonmarket activity and decrease its market activity.
  c) increase its market activity and decrease its nonmarket activity.
  d) increase both market and nonmarket activity.
  e) decrease both market and nonmarket activity.

17) As the wage rate continues to rise, a household will have a backward-bending supply of labour curve if
  a) the income effect is in the same direction as the substitution effect.
  b) the wage rate rises above the reservation wage.
  c) the substitution effect dominates the income effect.
  d) the income effect dominates the substitution effect.
  e) leisure is an inferior good.

18) Household savings are larger when either current income is
  a) low compared with expected future income or interest rates are high.
  b) low compared with expected future income or interest rates are low.
  c) high compared with expected future income or interest rates are high.
  d) high compared with expected future income or interest rates are low.
  e) above or below the reservation wage.

19) Whether a household's current income is high or low *compared with expected future income* is influenced by
  a) the stage of the life cycle the household is in.
  b) whether the household is rich or poor.
  c) whether interest rates are high or low.
  d) whether saving is high or low.
  e) all of the above.

20) In the short run, a firm faces a supply of capital that is
  a) perfectly elastic.
  b) perfectly inelastic.
  c) positively sloped.
  d) negatively sloped.
  e) backward bending.

21) If the desire for leisure increased, the wage rate would
  a) rise and the quantity of labour hired would fall.
  b) rise and the quantity of labour hired would rise.
  c) fall and the quantity of labour hired would fall.
  d) fall and the quantity of labour hired would rise.
  e) fall and the quantity of labour demanded would rise.

22) If the interest rate on capital in industry *A* is lower than the interest rate on capital in industry *B* then, in the long run,
  a) the supply of capital in industry *A* will decrease and the supply of capital in industry *B* will increase until the interest rates are equal.
  b) the supply of capital in industry *A* will increase and the supply of capital in industry *B* will decrease until the interest rates are equal.
  c) the supply of capital in industry *A* must be more elastic than the supply of capital in industry *B*.
  d) the supply of capital in industry *A* must be less elastic than the supply of capital in industry *B*.
  e) none of the above will occur.

23) Economic rent is the
  a) price paid for the use of a hectare of land.
  b) price paid for the use of a unit of capital.
  c) income required to induce a given quantity of a factor of production to be supplied.
  d) income received that is above the amount required to induce a given quantity of a factor of production to be supplied.
  e) transfer earnings of a factor of production.

24) Consider the supply schedule of a factor of production given in Table 15.1. If 4 units of the factor are supplied at a price of $8 per unit, what are the transfer earnings?
a) $8
b) $12
c) $20
d) $32
e) none of the above

Table 15.1

Price of a Factor ($)	Quantity of Factor Supplied
2	1
4	2
6	3
8	4
10	5

25) Consider the supply schedule of a factor of production given in Table 15.1. If 4 units of the factor are supplied at a price of $8 per unit, what is the economic rent?
a) $8
b) $12
c) $20
d) $32
e) none of the above

SHORT ANSWER

1) Why will an increase in the supply of a factor of production result in an increase in income if the demand for the factor has elasticity greater than 1, and result in a decrease in income if the elasticity of demand for the factor is less than 1?

2) Why is the demand for a factor of production given by its marginal revenue product curve?

3) Discuss the substitution and income effects on the quantity of labour supplied if the wage rate *decreases.*

4) Why do younger households tend to save less than older households?

5) Are prices of retail goods in Toronto's Yorkville district high because rents are high, or are rents high because prices are high? Explain.

PROBLEMS

1) Table 15.2 gives the total and marginal product schedules for a firm that sells its output in a competitive market and buys labour in a competitive market. Initially, the price at which the firm can sell any level of output is $5 per unit and the wage rate at which it can purchase any quantity of labour is $15 per unit.

Table 15.2

			P = $5		P = $3	
Quantity Labour (*L*)	Output (*Q*)	Marginal Product (MP_L)	Total Revenue (*TR*)	Marginal Revenue Product (MRP_L)	Total Revenue (*TR*)	Marginal Revenue Product (MRP_L)
0	0					
		12				
1	12					
		10				
2	22					
		8				
3	30					
		6				
4	36					
		4				
5	40					
		2				
6	42					

a) Complete the first two blank columns in Table 15.2 by computing the *TR* and MRP_L corresponding to a price of output = $5.
b) The text informs us that the values obtained for the marginal revenue product of labour (MRP_L) are the same when they are computed by either of the following formulas:

$$MRP_L = TR/ L$$
$$MRP_L = MR \times MP_L$$

where *TR* = the change in total revenue, *L* = the change in labour, *MR* = marginal revenue, and MP_L = marginal product of labour. Show that these two formulas are equivalent for the case when the quantity of labour changes from 1 to 2 units.
c) If the firm maximizes profit, what quantity of labour will it hire? How much output will it produce?
d) If total fixed cost is $125, what is the amount of profit?
e) What is its profit if the firm hires one more unit of labour than the profit-maximizing quantity? one less unit of labour than the profit-maximizing quantity?

f) Draw a graph of the demand for labour and the supply of labour and illustrate labour market equilibrium.

2) Now, suppose that the market demand for the output of the firm in problem 1 decreases, causing the price of output to decrease to $3 per unit. The total and marginal product schedules remain unchanged.
a) Complete the last two blank columns in Table 15.2 by computing the *TR* and MRP_L corresponding to price of output = $3.
b) If the wage remains at $15 per unit of labour, what is the profit-maximizing quantity of labour that the firm will hire? How much output will it produce?
c) Total fixed cost continues to be $125. What is the amount of profit?
d) Will the firm shut down in the short run? Explain.
e) Draw a new graph of the new labour market equilibrium.

3) The price of output for the firm in problem 2 remains at $3 but the wage now rises to $21 per unit of labour. The total and marginal product schedules remain unchanged.
a) What happens to the demand curve for labour (the *MRP* of labour curve)?
b) Under these circumstances, what is the profit-maximizing quantity of labour that the firm will hire? How much output will it produce?
c) Total fixed cost continues to be $125. What is the amount of profit?
d) Draw a graph of the labour market equilibrium.

4) A perfectly competitive firm in long-run equilibrium produces flubits using only two factors of production — labour and capital. Each factor is sold in a perfectly competitive factor market. Labour costs $30 per unit and capital costs $50 per unit.
a) Assuming the firm has hired the profit-maximizing quantity of capital in part (b) of this question, the marginal revenue product of labour curve is:

$$MRP_L = 110 - 8/5\ Q_L$$

where MRP_L is the marginal revenue product of labour and Q_L is the quantity (in units) of labour hired. How many units of labour does the firm hire?
b) Assuming the firm has hired the profit-maximizing quantity of labour in part (a) of this question, the marginal revenue product of capital curve is:

$$MRP_K = 125 - 75/40\ Q_K$$

where MRP_K is the marginal revenue product of capital and Q_K is the quantity (in units) of capital hired. How many units of capital does the firm hire?
c) The price of a flubit is $10.
i) How many flubits is the firm producing? (*Hint*: Remember that the firm is in long-run equilibrium.)
ii) What is the marginal (physical) product of the 25th unit of labour hired?

5) Table 15.3 gives the market labour demand and supply schedules.

Table 15.3

Wage Rate (dollars per hour)	Quantity of Labour Supplied (hours)	Quantity of Labour Demanded (hours)
0	0	240
1	20	200
2	40	160
3	60	120
4	80	80
5	100	40
6	120	0

a) What is the equilibrium wage rate and the quantity of labour hired?
b) What is the total amount of income received by labour in this market?
c) Represent the market graphically. Identify the equilibrium wage and quantity of labour.
d) How much of labour income constitutes transfer earnings? How much constitutes economic rent?
e) Now suppose that the demand for labour increases by 60 hours at each wage rate.
i) What are the new equilibrium wage rate and quantity of labour?
ii) What is the new total amount of labour income?
iii) How much of this income is transfer earnings? How much is economic rent?

ANSWERS

CONCEPT REVIEW

1) wages; interest; rent
2) increase; large; small
3) derived
4) hiring; labour; increase
5) negatively; marginal revenue product
6) right; right
7) higher; more
8) reservation
9) decrease; increase
10) capital; increase
11) economic rent; transfer

TRUE OR FALSE

1) F	6) T	11) F	16) T	21) F
2) T	7) T	12) T	17) T	22) T
3) T	8) F	13) T	18) F	
4) F	9) T	14) T	19) F	
5) F	10) F	15) F	20) T	

MULTIPLE-CHOICE

1) d	6) b	11) b	16) b	21) a
2) a	7) a	12) b	17) d	22) a
3) b	8) d	13) a	18) c	23) d
4) c	9) c	14) c	19) a	24) c
5) d	10) d	15) c	20) b	25) b

SHORT ANSWER

1) An increase in the supply of a factor of production will cause the price of the factor to decrease and the quantity of the factor hired to increase. Income received by the factor is equal to the price of the factor times the quantity hired. If the percentage increase in the quantity hired is greater than the percentage decrease in price (if the elasticity of demand for the factor is greater than 1), income will increase. Similarly, if the percentage increase in the quantity hired is less than the percentage decrease in price (if the elasticity of demand for the factor is less than 1), income will decrease.

2) The marginal revenue product curve for a factor of production gives its demand curve because firms are profit maximizers. As a consequence, they will hire an additional unit of a factor of production until the marginal cost of the factor (its price) is equal to the additional revenue from its use (its *MRP*). Thus, the quantity of the factor demanded at each price (the demand curve) is given by the *MRP* curve.

3) If the wage rate decreases, households will have a tendency to shift from work to leisure (the substitution effect), thus reducing the quantity of labour supplied. The lower wage also decreases the household's income and, thus, causes the household to reduce its demand for leisure and other normal goods (the income effect) thereby increasing the quantity of labour supplied.

4) Households will tend to save less when current income is low relative to expected future income and save more when current income is high relative to expected future income. Younger households are largely in this first situation while older households are largely in the second.

5) Rents are high because prices are high. Land in Yorkville has a perfectly inelastic supply, so the price of land (its rent) is determined entirely by demand for the land.

Demand is high because merchants know that the prime retail location will allow them to charge higher prices and potentially earn higher profits than in other locations.

PROBLEMS

1) a) The completed columns for *TR* and MRP_L corresponding to a price of output = \$5 are shown in Table 15.2 Solution on page 182. The values for *TR* are obtained by multiplying the quantity of output by the price of output (\$5). The values for MRP_L between any two quantities of labour are obtained by dividing the change in *TR* by the change in quantity of labour.

Table 15.2 Solution

			P = $5		P = $3	
Quantity Labour (L)	Output (Q)	Marginal Product (MP_L)	Total Revenue (TR)	Marginal Revenue Product (MRP_L)	Total Revenue (TR)	Marginal Revenue Product (MRP_L)
0	0		0		0	
		12		60		36
1	12		60		36	
		10		50		30
2	22		110		66	
		 8		40		24
3	30		150		90	
		 6		30		18
4	36		180		108	
		 4		20		12
5	40		200		120	
		 2		10		 6
6	42		210		126	

b) From part (a), the formula $MRP_L = \Delta TR / \Delta L$, yields a marginal revenue product of labour of 60 when the quantity of labour changes from 1 to 2 units. To confirm that the second formula ($MRP_L = MR \times MP_L$) gives the same answer when the quantity of labour changes from 1 to 2 units, substitute in the values for MR ($5, the price of an additional unit of output) and MP_L (12 units of output). This yields the same marginal revenue product of labour as above; $5 × 12 units = $60.

c) The firm maximizes profit by hiring labour up to the point where the *MRP* of labour is equal to the marginal cost of labour, (the wage rate). That point occurs at 5 units of labour. The *MRP* of moving from 4 to 5 units of labour is 20, and the *MRP* of moving from 5 to 6 units of labour is 10. Thus, by interpolation, the *MRP* at exactly 5 units of labour is 15 (midway between 20 and 10). So when 5 units of labour are hired, the *MRP* of labour is equal to the wage rate ($15). Given that 5 units of labour are hired, the profit-maximizing output will be 40 units (from Table 15.2 Solution).

d) To calculate profit, we must first calculate total revenue and then subtract total cost. Total revenue is $200 (40 units of output times $5 per unit) and total cost is also $200 — the sum of total variable (labour) cost of $75 (5 units of labour times $15 per unit) and total fixed cost of $125. Thus profit is zero.

e) If the firm hires one more unit of labour (6 units), total revenue will be $210 (42 units of output times the $5 price). Total cost will be the $125 fixed cost plus $90 in total variable cost (6 units of labour times the $15 wage rate) or $215. Thus profit will be a negative $5 (a $5 loss).

If the firm hires one less unit of labour (4 units), total revenue will be $180 (36 units of output times the $5 price). Total cost will be the $125 fixed cost plus $60 in total variable cost (4 units of labour times the $15 wage rate) or $185. Thus profit will be a negative $5 (a $5 loss).

f) The graph of labour market equilibrium appears in Figure 15.1. The demand for labour is given by the firm's MRP_L curve which is labelled D_0 (D_1 will be discussed in problem 2).

Notice that the values for *MRP* are plotted midway between the corresponding quantities of labour. For example, *MRP* of 60 is plotted midway between 1 and 2 units of labour.

Since the firm purchases labour in a perfectly competitive labour market, the supply of labour to the firm is perfectly elastic at the market wage rate. The labour supply curve is labelled $W =$ $15. The equilibrium is at the intersection of these curves, and corresponds to a wage rate of $15 and a quantity of labour hired of 5 units.

Figure 15.1

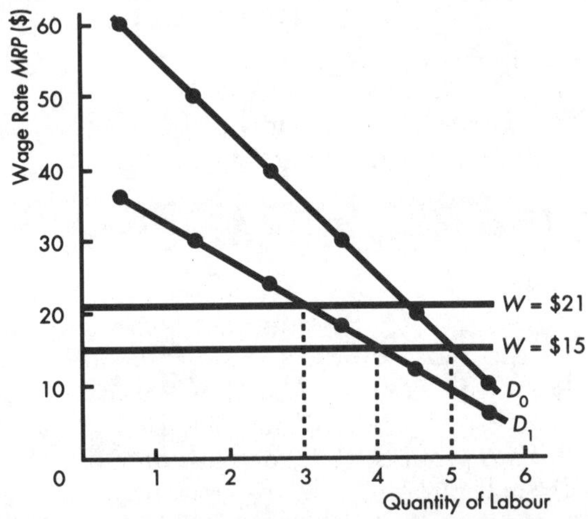

2) a) The completed columns for *TR* and MRP_L corresponding to price of output = $3 are shown above in Table 15.2 Solution. The values for *TR* are obtained by multiplying the quantity of output by the price of output ($3). The values for MRP_L between any two quantities of labour are obtained by dividing the change in *TR* by the change in quantity of labour.

b) If the wage rate remains at $15, the profit-maximizing quantity of labour will fall to 4 units since MRP_L equals the wage rate at 4 units of labour. The *MRP* of moving from 3 to 4 units of labour is 18, and the *MRP* of moving from 4 to 5 units of labour is 12. Thus, by interpolation, the

MRP at exactly 4 units of labour is 15 (midway between 18 and 12). Given that 4 units of labour are employed, the profit-maximizing output will be 36 units (from Table 15.2 Solution).

c) Profit equals total revenue minus total cost. Total revenue is $108 (36 units of output times $3 per unit) and total cost is $185 — the sum of total variable (labour) cost of $60 (4 units of labour times $15 per unit) and total fixed cost of $125. Thus profit is – $77, or a loss of $77.

d) The firm will not shut down since total revenue ($108) is enough to cover total variable cost ($60) and part of fixed cost. If the firm decided to shut down, it would lose the $125 of fixed cost rather than just $77.

e) The graph of labour market equilibrium appears in Figure 15.1. The new demand for labour is given by the firm's new MRP_L curve, which is labelled D_1. The supply of labour has not changed; it continues to be horizontal at $15, the competitive market wage. The new equilibrium is at the intersection of these curves, and corresponds to a wage rate of $15 and a quantity of labour hired of 4 units.

3) a) Since marginal revenue and the marginal product of labour are unaffected by a change in the wage rate, the demand curve for labour (the *MRP* of labour) will remain at D_1.

b) If the wage rate rises to $21, the profit-maximizing quantity of labour will fall to 3 units since MRP_L equals the wage rate at 3 units of labour. Given that 3 units of labour are employed, the profit-maximizing output will be 30 units (from Table 15.2 Solution).

c) Profit equals total revenue minus total cost. Total revenue is $90 (3 units of output times $3 per unit) and total cost is $188 — the sum of total variable (labour) cost of $63 (3 units of labour times $21 per unit) and total fixed cost of $125. Thus profit is – $98, or a loss of $98.

d) See Figure 15.1. The relevant demand for labour curve continues to be D_1, but the labour supply curve reflects the rise in the competitive wage rate; it is now horizontal at a wage rate of $21 (labelled $W = \$21$). The equilibrium is at the intersection of these curves and corresponds to a wage rate of $21 and a quantity of labour hired of 3 units.

4) a) By assuming that the firm has already hired its capital, we know (in principle) fixed costs and can calculate the profit-maximizing quantity of the variable factor (labour) by setting the MRP_L equal to the wage rate ($30).

$$30 = 110 - 8/5\ Q_L$$
$$8/5\ Q_L = 80$$
$$Q_L = 50$$

b) By assuming that the firm has already hired its labour, we can treat labour as the fixed cost and treat capital as the variable factor of production. Calculate the profit-maximizing quantity of the capital hired by setting the MRP_K equal to the cost of a unit of capital ($50).

$$50 = 125 - 75/40\ Q_K$$
$$75/40\ Q_K = 75$$
$$Q_K = 40$$

c) i) The fact that the firm is in long-run equilibrium provides the key to calculating the quantity of flubits produced. In long-run equilibrium, the firm earns zero profit, so total revenue is exactly equal to total cost.

We can calculate total cost by adding the costs of the (only) two factors of production. Labour cost is 50 units of labour times $30 per unit or $1,500. Capital cost is 40 units of capital times $50 per unit or $2,000. Total cost is, therefore, $3,500.

Total revenue must also be equal to $3,500. Since total revenue (*TR*) is just the price of output (*P*) times quantity sold (*Q*), we can calculate *Q* by substituting in the values we have for *TR* ($3,500) and *P* ($10).

$$TR = P \times Q$$
$$3{,}500 = 10 \times Q$$
$$Q = 350$$

ii) To calculate the marginal product of the 25th unit of labour, we begin by calculating the marginal *revenue* product of the 25th unit of labour. Substituting $Q_L = 25$ into the equation for MRP_L yields:

$$MRP_L = 110 - 8/5\ (25)$$
$$= 110 - 40 \text{ or } 70$$

One definition of the marginal revenue product of labour is the marginal product of labour (MP_L) times marginal revenue (*MR*) or $MRP_L = MP_L \times MR$. Rearranging to solve for MP_L yields:

$$MP_L = MRP_L / MR$$

Substituting in the values for the marginal revenue product of the 25th unit of labour (70) and for *MR* (the price of output $10) yields:

$$MP_L = 70/10 \text{ or } 7$$

5) a) The equilibrium wage rate is $4 per hour and the quantity of labour hired is 80 hours.

b) Total income is $4 per hour times 80 hours equals $320.

5) c) The supply and demand curves for labour are given in Figure 15.2.

Figure 15.2

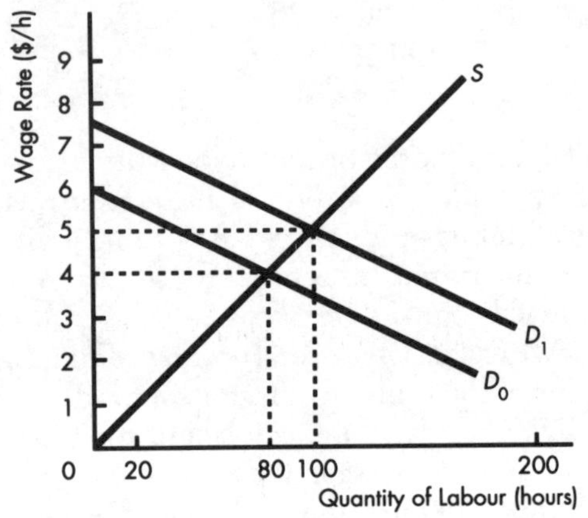

The supply of labour is given by S_0 and the initial demand for labour is represented by D_0. The equilibrium occurs at the intersection of these two curves. You can see that the equilibrium wage is $4 per hour and the quantity of labour is 80 hours.

d) Given that the supply of labour curve is a 45-degree line starting at the origin, half of income is transfer earnings (the area below the supply curve) and the other half is economic rent (the area above the supply curve). Since income is $320, each of these is $160.

e) i) Each entry in the last column of Table 15.3 will increase by 60 units. The new equilibrium wage rate is $5 per hour and the new equilibrium quantity of labour is 100 hours. The new labour demand curve appears in Figure 15.2 as D_1.

ii) Total income is now $5 per hour times 100 hours equals $500.

iii) Once again the slope of the labour supply curve (which has not changed) implies that income is split evenly between transfer earnings and economic rent. Each will be equal to $250.

Chapter 16 **Labour Markets**

Chapter in Perspective

Text Pages 405–436

Labour markets play a very important role in the economic well-being of almost every household since household income is determined largely by the operation of these markets. This chapter looks more carefully at labour markets to explain how wage rates and employment levels are determined. We investigate why some groups earn more than other groups: why skilled workers earn more than unskilled workers; why union workers earn more than nonunion workers; and why, on average, men earn more than women. We also examine the consequences of alternative labour payment schemes including legislated pay equity and performance-related compensation rules.

Learning Objectives

After studying this chapter, you will be able to:

- **Explain why university graduates earn more, on the average, than high school graduates.**
- **Explain why skilled workers earn more, on the average, than unskilled workers.**
- **Explain why union workers earn higher wages than nonunion workers.**
- **Explain why men earn more, on the average, than women.**
- **Predict the effects of pay equity legislation.**
- **Explain why some people are paid by the hour and others by formulas based on performance.**
- **Explain how performance-related compensation rules induce greater effort and higher profit.**

Helpful Hints

1) This chapter introduces the concept of a monopsonist, a firm that is the only buyer in a market such as labour, for example. The monopsonist faces an upward-sloping supply curve of labour and, as a result, its marginal cost of labour curve (*MCL*) is different from the labour supply curve.

   There is a close parallel between **a)** the relationship between the labour supply curve and the *MCL* curve for the monopsonist and **b)** the already familiar relationship (Chapter 13) between the demand curve and the marginal revenue curve (*MR*) for the monopolist. Both sets of relationships stem from the assumption of a single price for labour or output in the relevant market.

   The monopolist, as the only seller in an output market, faces a downward-sloping demand curve. The marginal revenue from the sale of an additional unit of output is *less* than the selling price because the monopolist must *lower* the price on all previous units as well. Thus, the *MR* curve lies *below* the demand curve for the monopolist.

   For the monopsonist in a labour market, the marginal cost of hiring an additional unit of labour is *higher* than the wage because the monopsonist must *raise* the wage on all previous units of labour as well. Thus, the *MCL* curve lies *above* the supply of labour curve for the monopsonist.

2) This chapter broadens our notion of equilibrium in the labour market by introducing the principal–agent model. A particular labour market may *not* establish a wage rate and a level of employment in the simple sense of the intersection of demand and supply curves. The broader notion of labour market equilibrium includes determination of quantity and type of compensation scheme of which time rates of pay (wage rates) are only one possibility. Equilibrium occurs when the market is at rest in the sense that no worker or firm has an incentive to change.

   The principal–agent model allows for an analysis of alternative types of compensation schemes. Since this model uses game theory, you will find it much easier to understand if you have mastered the discussion of game theory and payoff matrices in Chapter 14.

Key Figures and Table

Figure 16.1 Skill Differentials, text page 408
Different workers receive different wages depending on their level of skill. This figure shows how differences in wages can be explained using the model of competitive labour markets.

Part (a) of the figure shows that the demand for skilled labour is higher than the demand for unskilled labour because skilled labour has a higher marginal revenue product. The vertical distance between the two demand curves gives the difference in marginal revenue product, which is the marginal revenue product of the skill.

Part (b) gives the supply curves for skilled and unskilled labour. It illustrates that the supply curve for skilled labour will lie above the supply curve for unskilled labour because skills are costly to obtain. As a result, skilled labour must receive a higher wage in order to induce workers to obtain the skill. The vertical distance between the two labour supply curves gives the required additional wage.

Part (c) puts together the demand and supply curves from parts (a) and (b) in order to look at the equilibrium wage rate for each type of labour. Not surprisingly, the equilibrium wage rate for skilled workers will be higher than for unskilled workers.

Figure 16.4 A Union in a Competitive Labour Market, text page 412
This figure shows the consequences for the wage rate and quantity of labour employed when a union operates in a previously competitive labour market.

The competitive demand for labour and the competitive supply of labour are indicated by D_C and S_C, respectively. In the competitive market the equilibrium wage rate is $4 an hour and 100 hours of labour are employed.

The principal method by which a union causes the wage rate to rise is to restrict the supply of labour. Thus the union supply of labour is given by S_U. If this is all the union does, the wage rate will rise to $10 an hour and employment will fall to 62.5 hours. If, in addition to restricting supply, the union is also able to increase the demand for its labour, the union demand curve (D_U) will shift to the right of the competitive demand curve. In this case, the wage rate will be even higher, $16 an hour, and employment will rise to 75 hours.

Figure 16.8 Discrimination, text page 419
This figure illustrates how discrimination will affect wage rates and employment. Part (a) shows that discrimination against a particular group of workers (in this case, female investment advisors) will reduce wages and employment below what they would have been without discrimination. The prejudice of customers makes the marginal revenue product of the workers who are discriminated against (MRP_{DA}) lower than the marginal revenue product without discrimination (*MRP*).

Part (b) shows that customer prejudice in favour of a particular group (in this case, male investment advisors) makes the marginal revenue product of the workers who are discriminated in favour of (MRP_{DF}) higher than the marginal revenue product without discrimination. This will raise wages and employment above what they would have been without discrimination.

Figure 16.9 The Problem of Equal Pay for Work of Equal Value, text page 421
This figure illustrates the problems that will be created in two labour markets by an enforced wage. Part (a) shows the market for oil rig operators. The intersection of the marginal revenue product and supply curves of rig operators (MRP_R and S_R) determines the competitive equilibrium wage rate for rig operators (W_R).

Part (b) shows the market for nurses. The intersection of the marginal revenue product and supply curves of nurses (MRP_N and S_N) determines the competitive equilibrium wage rate for nurses (W_N), which is lower than the wage for rig operators.

If an "equal pay for work of equal value" scheme determines that the wage rates in the two markets should be equalized at a level (W_C) in between W_R and W_N, problems arise in both markets. The oil rig operator market will experience a labour shortage ($D_r - S_r$), forcing producers to find other ways of producing oil that use fewer operators. The nurses' market will experience unemployment ($S_n - D_n$) and some nurses will have to find different jobs.

Table 16.1 A Compact Glossary on Unions, text page 410
This table conveniently brings together much of the terminology associated with labour unions. It provides definitions of terms used frequently in analyzing the operation of unions in the economy.

SELF-TEST

CONCEPT REVIEW

1) The demand curve for skilled labour lies _______________ the demand curve for unskilled labour, because the marginal revenue product of skilled workers is _______________ than that of unskilled workers. The supply curve for skilled labour lies _______________ the supply curve for unskilled labour, because skills are costly to acquire.

2) Education and training can be viewed as investments in _______________ capital. The value of that capital is the _______________ _______________ of the extra future earnings that result from the increased education or training.

3) There are two main types of unions. A union that organizes workers with similar skills but who work for many different firms or industries is called a(n) _______________ union. A(n) _______________ union organizes workers with a variety of skills but who work for the same firm or industry.

4) A work arrangement in which all employees are required to join the labour union is called a(n) _______________ _______________. In a work arrangement where workers are not required to join the labour union, the _______________ _______________ makes it compulsory for all workers to contribute to the union.

5) A market in which there is only one buyer is called _______________. If there is only one firm that buys labour, the wage rate will be _______________ than the marginal cost of labour. A situation in which a single seller of labour, such as a union, faces a single buyer of labour is called _______________ monopoly.

6) Three possible explanations of wage differentials between the sexes are discussed in Chapter 16. The first explanation is discrimination. The second explanation is that the two groups have differences in _______________ capital. The third explanation is that there are differences in the degree of _______________ in market and non-market activities.

7) Equal pay for work of equal value involves paying the same _______________ for different jobs which are judged to be _______________.

8) A formula for calculating a person's income is called a(n) _______________ rule. If the formula is based solely on the number of hours the person works, it is called a(n) _______________ rate. If the formula is based on the amount of output the worker produces it is called a(n) _______________ rate. A rule that allocates a certain fraction of the firm's profit to employees is called _______________ - _______________.

9) Often, either worker effort or worker output are difficult, if not impossible, to observe. An individual who sets a rule for compensating workers, which motivates the worker to choose activities advantageous to the individual is called a(n) ______________ . Each worker in such a situation is called a(n) ______________ .

TRUE OR FALSE

_____ 1) The marginal revenue product of unskilled workers is lower than that of skilled workers.

_____ 2) The vertical distance between the labour supply curves for skilled and unskilled workers is the marginal revenue product of the skill.

_____ 3) The larger the marginal revenue product of the skill and the more costly it is to acquire, the smaller is the wage differential between skilled and unskilled workers.

_____ 4) A closed shop refers to a firm that is not operating because its workers are on strike.

_____ 5) A lockout occurs when a firm refuses to employ its workers or operate its plant.

_____ 6) Unions support minimum wage laws in part because they increase the cost of unskilled labour, a substitute for skilled union labour.

_____ 7) A firm that is a monopsonist in the labour market must compete with other firms for the labour it hires.

_____ 8) For a firm that is a monopsonist in the labour market, the supply curve of labour is the marginal cost of labour curve.

_____ 9) The more elastic is labour supply, the less opportunity a monopsonist has to make an economic profit.

_____ 10) In a monopsonistic labour market, the introduction of a minimum wage that is above the current wage will raise the wage but reduce employment.

_____ 11) In the case of bilateral monopoly in a labour market, the wage is indeterminate; the wage depends on the bargaining strength of the two traders.

_____ 12) The evidence suggests that, after allowing for the effects of skill differentials, union workers earn no more than nonunion workers.

_____ 13) Economic theory tells us that discrimination in employment will result in wage differentials.

_____ 14) If males on average earn more than females, we can conclude that there must be discrimination.

_____ 15) Compensation rules such as the minimum wage law are laws enacted by the government.

_____ 16) A principal sets a compensation rule to motivate an agent to choose activities advantageous to the agent.

_____ 17) Time-related compensation rules are more prevalent in situations where monitoring costs are high.

_____ 18) An efficient compensation rule delivers maximum expected profit to the agent and is acceptable to the principal.

_____ 19) The principal–agent model is used in this chapter to help us understand why discrimination exists.

_____ 20) With appropriate compensation rules, monitoring costs can be avoided.

MULTIPLE-CHOICE

1) Which of the following is *not* a reason why the wage of skilled workers exceeds the wage of unskilled workers?
   a) The market for skilled workers is more competitive than the market for unskilled labour.
   b) The marginal revenue product of skilled workers is greater than that of unskilled workers.
   c) The cost of training skilled workers is greater than the cost of training unskilled workers.
   d) Skilled workers have acquired more human capital than unskilled workers.
   e) The demand curve for skilled workers lies to the right of the demand curve for unskilled workers.

2) Other things remaining the same, if education costs rise substantially, we would expect to see
   a) a decrease in the marginal revenue product of skilled workers.
   b) a decrease in the demand for skilled workers.
   c) an increase in the supply of skilled workers.
   d) an increase in the wage of skilled workers.
   e) an increase in the number of skilled workers employed.

3) The economic value of the increase in human capital due to additional education is
   a) the money cost of the additional education.
   b) the money cost of the additional education plus forgone earnings.
   c) the present value of all expected future earnings.
   d) the present value of all extra expected future earnings that are the result of the additional education.
   e) none of the above.

4) A working arrangement in which all workers must be members of the union before they can be hired by the firm is called
   a) an open shop.
   b) a closed shop.
   c) a union shop.
   d) a craft shop.
   e) a professional association.

5) A union that organizes workers with a similar skill regardless of the firm or industry that employs them is
   a) an industrial union.
   b) a craft union.
   c) a local union.
   d) a national union.
   e) a public sector union.

6) Which of the following would unions be *least* likely to support?
   a) increasing the legal minimum wage
   b) restricting immigration
   c) encouraging imports
   d) increasing demand for the goods their workers produce
   e) increasing the marginal product of union labour

7) The most important way in which unions increase wages is by
   a) increasing the marginal (physical) product of labour.
   b) increasing the marginal revenue product of labour.
   c) increasing the demand for labour.
   d) decreasing the supply of labour.
   e) increasing the marginal cost of labour.

8) When compared to a competitive labour market with the same marginal revenue product and labour supply curves, a monopsonist labour market has
   a) a lower wage and lower employment.
   b) a lower wage and higher employment.
   c) a higher wage and lower employment.
   d) a higher wage and higher employment.
   e) an indeterminate outcome.

9) Figure 16.1 illustrates a monopsonist in the labour market (*MCL* = marginal cost of labour). The profit maximizing wage rate and quantity of labour hired will be
   a) $4 per hour and 800 hours of labour.
   b) $4 per hour and 400 hours of labour.
   c) $7 per hour and 600 hours of labour.
   d) $9 per hour and 400 hours of labour.
   e) none of the above.

Figure 16.1

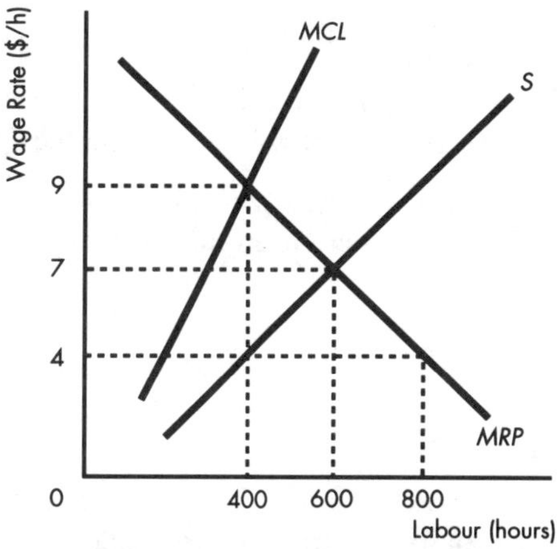

10) If the labour market illustrated in Figure 16.1 became competitive, the equilibrium wage rate and quantity of labour hired would be
   a) $4 per hour and 800 hours of labour.
   b) $4 per hour and 400 hours of labour.
   c) $7 per hour and 600 hours of labour.
   d) $9 per hour and 400 hours of labour.
   e) none of the above.

11) Wage differentials between males and females can be explained by
   a) occupational differences.
   b) human capital differences.
   c) degree of specialization differences.
   d) discrimination.
   e) all of the above.

12) If discrimination takes the form of restricting a group's access to education and training, the effect on this group of workers will be to shift the
   a) marginal revenue product curve to the right and increase the wage.
   b) marginal revenue product curve to the left and decrease the wage.
   c) marginal revenue product curve to the right and decrease the wage.
   d) supply of labour curve up and decrease the wage.
   e) supply of labour curve down and decrease the wage.

13) Consider two types of workers: types *A* and *B*. In competitive labour markets the wage paid to type *A* workers is substantially higher than the wage paid to type *B* workers. Suppose that a pay equity law is enacted and type *A* and *B* workers are judged to be comparable. Furthermore, assume that to equalize wages, the wage rate for type *B* workers rises and the wage rate for type *A* workers falls. We can conclude that employment of
   a) type *A* workers will rise while employment of type *B* workers will fall.
   b) type *A* workers will fall while employment of type *B* workers will rise.
   c) both types of workers will rise.
   d) both types of workers will fall.
   e) both types of workers will remain unchanged.

14) Laura is a barber who gets paid $15 for every haircut she gives. This compensation rule is an example of
   a) a commission.
   b) a time rate.
   c) a piece rate.
   d) a royalty.
   e) profit-sharing.

15) Commonly used compensation rules include
   a) payment based on group performance.
   b) time-related payment.
   c) absolute performance-related payment.
   d) relative performance-related payment.
   e) all of the above.

16) The general model we use to study compensation rules is called the
   a) bilateral monopoly model.
   b) principal–agent model.
   c) efficient compensation model.
   d) performance compensation model.
   e) monitoring cost model.

17) Which of the following compensation rules is most likely to be efficient in the case of a chief executive officer of a corporation?
   a) a commission on sales
   b) a share of total firm profits
   c) a salary based on years of employment
   d) a tournament-like prize
   e) both b) and d)

18) Which of the following compensation rules is most likely to be efficient in the case of a salesperson?
   a) an hourly wage rate
   b) a commission on sales
   c) a share of total firm profits
   d) a salary based on years of employment
   e) none of the above

19) An efficient compensation rule
   a) cannot incorporate the effects of luck.
   b) will not be accepted by the agent.
   c) splits revenues equally between the agent and principal.
   d) maximizes the agent's expected income.
   e) maximizes the principal's expected profit.

20) Which of the following cases is most likely to be characterized by a time rate of pay?
   a) Individual effort is readily observed but individual contribution to output is not.
   b) Individual effort is not readily observed but individual contribution to output is.
   c) Neither individual effort nor individual contribution to output is readily observable.
   d) Monitoring costs are very high.
   e) None of the above statements is most likely.

SHORT ANSWER

1) Members of labour unions earn wages well above the minimum wage. Even so, why is it in the interest of a union to support increases in the legal minimum wage?

2) Bob and Sue form a household. They have decided that Sue will fully specialize in market activity and Bob will pursue activities both in the job market and in the household. If most households are like Bob and Sue's, why would the result be a difference between the earnings of men and women, even if there is no discrimination?

3) Suppose the labour market for investment advisors is exactly as shown in Figure 16.8 on text page 419, where female advisors are discriminated against and male advisors are discriminated for. Explain the effects of introducing a scheme of "equal pay for work of equal value" that equalizes wage rates at $40,000 per year.

4) In a principal–agent model, what is the objective of the principal?

5) Many large firms are owned by a group of stockholders who hire managers to run the firm. Why is profit-sharing a good compensation scheme for top management in such a firm?

PROBLEMS

1) Figure 16.2 shows the demand and supply of skilled and unskilled labour. S_U and S_S are the supply

curves for unskilled and skilled workers, respectively, and D_U and D_S are the demand curves for unskilled and skilled workers, respectively.

Figure 16.2

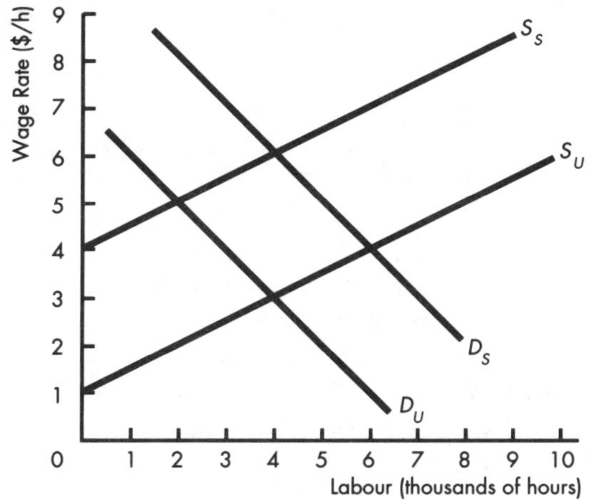

a) What is the marginal revenue product of skill if 5,000 hours of each kind of labour are hired?

b) What is the amount of extra compensation per hour required to induce the acquisition of skill at the same level of hiring?

c) What are the equilibrium wage and quantity of labour in the market for skilled labour?

d) What are the equilibrium wage and quantity of labour in the market for unskilled labour?

2) Yuri has an opportunity to increase his human capital by taking a training course that will raise his income by $100 every year for the rest of his life. Assume that there are no other benefits of the course. The cost of the course is $1,200 and Yuri's best alternative investment pays an interest rate of 10 percent per year for the rest of his life. Should Yuri pay the $1,200 and take the course? Explain.

3) Initially we observe an industry facing a competitive labour market in which the supply of labour comes from two sources: domestic workers and foreign workers. All workers have similar skills. Also assume that the output of the industry competes with imported goods.

a) In Figure 16.3, graphically represent the initial competitive labour market. Draw the labour demand and supply curves and identify the equilibrium wage rate and level of employment.

Figure 16.3

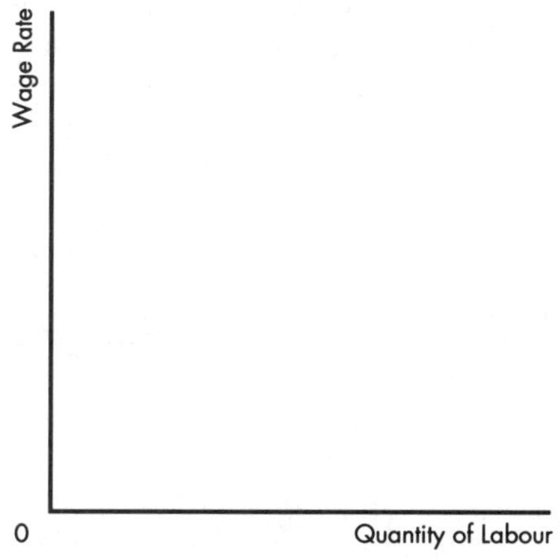

b) Now suppose a union consisting of domestic workers is formed. Through its support, a law is passed which prohibits firms from hiring foreign workers. What effect will this have on employment and the wage rate? Illustrate graphically using the graph in part (a).

c) Finally, the industry and union support the passage of a law that legally restricts imports which compete with industry output. Using the same graph, show the consequences for the wage rate and employment.

4) Figure 16.4 illustrates a profit-maximizing monopsonist in the labour market.

Figure 16.4

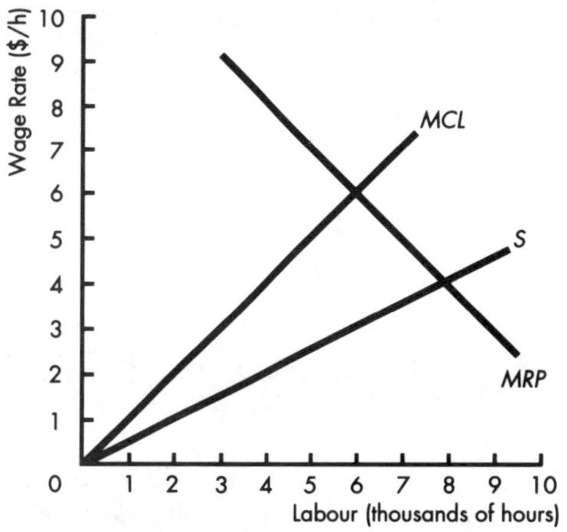

a) What wage rate will the monopsonist pay and how much labour will be employed? What is the value of labour's marginal revenue product at this level of employment?

b) If this were a competitive labour market with the same marginal revenue product curve, what would be the equilibrium wage rate and the level of employment?

c) Now, suppose the government imposes a minimum wage of $4 per hour. What wage rate will the monopsonist pay and how much labour will be employed now?

ANSWERS

CONCEPT REVIEW

1) above; greater; above
2) human; present value
3) craft; industrial
4) closed shop; Rand formula
5) monopsony; lower; bilateral
6) human; specialization
7) wages; comparable
8) compensation; time; piece; profit-sharing
9) principal; agent

TRUE OR FALSE

1) T	6) T	11) T	16) F
2) F	7) F	12) F	17) F
3) F	8) F	13) T	18) F
4) F	9) T	14) F	19) F
5) T	10) F	15) F	20) T

MULTIPLE-CHOICE

1) a	6) c	11) e	16) b
2) d	7) d	12) e	17) e
3) d	8) a	13) d	18) b
4) b	9) b	14) c	19) e
5) b	10) c	15) e	20) a

SHORT ANSWER

1) An increase in the minimum wage will increase the cost of hiring unskilled labour, which will tend to increase the demand for skilled labour, which is a substitute.

2) If Sue specializes in market activity while Bob is diversified, it is likely that Sue's earning ability will exceed Bob's due to the gains from her specialization. If most households followed this pattern of specialization, the income of women would exceed that of men even without discrimination.

3) The wages of female investment advisors will increase from $20,000 to $40,000 per year and employment will increase from 1,000 to 2,000. The wages of male investment advisors will decrease from $60,000 to $40,000 per year and employment will decrease from 3,000 to 2,000. The effects of the scheme will be to produce the competitive outcome that would have prevailed without discrimination. There is no excess demand or supply of either female or male advisors.

4) The principal wants to set a compensation rule that motivates the agent to make choices that are to the best advantage of the principal.

5) In this case the owners (stockholders) are the principals and the top managers are the agents. Neither the effort nor the output of the managers can be easily monitored. But since the decisions of managers have a direct and significant bearing on the profit of the firm, their incentive is to make decisions that maximize profit if they share in any increase in profit through a profit-sharing compensation scheme.

PROBLEMS

1) a) The marginal revenue product of skill is the difference between the marginal revenue products of skilled versus unskilled labour; the vertical distance between the demand curves for skilled and unskilled labour. In Figure 16.2 on page 191, the marginal revenue product of skill is $3 per hour when 5,000 hours of each kind of labour are employed.

b) Since labour supply curves give the minimum compensation workers are willing to accept in return for supplying a given quantity of labour, the extra compensation for skill is the vertical distance between the supply curves of skilled and unskilled labour. At 5,000 hours of employment for both kinds of labour, this is $3 per hour.

c) In equilibrium in the market for skilled labour, the wage rate will be $6 per hour and employment will be 4,000 hours of labour. This occurs at the intersection of the D_S and S_S curves.

d) In equilibrium in the market for unskilled labour, the wage rate will be $3 per hour and employment will be 4,000 hours of labour. This occurs at the intersection of the D_U and S_U curves.

2) Yuri should take the course only if the value of the course exceeds the cost of the course. The cost of the course is $1,200 while the value of the course is the present value of the extra $100 in income Yuri can expect to receive each year for the rest of his life. The present value of this income stream is the amount of money which, if invested today at 10 percent (Yuri's best alternative return), would yield an equivalent stream of income. Thus the present value of the extra income is $1,000. Since this is less than the cost of the training course, Yuri should not take it.

3) a) The initial competitive demand for labour and supply of labour curves are given by D_C and S_C respectively, in Figure 16.3 Solution (ignore the other curves for now). The equilibrium wage rate is denoted W_C and the competitive equilibrium level of employment is denoted Q_C.

b) If a law is passed prohibiting firms from hiring foreign workers, the labour supply curve (now under a union) will shift to the left (to S_U in Figure 16.3 Solution). This will have the effect of raising the wage rate to W_1 in the figure and decreasing the quantity of labour employed to Q_1 in the figure.

c) Restrictions on imports will increase the demand for the product produced in the industry and thus increase the derived demand (marginal revenue product) of labour in the industry. In Figure 16.3 Solution this is illustrated by a shift from D_C to D_U. The result will be a further increase in the wage rate to W_2 in the diagram and an increase in employment to Q_2 in the diagram. Whether the quantity of labour hired now exceeds the initial competitive quantity depends on the magnitude of the shift in the labour demand curve.

Figure 16.3 Solution

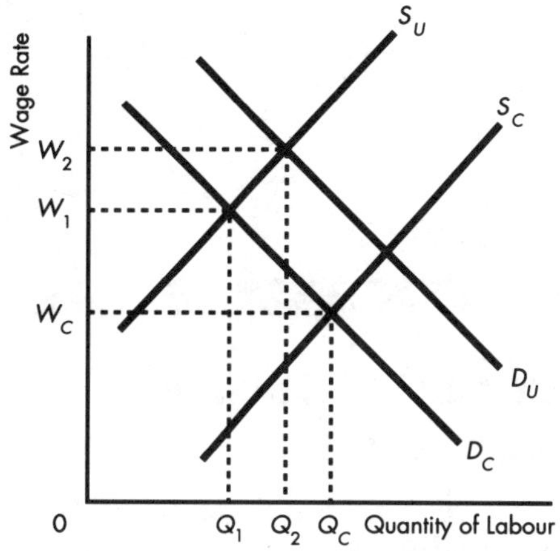

4) a) The profit-maximizing monopsonist will hire additional labour up to the point where the marginal cost of labour (*MCL*) equals the marginal revenue product of labour (*MRP*). Referring to Figure 16.4, this means that the monopsonist illustrated there will hire 6,000 hours of labour. The wage rate is given by the labour supply curve *S* and, for 6,000 hours of labour, will be $3 per hour. This is less than the $6 per hour marginal revenue product of labour.

b) In a competitive market, the wage rate would be $4 per hour and 8,000 hours of labour would be employed.

c) If the government establishes a minimum wage at $4 per hour, the marginal cost of labour to the monopsonist becomes constant at $4 per hour (up to 8,000 hours of labour). Thus, equating the marginal cost of labour and the marginal revenue product of labour leads to a wage rate of $4 and 8,000 hours of labour employed.

Chapter 17 Capital and Natural Resource Markets

Chapter in Perspective

Text Pages 437–464

This chapter continues a more detailed examination of markets for specific factors of production. In Chapter 16 we looked more closely at labour markets. Here we expand our understanding of capital and natural resource markets. What determines interest rates and stock prices? How are the prices of natural resources determined? Can we rely on market forces to regulate the use of exhaustible resources? These and related issues are discussed in this chapter.

Learning Objectives

After studying this chapter, you will be able to:

- **Define and distinguish among financial and real assets, capital, and investment.**
- **Define and distinguish between saving and portfolio choice.**
- **Describe the structure of capital markets in Canada today.**
- **Explain how interest rates and stock prices are determined and why the stock market fluctuates.**
- **Define natural resources and explain how their prices are determined.**
- **Explain how markets regulate the pace at which we use exhaustible resources such as oil.**

Helpful Hints

1) A profit-maximizing firm will hire an additional unit of a factor as long as the factor's use adds more to revenue than to cost; in other words, as long as its marginal revenue product (*MRP*) is greater than its marginal cost (*MC*). The profit-maximizing quantity will be the quantity at which the marginal revenue product of a factor is just equal to its marginal cost. Since, in a competitive market, the marginal cost is the price of the factor (P_F), this profit-maximizing condition becomes $MRP = P_F$ in a competitive factor market. This implies that the demand curve for a factor is given by its *MRP* curve.
2) The profit-maximizing condition given in *Hint 1* is easy to apply in the case of capital markets in which capital is rented. The profit-maximizing firm will rent capital up to the point at which the marginal revenue product per rental period is equal to the rental price.

   If, however, a firm considers purchasing capital rather than renting it, we must be careful in applying the profit-maximizing condition. The reason is that capital is generally operated over more than one period and will generate marginal revenue products that are distributed over time. The purchase price, however, must be paid now. Therefore, in order to compare the purchase price (P_F) with the stream of marginal revenue products, we must compute the present value of that stream.

   In the case of capital that will be used over more than one period, the profit-maximizing condition becomes: hire an additional unit of capital until the present value of the stream of marginal revenue products is equal to the price of the unit of capital. Since the net present value is defined as the difference between the present value of the stream of marginal revenue products and the price of the unit of capital, an equivalent condition is: hire capital until the net present value of the last unit of capital is zero. (If you need to review the concept of present value, return to Chapter 9.)

Key Figures and Tables

Figure 17.1 Capital Market Flows, text page 442
This diagram shows the major participants in capital markets and indicates the directions of interactions among them. Households purchase some capital directly (proprietorships and partnerships) and finance the purchase of other capital indirectly through the stock and bond markets and by making deposits in financial intermediaries. These financial intermediaries then use the deposited funds to make loans to households and firms. Financial intermediaries also buy and sell stocks and bonds. Firms finance capital purchases through direct purchase of capital by households, selling stocks and bonds, and by borrowing from financial intermediaries.

Figure 17.2 The Nation's Balance Sheet, text page 444
The nation's balance sheet combines the balance sheets of households, financial intermediaries, firms, and governments. Financial assets (in blue) and liabilities (in red) for each of these four sectors are shown in the top part of the figure as well as the direction of the flow of funds (by green arrows). The bottom part of the figure shows capital or real asset holdings (in orange) by each of the four sectors.

Note that total financial asset holdings of households greatly exceed their financial liabilities. Thus, households are net suppliers of funds to the other sectors through deposits in financial intermediaries, savings in life insurance and pension funds, and holding of stocks and bonds. Financial intermediaries have both financial assets and liabilities while firms and governments have only financial liabilities.

Figure 17.6 Capital Market Equilibrium, text page 451
Equilibrium in the capital market is achieved at the interest rate at which the quantity of capital demanded is equal to the quantity of capital supplied. For the example illustrated in this figure, the equilibrium interest rate is 6 percent and the equilibrium quantity of capital traded is $2 trillion.

Table 17.1 Balance Sheet of Rocky's Mountain Bikes as at January 1, 1991, text page 439
A balance sheet is a list of assets and liabilities. This table illustrates the concept of a balance sheet by reporting the assets and liabilities of the firm Rocky's Mountain Bikes. The firm's assets (items owned by the firm) are listed on the left-hand side of the table, and the firm's liabilities (money the firm owes — to the bank and to Rocky) are listed on the right. Note that the two sides of the balance sheet balance because total assets equal total liabilities.

Table 17.2 Financial Assets, Financial Liabilities, and Real Assets of Rocky's Mountain Bikes as at January 1, 1991, text page 440
This table uses the same information contained in the balance sheet of Table 17.1, but distinguishes between financial assets and real assets (capital). Some of the firm's assets and liabilities are financial and some of its assets are real assets.

The top part of the table lists the firm's financial assets and liabilities, which consist of cash in the bank (an asset), a bank loan (a liability), and Rocky's equity (also a liability of the firm). Net financial assets are financial assets minus financial liabilities. For this firm, net financial assets are –$225,000 since financial liabilities exceed financial assets.

The bottom part of the table lists the firm's real assets, which consist of its inventory of bikes and fixtures and fittings. Total capital is $225,000.

Table 17.5 Net Present Value of an Investment — Taxfile Inc., text page 445
A firm will decide to purchase an additional unit of capital if the net present value of the investment is positive; if the present value of the marginal revenue product of the investment is greater than the cost of the unit of capital. The calculation of net present value is illustrated in this table using the example of Tina's decision to purchase a new computer for her firm, Taxfile Inc.

Part (a) of the table reports the information necessary to compute the net present value of the investment: the price of the computer, the life of the computer, the marginal revenue product in each year, and the interest rate.

Part (b) uses this information to compute the present value of the flow of marginal revenue product.

In part (c), the cost of the computer is subtracted from the present value of the marginal revenue product of the computer to obtain the net present value of the investment. Since the net present value is positive, it pays Tina to buy the computer.

SELF-TEST

CONCEPT REVIEW

1) There are two broad classes of assets. Those that are paper claims against a household, firm, or the government are called ______________ assets and physical capital like buildings, factories, and machinery are called ______________ assets.

2) A quantity measured at a point in time, for example, the quantity of capital is called a(n) ______________ . A quantity measured per unit of time, for example, the amount of investment, is called a(n) ______________ .

3) The choices by households regarding which assets to hold and which liabilities to have are called ______________ choices. The purchase of new capital by a firm or a household is called ______________ .

4) Firms whose principal business is taking deposits, making loans, and buying securities are called financial ______________ .

5) A firm maximizes its net worth when the ______________ ______________ of the marginal revenue product of capital is equal to the price of capital. Thus, an increase in the interest rate means that the quantity of capital demanded will ______________ .

6) The quantity of capital supplied depends on the ______________ decisions of households. As the interest rate increases, the substitution effect causes a(n) ______________ in the quantity of capital supplied by the household; the income effect causes a(n) ______________ in the quantity of capital supplied if the household is a net borrower. If the proportion of young people in the population increases, we would expect to see the capital supply curve shift to the ______________ .

7) The ratio of the current price of a share of a stock to the most recent year's profit per share is called the ______________ – ______________ ratio. This ratio will fall if future profits are expected to ______________ .

8) A takeover occurs when the stock market value of a firm is ______________ than the present value of expected future profits from operating the firm. A merger occurs when the two firms involved think that by combining their assets, their combined stock market value will ______________ .

9) Natural resources that can only be used once and not replaced are called ______________ natural resources. According to the Hotelling Principle, the market for the stock of such a resource will be in equilibrium when the price of the resource is expected to rise over time, at a rate equal to the ______________ ______________ .

10) The price at which it no longer pays to use a natural resource is called its ______________ price.

11) The higher the interest rate, the ______________ will be the current price of a natural resource. The higher the marginal revenue product of a natural

resource, the _______________ will be its current price. The larger is the initial stock of a natural resource, the _______________ will be its current price.

TRUE OR FALSE

_____ 1) Net financial assets can be zero for a household but never negative.

_____ 2) If we add depreciation to net investment, we have gross investment.

_____ 3) Portfolio decisions determine a person's wealth.

_____ 4) The quantity of capital is an example of a flow.

_____ 5) Depositing wealth in a financial intermediary is generally safer than buying stocks or bonds.

_____ 6) If the price of a unit of capital exceeds the present value of its marginal revenue product, a profit-maximizing firm should buy it.

_____ 7) If the net present value of an investment is positive, a profit-maximizing firm will buy the item.

_____ 8) A new machine that is expected to last one year and, at the end of the year, increase firm revenue by $1,050, sells at a price of $1,000. The firm should buy the machine if the interest rate is 6 percent.

_____ 9) As the average age of the population increases, other things remaining unchanged, the supply of capital is likely to increase.

_____ 10) If a household has positive net financial assets, the income effect of a decrease in the interest rate will be to increase its saving.

_____ 11) In equilibrium, if financial asset *A* is riskier than financial asset *B*, it will have a higher rate of interest.

_____ 12) To say that the price of a bond has risen is the same as saying that the yield on the bond has declined.

_____ 13) The current price of a stock is the present value of the firm's expected future profits.

_____ 14) When current profit is quite high relative to expected future profits, the price–earnings ratio of the firm will be high.

_____ 15) Large stock price changes with low volume of trading implies wide agreement that something fundamental has changed.

_____ 16) A takeover of firm *A* by firm *B* would occur if firm *B* believes that the stock market value of firm *A* is greater than the present value of expected potential future profits.

_____ 17) While markets may be good at efficiently allocating goods that can be replaced or reproduced, they cannot allocate exhaustible natural resources efficiently.

_____ 18) If a cheap substitute for oil is developed, we would expect to see the choke price for oil decline.

_____ 19) The higher the interest rate, the lower is the current price of a natural resource.

_____ 20) The economic model of exhaustible natural resources implies that the market will provide an automatic incentive to conserve as the resource gets closer to being depleted.

MULTIPLE-CHOICE

1) Which of the following is a real asset?
   a) a shovel
   b) IBM stock
   c) money
   d) a General Motors bond
   e) all of the above

2) Which of the following is an example of a stock?
   a) investment
   b) depreciation
   c) capital
   d) income
   e) none of the above

3) The decline in the value of capital resulting from its use over time is given by
   a) the level of saving.
   b) investment.
   c) net investment.
   d) gross investment minus net investment.
   e) net present value.

4) Household determination of how much to hold in various assets and how much to owe in various liabilities is called
   a) investment.
   b) balance sheet decision making.
   c) portfolio choice.
   d) the price–earnings problem.
   e) the net present value problem.

5) Firms that are primarily engaged in taking deposits, making loans, and buying securities are called
   a) brokers.
   b) financial intermediaries.
   c) insurance companies.
   d) monopsonists.
   e) pension funds.

6) A profit-maximizing firm will choose to buy an extra unit of capital whenever
   a) the present value of the flow of marginal revenue product is greater than zero.
   b) the cost of capital exceeds the present value of the flow of marginal revenue product.
   c) the cost of capital equals the present value of the flow of marginal revenue product.
   d) net present value is greater than zero.
   e) none of the above occurs.

7) The higher the rate of interest, the
   a) higher the net present value of an investment.
   b) lower the present value of the flow of marginal revenue products of an investment.
   c) greater the quantity of capital demanded.
   d) greater the marginal revenue product of capital.
   e) lower the marginal revenue product of capital.

8) If the interest rate increases, the
   a) substitution effect encourages more saving only if the household is a net borrower.
   b) substitution effect encourages more saving only if the household is a net lender.
   c) income effect encourages more saving only if the household is a net borrower.
   d) income effect encourages more saving only if the household is a net lender.
   e) statements in b) and d) are true.

9) Which of the following would cause the supply of capital curve to shift to the right?
   a) an increase in the proportion of young households in the population
   b) an increase in the interest rate
   c) a decrease in the interest rate
   d) an increase in average household income
   e) an increase in the marginal revenue product of capital

10) Bond *A* is more risky than bond *B*. Then, in equilibrium,
   a) the interest rate on *A* must be higher than that on *B*.
   b) the interest rate on *A* must be lower than that on *B*.
   c) the interest rate on *A* must be equal to the interest rate on *B*.
   d) no one will want to buy bond *A*.
   e) only those who prefer risk will buy bond *A*.

11) A machine that costs $2,000 will generate marginal revenue product of $1,100 at the end of one year and the same amount at the end of two years. What is the net present value of the machine if the rate of interest is 10 percent?
   a) –$90.91
   b) –$49.90
   c) 0
   d) $90.91
   e) $1,909.09

12) The yield on a stock will rise when
   a) either the dividend increases or the share price of the stock increases.
   b) either the dividend increases or the share price of the stock decreases.
   c) either the dividend decreases or the share price of the stock increases.
   d) either the dividend decreases or the share price of the stock decreases.
   e) none of the above occurs.

13) A firm is expected to pay an $8 dividend per share of stock each year into the indefinite future. If the market rate of interest is 8 percent, what will be the price of a share of stock in this firm?
   a) $8
   b) $8.64
   c) $64
   d) $80
   e) $100

14) The price of a share of XYZ Corporation's stock is $80, and the current dividend payment is $4. What is the stock yield?
   a) 3.2 percent
   b) 4 percent
   c) 5 percent
   d) 8 percent
   e) 20 percent

15) A newly issued bond promises to pay $100 at the end of one year plus a $10 interest payment. If the price of the bond today is $98, what is its yield?
   a) 2 percent
   b) 8 percent
   c) 10 percent
   d) 11 percent
   e) 12 percent

16) An event occurs which almost everyone agrees will cause a decline in the future profit of the XYZ Corporation. Immediately after the event becomes known, what would we expect to observe with regard to XYZ stock?
   a) The stock price will fluctuate up and down with a high volume of trading.
   b) The stock price will fluctuate up and down with a low volume of trading.
   c) The stock price will fall gradually with a high volume of trading.
   d) The stock price will fall quickly with a low volume of trading.
   e) The stock price will fall quickly with a high volume of trading.

17) A *takeover* of a firm is likely to occur when
   a) the stock market value of the firm is higher than expected future profit from operating the firm.
   b) the stock market value of the firm is lower than expected future profit from operating the firm.
   c) current firm profit is higher than expected future profit from operating the firm.
   d) current firm profit is lower than expected future profit from operating the firm.
   e) interest rates are low.

18) Which of the following is an exhaustible natural resource?
   a) coal
   b) land
   c) water
   d) trees
   e) none of the above

19) The yield on a stock of a natural resource is the
   a) rate of interest on the loan used to buy the resource.
   b) marginal revenue product of the resource.
   c) marginal revenue product of the resource divided by its price.
   d) marginal revenue product of the resource multiplied by the market interest rate.
   e) rate of change in the price of the resource.

20) If the market for a stock of a natural resource is in equilibrium, then it must be that the price of the resource is
   a) expected to rise at a rate equal to the rate of interest.
   b) expected to fall at a rate equal to the rate of interest.
   c) equal to the choke price of the resource.
   d) equal to the marginal revenue product of the resource.
   e) equal to the Hotelling price of the resource.

21) The current price of a natural resource is higher when
   a) its marginal revenue product is lower.
   b) the stock of the resource remaining is larger.
   c) the interest rate is lower.
   d) the choke price is lower.
   e) none of the above is true.

SHORT ANSWER

1) Why does the quantity of capital demanded increase when the interest rate falls?

2) Suppose firms *A* and *B* earned the same amount of profit per share in the most recent year but the price of a share of stock in firm *A* is higher than for firm *B*.
   a) What does this imply about the two firms' price-earnings ratios?
   b) What does this reflect about expected future profits of the two firms?

3) Exxoff Oil Co. experiences a large and potentially very costly oil spill Sunday night. What can we infer about the degree of consensus among stock market participants' beliefs if on Monday
   a) the price of Exxoff stock declines significantly at the opening of the stock market and remains there?
   b) the price of Exxoff stock fluctuates narrowly all day with a large volume of trade?

4) Why will the market for the stock of an exhaustible natural resource be in equilibrium only if the price of the resource is expected to rise at a rate equal to the rate of interest?

5) Why does a higher interest rate imply a lower current price of an exhaustible resource?

PROBLEMS

1) Larry's Lawn Care began the year with a stock of capital equal to $100,000. The value of that stock of capital depreciated by 12 percent during the year. Larry also bought $10,000 worth of new lawn care equipment during the year. What was Larry's gross investment during the year? Net investment?

2) Larry's Lawn Care is considering the purchase of additional lawn mowers. These lawn mowers have a life of 2 years and cost $120 each. Marginal revenue products for each year are given in Table 17.1 on page 200.

Table 17.1

Number of Lawn Mowers	*MRP* in First Year	*MRP* in Second Year	*NPV* ($r = 0.05$)	*NPV* ($r = 0.10$)	*NPV* ($r = 0.15$)
1	100	80			
2	80	64			
3	72	62			

a) Complete Table 17.1 by computing net present values (*NPV*) if the interest rate is 5 percent ($r = 0.05$), 10 percent ($r = 0.10$), or 15 percent ($r = 0.15$).
b) How many lawn mowers will Larry's purchase if the interest rate is 15 percent? 10 percent? 5 percent?
c) Construct an approximate lawn mower demand curve for Larry's by graphically representing the three points identified in part (b) and drawing a curve through them.

3) The present value of expected future profits for Larry's Lawn Care is $400,000. There are 8,000 outstanding shares of stock in Larry's Lawn Care. The dividend paid in the current year was $7.50 a share.
   a) What is the market price of a share of Larry's Lawn Care stock?
   b) What is the stock yield?
   c) The city of Metropolis (in which Larry's operates) initiates a "Yard Beautiful" award with a cash prize. As a result, the present value of expected future profits for Larry's Lawn Care increases to $600,000.
      i) What is the market price of a share of Larry's Lawn Care stock now?
      ii) If the dividend remains at $7.50 a share, what is the stock yield?

4) Gunk is an exhaustible natural resource and we are running out of it. There are only 1,215 barrels of gunk remaining. Table 17.2 gives the marginal revenue product schedule for gunk.

Table 17.2

Barrels of Gunk per Year	Marginal Revenue Product (dollars)
0	14.64
133	13.31
254	12.10
364	11.00
464	10.00
555	9.09

   a) Draw a graph of the demand curve for gunk (as a flow).
   b) What is the choke price of gunk?
   c) Suppose that the interest rate is 10 percent.
      i) What is the current equilibrium price of a barrel of gunk? How did you determine this?
      ii) If the current year is year 1, complete Table 17.3 for each year until the stock of gunk is exhausted.

Table 17.3

Year	Price	Initial Stock of Gunk	Final Stock of Gunk
1		1,215	
2			
3			
4			
5			

ANSWERS

CONCEPT REVIEW

1) financial; real
2) stock; flow
3) portfolio; investment
4) intermediaries
5) present value; decrease
6) savings; increase; decrease; left
7) price–earnings; fall
8) lower; increase
9) exhaustible; interest rate
10) choke
11) lower; higher; lower

TRUE OR FALSE

1) F	6) F	11) T	16) F
2) T	7) T	12) T	17) F
3) F	8) F	13) T	18) T
4) F	9) T	14) F	19) T
5) T	10) F	15) T	20) T

MULTIPLE-CHOICE

1) a	8) d	15) e
2) c	9) d	16) d
3) d	10) a	17) b
4) c	11) a	18) a
5) b	12) b	19) e
6) d	13) e	20) a
7) b	14) c	21) c

SHORT ANSWER

1) Profit-maximizing firms will demand capital as long as the present value of the stream of future marginal revenue product from the new capital exceeds the price of the new capital; in other words, as long as net present value is positive. Since a lower interest rate implies that the present value of any given future stream of marginal revenue product will be larger, the net present value will be positive for a *larger* number of additional capital and thus more capital goods will be purchased. Therefore, the quantity of capital demanded increases as the interest rate falls.

2) a) The price–earnings ratio is the current price of a share of stock divided by the most recent profits per share. Thus, the price–earnings ratio of firm *A*'s stock is greater than the price–earnings ratio of firm *B*'s stock. This implies that, although the recent profits (per share) of the two firms may be the same, future profits (per share) for firm *A* are expected to be higher than for firm *B*.
   b) The price of a share of stock represents the present value of *expected* future profits, so a higher price implies higher expected future profits.

3) a) A significant decline in the price of Exxoff stock with little volume of trade implies that there is wide consensus that the oil spill means a significant reduction in the present value of future Exxoff profits.
   b) If, on the other hand, there is a large volume of trade in Exxoff stock with little net price movement, it must be that there is little consensus about the implications of the oil spill for the future profitability of Exxoff.

4) The yield on the stock of an exhaustible resource is the percentage rate of change in the price of the resource. In order for the market of the stock of the resource to be in equilibrium, there must be no incentive for movement into or out of the market. This will only be the case if the yield on the stock of the exhaustible resource is the same as the yield on other assets, which is given by the rate of interest.

5) In equilibrium, the current price of the resource will be the price which, if the price continues to increase at a rate equal to the interest rate, the choke price will be reached at the same time that the resource is depleted. A higher interest rate means that the price is expected to rise at a faster rate. Therefore, if it is to reach the choke price at the right time, it must start from a lower current price.

PROBLEMS

1) Gross investment is $10,000, the amount of the purchase of new capital. Net investment is –$2,000, the amount of gross investment minus depreciation of $12,000.

2) a) Completed Table 17.1 appears here as Table 17.1 Solution. *NPV* is calculated as the present value of the stream of marginal revenue products resulting from an investment minus the cost of the investment. For lawn mowers with a 2-year life, the *NPV* is calculated using the following equation:

$$NPV = \frac{MRP_1}{1+r} + \frac{MRP_2}{(1 t r)2} - P_L$$

In this equation, MRP_1 and MRP_2 are the marginal revenue products in the first and second years, respectively, and P_L is the price of a lawnmower. The values of MRP_1 and MRP_2 are given in Table 17.1 for 1, 2, and 3 lawnmowers and P_L is given as $120. The values for *NPV* given in Table 17.1 Solution are obtained by substituting these values into the above equation and evaluating the expression for the alternative values of *r*, the interest rate.

Table 17.1 Solution

Number of Lawn Mowers	*MRP* in First Year	*MRP* in Second Year	*NPV* (*r* = 0.05)	*NPV* (*r* = 0.10)	*NPV* (*r* = 0.15)
1	100	80	47.80	37.02	27.45
2	80	64	14.24	5.62	−2.04
3	72	62	4.81	−3.31	−10.51

b) If the interest rate is 15 percent, only one additional lawn mower will be purchased since the second lawn mower has negative net present value. If the rate of interest is 10 percent, 2 lawn mowers will be purchased, and if the rate of interest is 5 percent, 3 lawn mowers will be purchased.

c) The approximate lawn mower demand curve is illustrated in Figure 17.1. The curve indicates that, at an interest of 15 percent, one lawnmower will be demanded. At an interest rate of 10 percent, two lawnmowers will be demanded and, at an interest rate of 5 percent, three lawnmowers will be demanded.

Figure 17.1

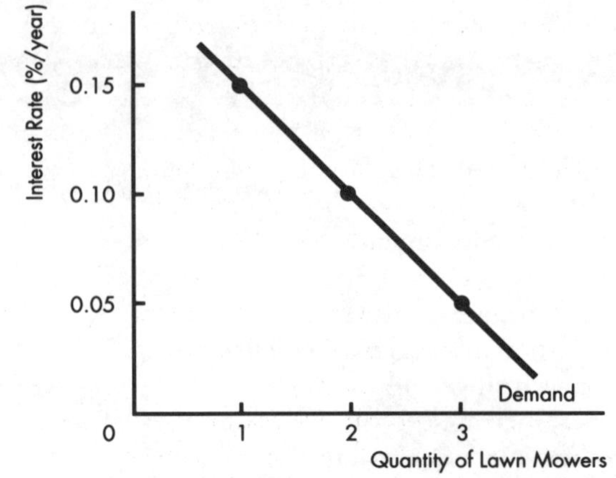

3) a) The market price of a share of Larry's Lawn Care stock will be the present value of expected future profits for the firm divided by the number of shares outstanding: $50.

b) The stock yield is 15 percent. This is the dividend ($7.50) as a percentage of the price of a share of stock ($50).

c) i) The price of a share of stock will increase to $75 (= $600,000/8,000).

ii) The stock yield will now be 10 percent. This is the dividend ($7.50) as a percentage of the new price of a share of stock ($75).

4) a) The demand curve for gunk is given by the marginal revenue product curve. It is illustrated in Figure 17.2.

Figure 17.2

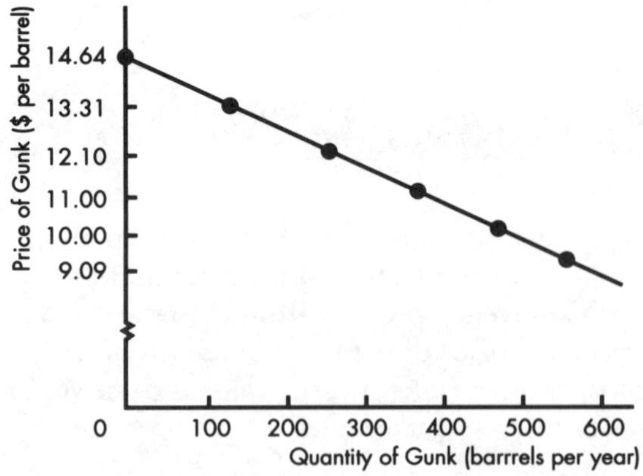

4) b) The choke price for gunk is $14.64. This is the price that is high enough that the resource will not be used at all.

c) i) If the interest rate is 10 percent, the current price of a barrel of gunk is $10. We know that the current (equilibrium) price must be such that if the price of gunk is increasing at a rate of 10 percent per year (equal to the rate of interest), the stock will be depleted just as the choke price is achieved. We can find the current price by noting that (1) the choke price is $14.64 and (2) the remaining stock is 1,215 barrels and working backwards.

Since the price of gunk is growing at the rate of 10 percent per year, the price in the year before the choke price is reached must be $14.64 (the choke price) divided by 1.10 (1 + the 10% growth rate of price) or $13.31. From Table 17.2 (and recognizing that gunk is just depleted as the $14.64 price is reached) we can infer that 133 barrels of gunk would be purchased in that year. Proceeding in a similar manner, working backward until all 1,215 barrels of gunk have been purchased, we discover that the current equilibrium price must be $10.

ii) Using the procedure outlined in part (c)(i), Table 17.3 can be completed as shown in Table 17.3 Solution.

Table 17.3 Solution

Year	Price	Initial Stock of Gunk	Final Stock of Gunk
1	10.00	1,215	751
2	11.00	751	387
3	12.10	387	133
4	13.31	133	0
5	14.64	0	

Chapter 18 The Distribution of Income and Wealth

Chapter in Perspective

Text Pages 465–488

Income is the payment by firms to owners of factors of production for the use of those resources. Individuals with more resources to sell or whose resources sell for a higher price will receive larger incomes. Thus, the distribution of income depends on the distribution of ownership of resources used in production and the market prices of those resources. In the last three chapters we learned that the prices of factors of production are determined in markets and we studied the operation of those markets.

In this chapter, we discuss the distribution of income and wealth in Canada, and address the following questions: How unequally are income and wealth actually distributed in Canada? What accounts for this inequality? What are the consequences of government policies intended to redistribute income or wealth? What are the major ideas that constitute a "fair" distribution of income?

Learning Objectives

After studying this chapter, you will be able to:

- **Describe the distribution of income and wealth in Canada today.**
- **Explain why the data on wealth distribution show greater inequality than the data on income distribution.**
- **Explain how the distribution of income arises from the prices of productive resources and the distribution of endowments.**
- **Explain how the distribution of income and wealth is affected by individual choices.**
- **Explain the different views about fairness in the distribution of income and wealth.**
- **Explain the effects of redistribution policies on the distribution of income and wealth.**

Helpful Hints

1) The major tool used by economists to picture the degree of inequality of income or wealth in an economy is the Lorenz curve. It is important to understand how to interpret such a curve. See Key Figure 18.3 below.

2) A major message of this chapter is that statistics used to construct Lorenz curves do not always give an accurate picture of inequality. It is important to understand why inaccurate pictures might arise.

   For example, you should understand why a distribution of wealth which excludes the value of human capital will give a distorted picture relative to the distribution of income.

   You should also understand why the distribution of annual (static) income will give a distorted picture relative to the distribution of lifetime (dynamic) income.

   Finally, you should understand why the distribution of before-tax, before-transfer income will give a distorted picture relative to the distribution of after-tax, after-transfer income.

3) The issue of fairness discussed in this chapter is a normative issue. Note, however, that the tradeoff between equity and economic efficiency (the so-called big tradeoff) is a positive issue.

Key Figures

Figure 18.3 Lorenz Curves for Income and Wealth, text page 469

A Lorenz curve is a useful way to represent the distribution of income or wealth. It plots the cumulative percentage of income earned by a given cumulative percentage of families. This figure gives Lorenz curves for Canada. The table gives the values of the cumulative percentage of income and wealth corresponding to various cumulative percentages of families.

For example, the table indicates that the lowest 20 percent of families earn approximately 5 percent of the income in Canada and hold zero percent of the wealth. Also, the highest 20 percent of families earn 43 percent of the income (the difference between 100 percent and 57 percent) and 73.3 percent of the wealth (the difference between 100 percent and 26.7 percent). This information is illustrated graphically in the Lorenz curves of the figure.

The farther a Lorenz curve is from the line of equality, the more unequal the distribution. It is readily seen that wealth is much more unequally distributed than income.

Figure 18.4 The Incidence of Low Income by Selected Family Characteristics, text page 471

This figure indicates the importance of certain family characteristics in influencing whether a household's income falls below a low-income cutoff. The most important characteristic influencing the incidence of low income is family type. Other important characteristics include the sex of the head of the household, whether the head is in or out of the labour force, the age of the head, and the geographical region of the household.

Figure 18.13 The Distribution of Wages, Hours, and Income, text page 481

The fact that the quantity of labour supplied increases as the wage rate increases implies that the distribution of income will be more unequal than the distribution of wage rates and is illustrated in this figure.

Part (a) of the figure shows a distribution of hourly wage rates, which is symmetric around the average wage rate of $5 per hour.

Part (b) shows the distribution of weekly income, which is *not* symmetric around the average weekly income of $128. More than half of the people earn less than the average income, and the range from the average to the highest income ($360) is much larger than the range from the average to the lowest income ($0).

These asymmetries, which make the distribution of income more unequal than the distribution of wage rates, are explained by the fact that the quantity of labour supplied increases as the wage rate increases.

SELF-TEST

CONCEPT REVIEW

1) Of the three basic factors of production, ______________ earns the largest share of total income.

2) The diagram used by economists to illustrate the cumulative percentage of households ranked from the poorest to the richest is called a(n) ______________ ______________. The straight line running through the middle of the diagram is called the line of ______________ .

3) The most important factor in determining whether a person receives a high income or a low income is ______________ .

4) An income tax system in which the marginal tax rate rises as income rises is called a(n) ______________ income tax. A(n) ______________ income tax is one in which the marginal tax rate falls with the level of income while for a(n) ______________ income tax, the marginal tax rate is constant for all levels of income.

5) The distribution of income that would prevail in the absence of government policies is called the ______________ distribution. The distribution that takes account of government policies is called the distribution after ______________ and ______________ .

6) A gift from one generation to the next is called a(n) ______________ .

7) The tendency for people to marry within their own socioeconomic class is called ______________ ______________. This tendency contributes to a(n) ______________ in the unequal distribution of wealth.

8) Theories of distributive justice that emphasize the equality of the outcomes of economic activity are called ______________ - ______________ theories while those emphasizing the equality of opportunity are called ______________ theories.

9) The ______________ theory states that the fairest outcome is the one that maximizes the sum of the utilities of all individuals in society.

10) According to the ______________ theory, the fairest distribution of income gives the poorest member of society the largest income possible.

TRUE OR FALSE

_____ 1) In Canada, the richest 5 percent of households own approximately 43 percent of total wealth.

_____ 2) In Canada, income is more unequally distributed than wealth.

_____ 3) The farther the Lorenz curve is from the line of equality, the more equal the distribution of income.

_____ 4) The distribution of income became much more unequal between 1951 and 1985.

_____ 5) Under a proportional income tax, total taxes rise as income rises.

_____ 6) Under a proportional income tax, the marginal tax rate does not change as income rises.

_____ 7) A regressive income tax redistributes income from the rich to the poor.

_____ 8) Compared to the market distribution of income, government benefits and taxes reduce the inequality of income distribution.

_____ 9) The financial wealth distribution ignores the distribution of human capital and thus overstates inequality among individuals.

_____ 10) Income is a stock of earnings received by an individual.

_____ 11) The value of a person's human capital is the sum of that person's lifetime earnings.

_____ 12) Because it does not take into account the family's stage in the life cycle, the measured distribution of annual income will *understate* the degree of inequality.

_____ 13) Wealthier families tend to leave larger bequests.

_____ 14) If debts could be bequeathed, the distribution of wealth would become more equal over time.

_____ 15) The existence of assortative mating tends to increase the inequality of the distribution of wealth.

_____ 16) A normal distribution is bell-shaped and is symmetric around the average.

_____ 17) The belief that everyone should have the same income and wealth is an example of a process theory of distributive justice.

_____ 18) The utilitarian theory is an example of an end-state theory of distributive justice.

_____ 19) Robert Nozick argues that a theory of distributive justice must be based on the mechanisms through which the distributions of income and wealth arise.

_____ 20) In general, reducing income inequality by redistributing income from the rich to the poor will lead to greater production of goods and services.

MULTIPLE-CHOICE

1) Which of the following statements is true?
   a) Labour earns the largest share of total income and that share has decreased slightly over the years.
   b) Labour earns the largest share of total income and that share has increased slightly over the years.
   c) Owners of capital earn the largest share of total income and that share has decreased slightly over the years.
   d) Owners of capital earn the largest share of total income and that share has increased slightly over the years.
   e) None of the above statements is true.

2) Differences in the wage rates received by different individuals reflect differences in
   a) marginal product of labour.
   b) natural ability.
   c) human capital.
   d) all of the above.
   e) none of the above.

3) The inequality in the distribution of wealth is
   a) less than the inequality in the distribution of income.
   b) decreased by the existence of assortative mating.
   c) a better measure of the inequality in the distribution of economic resources than is the inequality in the distribution of income.
   d) even greater if we look at the distribution of wealth among the richest 1 percent of all families.
   e) all of the above.

4) The wealthiest 20 percent of Canadian families own what percent of *total wealth*?
   a) 20 percent
   b) 43 percent
   c) 57 percent
   d) 73 percent
   e) 80 percent

5) The poorest 20 percent of Canadian families receive what percent of *total income*?
   a) 1 percent
   b) 5 percent
   c) 10 percent
   d) 20 percent
   e) 25 percent

6) Which diagram is used by economists to illustrate the distribution of income or wealth?
   a) Lorenz curve
   b) normal distribution
   c) Rawls curve
   d) Okun tradeoff curve
   e) none of the above

7) The most important factor influencing the incidence of low income is
   a) labour force status.
   b) sex of household head.
   c) age of household head.
   d) family type.
   e) geographical region.

8) If the marginal tax rate increases as income increases, the income tax is defined as
   a) progressive.
   b) proportional.
   c) negative.
   d) regressive.
   e) excessive.

9) The distribution of *annual income*
   a) understates the degree of inequality because it does not take into account the family's stage in its life cycle.
   b) understates the degree of inequality because it does not take into account the distribution of human capital.
   c) overstates the degree of inequality because it does not take into account the family's stage in its life cycle.
   d) overstates the degree of inequality because it does not take into account the distribution of human capital.
   e) is an accurate measure of the degree of inequality.

10) Consider the Lorenz curves in Figure 18.1. Which Lorenz curve corresponds to the greatest income *inequality*?
a) *A*
b) *B*
c) *C*
d) *D*
e) impossible to tell without additional information

Figure 18.1

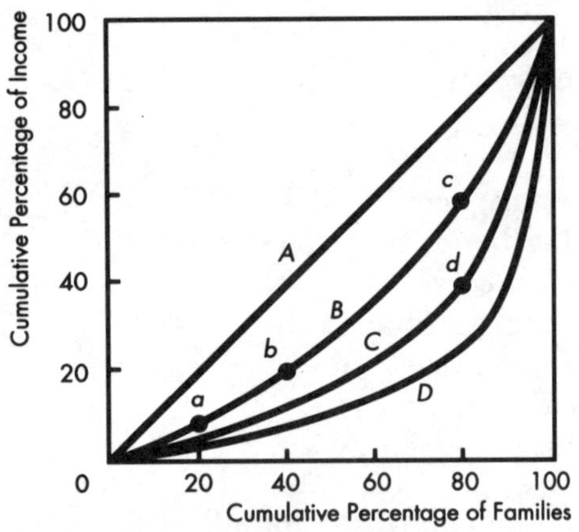

11) In Figure 18.1, what is curve *A* (a straight line) called?
a) market distribution line
b) line of equality
c) fairness line
d) Okun trade-off curve
e) none of the above

12) Which point in Figure 18.1 indicates that the richest 20 percent of families earn 40 percent of the income?
a) *a*
b) *b*
c) *c*
d) *d*
e) none of the above

13) The distribution of *wealth*
a) understates the degree of inequality because it does not take into account the family's stage in its life cycle.
b) understates the degree of inequality because it does not take into account the distribution of human capital.
c) overstates the degree of inequality because it does not take into account the family's stage in its life cycle.
d) overstates the degree of inequality because it does not take into account the distribution of human capital.
e) is an accurate measure of the degree of inequality.

14) Suppose that if a family earns zero income, it receives a monthly transfer payment of $1,000 from the government. If the family earns $400 in a month, the government payment drops to $700. What is the marginal tax rate in this case?
a) 0 percent
b) 10 percent
c) 40 percent
d) 50 percent
e) 75 percent

15) Even if the distribution of wages is symmetric, the distribution of income will be skewed because
a) abilities are distributed symmetrically.
b) abilities are distributed asymmetrically.
c) individuals tend to supply more labour at higher wages.
d) individuals tend to supply less labour at higher wages.
e) both b) and d) are true.

16) Which of the following *reduces* the inequality of income or wealth relative to the market distribution?
a) government payments to the poor
b) a regressive income tax
c) large bequests
d) assortative mating
e) all of the above

17) A theory of distributive justice that emphasizes the mechanism by which distribution takes place is
a) a utilitarian theory.
b) an end-state theory.
c) a Rawlsian theory.
d) a process theory.
e) an outcomes theory.

18) According to the Rawlsian theory, income should be redistributed if the
a) average person can be made better off.
b) poorest person can be made better off.
c) richest person can be made worse off.
d) wage rate is greater than the marginal product of labour.
e) wage rate is less than the marginal product of labour.

19) Which of the following is an example of an end-state theory of distributive justice?
a) marginal product theory
b) the theory of Robert Nozick
c) the utilitarian theory
d) the process theory
e) none of the above

20) Redistribution of income from the rich to the poor will lead to a reduction in total output. This is known as
   a) market distribution.
   b) the process theory of distributive justice.
   c) the end-state theory of distributive justice.
   d) the big tradeoff.
   e) the capitalist dilemma.

SHORT ANSWER

1) a) What is a Lorenz curve?
   b) What does it illustrate?

2) Explain the differences and connections between the concepts of wealth and income.

3) a) What are the two factors that determine a person's income?
   b) To what extent are these factors the result of forces beyond the control of the individual and to what extent are they the result of individual choice?

4) The two classes of theories of distributive justice are process theories and end-state theories.
   a) What is the principal characteristic of a process theory of distributive justice?
   b) Why is the utilitarian theory an end-state theory of distributive justice?

5) Why is there a "big tradeoff" between fairness and efficiency?

PROBLEMS

1) Table 18.1 gives information regarding the distribution of income in an economy which generates $100 billion in total annual income.

Table 18.1 Total Family Income

Percentage of Families	Total Income (billions of dollars)	Income Share (percent)	Cumulative Percentage of Families	Cumulative Percentage of Income
Poorest 20%	5			
Second 20%	10			
Third 20%	15			
Fourth 20%	20			
Richest 20%	50			

   a) Complete Table 18.1 by computing the entries in the last three columns.
   b) Draw the Lorenz curve for income in this economy and label it *A*.

2) Now suppose that a progressive income tax is levied on the economy. The distribution of after-tax income is given in Table 18.2. We have assumed that none of the revenue is redistributed to families in the economy. Note that total after-tax income is $71 billion.

Table 18.2 After-Tax Family Income

Percentage of Families	After-Tax Income (billions of dollars)	After-Tax Income Share (percent)	Cumulative Percentage of Families	Cumulative Percentage of After-Tax Income
Poorest 20%	5			
Second 20%	9			
Third 20%	12			
Fourth 20%	15			
Richest 20%	30			

   a) Complete Table 18.2.
   b) Draw the Lorenz curve for after-tax income on the same graph you used for problem 1(b) and label it *B*.
   c) What effect has the progressive income tax had on inequality?

3) Finally, suppose that, in addition, the government redistributes all of the tax revenue so that the after-transfer (after-tax) income distribution is that given in Table 18.3. For example, those in the poorest group receive transfer income in the amount of $10 billion so that their after-transfer income becomes $15 billion.

Table 18.3 After-Transfer Family Income

Percentage of Families	After-Transfer Income (billions of dollars)	After-Transfer Income Share (percent)	Cumulative Percentage of Families	Cumulative Percentage of After-Transfer Income
Poorest 20%	15			
Second 20%	16			
Third 20%	18			
Fourth 20%	20			
Richest 20%	31			

a) Complete Table 18.3.
b) Draw the Lorenz curve for after-transfer income on the same graph you used for 1(b) and 2(b) and label it *C*.
c) What effect has income redistribution through transfer payments had on inequality?

4) Consider an economy consisting of 100 individuals who are identical in every way. They each live to be 80 years old and no older. Between birth and the age of 20 years they earn zero income; between the ages of 21 and 35 they each earn an annual income of $30,000; between the ages of 36 and 50 they each earn an annual income of $40,000; between the ages of 51 and 65 they each receive an annual income of $60,000; and between the ages of 66 and 80 they each receive an annual income of $20,000. At any given time there are 20 individuals in each of the 5 age groups. For simplicity, we assume that there are no bequests. This information is summarized in Table 18.4.

Table 18.4 Lifetime Income Patterns

Age Group (years)	Number in Age Group	Individual Annual Income ($)
0 – 20	20	0
21 – 35	20	30,000
36 – 50	20	40,000
51 – 65	20	60,000
66 – 80	20	20,000

a) Draw the Lorenz curve for lifetime income in this economy and label it *A*.
b) Draw the Lorenz curve for annual income in this economy and label it *B*.
c) Which of these is a better measure of the inequality among individuals in this economy? Why?

ANSWERS

CONCEPT REVIEW

1) labour
2) Lorenz curve; equality
3) education
4) progressive; regressive; proportional
5) market; taxes; transfers
6) bequest
7) assortative mating; increase
8) end-state; process
9) utilitarian
10) Rawlsian

TRUE OR FALSE

1) T	5) T	9) T	13) T	17) F
2) F	6) T	10) F	14) T	18) T
3) F	7) F	11) F	15) T	19) T
4) F	8) T	12) F	16) T	20) F

MULTIPLE-CHOICE

1) b	5) b	9) c	13) d	17) d
2) d	6) a	10) d	14) e	18) b
3) d	7) d	11) b	15) c	19) c
4) d	8) a	12) c	16) a	20) d

SHORT ANSWER

1) a) The Lorenz curve gives a graphical representation of the distribution of income or wealth across some population.
b) The horizontal axis measures the cumulative percentage of families ranked from the poorest to the richest. The vertical axis measures the cumulative percentages of income or wealth. The farther the Lorenz curve is from the line of equality, the more unequal the distribution of income or wealth.

2) Wealth is the *stock* of assets owned by an individual while income is the *flow* of earnings received by an individual. The concepts are connected in that an individual's income is the earnings that flow from the person's stock of wealth.

3) a) A person's income is determined by the market prices for productive resource services and the quantity of resource services the person is able and willing to sell at those prices.
b) These two factors depend on a number of things, some of which are (at least partially) under the control of the individual and some of which are not.
The price of labour services, the wage rate, is determined in the market for labour. But, as we learned in Chapters 15 and 16, the wage rate will depend on the marginal product of labour, which is affected by individual choices about training and education as well as personal inherent ability.
The quantity of labour services supplied will also depend on personal choices about how to spend one's time. The quantity of other resource services supplied will also depend on personal choices as well as the individual's endowment of the factor.

4) a) A process theory of distributive justice focuses on the fairness of the *process* or *mechanisms* by which results are achieved instead of focusing on the results themselves.
b) The utilitarian theory suggests that the fairest system is one in which the sum of the utilities in the society is a maximum. Since the theory focuses on the *outcome* or the *ends*, it is an end-state theory of distributive justice.

5) If greater fairness means increasing the equality of income, it can only be achieved by income redistribution; the income of some must be taxed in order to make transfer payments to others. However, there are incentive effects that reduce the total amount of income available to be distributed.

If productive activities such as work are taxed, there will be a tendency to reduce time spent in those activities.

Furthermore, any redistribution program would require the use of resources to administer it and thus leave fewer resources for other productive activities. Therefore, we arrive at the insight: a more equally shared pie results in a smaller pie.

PROBLEMS

1) a) Table 18.1 is completed as Table 18.1 Solution. The income share for each group of families is the total income of that group as a percent of total income in the economy ($100 billion). The cumulative percentage of income (last column) is obtained by adding the percentage income share of the group (from the third column) to the total percentage income share of all poorer groups of families.

Table 18.1 Solution: Total Family Income

Percentage of Families	Total Income (billions of dollars)	Income Share (percent)	Cumulative Percentage of Families	Cumulative Percentage of Income
Poorest 20%	5	5	20	5
Second 20%	10	10	40	15
Third 20%	15	15	60	30
Fourth 20%	20	20	80	50
Richest 20%	50	50	100	100

1) b) The curve labelled *A* in Figure 18.2 is the Lorenz curve for total family income. This simply plots the values in the last two columns of Table 18.1 Solution.

Figure 18.2

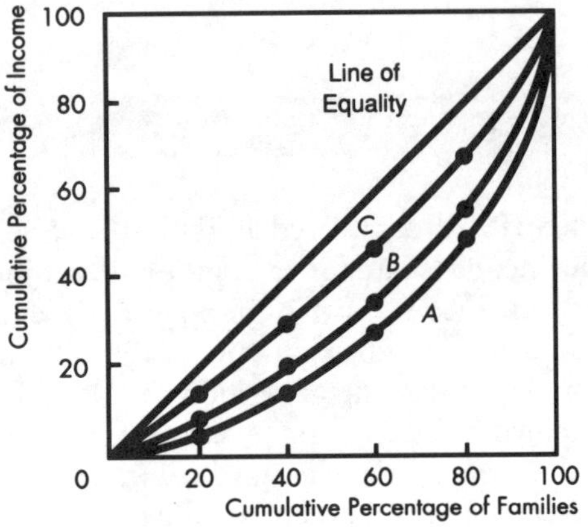

2) a) Table 18.2 is completed as Table 18.2 Solution.

Table 18.2 Solution: After-Tax Family Income

Percentage of Families	After-Tax Income (billions of dollars)	After-Tax Income Share (percent)	Cumulative Percentage of Families	Cumulative Percentage of After-Tax Income
Poorest 20%	5	7	20	7
Second 20%	9	13	40	20
Third 20%	12	17	60	37
Fourth 20%	15	21	80	58
Richest 20%	30	42	100	100

b) The curve labelled *B* in Figure 18.2 is the Lorenz curve for after-tax family income.

c) The progressive income tax has reduced inequality by taking a larger percentage of income from higher income groups.

3) a) Table 18.3 is completed as Table 18.3 Solution.

Table 18.3 Solution: After-Transfer Family Income

Percentage of Families	After-Transfer Income (billions of dollars)	After-Transfer Income Share (percent)	Cumulative Percentage of Families	Cumulative Percentage of After-Transfer Income
Poorest 20%	15	15	20	15
Second 20%	16	16	40	31
Third 20%	18	18	60	49
Fourth 20%	20	20	80	69
Richest 20%	31	31	100	100

b) The curve labelled *C* in Figure 18.2 is the Lorenz curve for (after-tax) after-transfer family income.

c) Income redistribution through transfer payments has reduced inequality.

4) a) Since each individual in the economy earns exactly the same lifetime income, the Lorenz curve for lifetime income coincides with the line of equality and is labelled *A* in Figure 18.3.

Figure 18.3

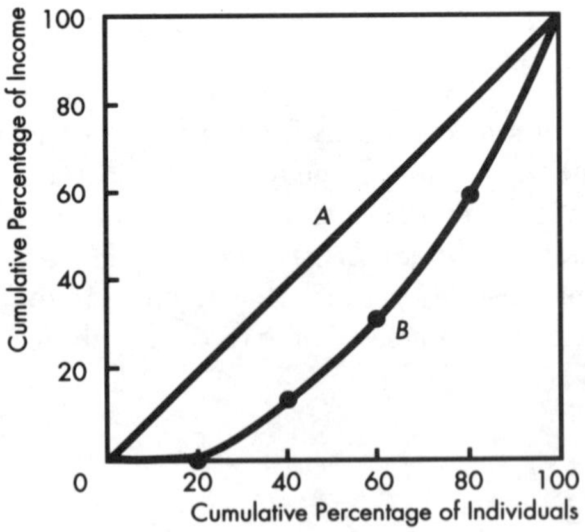

b) The Lorenz curve for annual income is labelled *B* in Figure 18.3. It reflects the fact that the poorest 20 percent of the individuals (0–20 years) receive 0 percent of the annual income; the second poorest 20 percent of the individuals (60–80 years) receive 13 percent of the annual income; the third poorest 20 percent of the individuals (21–35 years) receive 20 percent of the annual income; the fourth poorest 20 percent of the individuals (36–50 years) receive 27 percent of the annual income; and the richest 20 percent of the individuals (51–65 years) receive 40 percent of the income.

c) The distribution of lifetime income is a better measure of the degree of inequality. In this imaginary economy, all individuals are identical (equal), a fact that is reflected by equal lifetime incomes. The only reason annual income distribution in this economy is not equal is because the individuals are at different stages of identical life cycles.

Chapter 19 **Market Failure**

Chapter in Perspective

Text Pages 493–510

One of the conclusions of Chapter 12 is that competitive markets tend to be allocatively efficient. This fact suggests that, when there are competitive markets, there is no opportunity for the government to improve economic efficiency through programs which reallocate resources. In Chapters 13 and 14, however, we noted that when markets are not competitive, allocative efficiency is not achieved. In the face of monopoly or oligopoly, are there government policies that can improve efficiency? This question will be addressed in Chapter 21.

In this chapter we discover that there are circumstances in which even competitive markets fail to allocate goods and services efficiently. For example, if competitive markets are efficient, why is there so much pollution? As a result of such *market failure* to achieve efficiency, there are additional opportunities for government to improve allocation. This chapter begins a discussion of how an "ideal" government might proceed to do so. In the next chapter we examine the behaviour of actual governments.

Learning Objectives

After studying this chapter, you will be able to:

- **Describe the range of economic actions governments undertake.**
- **Outline the structure of the government sector of the Canadian economy.**
- **Distinguish between a normative and a positive analysis of government economic behaviour.**
- **Define market failure and explain how it might be overcome by government action.**
- **Distinguish between private goods and public goods.**
- **Explain the free-rider problem.**
- **Explain how government provision of public goods avoids the free-rider problem.**
- **Explain how property rights and taxes and subsidies may be used to achieve a more efficient allocation of resources when externalities are present.**

Helpful Hints

1) The criterion economists use to judge the success of the market (or any other institution for that matter) is allocative efficiency. Allocative efficiency means that the economy is producing all goods and services up to the point at which the marginal cost is equal to the marginal benefit. In such a state, no one can be made better off without making someone else worse off.

   When the market fails to achieve this "ideal" state of efficiency, we call it *market failure*. The market can fail by producing too little if the marginal benefit of the last unit exceeds the marginal cost. On the other hand, the market can fail by producing too much if the marginal cost of the last unit exceeds the marginal benefit.

2) All goods provided by the government are not necessarily public goods. A public good is defined by the characteristics of nonrivalry and nonexcludability, not by whether or not it is publicly provided. For example, many cities and communities provide swimming pools and residential garbage pickup. Neither of these is a pure public good in spite of the fact that they may be provided by the government. Indeed, in many other communities, the same services are provided by the private market.

3) It is important to understand why the properties of nonrivalry and nonexcludability associated with pure public goods imply that we obtain the marginal benefit curve for the economy as a whole differently than for private goods.

   A private good is a rival in consumption. Therefore, to obtain the demand curve for the whole economy, we sum the individual marginal benefit (demand) curves *horizontally*. However, the economy's marginal benefit curve for a public good is obtained by summing the individual marginal benefit curves *vertically*. This is the relevant marginal benefit curve for evaluating the efficient provision level of the public good. See the discussion of Key Figure 19.1.

4) A competitive market will result in the quantity traded at which the marginal private cost is equal to the marginal private benefit. The efficient quantity is the quantity at which marginal social cost is equal to marginal social benefit.

   The difference between *marginal social* and *marginal private cost* is external cost and the difference between *marginal social benefit* and *marginal private benefit* is external benefit.

   In most transactions, there are no affected third parties and so there are no external costs or benefits. This means that private and social costs and benefits coincide and competitive markets will be efficient. However, when third parties are affected, there are external costs or benefits and competitive markets will not be efficient.

5) Competitive markets with externalities are not efficient because some of the costs or benefits are *external*. If those costs or benefits could be *internalized* somehow, then the market would be efficient. There are two approaches to internalizing externalities that are discussed in this chapter.

   The first is to clearly define and strictly enforce property rights. Then costs imposed on nonparticipants in a transaction can be recovered through the legal process and will thus be borne by those making the transaction decision: the costs will become internal (private).

   The second approach to internalizing externalities is to tax activities that generate external costs and subsidize activities that generate external benefits. By charging a tax equal to the external cost, the entire cost becomes internal. Similarly, by paying a subsidy in the amount of external benefits, the entire benefit becomes internal.

6) The production of steel also produces pollution, which is an external cost. This means that the market will produce too much steel (and too much of the by-product, pollution). There are two important things to realize about the efficient level of steel production and thus the efficient level of pollution.
   a) If the production of steel is adjusted so that there is equality between marginal social cost and marginal social benefit, less steel will be produced and will sell at a higher price.
   b) The external cost will not be so great that the efficient level of steel production is zero. This means that the efficient (optimal) level of pollution will not be zero.

Key Figures

Figure 19.1 Benefits of a Public Good, text page 499
An individual's marginal benefit curve for either a private good or a public good indicates ability and willingness to pay. There is an important difference, however, in how we obtain the total economy's marginal benefit curve for private goods and public goods. The difference arises from the fact that private goods exhibit rivalry in consumption while public goods exhibit nonrivalry in consumption.

If one person consumes a unit of a private good, that unit cannot be consumed by anyone else. However, the consumption of a public good by one person does not reduce the amount available for others. This implies that the economy's marginal benefit curve (demand curve) for a private good is obtained by summing the individual marginal benefit (demand) curves *horizontally* (Chapter 7).

For a public good, however, the economy's marginal benefit curve is obtained by summing the individual marginal benefit curves *vertically*; by adding up the individual marginal benefits at each quantity. This is illustrated in the figure by considering an economy in which there are two individuals, Lisa and Max, who receive benefits from acid-rain check satellites, a public good. Their total and marginal benefits are reported in the table. Their marginal benefit curves are given in parts (a) and (b) of the figure. The economy's marginal benefit curve is given in part (c) as the *vertical* sum of the marginal benefit curves of Lisa and Max.

Figure 19.2 The Efficient Scale of Provision of a Public Good, text page 500

The efficient scale of provision of a public good is the amount that maximizes net benefit, which is total benefit minus total cost.

Part (a) of this figure graphs the total cost (*TC*) and total benefit (*TB*) curves. Net benefit is given by the vertical distance between the two curves. We find that this distance (net benefit) is a maximum at a quantity of two satellites. Thus two satellites is the efficient scale of provision.

Part (b) illustrates an alternative way to find the same result. The efficient scale of provision is achieved if satellites are produced up to the level at which marginal benefit equals marginal cost. The marginal benefit (*MB*) and marginal cost (*MC*) curves are shown in part (b). Marginal benefit equals marginal cost at a quantity of two satellites.

Figure 19.3 Taxing and Regulating an Externality, text page 503

If the production of a good or service produces external costs, a competitive market will result in a quantity which exceeds the allocatively efficient level. This figure illustrates that taxing the production of that good or service can induce the allocatively efficient quantity. The example used here is transportation services, which produce external costs. The demand curve for transportation services is the same as the marginal benefit curve. The marginal private cost (*MPC*) and marginal social cost (*MSC*) curves are *not* the same however. The *MPC* curve reflects the costs that directly accrue to the producer of transportation services. There are, however, other costs in the form of pollution and congestion that are imposed on others. The *MSC* curve reflects both the marginal cost incurred by the producer and these external costs.

The allocatively efficient quantity of transportation services occurs at Q_1, the intersection of the $D = MB$ curve and the *MSC* curve. A competitive market, however, will result in the quantity at which the *D* and *MPC* curves intersect since producers only take private costs into account; market price will be P_0 and quantity will be Q_0, which is greater than the allocatively efficient quantity.

If, however, a tax is levied on producers in the amount of the external costs, the *MSC* curve becomes the new relevant marginal cost curve for producers. As a result, the market price will rise to P_1 and the quantity will fall to Q_1, and allocative efficiency is achieved.

Figure 19.4 Subsidizing an External Benefit, text page 507

In cases of external benefits, a competitive market will result in a quantity that falls short of the allocatively efficient level. This occurs because the marginal social benefit associated with the good exceeds the marginal private benefit. In such a case, a subsidy can induce the market to achieve allocative efficiency.

This is illustrated in the figure using the example of education. The argument is similar to that of Figure 19.3, because there is a divergence between the marginal private benefit (*MPB*) curve and the marginal social benefit (*MSB*) curve for education. The allocatively efficient quantity is Q_1. A competitive market will result in a price of P_0 and quantity of Q_0, which is less than the allocatively efficient quantity. If the government subsidizes education so as to make it available for price P_1, the result will be the allocatively efficient quantity of Q_1.

SELF-TEST

CONCEPT REVIEW

1) If an unregulated market economy is unable to achieve allocative efficiency, in all circumstances, we have ______________ ______________ .

2) There are two classes of economic theories of government behaviour. Public ______________ theories predict that government will pursue actions that will achieve allocative efficiency. Public ______________ theories study the behaviour of government as the outcome of individual choices made by voters, politicians, and bureaucrats.

3) A good which, if consumed by one person, cannot be consumed by another is called a(n) ______________ good. There are two important features of such a good. The fact that Bob's consumption of a good means that Sue cannot consume the same good illustrates the feature of ______________ . If Sue has purchased a good, she owns it and can keep others from using it. This illustrates the feature of ______________ .

4) A good which, if consumed by one person, is necessarily also consumed by everyone else is called a(n) ______________ ______________ good.

5) Someone who consumes a good without paying for it is called a(n) ______________ ______________ . When such individuals are prevalent in the consumption of a particular good, the amount of that good provided by the private market will be ______________ than the allocatively efficient amount.

6) The maximum amount a person would be willing to pay for one more unit of public good is the ______________ ______________ of that good to the individual.

7) A cost or a benefit arising from a transaction which affects someone other than the direct parties in the transaction is called a(n) ______________ . When a chemical firm dumps its waste into the river, it kills a large number of fish downstream. This is an example of an external ______________ . When a neighbour plants flowers on the property line, you benefit. This is an example of an external ______________ .

8) A legally established title to the sole ownership of a resource is a(n) ______________ ______________ ______________ .

9) The marginal cost borne directly by the producer of a good is called the marginal ______________ cost. This marginal cost together with the marginal external cost is the marginal ______________ cost.

10) If there are external costs in the production of steel (for example pollution), the output of steel produced by the market will be ______________ than the allocatively efficient level.

TRUE OR FALSE

_____ 1) The government sector of the Canadian economy accounts for 33 percent of total economic spending.

_____ 2) Since 1940, the government's total share of spending has remained about the same.

_____ 3) Restriction of output by monopolies is an example of market failure.

_____ 4) All redistribution of income or wealth by the government can be explained as motivated by notions of equity or distributive justice.

_____ 5) The redistribution of income and wealth by the government arises partly from the rent-seeking activities of individuals in the economy.

_____ 6) According to the public choice theory of government behaviour, not only is there possibility of market failure, but there is also the possibility of "government failure."

_____ 7) The existence of public goods gives rise to the free-rider problem.

_____ 8) Any good made available by the government is a public good.

_____ 9) The excludability feature of private goods will lead to free-riders.

_____ 10) The economy's marginal benefit curve for a public good is obtained by adding the marginal benefits of each individual at each quantity of provision.

_____ 11) The private market will produce much less than the efficient quantity of pure public goods.

_____ 12) Net benefit is zero when the allocatively efficient level of output is obtained.

_____ 13) If negative externalities exist, marginal social cost and external cost are equivalent.

_____ 14) If the production of a good involves no external cost, then marginal social cost is equal to marginal private cost.

_____ 15) If, at the current level of production of good *A*, marginal social benefit is less than marginal social cost, then output of good *A* should increase to achieve allocative efficiency.

_____ 16) Externalities often arise from the absence of private property rights.

_____ 17) The existence of external benefits means that marginal social cost is less than marginal private cost.

_____ 18) When external costs are present, the private market will tend to produce more than the allocatively efficient level of output.

_____ 19) Externalities exist because someone is willfully trying to harm others.

_____ 20) The government can enhance allocative efficiency by subsidizing the production of goods that generate external benefits and taxing the production of goods that generate external costs.

MULTIPLE-CHOICE

1) Which of the following is *not* a source of market failure?
a) the existence of public goods
b) external costs
c) external benefits
d) an unequal distribution of income
e) the existence of monopolies

2) Which of the following statements about theories of government is *false*?
a) Positive theories explain the reasons for and effects of government policies.
b) Normative theories argue for the desirability of specific government policies.
c) Public choice theories are positive theories.
d) Public interest theories are normative theories.
e) The proposition that government can redistribute income from the rich to the poor is positive.

3) In an unregulated economy, if it is possible for someone to be made better off without making anyone worse off, then
a) income is distributed unfairly.
b) we have market failure.
c) allocative efficiency has been achieved.
d) net benefit is a maximum.
e) none of the above is true.

4) In the production of which of the following are we *least* likely to experience market failure?
a) education
b) national defense
c) bread
d) chemical fertilizer
e) parks

5) When market failure occurs, the government will act to reduce the level of inefficiency. This is a prediction of
a) an end-state theory of government behaviour.
b) a process theory of government behaviour.
c) a public interest theory of government behaviour.
d) a public choice theory of government behaviour.
e) a rent-seeking theory of government behaviour.

6) The efficient scale of provision of a public good occurs where
a) net benefit is at a maximum.
b) marginal benefit is at a maximum.
c) marginal benefit minus marginal cost equals zero.
d) marginal social cost is at a minimum.
e) both a) and c) are both true.

7) A good that exhibits both rivalry and excludability is a(n)
a) private good.
b) public good.
c) government good.
d) mixed good.
e) external good.

8) Governments provide pure public goods such as national defence because
a) governments are more efficient than private firms at producing such goods.
b) of the free-rider problems, which result in underproduction by private markets.
c) people do not value national defence very highly.
d) of the potential that private firms will make excess profits.
e) of external costs.

9) Which of the following goods has the nonexcludability feature?
a) city bus
b) toll-bridge
c) lighthouse
d) art museum
e) all of the above

10) The market demand curve for a *private* good is obtained by
a) summing the individual marginal cost curves horizontally.
b) summing the individual marginal cost curves vertically.
c) summing the individual marginal benefit curves horizontally.
d) summing the individual marginal benefit curves vertically.
e) none of the above methods.

11) The economy's total demand curve for a *public* good is obtained by
a) summing the individual marginal cost curves horizontally.
b) summing the individual marginal cost curves vertically.
c) summing the individual marginal benefit curves horizontally.
d) summing the individual marginal benefit curves vertically.
e) none of the above methods.

12) The *total benefit* of a given level of provision of a public good can be obtained by
a) adding the marginal benefit of each level of provision up to the given level.
b) adding the marginal benefit of each level of provision and then subtracting the marginal cost of each level of provision.
c) adding the net benefit of each level of provision up to the given level.
d) multiplying net benefit by the quantity of the public good provided.
e) none of the above methods.

13) An externality is
a) the amount by which price exceeds marginal private cost.
b) the amount by which price exceeds marginal social cost.
c) the effect of government regulation on market price and output.
d) someone who consumes a good without paying for it.
e) a cost or benefit that arises from a decision but is not borne by the decision maker.

14) Which of the following illustrates the concept of external cost?
a) Bad weather reduces the size of the wheat crop.
b) A reduction in the size of the wheat crop causes the income of wheat farmers to fall.
c) Smoking harms the health of the smoker.
d) Smoking harms the health of nonsmokers who are nearby.
e) Public health services reduce the transmission of disease.

15) Figure 19.1 depicts the demand for good *A* as well as the marginal private cost (*MPC*) and marginal social cost (*MSC*) associated with the production of good *A*. Production of the sixth unit of output generates an *external*
a) cost of $1.50.
b) cost of $3.
c) cost of $6.
d) benefit of $3.
e) benefit of $6.

Figure 19.1

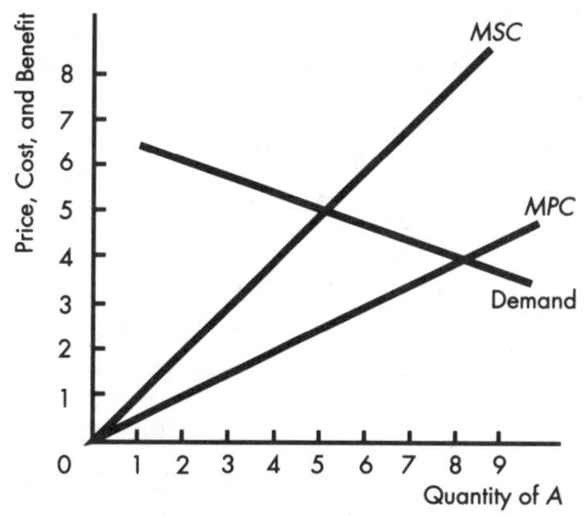

16) In Figure 19.1, how many units of good *A* will be produced in an unregulated market?
a) 0 units
b) 5 units
c) 6 units
d) 8 units
e) impossible to calculate without additional information

17) In Figure 19.1, what is the allocatively efficient quantity of good *A*?
a) 0 units
b) 5 units
c) 6 units
d) 8 units
e) impossible to calculate without additional information

18) Figure 19.2 depicts the demand curve for good *B* as well as the marginal social benefit (*MSB*) and marginal cost (*MC*) curves. How many units of good *B* will be produced and consumed in an unregulated market?
a) 0 units
b) 3 units
c) 5 units
d) 6 units
e) 9 units

Figure 19.2

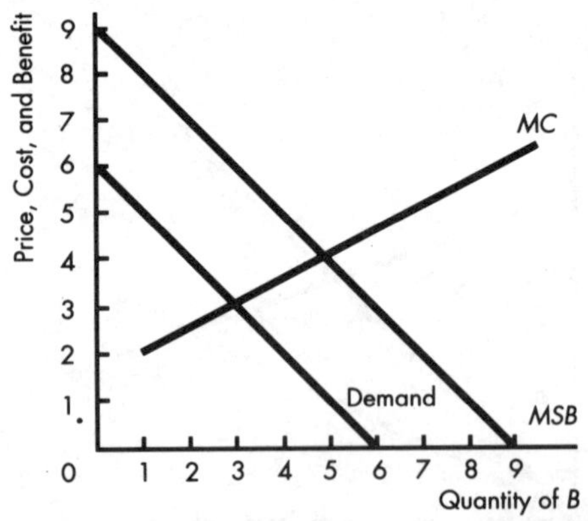

19) In Figure 19.2, what is the allocatively efficient quantity of good *B*?
a) 0 units
b) 3 units
c) 5 units
d) 6 units
e) 9 units

20) In Figure 19.2, which of the following government policies would induce the market to achieve allocative efficiency?
a) Tax the production of *B* in the amount of $3 per unit.
b) Tax the production of *B* in the amount of $4 per unit.
c) Subsidize the consumption of *B* in the amount of $1 per unit.
d) Subsidize the consumption of *B* in the amount of $3 per unit.
e) Subsidize the consumption of *B* in the amount of $4 per unit.

SHORT ANSWER

1) Explain the *nonrivalry* and *nonexcludability* features of a pure public good.

2) What is the free-rider problem?

3) Governments provide education for free, or at least at a price (tuition) much less than cost. What is the economic argument that supports this policy?

4) Explain how a tax can be used to achieve efficiency in the face of external costs.

5) a) The production of steel also produces pollution and thus generates an external cost. Suppose the government attempts to solve the problem by imposing a tax on steel producers (who also produce pollution). At the after-tax level of output, we observe that the original marginal social cost curve is below the demand curve. Is the after-tax level of output efficient?
b) If it is not, should steel production, and therefore pollution production, be increased or decreased?

PROBLEMS

1) Heritage Apartments has 100 residents who are concerned about security. Table 19.1 gives the total cost of hiring a 24-hour security guard service as well as the marginal benefit to each of the residents.

Table 19.1

Number of Guards	Total Cost per Day (dollars)	Marginal Benefit per Resident (dollars)	Marginal Benefit to All Residents (dollars)
1	300	10	
2	600	4	
3	900	2	
4	1,200	1	

a) Why is a security guard a public good for the residents of Heritage Apartments?
b) Why will zero guards be hired if each of the residents must act individually?
c) Complete the last column of Table 19.1 by computing the marginal benefit of security guards to all of the residents together.

2) Now suppose that the residents form an Apartment Council, which acts as a governing body in order to address the security issue.
   a) What is the optimal (allocatively efficient) number of guards? What is the net benefit at the optimal number of guards?
   b) Show that net benefit is less for either one less guard or for one more guard than the net benefit for the optimal number of guards.
   c) How might the Apartment Council pay for the optimal number of guards?

3) The first two columns of Table 19.2 give the demand schedule for education in Hicksville while the third column gives the marginal private cost. Since education generates external benefits, marginal social benefit, given in the last column, is greater than marginal private benefit.

Table 19.2

Quantity (number of students)	Marginal Private Benefit (dollars)	Marginal Private Cost (dollars)	Marginal Social Benefit (dollars)
100	500	200	800
200	400	250	700
300	300	300	600
400	200	350	500
500	100	400	400
600	0	450	300

   a) Represent the data in Table 19.2 graphically.
   b) What equilibrium price and quantity would result if the market for education is unregulated?
   c) What is the allocatively efficient quantity of students in Hicksville?

4) In an attempt to address the inefficient level of education in Hicksville, the Town Council has decided to subsidize schooling.
   a) The council offers $200 to each student who buys a year of education.
      i) Draw the new marginal private benefit curve, which includes the subsidy, on your graph and label it MPB_2.
      ii) What are the approximate new equilibrium price and quantity?
   b) The council increases the subsidy to $400.
      i) Draw another marginal private benefit curve, which includes the subsidy, on your graph and label it MPB_2.
      ii) What are the approximate corresponding equilibrium price and quantity?
   c) What level of subsidy will achieve the efficient quantity of education?

ANSWERS

CONCEPT REVIEW

1) market failure
2) interest; choice
3) private; rivalry; excludability
4) pure public
5) free rider; less
6) marginal benefit
7) externality; cost; benefit
8) private property right
9) private; social
10) greater

TRUE OR FALSE

1) T	6) T	11) T	16) T
2) F	7) T	12) F	17) F
3) T	8) F	13) F	18) T
4) F	9) F	14) T	19) F
5) T	10) T	15) F	20) T

MULTIPLE-CHOICE

1) d	6) e	11) d	16) d
2) d	7) a	12) a	17) b
3) b	8) b	13) e	18) b
4) c	9) c	14) d	19) c
5) c	10) c	15) b	20) d

SHORT ANSWER

1) A good has the nonrivalry feature if its consumption by one person does not reduce the amount available for others. The nonexcludability feature means that if the good is produced and consumed by one person, others cannot be excluded from consuming it as well.

2) The free-rider problem is the problem of unregulated markets producing too little of a pure public good because there is little incentive for individuals to pay for the good. The reason is that the person's payment will likely have no perceptible effect on the amount the person will be able to consume.

3) Government subsidizes education heavily. The economic argument is that education generates external benefits. In particular, when individuals are educated, society at large receives benefits beyond the private benefits that accrue to those choosing how much education to obtain.

4) The existence of external costs means that producers do not take into account all costs when deciding how much to produce. If a tax is levied that is exactly the amount of the external cost, the cost will no longer be external. As a result, the producer will take it into account and thus be induced to produce the efficient quantity.

5) a) Since the marginal social cost curve is below the demand curve at the after-tax output, marginal social cost is less than marginal benefit. This means that the tax has been set too high; it has been set at a level in excess of the external cost. As a result, the after-tax level of steel production will be less than the efficient level.
   b) The level of steel production and pollution production should be increased by decreasing the amount of the tax.

PROBLEMS

1) a) A security guard is a public good because, in this case, it has the features of nonrivalry and nonexcludability. It is nonrival because one resident's *consumption* of the security provided by a guard does not reduce the security of anyone else. The nonexcludability property is evidenced by the fact that once a security guard is in place, all residents enjoy the increased security; none can be excluded.
   b) If each resident must act individually in hiring a security guard none will be hired because each resident receives only $10 in benefit from the first guard, which costs $300 per day.
   c) The entries in the last column of Table 19.1 Solution are obtained by multiplying the marginal benefit per resident by the number of residents, 100. This multiplication is the numerical equivalent of summing the individual marginal benefit curves *vertically* for each quantity of guards.

Table 19.1 Solution

Number of Guards	Total Cost per Day (dollars)	Marginal Benefit per Resident (dollars)	Marginal Benefit to All Residents (dollars)
1	300	10	1,000
2	600	4	400
3	900	2	200
4	1,200	1	100

2) a) If the Apartment Council hires each guard for whom the marginal benefit exceeds the marginal cost, they will hire the optimal number of guards. The marginal cost of each additional guard is $300. The marginal benefit of the first guard is $1,000, so he will be hired. Similarly, the marginal benefit of the second guard is $400, and he will be hired.

   The marginal benefit of the third guard, however, is only $200, which is less than marginal cost. Therefore we conclude that the allocatively efficient (optimal) number of guards is two. For two guards, the net benefit is $800: total benefit ($1,400) minus total cost ($600).

b) For one guard, the net benefit is $700: total benefit ($1,000) minus total cost ($300). For three guards, the net benefit is also $700: total benefit ($1,600) minus total cost ($900). Thus, the net benefit of $800 is greater for two guards.

c) The Apartment Council might pay for the optimal number of guards by collecting a security fee of $6 per day from each of the one hundred residents in order to hire two security guards.

3) a) Figure 19.3 is a graphical representation of the data in Table 19.2 on page 221. The demand for education is given by the marginal private benefit curve (labelled *MPB*), the marginal private cost curve is labelled *MPC*, and the marginal social benefit curve is labelled *MSB*.

Figure 19.3

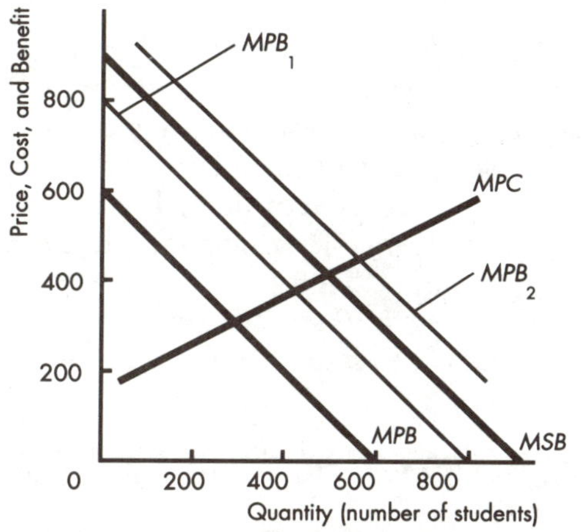

b) In an unregulated market, equilibrium price and quantity are determined by the intersection of the *MPB* and *MPC* curves. Thus, the equilibrium price would be $300 and the equilibrium quantity is 300 students.

c) Since there are no external costs, the efficient quantity is determined by the intersection of the *MPC* and *MSB* curves. This implies that allocative efficiency is attained at a quantity of 500 students.

4) a) i) The subsidy increases the marginal private benefit to each student by the amount of the subsidy, $200. The new *MPB* curve, labelled MPB_1, is included in Figure 19.3.

ii) The new equilibrium after the $200 subsidy is at the intersection of the *MPC* and MPB_1 curves. The price of a unit of education will be approximately $370 and there will be approximately 430 students.

b) i) With a subsidy of $400 per student, the *MPB* curve will shift to MPB_2 in Figure 19.3.

ii) With this subsidy the equilibrium will be at the intersection of the *MPC* and MPB_2 curves. The corresponding price of a unit of education will be approximately $430 and the number of students will be approximately 570.

c) In order to achieve an efficient outcome, the subsidy must make the *MPB* curve coincide with the *MSB* curve. This requires a subsidy of $300 per student.

Chapter 20 **Public Choice**

Chapter in Perspective

Text Pages 511–536

In Chapter 19, we learned that even when markets are competitive they are not always efficient. The existence of public goods and externalities implies an opportunity for government action to improve efficiency.

For example, because of the free-rider problem, government must generally produce pure public goods in order for the efficient quantity to be produced. But, we observe the government providing goods and services that do not have all of the features of public goods, such as garbage collection and mail service. Why? Even when a good provided by the government is a pure public good, will the quantity provided tend to maximize net benefit and thus be efficient?

In this chapter, our focus turns from the ideal to the actual behaviour of government. It presents public choice theory, which analyzes government actions as outcomes of interactions of participants in the *political marketplace*; voters, politicians, and bureaucrats.

Just as in markets for goods and services, participants in political markets pursue their own objectives. This powerful insight has significant implications for the behaviour of actual governments. We will discover why government actions can fail to achieve efficiency.

Learning Objectives

After studying this chapter, you will be able to:

- **Describe the components of the political marketplace.**
- **Define a political equilibrium.**
- **Explain how the main political parties choose their economic policy platforms.**
- **Explain how government bureaucracy interacts with politicians to determine the scale of provision of public goods and services.**
- **Explain why we vote for redistributions of income and wealth.**
- **Explain why we tax some goods at much higher rates than others.**
- **Predict the effects of taxes on prices, quantities produced, and profits.**
- **Explain why we subsidize the producers of some goods.**
- **Predict the effects of subsidies on prices, quantities produced, and profits.**

Helpful Hints

1) Public choice theory gives us a theory of the political marketplace that parallels the economic theory of markets for goods and services we have developed to this point. It is very useful to think about the analogy between the operation of political markets and ordinary markets.
   a) In political markets the demanders are voters, while in ordinary markets, the demanders are consumers. In both cases, demanders are concerned about their costs and benefits.
   b) The suppliers in political markets are politicians and bureaucrats, while in ordinary markets, the suppliers of goods and services are firms.
   c) In political markets, voters express their demands by means of votes, political contributions, and lobbying. This occurs because the suppliers (politicians) in this market are motivated by a desire to retain political office. In ordinary markets, consumers express their demands by means of dollars since suppliers are motivated by a desire to maximize profit.
   d) In both markets, equilibrium is a state of rest. In equilibrium there is no tendency to change because participants cannot become better off by making a different choice or by engaging in an additional transaction.

2) Understand the logic behind the median voter theorem. Politicians want to be elected and then remain in office. To do so, they must receive a majority of votes; they must win at least one more than 50 percent of the votes. Since all politicians realize this, the median voter, the "middle" voter, becomes the key voter. A politician who offers a platform that deviates from the preferences of the median voter will lose to a politician who offers a platform closer to those preferences.

3) Well-informed special interest groups are able to induce the government to conduct programs that do not maximize net benefits because most voters are *rationally* ignorant. For most voters, it does not pay to be well informed about any particular issue. As a result, a small, well-informed interest group will be able to have an influence on government programs that greatly exceeds its size relative to all voters.

4) From previous chapters we know that unregulated markets frequently fail to achieve allocative efficiency. In this chapter (and in the next), we learn that governments also frequently fail to achieve allocative efficiency. Since both markets and governments can fail, the relevant economic question in each case is: Which fails less?

5) The division of the burden of a tax is called tax incidence. Who pays an excise tax imposed on producers depends on the elasticities of demand and supply. The general principles of tax incidence are:
   a) The more inelastic the demand, the more consumers pay.
   b) The more elastic the demand, the more producers pay.
   c) The more inelastic the supply, the more producers pay.
   d) The more elastic the supply, the more consumers pay.

Key Figures

Figure 20.1 Provision of a Public Good in a Political System, text page 515

If voters are well informed and able to evaluate the benefits from alternative proposals, competition for votes among political parties will result in a political outcome that maximizes the net benefit of voters and is, therefore, allocatively efficient.

This is illustrated in the figure, which continues the example of acid-rain satellites used in Chapter 19. These satellites are public goods. The figure gives the total cost (*TC*) and total benefit (*TB*) curves (Figure 19.2(a) on text page 500). Net benefit is maximized when two satellites are provided.

There are two political parties, the Smokes and the Greens, with platforms that are identical in every way except for their proposals regarding the number of satellites to install.

If the Smokes propose to install 1 satellite and the Greens propose to install 4 satellites, the Smokes will win the election since net benefits are $1.5 billion if 1 satellite is installed but zero if 4 are installed.

If, on the other hand, the Greens propose 2 satellites, they will win the election because the net benefit for 2 satellites is $2.0 billion. The only way the Smokes can then avoid losing the election is to also propose 2 satellites.

Thus, if voters are in general agreement about the benefits and can readily calculate them, competition for voters between (among) political parties will produce the efficient scale of provision of a public good.

Figure 20.2 Principle of Minimum Differentiation, text page 518

There is a tendency for individual competitors to minimize the differences between themselves and other competitors in order to maximize their appeal to customers or voters. This is the principle of minimum differentiation and is illustrated in the figure by examining two competing ice cream vendors on a one-mile stretch of beach (from *A* to *B* in the figure).

Assuming that sunbathers are evenly distributed along the beach, the first vendor will locate at *C*, halfway between *A* and *B*, so that no potential customer is more than half a mile away. The interesting question is: Assuming that ice cream customers will buy from the nearest stand, where will a second vendor locate?

This figure helps us understand that the second vendor will want to locate right next to the first. At this location, the second vendor can expect to attract half of the ice cream customers on the beach. This is the best that can be done. At any other location (consider point *D*, for example), the vendor will attract less than half the customers.

Figure 20.3 The Median Voter Theorem, text page 519
The median voter theorem says that politicians will propose policies that maximize the net benefit of the median voter. This figure helps us clearly see the logic of the median voter theorem.

On any given political issue, there will be a range of views across voters. For example, in this figure, we consider the issue of what tax rate to charge polluters. If we arrange voters according to the tax rate they favour, the median voter is the one in the middle; half of the voters prefer a lower tax rate and half prefer a higher tax rate.

In the figure, the median voter prefers a tax rate of 30 percent. Since political parties want to be elected and then stay in office, they must obtain at least one more than 50 percent of the votes. As a result, a political party that proposes a tax rate of 30 percent will win against a party that proposes any other tax rate.

If, for example, a second party proposes any tax rate above 30 percent, the first party will obtain the votes of the median voter, who prefers a 30 percent rate, as well as the half of voters who prefer tax rates less than 30 percent and thus win the election.

Similarly, if the second party proposes any tax rate below that preferred by the median voter, the first party will again win the election. Therefore, the second party cannot hope to win unless it too proposes the tax rate preferred by the median voter.

Figure 20.4 Bureaucratic Overprovision, text page 523
This figure gives the same total benefit and cost curves depicted in Figure 20.1. In the earlier figure, it was shown that the efficient scale of provision is 2 acid-rain satellites and that if voters are well informed, the efficient scale would be achieved through the competitive political process. This will occur in spite of the fact that it is in the interest of the Ministry of the Environment to increase expenditure on satellites as far as possible.

However, if some voters are rationally ignorant, the environment bureaucracy may be able to increase its budget and the number of satellites above the level that maximizes the net benefit of voters.

Figure 20.5 An Excise Tax, text page 525
The effect of an excise tax on price and quantity traded is illustrated in this figure, using the market for gasoline as an example. Before the tax is imposed, the price of gasoline is 30¢ per litre and 400 million litres per day are traded.

Then a tax of 30¢ per litre is imposed. This causes the supply curve of gasoline to shift up by a vertical distance equal to the amount of the tax: from *S* to *S* + *tax*. The equilibrium price increases to 55¢ per litre and the equilibrium quantity traded falls to 300 million litres per day.

Note that even though the tax is 30¢ per litre, the equilibrium price rises by only 25¢ per litre. Thus, only 25¢ of the tax is borne by consumers and 5¢ is borne by the producer.

Figure 20.8 Subsidies, text page 529
The effects of a subsidy are just the opposite of those of an excise tax. Subsidizing the production of a good will lower the price of the good and increase the quantity traded. This is illustrated in the figure, using the market for wheat.

In the wheat market without a subsidy, the equilibrium price of wheat is $3.50 per bushel and 2 billion bushels per year are traded. A government subsidy of $1 per bushel will cause the supply curve for wheat to shift down by a vertical distance equal to the amount of the subsidy: from *S* to *S* minus the subsidy. The equilibrium price will fall to $3 per bushel and the quantity traded will rise to 3 billion bushels per year.

Wheat farmers receive just enough revenue (from the market price of $3 together with the subsidy of $1 per bushel) to cover their costs ($4 per bushel) of producing 3 billion bushels.

Figure 20.9 Subsidies with Quotas, text page 529
This figure is a continuation of the wheat market example of Figure 20.8. It shows the effects of the government imposing a quota on the production of wheat in addition to paying a subsidy. As in the previous figure, the equilibrium price without a subsidy is $3.50 per bushel and 2 billion bushels of wheat per year are traded.

The government introduces a subsidy of $1 per bushel, but now also introduces a quota of 2 billion bushels of wheat per year. With the quota, the market price and quantity will not change from their values before the subsidy and quota are implemented.

Thus, the producers receive $3.50 per bushel from consumers plus $1 per bushel from the government subsidy for a total of $4.50 per bushel. Since, at the quota amount, marginal cost is only $3.50 per bushel, the extra dollar per bushel is like a monopoly profit.

SELF-TEST

CONCEPT REVIEW

1) The theory that analyzes the "political market," using an approach similar to the economic analysis of ordinary markets, is called ______________ ______________ theory.

2) In this theory, there are three key groups of players. The ______________ are the consumers of the political process, while ______________ are elected officials. Finally, ______________ are appointed officials who work in the many ministries and agencies of government.

3) Just as firms in ordinary markets seek dollars, politicians seek ______________ . The objective of a(n) ______________ is to be elected and to remain in office.

4) If all voters have the same views and are able to correctly evaluate alternative government programs, political parties will produce platforms that ______________ the net benefit of the ______________ .

5) The tendency for competitors (for example, political parties) to make themselves almost identical in order to appeal to the maximum number of voters is called the principle of ______________ ______________ . There is also a tendency for political parties to choose platforms that appeal to the ______________ voter.

6) The theory of the behaviour of bureaucracy discussed in the text assumes that bureaucrats try to maximize the ______________ of the ministry in which they work. Since all bureaucrats in all ministries have this objective, there is a general ______________ pressure on government spending.

7) Since information is costly to obtain and voters are rational, only voters with a large direct interest in a political program will be well informed. As a result, the political equilibrium that emerges will tend to provide public goods on a scale that is ______________ than the scale that maximizes net benefit.

8) A new excise tax will shift the ______________ curve upward by the amount of the tax. The new equilibrium will be at a ______________ price and a ______________ quantity traded.

9) The loss of consumer surplus plus the loss of producer surplus associated with a tax is called the ______________ loss of the tax. This loss is ______________ , the more inelastic the demand for the good being taxed.

10) A subsidy shifts the ______________ curve of the subsidized good downward. Thus, the market price of the good will ______________ and the quantity traded will ______________ . If the subsidy is combined with a quota, the amount of the subsidy increases ______________ surplus.

TRUE OR FALSE

_____ 1) The public choice theory of government behaviour assumes that politicians and bureaucrats make decisions that are motivated only by concern for the public interest.

_____ 2) The only way voters can express their demands to politicians is through the votes they cast.

_____ 3) The Arrow Impossibility Theorem states that it is impossible to aggregate individual preferences to arrive at social preferences that can guide government policy.

_____ 4) Public choice theory assumes that voters will support policies that they believe will make them better off and oppose policies that they believe will make them worse off.

_____ 5) Political parties will tend to propose fundamentally different policies in order to give voters a clearer choice.

_____ 6) In order to be elected, a politician will tend to choose a platform that will appeal to the median voter.

_____ 7) The income redistribution plan that has the greatest chance of being accepted by voters is the one that maximizes the income of the median voter.

_____ 8) According to William Niskanen's theory of bureaucracy, the objective of bureaucrats is to maximize the net benefit of voters.

_____ 9) The ability of bureaucrats to increase the size of their agency's budget is constrained by the ability of politicians to collect sufficient taxes.

_____ 10) If voters are all well informed, there will be a tendency for government policies to be those which maximize net benefit.

_____ 11) It is irrational for voters to be uninformed about an issue as important as national defence.

_____ 12) When many voters are not well informed about the costs and benefits of a public good, there will be a tendency for less of that good to be produced than the quantity that maximizes net benefit.

_____ 13) An excise tax that is set as a fixed percentage of the value of the commodity is called a specific tax.

_____ 14) The more elastic demand is for a product, the larger the fraction is of an excise tax paid by the consumer.

_____ 15) The price of good *A* will rise by the full amount of a tax on *A* if the supply curve is perfectly elastic.

_____ 16) The deadweight loss arising from a tax is equal to the loss of consumer surplus minus the loss of producer surplus due to the increase in price.

_____ 17) Imposing a sales tax on a monopoly industry will raise the price but the quantity traded will remain unchanged.

_____ 18) Vote-seeking politicians will tend to impose heavier excise taxes on goods for which the demand is inelastic.

_____ 19) Subsidies to agriculture, especially when combined with quotas, are beneficial to consumers.

_____ 20) Subsidies combined with quotas generate an increase in producer surplus.

_____ 21) Most economists estimate that the GST (Goods and Services Tax) will have a larger deadweight loss than the manufacturers' sales tax that it replaced.

MULTIPLE-CHOICE

1) Public choice theory
   a) argues that government has a tendency to conduct policies that help the economy toward allocative efficiency.
   b) argues that politicians and bureaucrats tend to be more concerned about the public interest than individuals in the private sector.
   c) argues that the public choices of government maximize net benefits.
   d) applies economic tools used to analyze markets to the analysis of government behaviour.
   e) applies the tools of political analysis to the analysis of economic markets.

2) According to public choice theory, a voter will favour a candidate whose political program is
   a) perceived to offer the greatest personal benefit to the voter.
   b) best for the majority of the people.
   c) closest to allocative efficiency.
   d) favoured by the median voter.
   e) all of the above.

3) Public choice theory assumes that those involved in the political process are generally motivated by
   a) self-interest.
   b) the desire to achieve allocative efficiency.
   c) dishonesty.
   d) public spirit.
   e) the desire for maximum profit.

4) If voters have similar views and are well informed, the quantity of national defence provided by the government will tend to be
   a) greater than the allocatively efficient quantity.
   b) less than the allocatively efficient quantity.
   c) the least costly quantity.
   d) the quantity that maximizes net benefit.
   e) the quantity that maximizes the Ministry of Defence budget.

5) Competition between two political parties will cause those parties to propose policies
   a) that are quite different.
   b) that are quite similar.
   c) of rational ignorance.
   d) that reduce the well-being of middle income families and increase the well-being of the rich and the poor.
   e) that equate total costs and total benefits.

6) On any given spending issue subject to a vote, the median voter is the one who favours
   a) the least spending.
   b) the most spending.
   c) the efficient level of spending.
   d) the average level of spending.
   e) spending more than the level favoured by half the voters and less than the level favoured by half the voters.

7) Voters are asked to vote for either proposition *A* or proposition *B*. Proposition *A* will win if it
   a) is closer to allocative efficiency.
   b) is supported by bureaucrats.
   c) is preferred by the median voter.
   d) generates greater social benefits than social costs.
   e) generates the fewest negative externalities.

8) The tendency for redistribution policies to be stable for long periods of time is best explained by
   a) the trade-off between redistribution and the average level of income.
   b) the range of differences among voters.
   c) the principle of minimum differentiation.
   d) the principle of rational ignorance.
   e) lobbying.

9) The claim that bureaucrats will attempt to maximize the budget of their agency follows from the assumption that bureaucrats
   a) have a superior understanding of the public interest.
   b) have an inferior understanding of the public interest.
   c) are motivated by the same forces of self-interest that motivate individuals in the private sector.
   d) are less honest than individuals in the private sector.
   e) are more honest than individuals in the private sector.

10) Rational ignorance
   a) results when the cost of information exceeds the benefits of having the information.
   b) allows special interest groups to exert political influence.
   c) combined with special interest groups can yield allocative inefficiency in the provision of public goods.
   d) results in all of the above.
   e) results in none of the above.

11) The budget of a government bureau is likely to increase beyond the quantity that maximizes net benefit of the economy if
   a) voters are well informed.
   b) there is rational voter ignorance combined with special interest lobbying.
   c) it is allocatively efficient to do so.
   d) bureaucrats are rationally ignorant.
   e) there are negative externalities.

12) According to public choice theory, a voter will tend to be well informed if the issue in question
   a) is complicated and difficult to understand.
   b) affects everyone a little.
   c) is of special interest to a small group to which the voter does not belong.
   d) has a large direct effect on the voter.
   e) is important even if it does not directly affect the voter.

13) A sales tax that collects 5 percent of the amount of a purchase is an example of a(n)
   a) specific tax.
   b) proportional income tax.
   c) flat tax.
   d) *ad valorem* tax.
   e) deadweight tax.

14) In general, a tax of $3 per unit of good *A* will shift the supply curve of *A* up by
   a) $3 and increase the price of *A* by $3.
   b) $3 and increase the price of *A* by less than $3.
   c) $3 and increase the price of *A* by more than $3.
   d) more than $3 and increase the price of *A* by $3.
   e) less than $3 and increase the price of *A* by $3.

15) The deadweight loss due to a price increase resulting from a tax is the loss of
a) consumer surplus.
b) producer surplus.
c) consumer surplus plus the loss of producer surplus.
d) consumer surplus minus the loss of producer surplus.
e) tax revenue from the decreased quantity traded.

16) The deadweight loss created by a new tax is zero if the
a) supply curve is perfectly inelastic.
b) supply curve is perfectly elastic.
c) demand curve is more elastic than the supply curve.
d) demand curve is less elastic than the supply curve.
e) industry is perfectly competitive.

17) Figure 20.1 gives the demand and supply for imported cheese. If the government imposes a $3 tax per kilogram of imported cheese, price will increase by
a) $3 to $7.
b) $3 to $6.
c) $2 to $6.
d) $2 to $5.
e) none of the above.

Figure 20.1

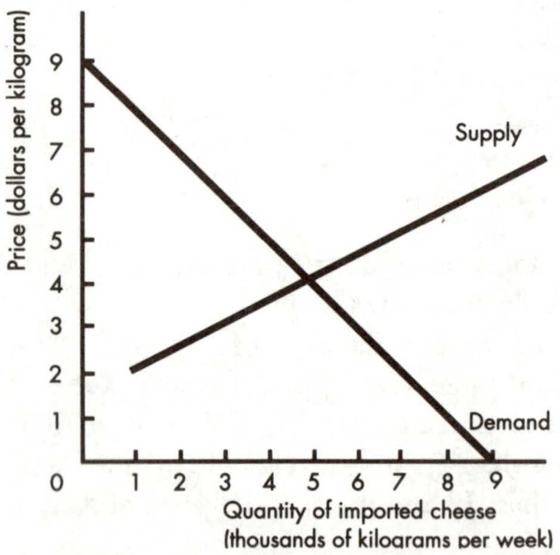

18) Consider again the $3 per kilogram tax discussed in the previous question. How is the burden of the tax shared between consumers and producers?
a) The entire $3 is borne by consumers in the form of a higher price.
b) The entire $3 is borne by producers in the form of lower sales.
c) The entire $3 is borne by producers in the form of lower receipts per unit.
d) $2 is borne by producers in the form of lower receipts per unit and $1 is borne by consumers in the form of a higher price.
e) $2 is borne by consumers in the form of a higher price and $1 is borne by producers in the form of lower receipts per unit.

19) The tax incidence on consumers will be greater the more
i) elastic is demand.
ii) inelastic is demand.
iii) elastic is supply.
iv) inelastic is supply.
a) ii) only
b) i) and iii)
c) i) and iv)
d) ii) and iii)
e) ii) and iv)

20) If the government subsidizes the production of a good, the
a) supply curve will shift downward, price will fall, and quantity traded will increase.
b) supply curve will shift upward, price will rise, and quantity traded will decrease.
c) supply curve will shift upward, price will rise, and quantity traded will increase.
d) demand curve will shift upward, price will rise, and quantity traded will increase.
e) demand curve will shift downward, price will fall, and quantity traded will decrease.

SHORT ANSWER

1) Briefly compare an equilibrium in a political market to an equilibrium in a market for goods and services.

2) The median voter theorem states that political candidates and parties will try to appeal to the median voter. Explain why the theorem holds.

3) Explain why it may be rational for voters to be ignorant.

4) Why does the imposition of an excise tax cause the supply curve of the taxed good to shift upward?

5) How would public choice theory explain the existence of the system of agricultural subsidies and quotas in Canada?

PROBLEMS

1) Two candidates are competing in an election for president of the Economics Club. The only issue dividing them is how much will be spent on the annual Economics Club party. It is well known that the seven voting members of the club (*A* through *G*) have preferences as shown in Table 20.1.

Table 20.1

Voting Member	Proposed Amount (dollars)
A	10
B	20
C	30
D	40
E	50
F	60
G	70

These are strongly held preferences regarding exactly how much should be spent on the party.

a) How much will each candidate propose to spend?

b) To demonstrate that your answer to part (a) is correct, consider the outcome of the following two contests.

i) Candidate 1 proposes the amount you gave in part (a) and candidate 2 proposes $1 less. Which candidate will win? Why?

ii) Candidate 1 proposes the amount you gave in part (a) and candidate 2 proposes $1 more. Which candidate will win? Why?

c) Suppose that the Sociology Club is also electing a president and that the same single issue prevails. It is well known that the seven voting members of the Sociology Club have the following strongly held preferences regarding exactly how much should be spent on their party.

Table 20.2

Voting Member	Proposed Amount (dollars)
T	0
U	0
V	0
W	40
X	41
Y	42
Z	43

How much will each of the two candidates propose in this case?

2) Table 20.3 gives three alternative income distributions for five individuals, *A* through *E*. Currently income is distributed according to distribution 1 (given in the second column of the table). Consider alternative proposed distributions 2 and 3 one at a time.

Table 20.3

Individual	Distribution 1 (dollars)	Distribution 2 (dollars)	Distribution 3 (dollars)
A	0	200	150
B	200	300	250
C	400	350	450
D	700	600	600
E	1,000	850	850

a) If distribution 2 is proposed as an alternative to distribution 1, will it have majority support? Why or why not?

b) If distribution 3 is proposed as an alternative to distribution 1, will it have majority support? Why or why not?

3) Figure 20.2 on page 232 gives the supply and demand for movie tickets in Ourtown. The market is initially in equilibrium (point *a*) with a price of $5 per ticket and 5,000 tickets sold per week. Suppose that the town government establishes a new tax of $2 per movie ticket.

Figure 20.2

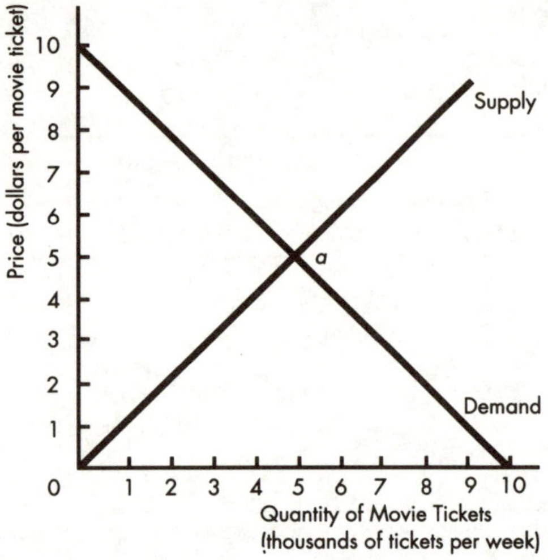

Figure 20.3

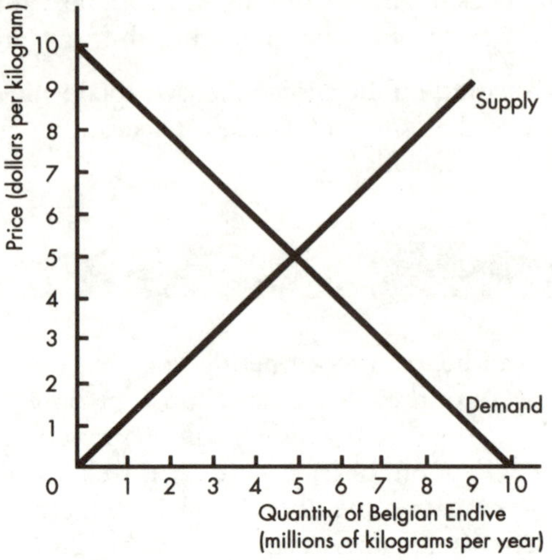

a) Illustrate the effect of the new tax graphically. What will be the new equilibrium price and quantity traded?
b) How much of the $2 tax is borne by consumers in the form of a higher price and how much is borne by movie ticket sellers in the form of reduced revenue per ticket?
c) How much tax revenue will be collected each week?
d) How much consumer surplus will be lost due to the tax? How much producer surplus will be lost? What is the deadweight loss of the tax?

4) The supply and demand for Belgian endive (a leafy salad vegetable) are given in Figure 20.3. Since this is a competitive market, the supply curve is the same as the industry marginal cost curve (the horizontal sum of the marginal cost curves for each producer). The competitive equilibrium price and quantity traded are $5 per kilogram and 5 million kilograms per year respectively. There are 1,000 Belgian endive farmers who are identical in every relevant way. Suppose that their member of parliament successfully establishes a government subsidy for Belgian endive in the amount of $2 per kilogram.
a) Illustrate the effect of the subsidy graphically. What will be the new equilibrium price and quantity traded?
b) What is the total amount of the subsidy paid? How much is received by each farmer? If there are 100 million taxpayers, how much of the subsidy will each pay on average?
c) Is price equal to the (after-subsidy) marginal cost?
d) Does producer surplus increase or decrease with the subsidy? By how much?

5) Now suppose that in addition to the subsidy of $2 per kilogram, a quota of 5 million kilograms of Belgian endive per year is established.
a) What are the resulting equilibrium price and quantity traded?
b) What is the total amount of the subsidy paid?
c) Is price equal to the (after-subsidy) marginal cost?
d) Does producer surplus increase or decrease with the addition of the quota? By how much?

6) Suppose the Belgian endive farmers are able to choose the level of the government imposed quota while retaining the $2 per kilogram subsidy. What quota level would they choose? Why? (*Hint*: How would a cartel choose a restricted level of output?)

ANSWERS

CONCEPT REVIEW

1) public choice
2) voters; politicians; bureaucrats
3) votes; politician
4) maximize; voters
5) minimum differentiation; median
6) budget; upward
7) greater
8) supply; higher; lower
9) deadweight; less
10) supply; fall; increase; producer

TRUE OR FALSE

1) F	8) F	15) T
2) F	9) T	16) F
3) T	10) T	17) F
4) T	11) F	18) T
5) F	12) F	19) F
6) T	13) F	20) T
7) T	14) F	21) F

MULTIPLE-CHOICE

1) d	6) e	11) b	16) a
2) a	7) c	12) d	17) c
3) a	8) a	13) d	18) e
4) d	9) c	14) b	19) b
5) b	10) d	15) c	20) a

SHORT ANSWER

1) In both cases, the equilibrium is a state of rest in the sense that no group has an incentive to change their choices. In the case of equilibrium in an ordinary market for goods and services, neither demanders nor suppliers are able to make an exchange that will make them better off. Similarly, when a political market is in equilibrium, neither demanders (voters) nor suppliers (politicians and bureaucrats) are able to make an alternative choice that will make them better off.

2) The median voter theorem holds because the objective of politicians is to be elected and then re-elected to political office. In order to do so they must capture at least one more than 50 percent of the votes. Since all politicians are aware of this fact, the voter that can just put them over 50 percent becomes the key voter. That voter is the median voter. Politicians must choose a platform that appeals to the median voter in order to be elected.

3) Most issues have only a small and indirect effect on most voters. In such cases it would be irrational for a voter to spend much time and effort to become well informed because the additional cost would quickly exceed any additional benefit. Only if the voter is significantly and directly affected by an issue will it pay to become well informed. As a result, most voters will be rationally ignorant regarding any given issue.

4) When an excise tax is imposed on a supplier, it raises the minimum price the supplier must receive in order to be willing to offer any given quantity for sale. This is nothing more than an upward shift in the supply curve. It is useful to think of a new excise tax as an increase in the cost of production.

5) Public choice theory would explain the existence of the system of agricultural subsidies and quotas as the expected and inefficient consequence of rational voter ignorance and well-informed special interest groups. The costs borne by each of the great majority of consumers (voters) is small, so they will not be well informed or well organized.

On the other hand, the agricultural producers who benefit from the system are much fewer in number and will each benefit significantly. Thus, producers will tend to be well informed and well organized and will have a significant political impact. The resulting system will benefit producers at the expense of consumers.

PROBLEMS

1) a) Each candidate will propose spending $40 since that is the preference of the median voter (voter *D*).

b) i) Candidate 1 will win because *D*, *E*, *F*, and *G* will vote for that candidate since $40 comes closer to matching their preferences than the $39 proposed by candidate 2. Only *A*, *B*, and *C* will vote for candidate 2.

ii) Candidate 1 will win because *A, B, C,* and *D* will vote for that candidate while only *E, F,* and *G* will vote for candidate 2.

c) Once again, the candidates will both propose spending $40 on the party since that is the preference of the median voter. Note that in this case, the median voter's view is not "average."

2) a) Only *A* and *B* are better off under distribution 2. Distribution 2 will receive the support of only *A* and *B* with *C, D,* and *E* opposed. Note particularly that the median voter (*C*) is worse off under distribution 2.

b) Distribution 3 will receive majority support since it makes the median voter better off. It will be supported by *A, B,* and *C* and opposed by *D* and *E.*

3) a) The new tax shifts the supply curve for movie tickets up by $2, the amount of the tax. In Figure 20.2 Solution, the new curve is labelled S_1. The new equilibrium (point *b*) price and quantity traded are $6 per ticket and 4,000 tickets per week, respectively.

Figure 20.2 Solution

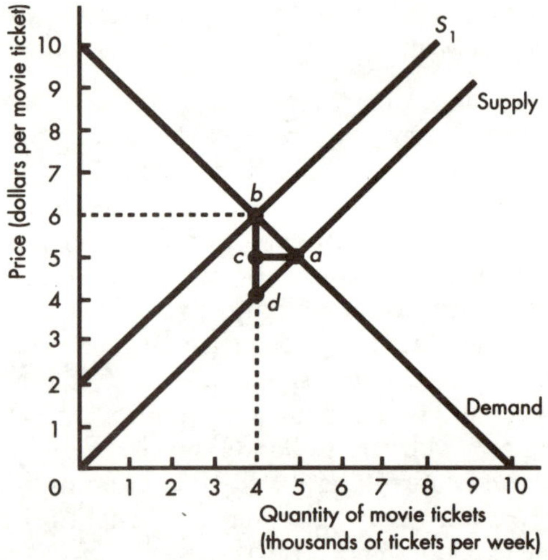

b) Of the $2 tax, $1 is borne by consumers since the price of a ticket rises from $5 to $6 and $1 is borne by sellers, since the revenue per ticket they receive falls from $5 to $4.

c) Total tax revenue will be $8,000 per week: $2 per ticket times 4,000 tickets sold.

d) The loss of consumer surplus is given by the area of triangle *abc* in Figure 20.2 Solution and is equal to $500 ($1/2bh$). Similarly, the loss of producer surplus is given by the area of triangle *adc*, and is equal to $500. Thus the deadweight loss is $1,000, the sum of consumer and producer surplus.

4) a) The subsidy shifts the supply curve for Belgian endive down by $2, the amount of the subsidy. The new supply curve is labelled S_1 in Figure 20.3 Solution. The new equilibrium price is $4 per kilogram and the quantity traded is 6 million kilograms per year.

Figure 20.3 Solution

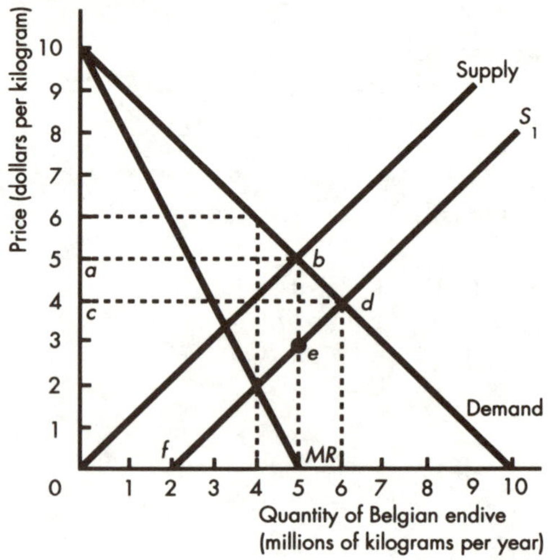

b) The total subsidy paid is $12 million: $2 per kilogram times 6 million kilograms of Belgian endive. This amounts to $12,000 received by each farmer but the 100 million taxpayers will pay an average of only 12 cents each.

c) Yes, price is equal to the after-subsidy marginal cost.

d) Producer surplus increases by $3.5 million, from $12.5 million before the subsidy to $16 million after the subsidy. Recall that producer surplus is the amount by which revenue exceeds the opportunity cost of production (Chapter 13). Graphically, it is given by the area below the price and above the relevant marginal cost curve. The producer surplus before the subsidy is given by the area of triangle 0*ab* ($12.5 million), while the producer surplus after the subsidy is given by the area of trapezoid 0*cdf* ($16 million ($1/2h(a+b)$)).

5) a) If a quota is established at 5 million kilograms per year, the price will be $5 per kilogram and the quantity traded will be 5 million kilograms.

5) **b)** The total amount of the subsidy is \$10 million: \$2 per kilogram times 5 million kilograms.

c) Under the quota, price is \$5 per kilogram, but marginal cost (given by S_1) is only \$3 per kilogram, so price exceeds marginal cost as in the case of monopoly.

d) The producer surplus increases by \$4.5 million to \$20.5 million. Graphically, the producer surplus after the quota is given by the area of the five-sided figure 0*abef* in Figure 20.3 Solution, which is \$20.5 million.

6) If the Belgian endive producers can choose the quota, they will set it so as to maximize industry profit. This level of output occurs when marginal revenue is equal to marginal cost for the industry.

The marginal revenue curve is labelled *MR* in Figure 20.3 Solution and S_1 is the industry marginal cost curve given the subsidy. The profit-maximizing output, and thus the quota that would be chosen by the farmers, is 4,000 kilograms per year.

In the situation described here, Belgian endive farmers will have, with the necessary help of the government, formed a cartel in which the government will enforce the output restrictions.

Chapter 21 Competition Policy

Chapter in Perspective

Text Pages 537–560

This is the last of three chapters on the allocative role of government. The existence of market failure provides opportunities for government to improve allocative efficiency.

We begin by examining the ways government attempts to compensate for market failure. We will identify the gains from trade and analyze who stands to gain and who stands to lose from various types of government intervention. Since such intervention is supplied by politicians and bureaucrats, we will also use the public choice theory developed in the last chapter to look at their economic behaviour.

While there are government policies that can induce noncompetitive industries to come closer to allocative efficiency, we will find that regulation does not always serve the public interest.

Learning Objectives

After studying this chapter, you will be able to:

- **Define regulation.**
- **Describe the main trends in regulation and deregulation.**
- **Explain what a Crown corporation is.**
- **Describe the main elements of Canada's anti-combine law.**
- **Explain how anti-combine law has evolved in Canada.**
- **Distinguish between the public interest and capture theories of government intervention in the marketplace.**
- **Explain how the regulation of natural monopolies affects prices, outputs, profits, and the distribution of the gains from trade between consumers and producers.**
- **Explain how Crown corporations' outputs, costs, and prices are determined, and how these corporations distribute the gains from trade between consumers and producers.**
- **Explain how anti-combine laws affect prices, outputs, profits, and the distribution of the gains from trade between consumers and producers.**

Helpful Hints

1) Consider Figure 21.1, which depicts revenue and marginal cost curves for an industry. Using this figure, it is helpful to think of regulation as determining how the potential total surplus (the area of triangle *abc*) is divided among consumer surplus, producer surplus, and deadweight loss.

Figure 21.1

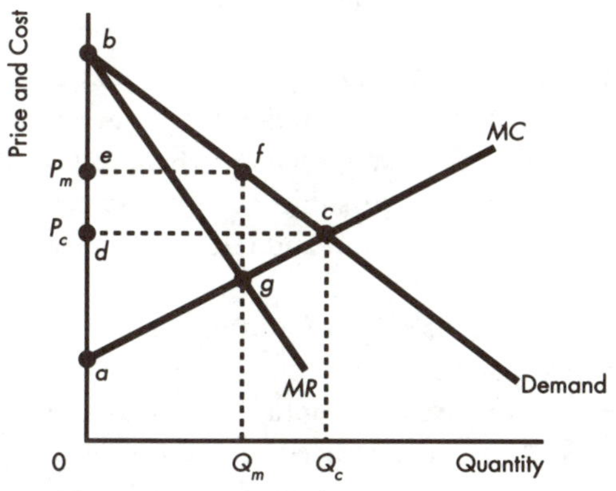

If the industry is perfectly competitive, then the quantity traded will be Q_c and the market price will be P_c. Total surplus is maximized and is given by the area of the triangle *abc*. Total surplus is equal to the sum of consumer surplus given by the area of triangle *dbc* and producer surplus given by the area of the triangle *adc*. There is no deadweight loss.

If the industry is a profit-maximizing monopoly, output will be Q_m and the price will be P_m. In this case, total surplus is represented by the area of trapezoid *abfg*. Because of monopoly restriction of output, total surplus under monopoly is less than under competition. The difference is the deadweight loss from monopoly, the amount of total surplus that is lost when we go from competition to monopoly. The deadweight loss is given by the area of the triangle *gfc*. Total surplus can be divided into consumer surplus given by the area of triangle *ebf* and producer surplus given by the area of trapezoid *aefg*. Consumer surplus is quite small but producer surplus is at a maximum.

Of course, actual output may be between these bounds. As output moves from Q_c to Q_m, consumer surplus decreases while producer surplus and the deadweight loss both increase. If this industry is regulated, the public interest theory of intervention predicts that the result will be a level of output close to Q_c, while the capture theory of intervention predicts a level of output closer to Q_m.

Key Figures and Tables

Figure 21.1 Natural Monopoly: Marginal Cost Pricing, text page 543

Natural monopolies are heavily regulated. A natural monopoly has decreasing average total cost (*ATC*) over the entire range of market demand. Thus marginal cost (*MC*) is less than *ATC*. This figure illustrates a marginal cost pricing rule as applied to a natural monopoly.

The specific example of a natural monopoly examined here is railway services. Note that the *ATC* curve is always decreasing and marginal cost is constant at 2¢ per tonne. Setting the price at marginal cost maximizes total surplus and results in a quantity carried of 8 billion tonnes per year. The consumer surplus is indicated by the area of the green triangle.

The producer will make a loss on each tonne equal to the difference between *ATC* at 8 billion tonnes and the price of 2¢ (the height of the red arrow).

Figure 21.2 Natural Monopoly: Average Cost Pricing, text page 544

This figure uses the same railway services example as Figure 21.1 to illustrate an average cost pricing rule as applied to a natural monopoly. The price is set equal to average total cost — at the intersection of the *ATC* curve and the demand curve.

Average cost pricing gives a price of 4¢ per tonne and results in 6 billion tonnes per year. The railway is now breaking even, but consumer surplus is less than under marginal cost pricing and there is a deadweight loss generated equal to the area of the grey triangle. This is the outcome predicted by the public interest theory of intervention.

Figure 21.3 Natural Monopoly: Profit Maximization, text page 545

If the railway is able to maximize profit, it will equate marginal cost (*MC*) and marginal revenue (*MR*). The resulting price, given by the demand curve, will be 6¢ per tonne and 4 billion tonnes per year will be sold.

Since the price is above average total cost, the railway will now be making a profit as indicated by the area of the blue rectangle in the figure. Consumer surplus (the area of the green triangle) has declined even further, and the deadweight loss has increased to the area of the grey triangle. This is the outcome predicted by the capture theory of intervention.

Figure 21.5 Collusive Oligopoly, text page 547
From Chapter 14, we know that an oligopoly industry can make monopoly profits if the firms in the industry form a cartel and enter into a collusive agreement. Because each firm has an incentive to cheat, however, it is difficult to enforce the cartel agreement. As a result, an oligopoly may "demand" regulation, which has the effect of having the government regulatory agency enforce the collusive agreement that generates monopoly profits for the industry. This is illustrated in the figure using the example of a ten-firm trucking industry.

Under competition or public interest regulation, the *MC* curve is the industry supply curve and the price will be $20 per trip and 300 trips per week will be made. However, the industry can maximize profit if it can obtain regulation that restricts output to the level at which industry marginal cost is equal to industry marginal revenue and sets the price accordingly. In this example, producer interest regulation would restrict industry output to 200 trips per week and the price would be set at $30 per trip.

Figure 21.6 Public Enterprise, text page 550
This figure illustrates the operation of a Crown corporation, continuing with the example of a railway from Figures 21.1 through 21.4.

Part (a) of the figure shows that the Crown corporation will achieve allocative efficiency if it produces the output such that price equals marginal cost. Output is 8 billion tonnes per year and price (and marginal cost) are 2¢ per tonne. Because that price is below average total cost, the corporation must receive a subsidy per unit equal to the difference between average total cost and price (marginal cost). That subsidy is collected by taxation in other areas, reducing the consumer surplus area in Figure 21.1 by the total amount of the subsidy to yield the consumer surplus area in this figure. This outcome maximizes consumer surplus and achieves economic efficiency.

Part (b) of the figure illustrates the operation of the Crown corporation, if we assume that the corporation bureaucrats maximize their budget but still obey the marginal cost pricing rule. Output will remain at the economically efficient level of 8 billion tonnes per year and the price remains at 2¢ per tonne. But the bureaucrats pad costs up to a maximum level that completely exhausts the consumer surplus (ATC_1(padded)). This outcome is efficient but maximizes the benefit of the producer by squeezing consumer surplus to zero.

Part (c) of the figure illustrates the admittedly improbable case of budget maximization at a zero price of output. At the new output of 10 billion tonnes per year, a deadweight loss exists because marginal cost (2¢) is less than marginal benefit (0¢). The bureaucrats again pad costs up to a maximum level that completely exhausts the consumer surplus (ATC_2(padded)). This outcome is inefficient and maximizes the benefit of the producer by squeezing consumer surplus to zero.

Table 21.1 Federal Regulatory Agencies, text page 542
This table lists the major federal regulatory agencies, together with a brief statement of their responsibilities. The predominant sectors subject to regulation are agriculture, energy, transportation, and telecommunications.

Table 21.3 Canada's Anti-Combine Law: A Compact History, text page 554
This table chronicles the original Canadian anti-combines law of 1889 and the subsequent ammendments and changes in the law up to the most recent Competition Act of 1986.

Table 21.4 Canada's Anti-Combine Law: The Law Today, text page 555
The most important features of the Competition Act of 1986 — regarding a firm's abuse of its dominant position and merger — are summarized in this table.

Table 21.5 Landmark Anti-Combine Cases, text page 556
This table briefly summarizes the most important anti-combines cases that have been decided by Canadian courts. The cases are divided into three broad areas: (a) collusive agreements, (b) monopolies, and (c) mergers. Each case is identified by year, charge, verdict, and importance of the precedent set.

SELF-TEST

CONCEPT REVIEW

1) There are three principal ways in which the government intervenes in monopolistic and oligopolistic markets. The first of these is ______________, which consists of rules administered by a government agency and intended to restrict the behaviour of firms. The second is ______________, which places a corporation under public ownership. The third is ______________ – ______________ ______________, which legally prohibit certain kinds of monopoly practice.

2) The difference between the most that consumers are willing to pay and the amount they actually pay is called ______________ ______________. The difference between the revenue received by a producer and the opportunity cost of production is called ______________ ______________. The sum of these is ______________ ______________.

3) Allocative efficiency is achieved when total surplus is ______________.

4) The larger the consumer surplus per buyer resulting from intervention, the ______________ is the demand for intervention by buyers. The larger the producer surplus per seller resulting from intervention, the ______________ is the demand for intervention by sellers.

5) The ______________ ______________ theory of intervention claims that intervention is supplied in order to attain allocative efficiency. The ______________ theory of intervention states that intervention is intended to maximize producer surplus.

6) The process of selling a publicly owned corporation to private shareholders is called ______________.

7) The pricing rule that maximizes total surplus and achieves allocative efficiency is the ______________ ______________ pricing rule.

8) When a regulatory agency sets the price of a regulated natural monopolist so that the regulated firm is able to earn a specified target percent return on its capital, it is using ______________ ______________ ______________ regulation. If the target rate of return is a normal rate of return, this form of regulation gives the same result as the ______________ ______________ pricing rule.

9) An efficient Crown corporation will produce an output such that price equals ______________ ______________.

10) The current anti-combine law in Canada is called the ______________ ______________ of 1986.

TRUE OR FALSE

_____ 1) Regulation and privatization are the two main ways that the government intervenes in the operation of monopolistic and oligopolistic markets.

_____ 2) A regulatory agency determines the technology that individual firms must use in production.

_____ 3) In a monopoly industry, producer surplus is maximized at the profit-maximizing level of output.

_____ 4) In a monopoly industry, total surplus is maximized at the profit-maximizing level of output.

_____ 5) For a given consumer surplus, the smaller the number of households who share that surplus, the smaller is the demand for the intervention that creates it.

_____ 6) Intervention is supplied by politicians and bureaucrats.

_____ 7) Evidence of higher-than-normal rates of return for regulated natural monopolies would match the predictions of the capture theory.

_____ 8) The evidence that producers are strongly supporting deregulation matches the predictions of the capture theory.

_____ 9) According to the public interest theory of intervention, all government intervention will move the economy closer to allocative efficiency.

_____ 10) According to the capture theory, government regulatory agencies eventually capture the profits of the industries they regulate.

_____ 11) A natural monopoly will always produce on the downward-sloping portion of its average total cost curve.

_____ 12) For a natural monopoly, marginal cost will always be less than average total cost.

_____ 13) An average cost pricing rule will achieve allocative efficiency.

_____ 14) In practice, rate of return regulation is equivalent to marginal cost pricing.

_____ 15) Under rate of return regulation, firms can get closer to maximizing producer surplus if they inflate their costs.

_____ 16) If, after deregulation of an industry, its prices and profits fall, we can reasonably conclude that the regulation was serving the interest of consumers.

_____ 17) According to the public interest theory, regulators will regulate a cartel to make sure that firms do not cheat on the collusive cartel agreement to restrict output.

_____ 18) An efficiently operated Crown corporation will maximize total surplus.

_____ 19) The Competition Act is enforced by a quasi-judicial tribunal rather than by the courts.

_____ 20) Anti-combines laws have generally been directed towards achieving allocative efficiency and serving the public interest.

MULTIPLE-CHOICE

1) Which of the following is *not* a federal regulatory agency?
   a) Atomic Energy Control Board
   b) CRTC
   c) Petro-Canada
   d) Canadian Transport Commission
   e) National Farm Products

2) The difference between the maximum amount consumers are willing to pay and the amount they actually do pay for a given quantity of a good is called
   a) government surplus.
   b) consumer surplus.
   c) producer surplus.
   d) total surplus.
   e) deadweight surplus.

3) Total surplus is given by the sum of
   a) the gain from trade accruing to consumers and the gain from trade accruing to producers.
   b) the gain from regulation and the gain from anti-combines laws.
   c) revenues received by firms and government subsidies.
   d) consumer payments and producer profit.
   e) none of the above.

4) Total surplus is maximized when
   a) marginal cost equals marginal revenue.
   b) marginal cost equals average total cost.
   c) price equals marginal cost.
   d) price equals average total cost.
   e) price equals average variable cost.

5) In a monopoly industry, producer surplus is maximized when
   a) marginal cost equals marginal revenue.
   b) marginal cost equals average total cost.
   c) price equals marginal cost.
   d) price equals average total cost.
   e) price equals average variable cost.

6) A large demand for intervention by *producers* will result when there is a
   a) small consumer surplus per buyer.
   b) large consumer surplus per buyer.
   c) large number of buyers.
   d) small producer surplus per firm.
   e) large producer surplus per firm.

7) In a political equilibrium,
   a) allocative efficiency must be achieved.
   b) no one wants to change their proposals.
   c) firms will be making zero economic profit.
   d) all parties will agree that the appropriate level of regulation has been achieved.
   e) all of the above are true.

8) Which of the following is consistent with the public interest theory of intervention?
   a) regulation of a natural monopolist by setting price equal to marginal cost
   b) regulation of a competitive industry in order to increase output
   c) regulation of the airline industry by establishing minimum airfares
   d) regulation of agriculture by establishing barriers to exit from the industry
   e) none of the above

9) Which of the following is consistent with the capture theory of intervention?
 a) regulation of a natural monopolist by setting price equal to marginal cost
 b) regulation of a competitive industry in order to increase output
 c) regulation of the airline industry by establishing minimum airfares
 d) regulation of agriculture by establishing barriers to exit from the industry
 e) none of the above

10) Which of the following is *least* likely to be a *natural monopoly*?
 a) subway service
 b) electric utilities
 c) water and sewer service
 d) taxi cab service
 e) cable TV service

11) Figure 21.2 gives the revenue and cost curves for an industry. This industry will become a natural monopoly because
 a) one firm can supply the entire market at a lower price than can two or more firms.
 b) there are decreasing returns to scale over the entire range of demand.
 c) there are diseconomies of scale over the entire range of demand.
 d) even a single firm will be unable to earn a positive profit in this industry.
 e) all of the above are true.

Figure 21.2

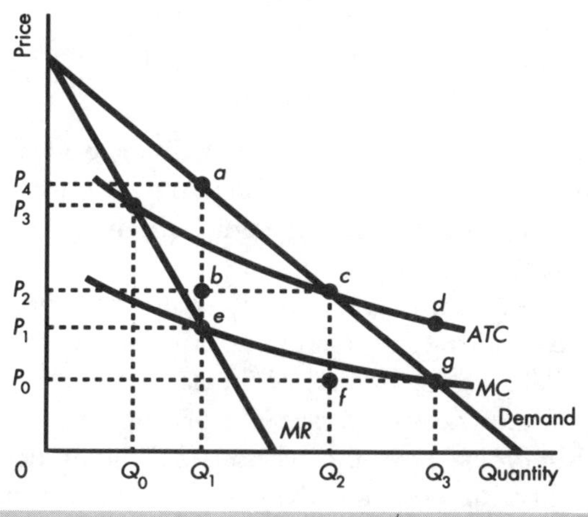

12) Consider the natural monopoly depicted in Figure 21.2. If the firm is unregulated and operates as a private profit-maximizer, what output will it produce?
 a) 0, because the firm suffers economics losses when $P = MC$
 b) Q_0
 c) Q_1
 d) Q_2
 e) Q_3

13) Consider the natural monopoly depicted in Figure 21.2. If a regulatory agency sets a price just sufficient for the firm to earn normal profits, what output will it produce?
 a) 0, because the firm suffers economics losses when $P = MC$
 b) Q_0
 c) Q_1
 d) Q_2
 e) Q_3

14) Consider the natural monopoly depicted in Figure 21.2. Total surplus is a maximum when quantity is
 a) Q_0 and price is P_3.
 b) Q_1 and price is P_1.
 c) Q_1 and price is P_4.
 d) Q_2 and price is P_2.
 e) Q_3 and price is P_0.

15) Consider the natural monopoly depicted in Figure 21.2. Producer surplus is a maximum when quantity is
 a) Q_0 and price is P_3.
 b) Q_1 and price is P_1.
 c) Q_1 and price is P_4.
 d) Q_2 and price is P_2.
 e) Q_3 and price is P_0.

16) Consider the natural monopoly depicted in Figure 21.2. If a regulator uses a marginal cost pricing rule, what line segment gives the amount of subsidy (per unit of output) that will be required to assure that the monopolist will remain in business?
 a) *ba*
 b) *ea*
 c) *fc*
 d) *gd*
 e) *eb*

17) Consider the natural monopoly depicted in Figure 21.2. What region in the graph represents the deadweight loss arising from an average cost pricing rule?
 a) *abc*
 b) *cdg*
 c) *cfg*
 d) *aeg*
 e) none of the above

18) A monopolist under rate of return regulation has an incentive to
   a) pad costs.
   b) produce more than the efficient quantity of output.
   c) charge a price equal to marginal cost.
   d) maximize consumer surplus.
   e) do both (a) and (b).

19) The demand for intervention depends on
   a) consumer surplus per buyer.
   b) number of buyers.
   c) producer surplus per firm.
   d) number of firms.
   e) all of the above.

20) A Crown corporation which maximizes its budget together with marginal cost pricing will
   a) produce the efficient level of output.
   b) produce more than the efficient level of output.
   c) maximize consumer surplus.
   d) maximize producer surplus.
   e) do both (a) and (d).

SHORT ANSWER

1) Regulation of monopoly is necessary because of the tension between the public interest and the producer's interest. Explain.

2) In the regulation of a natural monopoly, when would an average cost pricing rule be better than a marginal cost pricing rule?

3) Why is rate of return regulation equivalent to average cost pricing?

4) What, if anything, can the behaviour of prices and profits following deregulation of an industry tell us about whether regulation favoured consumers or producers?

5) Explain the problem that the recent deregulation process poses for the capture theory of intervention.

PROBLEMS

1) a) It has been suggested that government should eliminate monopoly profit by taxing each unit of monopoly output. What effect would such a policy have on the quantity a monopolist produces and the price it charges?
   b) What is the effect on economic efficiency?

2) The demand for Aerodisks, a disk made from a unique material that flies a considerable distance when thrown, is given by this equation:

$$P = 10 - 0.01\,Q_D$$

The corresponding marginal revenue (MR) equation is

$$MR = 10 - 0.02\,Q$$

The Aerodisk Company is a natural monopoly. The firm's total fixed cost is $700 and the marginal cost is constant at $2 per disk. (*Note*: This implies that average variable cost is also constant at $2 per disk.) Suppose that the Aerodisk Company is not regulated.
   a) What will be the quantity sold and the price of an Aerodisk?
   b) How much is total profit or loss?
   c) How much is producer surplus?
   d) How much is consumer surplus?
   e) How much is total surplus?

3) Now suppose that the Aerodisk Company becomes regulated and that the regulator uses a marginal cost pricing rule.
   a) What will be the quantity sold and the price of an Aerodisk?
   b) How much is total profit or loss?
   c) How much is producer surplus?
   d) How much is consumer surplus?
   e) How much is total surplus?

4) Suppose that the regulator of the Aerodisk Company uses an average cost pricing rule.
   a) What will be the price of an Aerodisk and how many will be sold?
   b) How much is total profit or loss?
   c) How much is producer surplus?
   d) How much is consumer surplus?
   e) How much is total surplus?

5) Since the Aerodisk Company will make a loss under marginal cost pricing, the government must subsidize the production of Aerodisks in order for the firm to be willing to produce.
   a) What is the total subsidy necessary under a marginal cost pricing rule to leave the firm with a zero profit?
   b) What is the amount of the deadweight loss associated with an average cost pricing rule?
   c) In order to pay the necessary subsidy under the marginal cost rule, the government must raise tax revenue in the amount of the subsidy. If the deadweight loss associated with the tax is $100, which pricing rule is superior?

6) Figure 21.3 illustrates the industry demand, marginal revenue (*MR*), and marginal cost (*MC*) curves in an oligopoly industry. The industry is regulated.
   a) What price and quantity will be predicted by the public interest theory of regulation? Why?
   b) What price and quantity will be predicted by the capture theory of regulation? Why?
   c) Can you explain why the firms in this industry might be demanders of regulation?

Figure 21.3

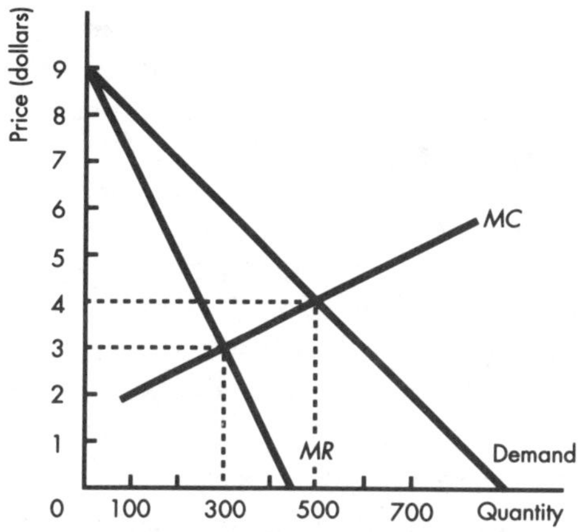

ANSWERS

CONCEPT REVIEW

1) regulation; nationalization; anti-combine laws
2) consumer surplus; producer surplus; total surplus
3) maximized
4) larger; larger
5) public interest; capture
6) privatization
7) marginal cost
8) rate of return; average cost
9) marginal cost
10) Competition Act

TRUE OR FALSE

1) F	6) T	11) T	16) F
2) F	7) T	12) T	17) F
3) T	8) F	13) F	18) T
4) F	9) T	14) F	19) T
5) F	10) F	15) T	20) T

MULTIPLE-CHOICE

1) c	6) e	11) a	16) d
2) b	7) b	12) c	17) c
3) a	8) a	13) d	18) a
4) c	9) c	14) e	19) e
5) a	10) d	15) c	20) e

SHORT ANSWER

1) It is in the public interest to achieve allocative efficiency; to expand output to the level that maximizes total surplus. On the other hand, it is in the interest of the monopoly producer to restrict output in order to maximize producer surplus and thus, monopoly profit.

Since these interests are not the same, monopoly must be regulated in order to achieve allocative efficiency. The public interest theory of regulation suggests that this is the principle that guides regulation of monopoly industries.

2) An average cost pricing rule will create a deadweight loss but so will a marginal cost pricing rule, through the need to impose a tax.
   Since, for a natural monopoly, marginal cost is less than average total cost, regulation by use of a marginal cost pricing rule requires the government to pay a subsidy in order for the firm to be willing to produce at all.
   In order to pay that subsidy the government must levy a tax, which will impose a deadweight loss on the economy. If the deadweight loss associated with the tax (for example, the deadweight loss of the marginal cost pricing rule with its attendant subsidy) is greater than the deadweight loss of an average cost pricing rule, the average cost pricing rule is superior.

3) The key here is to recall that economic cost includes a normal rate of return. Thus, because rate of return regulation sets a price that allows the firm to achieve a normal rate of return, it is setting the price equal to average total cost.

4) If, after deregulation of an industry, prices and profits fall, we can conclude that the regulation must have favoured producers.

5) The capture theory predicts that producers will capture the regulatory process and use it to maximize producer surplus. But if the producer lobby was strong enough to achieve regulation, why have producers been unable to stop deregulation? A further question is why do many producers *favour* deregulation? The capture theory has no good answers to these questions.

PROBLEMS

1) a) Imposing a tax on each unit sold by a monopolist will increase marginal cost. As a consequence the profit-maximizing monopolist will raise the price and reduce the quantity produced.
   b) The tax will certainly reduce the profit of the monopolist and may even eliminate it, but the consequence will be to make the inefficiency due to monopoly even worse. This is illustrated in Figure 21.4. The curve *MC* is the marginal cost curve before the tax. An unregulated monopolist will produce amount Q_2, while the economically efficient output is Q_3. The tax, however, causes the monopolist to reduce output from Q_2 to Q_1 which moves the market outcome farther away from efficiency.

Figure 21.4

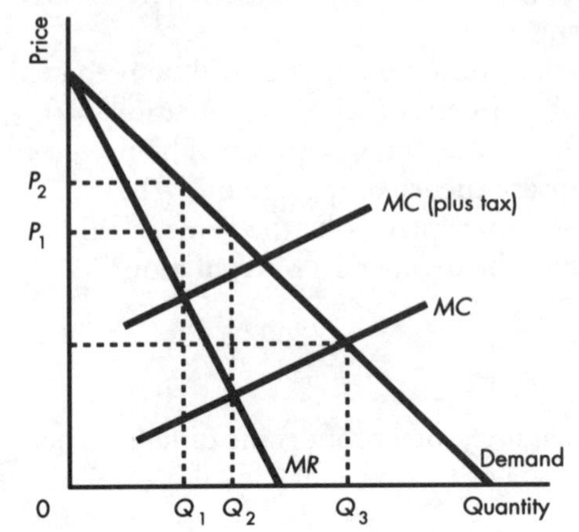

2) Figure 21.5 will be helpful in answering questions about the Aerodisk market. It gives the relevant revenue and cost curves for the aerodisk Company.

Figure 21.5

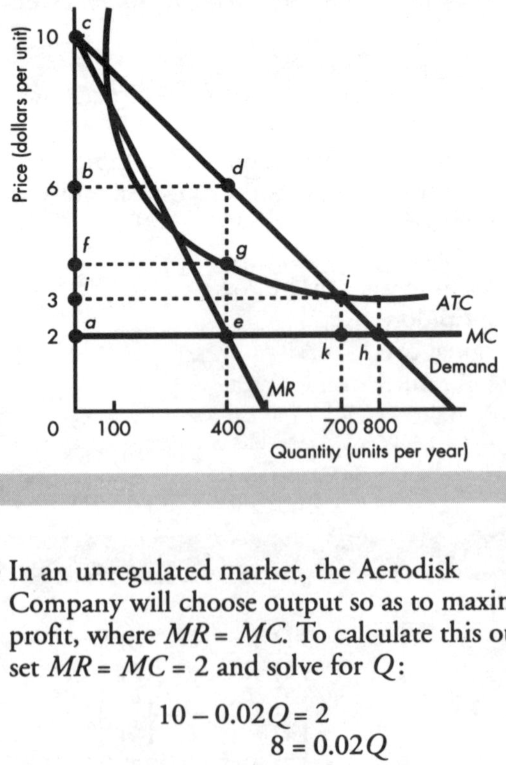

a) In an unregulated market, the Aerodisk Company will choose output so as to maximize profit, where $MR = MC$. To calculate this output, set $MR = MC = 2$ and solve for Q:

$$10 - 0.02Q = 2$$
$$8 = 0.02Q$$
$$400 = Q$$

To calculate price, substitute $Q = 400$ into the demand equation:

$$
\begin{aligned}
P &= 10 - 0.01Q_D \\
&= 10 - 0.01\,(400) \\
&= 10 - 4 \\
&= 6
\end{aligned}
$$

400 Aerodisks will be produced and sold at a price of $6 each.

b) To determine total profit, we first determine average total cost (*ATC*) when output (*Q*) is 400 units.

$$
\begin{aligned}
ATC &= AFC + AVC \\
&= (TFC/Q) + AVC \\
&= (700/400) + 2 \\
&= 3.75
\end{aligned}
$$

Therefore, total profit is the difference between price (average revenue) and *ATC* times the quantity sold. This is equal to $900 and is represented in Figure 21.5 by the region *fbdg*.

c) Producer surplus is the difference between the producer's revenue and the opportunity cost of production. Total revenue is $2,400 ($6 × 400 units) and total opportunity cost is $800 ($2 × 400 units). Thus, producer surplus is $1,600. Graphically producer surplus is the area of the rectangle *abde* in Figure 21.5.

d) Consumer surplus is readily obtained graphically as the area in the triangle denoted *bcd* in Figure 21.5. The area of that triangle is $800.

e) Total surplus is $2,400, the sum of producer and consumer surplus.

3) a) Under a marginal cost pricing rule, the price of an Aerodisk will be equal to marginal cost or $2. To calculate the quantity sold, substitute the price into the demand equation:

$$
\begin{aligned}
P &= 10 - 0.01Q_D \\
2 &= 10 - 0.01Q_D \\
0.01Q_D &= 8 \\
Q_D &= 800
\end{aligned}
$$

b) To determine the amount of profit or loss, we must first determine *ATC* when output is 800. Using the procedure in the previous problem, we find that at $Q = 800$, *ATC* is $2.875, which is greater than price by $0.875 (87.5¢). Therefore, the Aerodisk Company will make a loss in the amount of $700 (0.875 x 800). Alternatively, since *MC* is constant, if the price is set equal to *MC* which is equal to *AVC*, the total loss will be just *TFC* or $700.

c) Producer surplus is zero.

d) Consumer surplus is given by the area of the triangle *ach* in Figure 21.5, which is $3,200.

e) Total surplus is $3,200 (a maximum).

4) a) Computation of *ATC* at various levels of output allows us to determine that the *ATC* curve crosses the demand curve when $Q = 700$ and $ATC = \$3$. Thus, under an average cost pricing rule, the price of an Aerodisk will be $3 and 700 units will be sold.

b) Since price is equal to average total cost, profit is zero.

c) Producer surplus is $700, the area of the rectangle *aijk* in Figure 21.5.

d) Consumer surplus is $2,450, the area of the triangle *ijc* in Figure 21.5.

e) Total surplus is $3,150.

5) a) The total subsidy is equal to the loss under marginal cost pricing. In problem 3(b) we computed this to be $700.

b) The deadweight loss associated with the average cost pricing rule is the loss of total surplus relative to the marginal cost pricing rule. We have computed the total surplus under marginal cost pricing ($3,200) in problem 3(e) and the total surplus under average cost pricing ($3,150) in problem 4(e). The deadweight loss is the difference: $50.

c) The average cost pricing rule is superior because it has the smaller deadweight loss.

6) a) The public interest theory predicts that regulators will set price and quantity so as to maximize total surplus. This means that they will choose quantity (and price) where *MC* is equal to demand. This corresponds to a quantity of 500 units and a price of $4 per unit.

b) The capture theory predicts that the regulator will choose quantity and price so as to maximize the profit of the industry. This is the quantity that would be chosen by a profit-maximizing monopolist, 300 units, where $MC = MR$. The highest price that could be charged and still sell that quantity can be read from the demand curve: $6 per unit.

c) Firms in the industry would be demanders of regulation if the regulation had the effect of increasing profit to the industry. As we discovered in Chapter 14, cartels are unstable because there is always an incentive to cheat on output restriction agreements and it is very difficult to enforce the agreements. If, however, the firms in an industry can get the government, through regulation, to enforce a cartel agreement, they will want to do it.

Chapter 36 Trading with the World

Chapter in Perspective

Text Pages 967–992

Trade issues seem to be constantly in the news, partially because Canada is a nation that is heavily involved in international trade. In recent years that involvement has grown with the signing of the Canada–United States Free Trade Agreement. This agreement will drastically reduce barriers to trade between the two countries and will change what our country produces and consumes. This agreement met much opposition when it was first signed and many Canadians blame it for a score of current economic problems.

There are many other trade issues in the news. These include the European Community's move toward a single trading bloc in 1992 and the recent series of General Agreement on Tariffs and Trade (GATT) talks on agricultural subsidies. This chapter addresses these and other trade issues.

We first address the basic issue of why do nations trade? What is the nature of the gains that make trade worthwhile? What determines the type of goods a country will import and the type it will export? We then turn to questions on more difficult issues such as the following: If there are significant gains to free trade, why do countries frequently restrict imports? What are the effects of a tariff or a quota or some other trade restriction?

These are timely issues, which are not widely understood, and which will likely become increasingly important.

Learning Objectives

After studying this chapter, you will be able to:

- **Describe the trends and patterns in international trade.**
- **Explain comparative advantage.**
- **Explain why all countries can gain from international trade.**
- **Explain how prices adjust to bring about balanced trade.**
- **Explain how economies of scale and diversity of taste lead to gains from international trade.**
- **Explain why trade restrictions lower the volume of imports and exports and lower our consumption possibilities.**
- **Explain why we have trade restrictions even though they lower our consumption possibilities.**

Helpful Hints

1) It is useful to recall the discussion of opportunity cost, comparative advantage, and gains from trade in Chapter 3. This chapter applies the fundamental concepts of opportunity cost and comparative advantage to the problem of trade between nations. The basic principles are the same whether we are talking about trade between individuals in the same country or between individuals in different countries.

   Many students (and others involved in debates about trade) seem confused by the concept of comparative advantage, partially because they implicitly conceive of *absolute advantage* as the sole reason for trade. A country has an absolute advantage if it can produce all goods using less inputs than another country. However, such a country can still gain from trade.

   To see this, consider comparing California to Saskatchewan. California has better weather and in combination with widespread irrigation has an absolute advantage in the production of all agricultural products — indeed, California frequently has more than one harvest a year! This would seem to imply that California has no need to trade with Saskatchewan. However, Saskatchewan has a *comparative advantage* in the production of wheat. Therefore, California will specialize in fruits and trade them for wheat. California could easily grow its own wheat, but to do so would have too high an opportunity cost — the lost fruit crops. By specializing and trading, both California and Saskatchewan can gain.

2) In addition to the gains from trade, this chapter also discusses the economic effects of trade restrictions. One of the important things we learn is that the economic effects of a tariff and a quota are the same. A voluntary export restraint (VER) is also a quota but a quota imposed by the exporting country rather than the importing country.

   All these trade restrictions raise the domestic price of the imported good, and reduce the volume and value of imports. They will also reduce the value of exports by the same amount as the reduction in the value of imports. The increase in price that results from each of these trade restrictions produces a gap between the domestic price of the imported good and the foreign supply price of the good.

   The difference between the alternative trade restrictions lies in which party captures this excess. In the case of a tariff, the government receives the tariff revenue. In the case of a quota imposed by the importing country, domestic importers who have been awarded a licence to import, capture this excess through increased profit. When a VER is imposed, the excess is captured by foreign exporters who have been awarded licences to export by their government.

3) The major point of this chapter is that gains from free trade can be considerable. Why then do countries have such a strong tendency to impose trade restrictions? The key is that while free trade creates overall benefits to the economy as a whole, there are both winners and losers. The winners gain more in total than the losers lose, but the latter tend to be concentrated in a few industries.

   It is therefore not surprising that free trade will be resisted by some acting on the basis of rational self-interest. Even though only a small minority benefit from any given trade restriction, while the overwhelming majority will be hurt, it is not surprising to see trade restrictions implemented. The reason is that the cost of a given trade restriction to each of the many is individually quite small, while the benefit to each of the few will be individually large. Thus, the few will have a significant incentive to see that restriction takes place, while the many will have little incentive to expend time and energy in resisting trade restriction.

Key Figures

Figure 36.1 Canadian Exports and Imports, text page 970
This figure shows the major types of goods and services that Canada exports and imports. Surprisingly, our major export is motor vehicles and motor vehicles parts, as is our major import, due in no small part, to the Auto Pact trade agreement. Less surprisingly, our next most important export category is lumber, pulp, and paper. Other major imports include consumer goods and electronic equipment.

Figure 36.4 Opportunity Cost in Pioneerland, text page 973
This figure shows the production possibility frontier for the imaginary country of Pioneerland. Currently it is producing and consuming 15 billion bushels of grain and 8 million cars a year at point *a* on the production possibility frontier. Opportunity cost is measured as the slope of the production possibility frontier at this point. At point *a*, 1 car costs 9,000 bushels of grain, or 9,000 bushels cost 1 car.

Figure 36.5 Opportunity Cost in Magic Empire, text page 973
This figure shows the production possibility frontier for the imaginary country of Magic Empire. Currently it is producing and consuming 18 billion bushels of grain and

4 million cars a year at point a' on the production possibility frontier. Opportunity cost is measured as the slope of the production possibility frontier at this point. At point a', 1 car costs 1,000 bushels of grain, or 1,000 bushels cost 1 car.

Figure 36.6 International Trade in Cars, text page 975
The price at which a good trades internationally and the quantity traded are determined by the international market for the good. This figure illustrates a hypothetical international market for cars using the example of Pioneerland and Magic Empire.

Magic Empire has a comparative advantage in the production of cars and so supplies cars to the world market. At higher prices, Magic Empire is willing to supply more cars, although it must receive at least 1,000 bushels of grain (its opportunity cost of a car) to be willing to produce.

The supply curve in the figure gives Magic Empire's export supply of cars. Similarly, the demand curve in the figure gives Pioneerland's import demand for cars. It shows that as the price of a car falls, the quantity of cars that Pioneerland wants to import increases although it will not buy any cars at a price above 9,000 bushels of grain (its opportunity cost of a car). The equilibrium price when trade takes place is at the intersection of these two curves. The price of a car (under free trade) is 3,000 bushels of grain, and 4 million cars per year are imported by Pioneerland from Magic Empire.

Figure 36.7 Expanding Consumption Possibilities, text page 976
This figure clearly illustrates the gains from trade experienced by Pioneerland and Magic Empire. Without trade, each country consumes what it produces. Its consumption is constrained by the production possibility frontier. The gain from trade for each country is that, with trade, while production is constrained by the production possibility frontier, consumption can exceed that frontier. Consumption is only constrained by the consumption possibility curve which (except for a single point) lies beyond the production possibility curve

Part (a) of the figure shows the situation for Pioneerland. Without trade, Pioneerland produces and consumes at point a: 8 million cars and 15 billion bushels of grain. With trade (at 1 car trading for 3,000 bushels of grain), Pioneerland produces at point b: 5 million cars and 30 billion bushels of grain.

But, because of trade, consumption can be different. Indeed, with trade, Pioneerland consumes at point c: 9 million cars and 18 billion bushels of grain. This is 1 million more cars and 3 billion more bushels of grain than were consumed without trade (at point a). This additional consumption is the gain from trade for Pioneerland. A similar analysis in part (b) illustrates that Magic Empire also gains from trade.

Figure 36.9 The Effects of a Tariff, text page 982
The effects of a tariff on the price of a good and the quantity traded are shown in this figure by using the Pioneerland and Magic Empire example of trade in cars. Pioneerland imposes a tariff of $4,000 per car on cars imported from Magic Empire. This shifts the export supply curve upward by $4,000 because the price must include the supply price received by Magic Empire and the tariff. Thus, the price of a car in Pioneerland increases from $3,000 to $6,000 and the quantity of cars traded falls to 2 million per year. The total revenue from the tariff (which is received by the government of Pioneerland) is $8 billion: $4,000 per car times 2 million cars. Although this figure does not show it directly, Pioneerland's grain exports will also decrease because Magic Empire's income from the export of cars has fallen.

Figure 36.10 The Effects of a Quota, text page 986
This figure illustrates the effects of a quota on domestic price and quantity traded again using the Pioneerland and Magic Empire example. Pioneerland imposes a quota of 2 million cars per year. This restriction is indicated in the graph by a vertical line. This becomes the effective supply curve for the purpose of determining the price, which turns out to be $6,000. The quantity traded, of course, is 2 million cars per year, the quota limit. At 2 million cars, Magic Empire is willing to supply cars for $2,000 each. This $4,000 per car difference between the selling price and the price received by the exporter is captured by whoever has the import rights.

SELF-TEST

CONCEPT REVIEW

1) The goods and services purchased from people in foreign countries are called ______________ . The goods and services sold to people in foreign countries are called ______________ . The value of exports minus the value of imports is called the ______________ of ______________ .

2) A country is said to have a(n) ______________ ______________ in the production of a good if it can produce that good at a lower opportunity cost than any other country. A country is said to have a(n) ______________ ______________ if for all goods its output per unit of inputs is higher than any other country.

3) The restriction of international trade is called ______________ . A tax imposed by the importing country on an imported good is called a(n) ______________ . The result of imposing such a tax is to ______________ the price that consumers in the importing country pay and ______________ the quantity traded. When such a tax is imposed, the tax revenue is received by the ______________ .

4) The international agreement that came into law on January 1, 1989, which reduces trade barriers between Canada and the United States, is the ______________ – ______________ ______________ ______________ ______________ Agreeement.

5) A restriction that specifies a limit on the quantity of a particular good that can be imported is called a(n) ______________ . The result of such a limit is to ______________ the price that consumers in the importing country pay. The extra revenue from such a limit is received by the ______________ .

6) An agreement between two governments in which the government of the exporting country agrees to restrict the quantity of its exports to the importing country is called a(n) ______________ ______________ ______________ . Such an agreement will ______________ the price that consumers in the importing country pay for the good.

7) When a good is sold in a foreign market at a lower price than in a domestic market or for a price that is lower than the cost of production it is called ______________ .

8) A tariff that enables domestic producers to compete with subsidized foreign producers is called a ______________ ______________ .

TRUE OR FALSE

____ 1) Canada imports more manufactured goods than it exports.

____ 2) Canada is a net exporter of agricultural products.

____ 3) When a Canadian citizen stays in a hotel in France, Canada is exporting a service.

____ 4) Canada's most important trading partner is Japan.

____ 5) If there are two countries, *A* and *B*, and two goods, *X* and *Y*, and country *A* has a comparative advantage in the production of *X*, then country *B* must have a comparative advantage in the production of *Y*.

____ 6) If country *A* must give up 3 units of *Y* to produce 1 unit of *X* and *B* must give up 4 units of *Y* to produce 1 unit of *X*, then *A* has a comparative advantage in the production of *X*.

____ 7) If countries specialize in goods for which they have a comparative advantage, then some countries will gain and others will lose, but the gains will be larger than the losses.

____ 8) Trading according to comparative advantage allows all trading countries to consume outside their production possibility frontiers.

____ 9) If a country has an absolute advantage, it will not benefit from trade.

____ 10) Countries may exchange similar goods for each other due to economies of scale in the face of diversified tastes.

____ 11) When governments impose tariffs, they are increasing their country's gain from trade.

____ 12) Tariffs in Canada are much higher than they were before World War II.

_____ 13) The Canada–United States Free Trade Agreement will raise trade barriers.

_____ 14) A tariff on a good will raise its price and reduce the quantity traded.

_____ 15) A tariff not only reduces the total value of imports but it reduces the total value of exports as well.

_____ 16) A quota will cause the price of the imported good to fall.

_____ 17) The government will raise no revenue from a quota.

_____ 18) The excess revenue created by a voluntary export restraint is captured by the exporter.

_____ 19) Japan is dumping steel if it sells it in Japan at a lower price than it sells it in Canada.

_____ 20) Elected governments are likely to be slow to reduce trade restrictions even though the gains would be much larger than the losses because there would be many fewer losers than gainers.

MULTIPLE-CHOICE

1) Canada is a net
   a) exporter of manufactured goods and a net importer of crude petroleum.
   b) exporter of manufactured goods and a net exporter of agricultural products.
   c) importer of manufactured goods and a net importer of forestry products.
   d) importer of manufactured goods and a net exporter of agricultural products.
   e) importer of travel and a net exporter of textiles and footwear.

2) Which of the following is a Canadian service export?
   a) A Canadian citizen buys a restaurant meal while travelling in Switzerland.
   b) A Swiss citizen buys a restaurant meal while travelling in Canada.
   c) A Canadian citizen buys a clock made in Switzerland.
   d) A Swiss citizen buys a computer made in Canada.
   e) Both a) and b) are Canadian service exports.

3) Canada recently signed a free trade agreement with
   a) the United States.
   b) Japan.
   c) Mexico.
   d) the European Community.
   e) Great Britain.

4) Suppose there are two countries, *A* and *B*, producing two goods, *X* and *Y*. Country *A* has a comparative advantage in the production of good *X* if less
   a) of good *Y* must be given up to produce one unit of *X* than in country *B*.
   b) labour is required to produce one unit of *X* than in country *B*.
   c) capital is required to produce one unit of *X* than in country *B*.
   d) labour and capital are required to produce one unit of *X* than in country *B*.
   e) of good *X* must be given up to produce one unit of *Y* than in country *B*.

5) Suppose there are two countries, *A* and *B*, producing two goods, *X* and *Y* and country *A* has a comparative advantage in the production of *X*. If the countries trade, the price of *X* in terms of *Y* will be
   a) greater than the opportunity cost of *X* in country *A* and less than the opportunity cost of *X* in country *B*.
   b) less than the opportunity cost of *X* in country *A* and greater than the opportunity cost of *X* in country *B*.
   c) greater than the opportunity cost of *X* in both countries.
   d) less than the opportunity cost of *X* in both countries.
   e) dependent on the relative size of each economy.

6) Compared to a no-trade situation, international trade according to comparative advantage allows each country to consume
   a) more of the goods it exports but less of the goods it imports.
   b) more of the goods it imports but less of the goods it exports.
   c) more of both goods it exports and goods it imports.
   d) less of both goods it exports and goods it imports.
   e) either a) or b); depending on the price of the goods.

7) In country *A*, it requires one unit of capital and one unit of labour to produce a unit of *X* and it requires two units of capital and two units of labour to produce a unit of *Y*. What is the opportunity cost of good *X*?
   a) the price of a unit of capital plus the price of a unit of labour
   b) one unit of capital and one unit of labour
   c) two units of capital and two units of labour
   d) one half unit of *Y*
   e) two units of *Y*

8) If country *A* has an absolute advantage in the production of everything,
   a) no trade will take place because country *A* will have a comparative advantage in everything.
   b) no trade will take place because no country will have a comparative advantage in anything.
   c) trade will probably take place and all countries will gain.
   d) trade will probably take place but country *A* will not gain.
   e) trade will probably take place but country *A* will be the only one to gain.

9) The imposition of a tariff on imported goods will increase the price consumers pay for imported goods and
   a) reduce the volume of imports and the volume of exports.
   b) reduce the volume of imports and increase the volume of exports.
   c) reduce the volume of imports and leave the volume of exports unchanged.
   d) will not affect either the volume of imports or the volume of exports.
   e) increase the volume of imports but decrease the volume of exports.

10) Who benefits from a tariff on good *X*?
   a) domestic consumers of good *X*
   b) domestic producers of good *X*
   c) foreign consumers of good *X*
   d) foreign producers of good *X*
   e) no one

11) Which of the following is most responsible for significant reduction in trade restrictions since World War II?
   a) the Smoot–Hawley Act
   b) the voluntary exports restraint agreement between the United States and Japan
   c) the United Nations
   d) the General Agreement on Tariffs and Trade
   e) the Free Trade Agreement

12) A tariff on good *X* which is imported by country *A* will cause the
   a) demand curve for *X* in country *A* to shift upward.
   b) demand curve for *X* in country *A* to shift downward.
   c) supply curve of *X* in country *A* to shift upward.
   d) supply curve of *X* in country *A* to shift downward.
   e) demand and the supply curve of *X* in country *A* to shift upward.

13) Country *A* and country *B* are currently engaging in free trade. Country *A* imports good *X* from country *B* and exports *Y* to *B*. If country *A* imposes a *tariff* on *X*, country *A*'s *X*-producing industry will
   a) expand and its *Y*-producing industry will contract.
   b) expand and its *Y*-producing industry will expand.
   c) contract and its *Y*-producing industry will contract.
   d) contract and its *Y*-producing industry will expand.
   e) expand and its *Y*-producing industry will be unchanged.

14) Country *A* and country *B* are currently engaging in free trade. Country *A* imports good *X* from country *B* and exports *Y* to *B*. If country *A* imposes a *quota* on *X*, country *A*'s *X*-producing industry will
   a) expand and its *Y*-producing industry will contract.
   b) expand and its *Y*-producing industry will expand.
   c) contract and its *Y*-producing industry will contract.
   d) contract and its *Y*-producing industry will expand.
   e) expand and its *Y*-producing industry will be unchanged.

15) When a *tariff* is imposed, the gap between the domestic price and the export price is captured by
   a) consumers in the importing country.
   b) the person with the right to import the good.
   c) the domestic producers of the good.
   d) foreign exporters.
   e) the government of the importing country.

16) When a *quota* is imposed, the gap between the domestic price and the export price is captured by
   a) consumers in the importing country.
   b) the domestic producers of the good.
   c) the government of the importing country.
   d) foreign exporters.
   e) the person with the right to import the good.

17) When a voluntary export restraint agreement is reached, the gap between the domestic price and the export price is captured by
a) consumers in the importing country.
b) the person with the right to import the good.
c) the government of the importing country.
d) foreign exporters.
e) the domestic producers of the good.

18) Country *A* imports good *X* from country *B* and exports *Y* to *B*. Which of the following is a reason why country *A* might prefer arranging a voluntary export restraint rather than a quota on *X*?
a) to not reduce the volume of its own exports of *Y*
b) to prevent country *B* from retaliating by restricting country *A*'s exports
c) to keep the domestic price of *X* low
d) to increase government revenue
e) it helps domestic producers more than a quota

19) If we import more than we export *ceteris paribus*, then
a) we are going to be unable to buy as many foreign goods as we desire.
b) we will make loans to foreigners to enable them to buy our goods.
c) we will have to finance the difference by borrowing from foreigners.
d) the budget deficit increases.
e) both c) and d) are true.

20) The implementation of the Canada–United States Free Trade Agreement has revealed that
a) Canada has been severely damaged by the agreement.
b) Canada has been helped enormously by the agreement.
c) free trade does not work.
d) all losers from free trade will be compensated.
e) it is too early to isolate the effects of the agreement and, therefore, it is too early to arrive at any conclusions on its worth.

SHORT ANSWER

1) How is it that *both* parties involved in trade can gain?

2) How does a tariff on a particular imported good affect the domestic price of the good, the export price, the quantity imported, and the quantity of the good produced domestically?

3) How does a tariff on imports affect the exports of the country?

4) How does a quota on a particular imported good affect the domestic price of the good, the export price, the quantity imported, and the quantity of the good produced domestically?

5) Why might a government prefer a quota to a tariff?

PROBLEMS

1) Consider a simple world in which there are two countries, Atlantis and Beltran, each producing two goods, food and cloth. The production possibility frontier for each country is given in Table 36.1.
a) Assuming a constant opportunity cost in each country, complete the table.
b) What is the opportunity cost of food in Atlantis? of cloth?
c) What is the opportunity cost of food in Beltran? of cloth?
d) Draw the production possibility frontiers on separate graphs.

Table 36.1

Atlantis		Beltran	
Food (units)	Cloth (units)	Food (units)	Cloth (units)
0	500	0	800
200	400	100	600
400		200	
600		300	
800		400	
1,000		—	—

2) Suppose that Atlantis and Beltran engage in trade.
a) In which good will each country specialize?
b) If 1 unit of food trades for 1 unit of cloth, what will happen to the production of each good in each country?
c) If 1 unit of food trades for 1 unit of cloth, draw the consumption possibility frontiers for each country on the corresponding graph from problem 1(d).
d) Before trade, if Atlantis consumed 600 units of good, the most cloth it could consume was 200 units. After trade, how many units of cloth can be consumed if 600 units of food are consumed?

3) Continue the analysis of Atlantis and Beltran trading at the rate of 1 unit of food for 1 unit of cloth.

3) a) If Atlantis consumes 600 units of food and 400 units of cloth, how much food and cloth will be consumed by Beltran?
b) Given the consumption quantities and the production quantities from problem 2(b), how much food and cloth will Atlantis and Beltran import and export?

4) Figure 36.1 gives the import demand curve for shirts for country *A*, labelled *D*, and the export supply curve of shifts for country *B*, labelled *S*.
a) What is the price of a shirt under free trade?
b) How many shirts will be imported by country *A*?

Figure 36.1

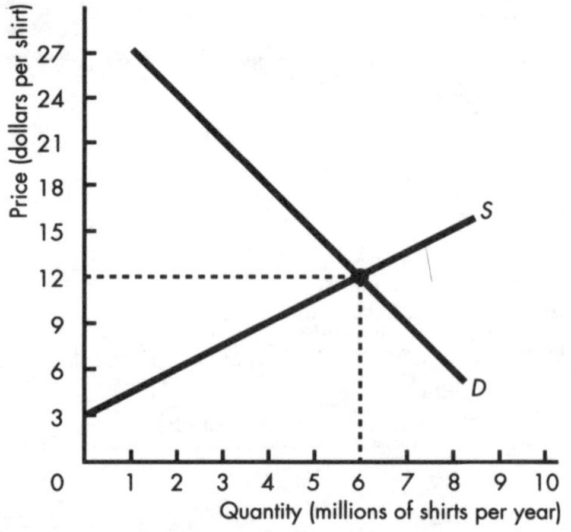

5) Suppose the shirtmakers in country *A* of problem 4 are concerned about foreign competition and, as a result, the government of country *A* imposes a tariff of $9 per shirt. Using Figure 36.1, answer the following questions:
a) What will happen to the price of a shirt in country *A*?
b) What is the price the exporter will actually receive?
c) How many shirts will be imported by country *A*?
d) What is the revenue from the tariff? Who captures it?

6) Suppose that instead of a tariff, country *A* imposes a quota of 4 million shirts per year. Again, use Figure 36.1 to answer the following questions:
a) What will be the price of a shirt in country *A*?
b) What price will the exporter actually receive?
c) How many shirts will be imported by country *A*?
d) What is the difference between the total amount paid by consumers and the total amount received by exporters — the "excess profit?" Who captures it?

ANSWERS

CONCEPT REVIEW

1) imports; exports; balance; trade
2) comparative advantage; absolute advantage
3) protectionism; tariff; increase; decrease; government
4) Canada–United States Free Trade
5) quota; raise; importer
6) voluntary export restraint; raise
7) dumping
8) countervailing duty

TRUE OR FALSE

1) T	6) T	11) F	16) F
2) T	7) F	12) F	17) T
3) F	8) T	13) F	18) T
4) F	9) F	14) T	19) F
5) T	10) T	15) T	20) T

MULTIPLE-CHOICE

1) d	6) c	11) d	16) e
2) b	7) d	12) c	17) d
3) a	8) c	13) a	18) b
4) a	9) a	14) a	19) c
5) a	10) b	15) e	20) e

SHORT ANSWER

1) In order for two potential trading partners to be willing to trade, they must have different comparative advantages; that is to say, different opportunity costs. If they do, then they will trade and both parties will gain. If the parties do not trade, they will each face their own opportunity costs. A price at which trade takes place must be somewhere between the opportunity costs of the two traders. This means that the party with the lower opportunity cost of the good in question will gain because it will receive a price above its opportunity cost. Similarly, the party with the higher opportunity cost will gain because it will pay a price below its opportunity cost.

2) A tariff on an imported good will *raise its price to domestic consumers* as the export supply curve shifts upward. The export price is determined by the original export supply curve. As the domestic price of the good rises, the quantity of the good demanded falls, and thus the relevant point on the original export supply curve is at a lower quantity and a *lower export price.* This lower quantity means that the quantity imported falls. The rise in the domestic price will also lead to an *increase in the quantity of the good supplied domestically.*

3) When country *A* imposes a tariff on its imports of good *X*, not only does the volume of imports shrink, but the volume of exports of *Y* to country *B* will shrink by the same amount. Thus a balance of trade is maintained. As indicated in the answer to Short Answer question 2, the export price of good *X* falls when a tariff is imposed. This fall in the price received by the exporter means that the price of imports in the foreign country has risen; in other words, if the amount of *Y* that country *B* receives for an *X* has fallen, the quantity of *X* that must be given up to obtain a *Y* has increased. This implies that the quantity of *Y* (*A*'s export) demanded by country *B* will fall and thus *A*'s exports decline.

4) The effect of a quota on the domestic price of the good, the export price, the quantity imported, and the quantity of the good produced domestically are exactly the same as the effects of a tariff discussed in the answer to Short Answer 2. The only difference here is that the increase in the domestic price is not the result of a vertical shift in the export supply curve but the result of the fact that the quota forces a vertical effective export supply curve at the quota amount.

5) The effects of tariffs and quotas on prices and quantities were discussed in the solution to Short Answer questions 2 to 4. The difference is that the excess revenue raised by a tariff is captured by the government, whereas the excess revenue raised by a quota is captured by those persons who have been given the right to import by the government. In either case the government is in a position to benefit. It may prefer to use quotas in order to reward political supporters by giving them rights to import and thus allowing them to capture large profits. Second, quotas give the government more precise control over the quantity of imports. Also, it is politically easier to impose a quota than a tariff.

PROBLEMS

1) a) Completed Table 36.1 is shown here as Table 36.1 Solution. The values in the table are calculated using the opportunity cost of each good in each country. See parts (b) and (c) below.

Table 36.1 Solution

Atlantis		Beltran	
Food (units)	Cloth (units)	Food (units)	Cloth (units)
0	500	0	800
200	400	100	600
400	300	200	400
600	200	300	200
800	100	400	0
1,000	0	—	—

b) In order to increase the output (consumption) of food by 200 units, cloth production (consumption) falls by 100 units in Atlantis. Thus the opportunity cost of a unit of food is 1/2 unit of cloth. This opportunity cost is constant as are all others in this problem, for simplicity. Similarly, the opportunity cost of cloth in Atlantis is 2 units of food.

c) In Beltran a 100-unit increase in the production (consumption) of food requires a reduction in the output (consumption) of cloth of 200 units. Thus the opportunity cost of food is 2 units of cloth. Similarly the opportunity cost of cloth in Beltran is 1/2 units of food.

d) Figure 36. 2, parts (a) and (b) on page 404 illustrate the production possibility frontiers for

Atlantis and Beltran, respectively labelled PPF_A and PPF_B. The rest of the diagram is discussed in the solution to problems 2 and 3.

Figure 36.2

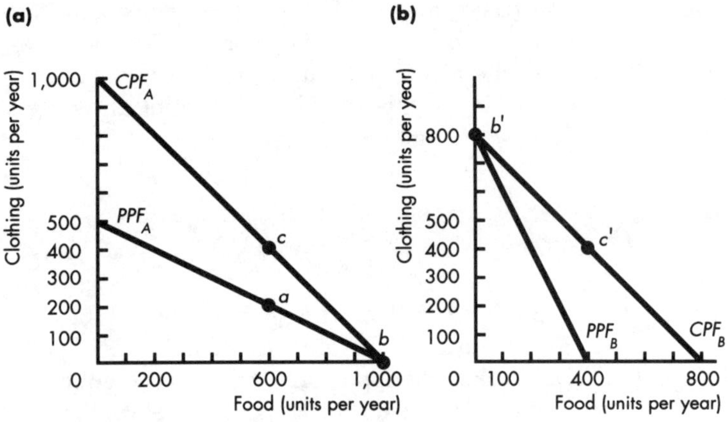

2) a) We see from the solution to problems 1(b) and (c) that Atlantis has a lower opportunity cost (1/2 unit of cloth) in the production of food. Therefore, Atlantis will specialize in the production of food. Beltran, with the lower opportunity cost for cloth (1/2 unit of food), will specialize in cloth.

b) Each country will want to produce every unit of the good in which they specialize as long as the amount they receive in trade exceeds their opportunity cost. For Atlantis, the opportunity cost of a unit of food is 1/2 unit of cloth but it can obtain 1 unit of cloth in trade. Because the opportunity cost is constant (in this simple example), Atlantis will totally specialize by producing all of the food it can: 1,000 units per year, point *b* in Figure 36.2 (a). Similarly, in Beltran, the opportunity cost of a unit of cloth is 1/2 unit of food but a unit of cloth will trade for 1 unit of food. Since the opportunity cost is constant, Beltran will totally specialize in the production of cloth and will produce 800 units per year, point *b*' in Figure 36.2(b).

c) The consumption possibility frontiers for Atlantis and Beltran, labelled CPF_A and CPF_B, are illustrated in Figure 36.2, parts (a) and (b), respectively. These frontiers are straight lines that indicate all the combinations of food and cloth that can be consumed with trade. The position and slope of the consumption possibility frontier for an economy depends on the terms of trade between the goods and the production point of the economy.

The consumption possibility frontier for Atlantis (CPF_A), for example, is obtained by starting at point *b* on PPF_A, the production point, and examining possible trades. For example, if Atlantis traded 400 units of the food it produces for 400 units of cloth, it would be able to consume 600 units of food (1,000 units produced minus 400 units traded) and 400 units of cloth, which is represented by point *c*.

d) If Atlantis consumes 600 units of food, trade allows consumption of cloth to be 400 units, 200 units more than possible without trade. The maximum amount of cloth that can be consumed without trade is given by the production possibility frontier. If food consumption is 600 units, this is indicated by point *a* on PPF_A. The maximum amount of cloth consumption for any level of food consumption with trade is given by the consumption possibility frontier. If food consumption is 600 units, this is indicated by point *c* on CPF_A.

3) a) Since Atlantis produces 1,000 units of food per year (point *b* on PPF_A), to consume 600 units of food and 400 units of cloth (point *c* on CPF_A) it must trade 400 units of food for 400 units of cloth. This means that Beltran has traded 400 units of cloth for 400 units of food. Since Beltran produces 800 units of cloth, this suggests that Beltran must consume 400 units of food and 400 units of cloth (point *c*' on CPF_B).

b) Atlantis exports 400 units of food per year and imports 400 units of cloth. Beltran exports 400 units of cloth per year and imports 400 units of food.

4) a) The price of a shirt under free trade will occur at the intersection of country *A*'s import demand curve for shirts and country *B*'s export supply curve of shirts. This occurs at a price of $12 per shirt.

b) Country *A* will import 6 million shirts per year.

5) a) The effect of the $9 per shirt tariff is to shift the export supply curve (*S*) upward by $9. This is shown as a shift from *S* to *S*' in Figure 36.1 Solution. The price is now determined by the intersection of the *D* curve, which is unaffected by the tariff, and the *S*' curve. The new price of a shirt is $18.

Figure 36.1 Solution

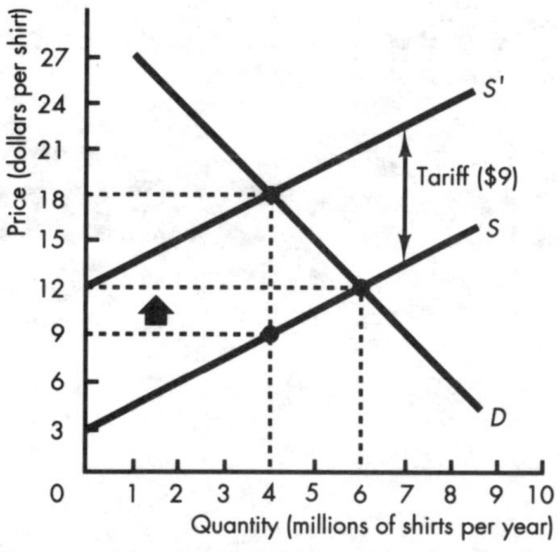

Figure 36.3

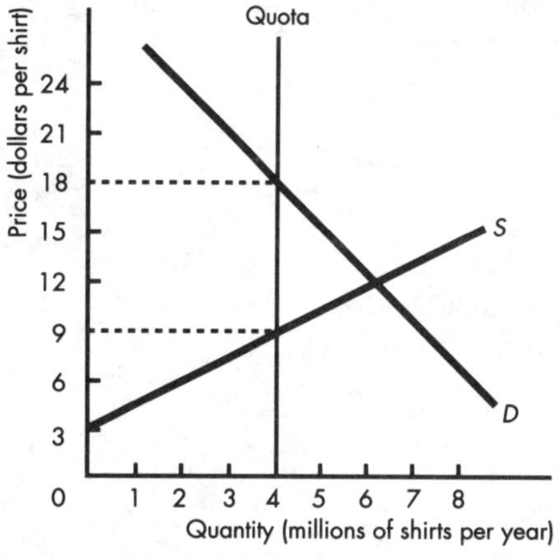

b) Of this $18, $9 is the tariff, so the exporter only receives the remaining $9.

c) Country *A* will now import only 4 million shirts per year.

d) The tariff revenue is $9 (the tariff per shirt) times 4 million (the number of shirts imported), which is $36 million. This money is received by the government of country *A*.

6) a) The quota restricts the quantity that can be imported to 4 million shirts per year regardless of the price and is represented by a vertical line in Figure 36.3 (which corresponds to Figure 36.1). The market for shirts will thus clear at a price of $18 per shirt.

b) This $18 price is received by the people who are given the right to import shirts under the quota. The amount received by the exporter is $9, given by the height of the *S* curve at a quantity of 4 million shirts per year.

c) Country *A* will import 4 million shirts per year, the quota limit.

d) The "excess profit" is $9 per shirt (the $18 received by the importer minus the $9 received by the exporter) times 4 million shirts, which is $36 million. This is captured by the importers who have been rewarded by the government of country *A* because they have been given the right to import under the quota. This is essentially a right to make an "excess profit."

Chapter 39 Comparing Economic Systems

Chapter in Perspective

Text Pages 1035 – 1060

Through the first 38 chapters of the text, we have looked to capitalist economies in general and the Canadian economy in particular, both as the object of description and as a source of examples. However, much of the world's population lives in countries with economic systems that are certainly not capitalist. In this chapter we briefly examine alternative economic systems. We compare the capitalist and socialist economic systems in terms of structure, operation, and results. We also examine the range of economic systems that lie somewhere between the extremes of pure capitalism and pure socialism.

Learning Objectives

After studying this chapter, you will be able to:

- **Explain why the economic problem of scarcity is common to all economic and political systems.**
- **Describe the various political systems that have been proposed to deal with the economic problem.**
- **Explain the difference between capitalism and socialism.**
- **Describe the varieties of capitalism in the United States, Japan, and Western Europe.**
- **Describe the main features of the economy of the Soviet Union.**
- **Explain the economic restructuring — or *perestroika* — being undertaken in the Soviet Union.**
- **Describe the economic reforms being undertaken in China.**
- **Assess the efficiency of alternative economic systems.**

Helpful Hints

1) It is appropriate that the textbook ends where it began, emphasizing the universal problems that face any economy regardless of the kind of economic system that organizes its economic activity. Foremost among these is the fundamental and universal problem of scarcity, which makes choice necessary. No economic system can eliminate scarcity. Each simply confronts the problem in a different way. Furthermore, we find, once again, that opportunity cost is a consequence of choice necessitated by scarcity and not a consequence of the kind of economic system in place. Regardless of how choices are made, the cost of any action is the value of the best forgone alternative.

   An additional underlying notion that is relevant, under any economic system, is the postulate of the rationality of economic agents that has been maintained throughout the text. In particular, we have assumed that individuals will pursue their own best interest as they understand it. This is a postulate about basic human attributes and is independent of economic environment. It is the case, however, that the specific way in which that pursuit of self-interest will manifest itself is different under different economic systems, since alternative systems provide different incentives and constraints. Socialism does not change the desire to pursue one's interest as indicated by the fact that managers of socialist enterprises receive bonuses if they achieve certain targets.

2) The topic of this chapter is of great current practical interest and likely will continue to be by the time you read it. Much of the socialist world is in a process of reform. In addition to the ongoing economic reforms in China and *perestroika* in the Soviet Union, great changes are taking place in other socialist countries like Poland, Hungary, and Czechoslovakia. The greatest change is the recent reunification of Germany. It will be interesting for you to examine these changes in light of the principles taught here.

Key Figures and Tables

Figure 39.1 Alternative Economic Systems, text page 1039
Alternative economic systems differ in two dimensions: (1) the degree to which resources are allocated by markets and (2) the degree to which capital is owned by individuals. This figure creates a diagram in these two dimensions in order to easily compare the economic systems of different countries.

On the vertical scale, the range of methods by which resources are allocated is given with pure market allocation at the top and pure planning at the bottom. On the horizontal scale, the range of capital ownership patterns is given with all capital owned by individuals at the left and all capital owned by the state at the right. Using these two scales we can place a country in the figure according to its actual system.

The upper-left corner of the space corresponds to capitalism because all capital is owned by individuals and all resources are allocated by markets. Similarly, the lower-right corner corresponds to socialism, the lower-left corner corresponds to welfare state capitalism, and the upper-right corner corresponds to market socialism. It is useful to note that no country is located exactly at a corner. This reflects the fact that all countries have elements of both capitalism and socialism but differ in degree.

Figure 39.2 Organization Chart of the Soviet Union, text page 1044
This figure illustrates the organizational structure by which management of the economy in the Soviet Union takes place. A key feature of this organization is its dual structure: a state organization and a party organization. The party organization dominates, but the detailed planning and implementation of plans is carried out by the state organization.

Note in particular the line connecting GOSPLAN, the central planning committee, which is in the state organization, and the Politburo, the party group that is dominant in terms of real power. There are also connections between regional and local state ministries and regional and state party organizations, with the real power residing in the party organizations. It is also important to note the mammoth dimensions of this structure at the national, regional, and local levels. An immense bureaucracy is required to accomplish the tasks associated with drawing up and implementing the detailed economic plans in the Soviet Union.

Figure 39.3 Consumer Goods Balance, text page 1046
One of the planning goals in the Soviet Union is consumer goods balance: balance between the quantity of each consumer good demanded and the quantity supplied. This figure illustrates three ways in which balance can be achieved if, at the price set by the planners, there is an excess of quantity demanded over quantity supplied. It uses the example of shoes.

In the case of an excess demand for shoes at the set price, planners face three options for achieving balance. The first of these, illustrated in part (a) of the figure, is to increase the production of shoes. This amounts to increasing the supply by enough to meet the demand at the existing price.

The second option, illustrated in part (b), is to reduce the demand for shoes by decreasing after-tax income through an increase in income taxes. This causes the demand curve for shoes to shift to the left by just enough to reduce the quantity of shoes demanded at the set price so that it equals the quantity of shoes supplied.

The third option, illustrated in part (c), is to raise the price of shoes through the use of a turnover tax. If the tax is chosen appropriately, the price of shoes will rise by just enough so that the quantity of shoes demanded will fall (a movement along the D_0 curve) to the quantity of shoes supplied. See problem 1 on page 430 for more discussion of consumer goods balance.

Figure 39.5 Prices and Quantities Under Socialism, text page 1051

The results of this figure should be compared with those of Figure 39.4 on text page 1050, which show the price and quantity that would result in a capitalist economy. The demand curves under capitalism and socialism will be the same, but there are two other key reasons why the outcome under socialism will be different than the outcome under capitalism.

First, the relevant supply curve is likely to be higher than (to the left of) the supply curve under capitalism because the manager under socialism has an incentive to be inefficient. This result occurs because capital is owned by the state rather than individuals.

Second, resources are allocated by planning rather than markets, which implies that output may be set (by the planner) at a level which does not clear the market. In this example, the output target is too low and there is excess demand at the set price. As a result, a turnover tax is imposed to raise the price and achieve consumer goods balance. The overall result is that the socialist economy will produce a lower quantity of shoes and charge a higher price than the capitalist economy.

Figure 39.6 Prices and Quantities Under Market Socialism, text page 1052

This figure should also be compared with Figures 39.4 and 39.5 on text pages 1050 and 1051. It shows the price and quantity of shoes that would result in a market socialist economy. The difference between the results here and those under socialism, discussed previously, is a consequence of the main difference between the market socialist and a socialist economic system.

In both cases, capital is owned by the state and so there is likely to be a disincentive for managers to be efficient. Thus the supply curve would again be higher than under capitalism. However, under market socialism, markets are used for allocation rather than allocating through central planning. As a result, the price of shoes would adjust to clear the market at the intersection of the demand and supply curves.

In this example, the market clears at a price of P_{MS} and a quantity of Q_{MS}. The price is higher than under capitalism but lower than under socialism. The quantity is lower than under capitalism but higher than under socialism.

Table 39.1 A Compact Summary of Key Periods in the Economic History of the Soviet Union, text page 1043

In order to understand the nature and consequences of Soviet socialism, it is important to have a knowledge of the economic history of the Soviet Union since the Bolshevik revolution. The key aspects of that history are summarized here. As a consequence of the Bolshevik revolution under Lenin, the Soviet economic system began to change, but the fundamental changes took place under Stalin during the 1930s. The system that is described in this chapter was largely put in place by Stalin. Finally, the effects of Gorbachev's *perestroika* on the Soviet economic system remain to be seen.

Table 39.3 A Compact Summary of Key Periods in the Economic History of the People's Republic of China, text page 1048

The People's Republic of China was established in 1949. Since then, the Chinese economic system has undergone several changes. Although at first Mao Zedong followed the Soviet model of socialism, in 1958 he initiated the Great Leap Forward, which was a significant economic reform. It was an economic failure. During the cultural revolution, real GDP actually fell. Since the reforms of 1978 initiated by Deng Xiaoping, however, China has experienced a very rapid rate of growth. These reforms introduced many elements of capitalism into the Chinese economy.

SELF-TEST

CONCEPT REVIEW

1) The universal, fundamental economic problem of ______________ cannot be abolished by any economic system.

2) Private ownership of capital and reliance on market allocation of resources are the principal characteristics of the economic system known as ______________. The economic system based on state ownership of capital and centrally planned allocation of resources is called ______________.

3) An in-between economic system that combines state ownership of capital with market allocation of resources is called ______________ ______________. Another in-between economic system with private ownership of capital, but a high degree of state intervention in the allocation of resources is called ______________ ______________ ______________.

4) A variant of socialism in which income is distributed on the basis of need rather than contribution is called ______________.

5) An industry owned and operated by a publicly owned authority, directly responsible to the government, is called a(n) ______________ industry. The process of selling state-owned enterprises is called ______________.

6) The state planning committee responsible for drawing up and implementing the Soviet Union's economic plans is called ______________. Every five years, this committee draws up a ______________ - ______________ ______________, which gives a broad outline of the goals of the economy over the next five years.

7) A tax on a consumer good in the Soviet Union, which is designed to raise its price by enough to achieve a balance between the quantity of the good demanded and quantity supplied, is called a(n) ______________ tax. The achievement of a balance between the quantity demanded and supplied for each raw material and intermediate good used in the production of final goods is called ______________ ______________.

8) The term that is used to refer to the "restructuring" plans of Mikhail Gorbachev in the Soviet Union is ______________.

TRUE OR FALSE

_____ 1) Scarcity is a greater problem for capitalist economies than for socialist economies.

_____ 2) All economic systems attempt to get onto the production possibility frontier.

_____ 3) Under capitalism, all capital is owned by the state.

_____ 4) Under socialism, resources are allocated by central planning.

_____ 5) Under market socialism, there is decentralized planning.

_____ 6) Under capitalism, individual preferences are paramount.

_____ 7) Great Britain is an example of a pure capitalist economy.

_____ 8) The scale of government is larger in Japan than in most other capitalist countries.

_____ 9) In Japan, government economic intervention through the Ministry of Trade and Industry has been pro-business.

_____ 10) In recent years, European welfare states have increasingly been selling state-owned enterprises to private groups.

_____ 11)The architect of the economic management system that has been used by the Soviet Union since the 1930s was Vladimir Lenin.

_____ 12) The state planning committee in the Soviet Union that draws up and implements annual and five-year plans is the Communist Party Congress.

_____ 13) The annual plan in the Soviet Union tries to balance the quantities demanded and supplied for each category of consumer goods and services.

_____ 14) If, in the Soviet Union, the quantity of a consumer good supplied exceeds the quantity demanded, a turnover tax is likely to be applied to bring consumer goods balance.

_____ 15) Private plots constitute about 25 percent of the agricultural land of the Soviet Union but produce less than 3 percent of total agricultural output.

_____ 16) The Great Leap Forward initiated in 1958 by Mao Zedong was one of the significant economic successes in modern China.

_____ 17) Economic growth rates in China have increased considerably since the market-oriented economic reforms initiated by Deng Xiaoping in 1978.

_____ 18) The highest economic growth rates over the last forty years have been achieved by socialist countries.

_____ 19) Productivity is higher in capitalist countries than in socialist countries.

_____ 20) Income distribution is about as unequal in the Soviet Union as it is in welfare state economies of Western Europe like the United Kingdom.

MULTIPLE-CHOICE

1) The best any economic system can do is to
a) produce on its production possibility frontier.
b) produce above its production possibility frontier.
c) produce below its production possibility frontier.
d) eliminate scarcity.
e) produce a fair distribution of individual incentives.

2) Which economic system is characterized by private ownership of capital and considerable state intervention in the allocation of resources?
a) capitalism
b) socialism
c) market socialism
d) welfare state capitalism
e) communism

3) Which economic system is characterized by private ownership of capital and reliance on market allocation of resources?
a) capitalism
b) socialism
c) market socialism
d) welfare state capitalism
e) communism

4) Which economic system is characterized by state ownership of capital and reliance on market allocation of resources?
a) capitalism
b) socialism
c) market socialism
d) welfare state capitalism
e) communism

5) Which economic system is characterized by state ownership of capital and centrally planned allocation of resources?
a) capitalism
b) socialism
c) market socialism
d) welfare state capitalism
e) communism

6) What is the principal difference between communism and socialism?
a) There is central planning under communism but not under socialism.
b) Capital is owned by the state under communism but privately owned under socialism.
c) Income is to be distributed according to need under communism and according to contribution under socialism.
d) Income is to be distributed according to contribution under communism and according to need under socialism.
e) Income is to be generated according to ability under communism and according to state need under socialism.

7) Which of the following has a predominantly socialist economic system?
a) China
b) Great Britain
c) Japan
d) Sweden
e) Canada

8) Which of the following is *not* a feature of the Japanese economy that appears to be responsible for its dramatic economic success?
a) reliance on free-market, capitalist methods
b) an abundance of natural resources
c) small scale of government
d) pro-business government intervention by the Ministry of Trade and Industry
e) loyal and co-operative people

9) Which of the following does *not* exist in the Soviet Union?
a) money
b) state enterprises
c) markets of any kind
d) a central planning committee
e) resource markets

10) Which of the following methods is most often used by Soviet planners to achieve consumer goods balance if there is an excess of quantity demanded over quantity supplied at the price set by planners?
a) increasing production
b) increasing income taxes
c) lowering wages
d) imposing a turnover tax
e) imposing a quota

11) The Soviet Union allocates raw materials and intermediate goods by using
a) market prices.
b) materials balancing.
c) a survey of the needs of state enterprise managers.
d) feedback from the workers.
e) labour balancing.

12) Which of the following is *not* an element of *perestroika*?
a) elimination of the dominance of the Communist party
b) establishment of a direct link of incomes to performance
c) increased independence for state enterprises
d) reform of accounting methods to calculate enterprises' full cost, revenue, and profit
e) requirements that each enterprise achieve the "highest end results"

13) During the Great Leap Forward in China under Mao Zedong,
a) there was a dramatic increase in agricultural production but not industrial production.
b) the application of new technologies resulted in a significant general increase in production.
c) China experienced very slow economic growth.
d) China became a major exporter of grains and cotton.
e) China's educational sector boomed.

14) From which year does the People's Republic of China date?
a) 1917
b) 1927
c) 1936
d) 1949
e) 1967

15) The economic reforms of 1978, under Deng Xiaoping,
a) moved China off the "capitalist road" it had been on under Mao Zedong.
b) abolished collectivized agriculture.
c) have resulted in slower economic growth in China.
d) have made China more dependent on food imports.
e) led to the closing of universities and schools.

16) Under socialism, when managers of state enterprises are rewarded for reaching the target levels of production, managers have an incentive to produce
a) efficiently, but they do not know how.
b) efficiently, but there are generally shortages of inputs.
c) efficiently, and usually do.
d) inefficiently, as they produce too much output because they are paid per unit of output.
e) inefficiently, as they produce too little output to lower future production quotas.

17) Which of the following countries has an economic system closest to market socialism?
a) Japan
b) Soviet Union
c) Yugoslavia
d) Hungary
e) both c) and d)

18) The Soviet Union's basic plan is centred around five basic balances, which include all of the following *except* the
a) foreign exchange balance.
b) consumer goods balance.
c) labour balance.
d) credit balance.
e) materials balance.

19) The rate of economic growth in the Soviet Union over the period 1950–1980 was
a) greater than in the United States but less than in Japan.
b) greater than in both the United States and Japan.
c) greater than in Japan but less than in the United States.
d) less than in both the United States and Japan.
e) about the same as in both the United States and Japan.

20) Which of the following is true?
a) Socialist economies have much more equal distributions of income than capitalist or welfare state capitalist countries.
b) Socialist economies tend to grow more slowly when they relax their central planning and command mechanisms and rely on markets and decentralized incentive.
c) Productivity is higher in capitalist economies than in socialist economies.
d) Socialist economies can grow quite rapidly without squeezing consumption to levels below those that would be tolerated in capitalist economies.
e) Socialist economies have much less equal distributions of income than capitalist or welfare state capitalist countries.

SHORT ANSWER

1) Distinguish between a capitalist economic system and a welfare state capitalist system.

2) How do planners in the Soviet Union achieve consumer goods balance if the quantity of a good demanded is greater than the quantity supplied at the price set by the planners?

3) How do planners in the Soviet Union achieve materials balance if the quantity of coal demanded turns out to be greater than the quantity supplied? (Note that coal is used by households for heating and for the production of other goods.)

4) Briefly describe the economic reforms proclaimed by Deng Xiaoping in China in 1978. What has been their effect?

5) How do capitalist countries and socialist countries compare with regard to productivity?

PROBLEMS

1) Rogaria is a socialist country. The annual plan of the Central Planning Committee (CPC) of Rogaria has set the target quantity of shoes to be produced at 2 million pairs. Suppose that the target is just reached. The average cost of producing a pair of shoes is 4 cubles where the cuble is the currency of Rogaria. The CPC, which is not motivated by a desire for profit, sets the price of a pair of shoes at 4 cubles.

Figure 39.1 illustrates these facts and also gives the demand curve for shoes in Rogaria (labelled D_0). As the figure shows, consumer goods balance is not achieved: at the set price the quantity of shoes demanded exceeds the quantity supplied.

Consider each of the following three possible ways for the CPC to achieve consumer goods balance. Illustrate each graphically to show that consumer goods balance is achieved.

a) Increase the output of shoes.

b) Increase the income tax rate in order to reduce the demand for shoes.

c) Impose a turnover tax in the appropriate amount.

i) What is the amount (per pair of shoes) of the turnover tax?

ii) How much tax revenue will be collected?

Figure 39.1

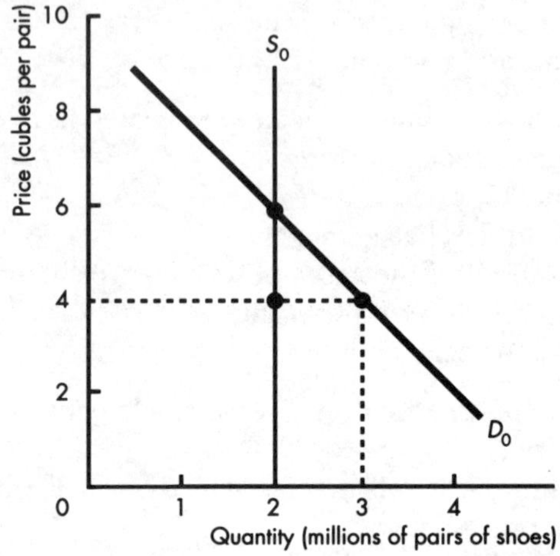

2) This problem allows you to think about achieving materials balance in Bulmania, another socialist country. Only three materials are used in Bulmania: coal, electric power, and nylon. The materials balance schedule is given in Table 39.1 on page 431, which is similar to Table 39.2 on text page 1047.

a) Assuming that the plan is in balance, complete the blank entries in the table.

b) The plan is now in balance. Suppose, however, that the quantity of electric power demanded by coal producers turns out to be 2,500 kilowatt-hours rather than the expected 2,000 kilowatt-hours. Everything else in the table remains unchanged. This, of course, implies that materials balance will not be achieved and planners must resolve the imbalance. Consider each of the following possible responses planners could make to achieve materials balance. For each, discuss the effects on the materials balance schedule. Be sure to indicate all entries in the table that would be affected.

i) Increase the production of electric power.

ii) Decrease the production of coal.

iii) Decrease the production of nylon.

iv) Decrease the domestic consumption of electric power.

Table 39.1 Materials Balance in Bulmania

	Quantity Supplied			Quantity Demanded				
				Intermediate Goods			Final Goods	
Material	Production	Inventories	Imports	Coal	Electric Power	Nylon	Domestic	Foreign
Coal (tonnes)	490	10	0	50	300	50		25
Electric power (kWh)	10,000	0	0	2,000	1,000	1,500		0
Nylon (metres)	20,000	200	2,000	0	0	0		0

3) Suppose an industry in a socialist economy is being converted to market socialism. Show what happens to price and quantity graphically. Is the new system more or less efficient? Is it the most efficient system?

4) Consider the East German market for widgets. These goods were not produced in East Germany before unification, and the only supply is smuggled in from West Germany. However, after unification, they become readily available in East Germany at the West German price. Show the impacts of this change on a graph of the East German market.

ANSWERS

CONCEPT REVIEW

1) scarcity
2) capitalism; socialism
3) market socialism; welfare state capitalism
4) communism
5) nationalized; privatization
6) GOSPLAN; five-year plan
7) turnover; materials balance
8) *perestroika*

TRUE OR FALSE

1) F	6) T	11) F	16) F
2) T	7) F	12) F	17) T
3) F	8) F	13) T	18) F
4) T	9) T	14) F	19) T
5) T	10) T	15) F	20) T

MULTIPLE-CHOICE

1) a	6) c	11) b	16) e
2) d	7) a	12) a	17) e
3) a	8) b	13) c	18) a
4) c	9) e	14) d	19) a
5) b	10) d	15) b	20) c

SHORT ANSWER

1) Both capitalism and welfare state capitalism are characterized by private ownership of capital. They differ with regard to the role of the state in the allocation of resources. Capitalism relies on market allocation of resources, while welfare state capitalism is characterized by a significant degree of state intervention in the allocation of resources.

2) Soviet planners seek for consumer goods balance: balance between the quantity of each consumer good demanded and the quantity supplied. If it turns out that, at the set price, the quantity demanded is greater than the quantity supplied, planners face three choices. They can increase output, decrease after-tax income (through an income tax increase) and thus decrease demand, or they can raise the price and thus decrease the quantity demanded. The easiest, and most likely, response is to raise the price by imposing a turnover tax (like an excise tax) on the good.

3) Soviet planners also seek materials balance: balance between the quantity of each raw material or intermediate good demanded and the quantity supplied. Coal is one of these raw materials. If it turns out

that the quantity of coal demanded is greater than the quantity supplied, planners have three options.

First, they can plan to produce more coal in order to meet the quantity demanded. Second, they can plan to reduce production of goods for which coal is an input. This will reduce the quantity of coal demanded. It will also disrupt the production plans of other goods since many of the goods that use coal as an input are inputs to other processes (steel, for example). A third alternative is to reduce the amount of coal provided to households for heating purposes. This is the easiest and therefore the most likely alternative.

4) In 1978 Deng Xiaoping abolished collective agriculture (state-owned and state-operated farms) and raised prices paid to farmers for many crops. Agricultural land was leased to farmers for the payment of a fixed tax and a commitment to sell part of its output to the state. The main thing is that individual farmers were free to decide what to plant and how to produce.

Since farmers were now able to profit from their productivity, there were new incentives for efficiency. The effects have been striking. The production of agricultural products increased dramatically with the output of some products (those for which the set price was increased the most) increasing by many times their previous level. China went from being the world's largest importer of agricultural products to being an exporter of these products. The overall growth rate in the economy increased to 7 percent per year.

5) Because of the disincentives for efficiency in socialist economies, productivity is higher in capitalist economies. Studies that compare productivity in the Soviet Union and the United States suggest that output per unit of input in the Soviet Union is less than half what it is in the United States.

PROBLEMS

1) a) The effect of an increase in the output of shoes is illustrated in Figure 39.2. In order to achieve balance, the CPC must increase the output of shoes to 3 million pairs since that is the quantity demanded at 4 cubles. This is shown by the curve labelled S_1. In this case, balance is achieved at point *a*, because the quantity of shoes supplied increases to meet the quantity demanded at the price of 4 cubles per pair, which is 3 million shoes.

Figure 39.2

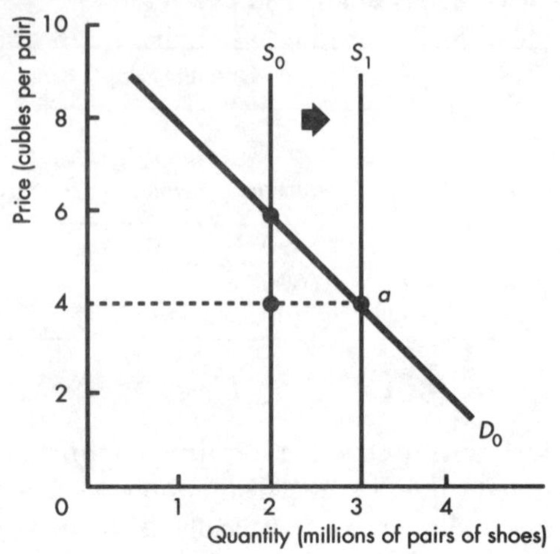

b) The effect of a decrease in the demand for shoes induced by an increase in income tax rates is shown in Figure 39.3. The objective of the planner is to reduce the quantity of shoes demanded at 4 cubles from 3 million pairs to 2 million pairs. Thus, the planner wants to choose the income tax rate increase so as to shift the demand curve for shoes to the left by 1 million shoes, from D_0 to D_1. In this case, balance is achieved at point *b*.

Figure 39.3

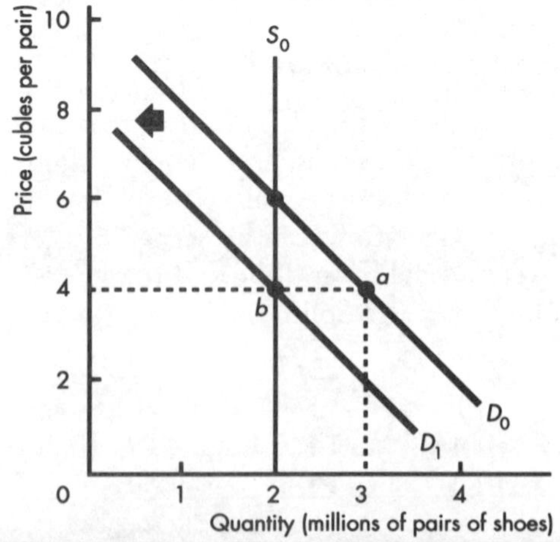

c) The effect of imposing an appropriate turnover tax on shoes is shown in Figure 39.4 on page 433. The planner desires to raise the price of a pair of shoes enough to decrease the quantity of shoes demanded from 3 million to 2 million pairs. This will be done by adding a turnover tax to the 4 cuble cost of producing a pair of shoes.

Note from the figure that the quantity of shoes demanded is 2 million pairs (on demand curve D_0) if the price is 6 cubles per pair. This price would be achieved if a turnover tax of 2 cubles per pair of shoes is imposed. Thus, balance is achieved at point *c*.

i) As indicated above, the tax must be 2 cubles per pair of shoes.

ii) The tax revenue will be 4 million cubles: 2 cubles per pair of shoes times 2 million pairs of shoes.

Figure 39.4

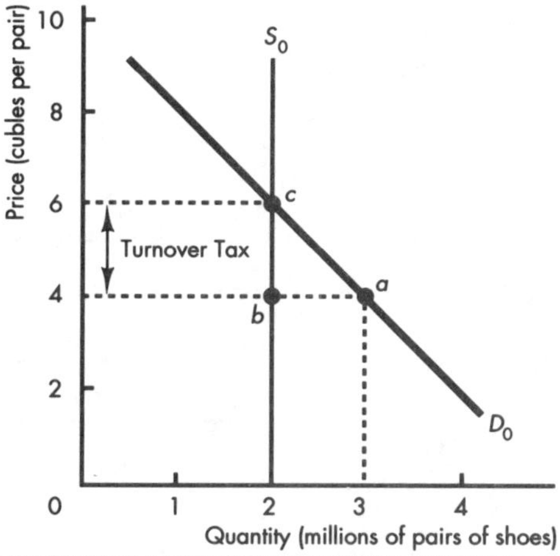

2) a) Quantity supplied of each good must equal total quantity demanded. Coal, for example, has a supply of 500 tonnes, and therefore domestic final demand must equal 75 tonnes for balance. Similar calculations can be carried out for electric power and nylon, and the end results are presented in Table 39.1 Solution.

b) i) Increasing the production of electric power would have a more significant effect on the materials balance schedule than just increasing the entry indicating the quantity of electric power supplied from production.

An increase in production of electric power requires more coal and electric power. So, in order for balance to be achieved, it would also be necessary to increase coal production to further increase electric power by enough to meet the additional demand for those inputs in the production of the additional electric power.

ii) If the production of coal is reduced in order to achieve materials balance, all inputs required to produce coal and all products for which coal is an input will be affected. In particular, not only will less electric power be needed to produce coal (the original desired effect), but less coal will be needed in the production of coal.

Furthermore, a reduction in coal production means that less electric power and nylon can be produced. The output of final goods will also be affected. Thus, this response by planners would end up changing most of the entries in the table.

iii) The effects from a reduction in the production of nylon are not as pervasive because nylon is not used in the production of other goods; it is not an intermediate good. However, a reduction in output of nylon would not only reduce the quantity of electric power demanded (the desired effect) but it would also reduce the demand for coal. It would also reduce the quantity of nylon available for domestic consumption.

iv) The simplest response would be to reduce domestic consumption of electric power by 500 kilowatt-hours. This would achieve materials balance without affecting the interdependent production processes.

Table 39.1 Solution: Materials Balance in Bulmania

	Quantity Supplied			Quantity Demanded				
				Intermediate Goods			Final Goods	
Material	Production	Inventories	Imports	Coal	Electric Power	Nylon	Domestic	Foreign
Coal (tonnes)	490	10	0	50	300	50	75	25
Electric power (kWh)	10,000	0	0	2,000	1,000	1,500	1,500	0
Nylon (metres)	20,000	200	2,000	0	0	0	22,200	0

3) Figure 39.5 shows the industry. When the industry is run by planners, a quantity of Q_S is set to be produced, at a price of P_S (perhaps with the use of a turnover tax). Under capitalism, we would have the supply curve *S* and the demand curve *D*, producing an equilibrium price of P_C and an equilibrium quantity of Q_C. This is the most efficient level of production. Under market socialism, the supply curve becomes S_{MS}, higher than the capitalist curve since the managers of enterprises do not have correct incentives. This leads to a production of Q_{MS}, higher than the socialist case but lower than the capitalist case, at a price of P_{MS}, higher than the capitalist case but lower than the socialist case. Therefore, the market socialist case is more efficient than the pure socialist case, but less efficient than the capitalist case.

4) Figure 39.6 shows the East German market for widgets. Initially, the only supply is the amount that can be smuggled in, S_{BM}. This leads to a price of P_{BM} on the black market. After unification, widgets become readily available at the West German price, so that the new supply curve is S_{WG}. This leads to a price of P_{WG}, and a quantity of Q_U.

Figure 39.5

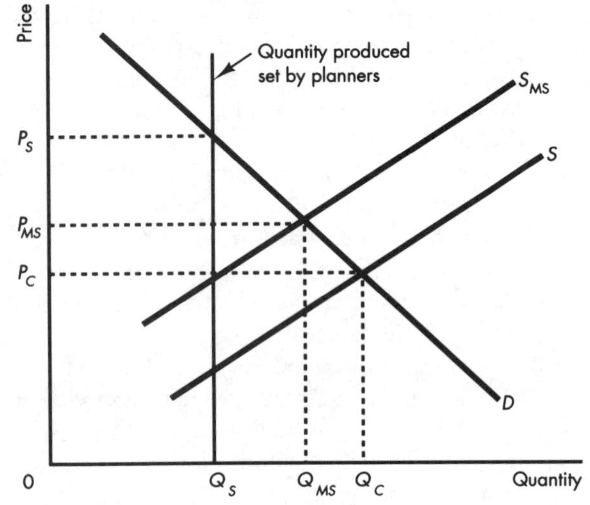

Figure 39.6

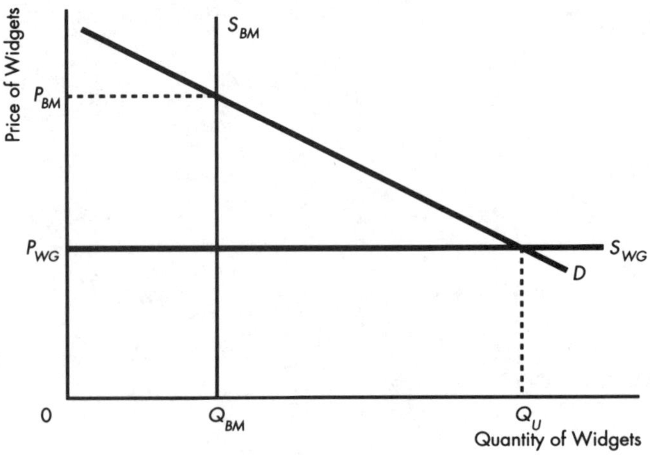